WE·THE
PEOPLE

HOUGHTON MIFFLIN

Explore
Our Land

WE·THE PEOPLE

Explore Our Land

New York, New York

Sarah Bednarz
Catherine Clinton
Michael Hartoonian
Arthur Hernandez
Patricia L. Marshall
Pat Nickell

HOUGHTON MIFFLIN   BOSTON · MORRIS PLAINS, NJ

California · Colorado · Georgia · Illinois · New Jersey · Texas

AUTHORS

Sarah Bednarz
Assistant Professor
Texas A&M University
College Station, TX

Arthur Hernandez
Associate Professor
Division of Education
College of Social and
Behavioral Sciences
University of Texas at
San Antonio
San Antonio, TX

Catherine Clinton
W.E.B. Du Bois Institute
Fellow
Harvard University
Cambridge, MA

Patricia L. Marshall
Assistant Professor
Department of Curric-
ulum and Instruction
College of Education
and Psychology
North Carolina State
University
Raleigh, NC

Michael Hartoonian
Professor and Director
Carey Center
Hamline University
St. Paul, MN

Pat Nickell
Director
High School Curriculum
and Instruction
Fayette County Schools
Lexington, KY

Susan Buckley General Editor

Acknowledgments appear on page 525.
2003 Impression
Copyright © 2000 by Houghton Mifflin Company. All rights reserved.

Printed in the U.S.A. ISBN: 0-618-04578-3   6789-VH-06 05 04 03 02 01

CONSULTANTS

Felix D. Almárez, Jr.
Department of History
University of Texas
San Antonio, TX

Manley A. Begay, Jr.
John F. Kennedy School
of Government
Harvard University
Cambridge, MA

William Brinner
University of California
Berkeley, CA

Phap Dam
Director of World
Languages
Dallas Independent
School District
Dallas, TX

Philip J. Deloria
Department of History
University of Colorado
Boulder, CO

Jorge I. Domínguez
The Center for
International Affairs
Harvard University
Cambridge, MA

Kenneth Hamilton
Department of History
Southern Methodist
University
Dallas, TX

Charles Haynes
Freedom Forum First
Amendment Center
Vanderbilt University
Nashville, TN

Roberta Martin
East Asian Institute
Columbia University
New York, NY

Shabbir Mansuri
Founding Director
Council on Islamic
Education
Susan Douglas
CIE Affiliated Scholar

Acharya Palaniswami
Editor
Hinduism Today
Kapaa, HI

Linda Reed
Department of History
Princeton University
Princeton, NJ

Dahia Ibo Shabaka
Director of Social Studies
Detroit Public Schools
Detroit, MI

Ken Tanaka
Institute of Buddhist
Studies
Graduate Theological
Union
Berkeley, CA

Ling-chi Wang
Department of Asian
American Studies
University of California
Berkeley, CA

TEACHER REVIEWERS

Kindergarten/Grade 1: Wayne Gable, Langford Elementary, Austin Independent School District, TX • **Donna LaRoche,** Winn Brook School, Belmont Public Schools, MA • **Gerri Morris,** Hanley Elementary School, Memphis City Schools, TN • **Eddi Porter,** College Hill Elementary, Wichita School District, KS • **Jackie Day Rogers,** Emerson Elementary, Houston Independent School District, TX • **Debra Rubin,** John Moffet Elementary, Philadelphia School District, PA

Grade 2: Rebecca Kenney, Lowery Elementary School, Cypress-Fairbanks School District, TX • **Debbie Kresner,** Park Road Elementary, Pittsford Central School District, NY • **Karen Poehlein,** Curriculum Coordinator, Buncombe County School District, NC

Grade 3: Bessie Coffer, RISD Academy, Richardson School District, TX • **Shirley Frank,** Instructional Specialist, Winston-Salem/Forsyth County Schools, NC • **Elaine Mattson,** Aloha Park Elementary, Beaverton School District, OR • **Carmen Sanchez,** Greenbrier Elementary, Fort Worth School District, TX • **Irma Torres,** Galindo Elementary School, Austin Independent School District, TX

Grade 4: Patricia Amendariz, Lamar Elementary, El Paso Independent School District, TX • **Lenora Barnes,** Duncan Elementary, Lake County School District, IN • **Dianna Deal,** Park Hill Elementary, North Little Rock School District, AR • **Karen Dodson,** Martin Elementary, Alief Independent School District, TX • **Linda Johnson,** Memorial Drive Elementary, Spring Branch School District, TX • **Marina Lopez,** Hillside Elementary, El Paso Independent School District, TX • **Becky Murphy,** Butler Elementary, Springfield School District, IL • **Ann Powell,** Austin Independent School District, TX • **Sumner Price,** Legion Park Elementary, East Las Vegas School District, NM • **Sara Stultz,** Richland Elementary, Richardson Independent School District, TX • **Jim Wilkerson,** Glenoaks Elementary School, Northside Independent School District, TX

Grade 5: Pat Carney-Dalton, Lower Salford Elementary School, Souderton School District, PA • **Janice Hunt,** Dearborn Park Elementary, Seattle Public Schools, WA • **Debbie Ruppell,** Dover Elementary, Dover Union Free School District, NY • **Jon Springer,** Bethany Elementary, Beaverton School District, OR • **Nancy Watson,** Weeks Elementary, Kansas City School District, MO • **Gloria Wilson,** Forest Park Elementary, Little Rock School District, AR

Grade 6: Marcia Baynes, The Longfellow School, Middlesex County Schools, MA • **Diane Bloom,** Steelman School, Eatontown School District, NJ • **Hillary Callahan,** Coordinator of Language Arts, Roanoke City Schools, VA • **Tom Murphy,** Carusi Elementary, Cherry Hill School District, NJ • **Mark Newhouse,** A.T. Morrow School, Central Islip School District, NY • **Dot Scott,** Meadow Creek Elementary, Hurst-Euless-Bedford Independent School District, TX

CONTENTS

UNIT 2 A Nation of Many Peoples

THEME: CITIZENSHIP

UNIT 3 The Northeast

THEME: LAND AND SEA

Philadelphia Museum of Art

UNIT 4   The South

THEME: RIVERS AND COASTS

UNIT 5 The Midwest

THEME: PRAIRIES AND PLAINS

FEATURES

American Voices

" It is a fertile land with fine crystalline waters . . ."

Father Jeronimo de Zarate Salmeron

" *Oh beautiful for spacious skies . . .*"

Katharine Lee Bates

" *If a nation expects to be ignorant and free . . . it expects what never was and never will be.*"

Thomas Jefferson

" *Lift every voice and sing*
Till earth and heaven ring,
Ring with the harmonies of Liberty."

James Weldon Johnson

> *" America is not anything if it consists of each of us. It is something only if it consists of all of us."*
>
> **Woodrow Wilson**

We are the

Spirit of America!

Understanding Geography

"*Wonderful Earth, only you live forever.*"

Kiowa song

· THEME ·

Our Land

❝ *The land in the United States is special because it's like a salad, a little bit of everything helping to make our country great.* ❞

Anitoshia Johnson, Fourth Grade
Gary, IN

Where do you live? In the United States, of course! That's only one way to describe it, though. You also live in a community, a state, and a region. The land and climate of each region and of the entire nation affect how people there live and work. Learning about geography can help you answer many questions about the regions of our land, the United States.

 Theme Project

Create a Geographic Dictionary

You are a geographer who wants to explain different geographic features to students. You can show what those features look like by making a three-dimensional geographic dictionary.

- List the features covered in this unit and identify where they are located in the United States.
- Draw or find pictures of some of the features.
- Build models of some of the features.

RESEARCH: Find photographs or maps of your state that show examples of as many features as possible.

◀ Yosemite National Park, California, in winter

WHEN & WHERE
ATLAS

Land can influence history in many ways. An area's physical features can affect how it is settled, the way people live, and why some towns grow more than others. This map shows some important physical features of the United States and North America. These features have had a big impact on people in the United States.

In this unit, you will learn about the land and climate of the United States. You will also learn what geographers do, the kinds of questions they ask, and how they use regions to understand the world. As you learn about geography, you too can better understand the world around you.

Unit 1 Chapters

Unit Timeline

10,000 years ago

Mount Rainier

This mountain is also a volcano.
Chapter 1, Lesson 2

Arches National Park

What carved this rock into an arch?
Chapter 2, Lesson 1

CANADA

ROCKY MOUNTAINS

Missouri River

Seattle
Mount
St. Helens
8364 ft.

GRAND TETON
NATIONAL PARK

WEST

Pikes
Peak
14,110 ft.

Phoenix

Los Angeles

Bismarck

GREAT PLAINS

GREAT

MIDWEST

Des
Moines

Hutchinson

Mississippi River

GREAT LAKES

Gary

NORTHEAST

Boston

New York

APPALACHIAN MOUNTAINS

SOUTH

Atlanta

Charleston

Rio Grande

Houston

MEXICO

Gulf
of
Mexico

Miami

ATLANTIC
OCEAN

Tropic of Cancer

N
W   E
S

30°W   120°W   110°W   100°W   80°W   70°W   60°W   50°W   40°W

Today

The Water Cycle

You call it rain. Find out another word for this wet stuff from the sky. *Chapter 2, Lesson 3*

The Oregon Trail

To which region did this trail lead? *Chapter 3, Lesson 2*

Astoria
Oregon City
OREGON
Pacific Ocean
Columbia River
ROCKY Mountains
Missouri River
Oregon Trail
Great Salt Lake
N
0   125   250 miles

Writing in Chinese

Find out what writing system you use. *Chapter 3, Lesson 3*

The World of Geography

Chapter Preview: *People, Places, and Events*

Long Ago

The Grand Canyon

What is geography all about? Find some answers to this question. *Lesson 1, Page 14*

Boston, Massachusetts

What would a geographer ask about a town like this one? *Lesson 1, Page 15*

A Dam

Learn how people can shape the world around them. *Lesson 1, Page 19*

What Is Geography?

Main Idea Geography is the study of the physical world and the people and things that live there.

> "**W**e are now ready to start on our way down the Great Unknown . . ."
>
> John Wesley Powell, August 13, 1869

Key Vocabulary
geography
environment
hemisphere
adapt

Key Places
Grand Canyon

John Wesley Powell's Great Unknown was the Grand Canyon. In the 1860s, most people knew very little about the canyon. It wasn't on any maps of the United States. So Powell decided to explore it. He led his first expedition into the canyon in 1869.

Powell wanted to learn about the Grand Canyon. You, too, can learn about places and what makes them special. One way to learn about a place is to ask questions. If you ask the right ones, you can explore amazing unknown places.

◀ The Teton Range in Wyoming is part of the Rocky Mountains.

Today

Geographer Kevin Scott

This man studies volcanoes and landslides. *Lesson 2, Page 26*

Mount St. Helens

When this volcano erupted, it knocked down trees 17 miles away. *Lesson 2, Page 27*

Penguin on Patrol

What's this bird doing with a backpack? *Lesson 2, Page 29*

Where Is It?

Where is the Grand Canyon? It is located on the Colorado River, in northwestern Arizona. Arizona is in the southwestern part of the United States.

ARIZONA

Where, What, and Why

Focus *What questions do geographers ask?*

Powell probably asked himself many questions about the Grand Canyon. Some of them might have been questions such as: How long is it? Which people and what kinds of animals and plants live there? What does the land there look like? Why does it look that way?

What kinds of questions are these? Are they music questions? Of course not! Are they math questions? Not exactly, even though the answers may use numbers. Are they history questions? No! These are geography questions.

The term *geography* comes from words that mean "earth" and "to write." So **geography** involves writing about, or describing, the earth. Geographers ask questions about the surface of the earth. They ask about the way people and other living things use the earth as their home. Some of the most important geography questions are: Where is it? What is it like there? Why is it there? These are the kind of questions John Wesley Powell might have asked about the Grand Canyon. On these two pages you can find some answers.

What Is It Like There?

The Grand Canyon is in a dry area of the United States. It gets hot in the summer and cold in the winter. Cactus plants and pine trees grow in the area. Bighorn sheep and mule deer also live there.

Where Is It?

People like to find their hometowns on a map or globe. It's fun to find other places, too. Where is the highest point in your state? Where is your state's biggest city? Where is your country's capital? Where in the United States does it snow most?

Lots of geography questions start with *where*. These are questions about location. Location is the position of a place.

What Is It Like There?

People also ask questions about what places are like. Can you describe the southern part of the United States? What does the area around the country's largest lakes look like? What plants and animals live there? What is the weather like? The answers to these questions tell what you would find in these places.

Why Is It There?

When people see what a place is like, they also ask why it is that way. Why do some plants grow in the southwestern part of the United States but not in other places? Why is the country's biggest city located where it is? *Why?* is one of the geographer's most important questions.

Why Is It There?

The Grand Canyon formed when the Colorado River cut through the rocks around it. While the river cut through the rocks, the land around the river was rising. Over millions of years, these forces created the Grand Canyon.

Dr. Ricki Sanders

Dr. Ricki Sanders is a geographer at Temple University in Philadelphia, Pennsylvania. She is working on new and exciting ways to teach geography. Dr. Sanders is also interested in how geographers solve problems.

Geographers can learn a lot by asking why. Asking that question helps people learn how the land came to be the way it is. It can also help us understand how our surroundings change. Another word for those surroundings is the **environment**. Today, many people are interested in the environment we share. They work to keep it clean and healthy.

People never stop learning about geography. The world is a fascinating place. You can always ask more questions to understand it better. If you ask these kinds of questions, you're thinking like a geographer.

Where in the World Are You?

Focus *How could you describe where you live?*

If someone asked you where you live, how would you answer? It might depend on whom you were talking to. Here are some answers you could give.

From Neighborhoods to Nations

If classmates asked, you might tell them the name of your street or your neighborhood. If you traveled to another city, you'd probably tell people the town or city you live in. If you went to another state, you might tell people there the state you live in. If you traveled to another country, like Mexico or Japan, you might say your home was in the United States.

Continents and Hemispheres

You could give other answers as well. Do you remember which continent you live on? Continents are the earth's large land masses. You probably already know that the United States is on the continent of North America.

Geographers also divide the earth into halves, called **hemispheres**. The equator is an imaginary line around the middle of the earth. It divides the world into the Northern and Southern hemispheres. The United States is in the Northern Hemisphere. The prime meridian and the International Date Line are imaginary lines that run from the North Pole to the South Pole. They divide the world into Eastern and Western hemispheres. The United States is in the Western Hemisphere. You could also add that your home was on planet earth.

The girl in this photo is showing you one answer to the question, "Where do you live?" You might choose to give a different answer to that question. There are many ways to describe where you live.

1 You live in a neighborhood in a town or city.

2 Your town or city is in a state.

3 Your state is part of the United States of America.

4 The United States is in the Northern and Western hemispheres.

The United States is one of many nations on the planet earth. **Map Skill:** *Does the equator run through any part of the United States?*

Ask Yourself

People use their mental maps every day. In fact, you couldn't get through your day without mental maps. What are three ways in which you use mental maps?

? ? ? ? ? ? ? ? ? ? ? ? ?

Everyone uses maps to get around. A map that you carry in your mind is called a mental map. Sometimes, when people give directions, they draw their mental maps on paper.

Maps

Maps can show the different ways to describe where you live. Most maps are drawings or pictures of the earth's surface. They hold lots of information about locations. Some maps show where mountains are and where the land is flat. Some maps show cities and roads. Maps can also show counties, states, and countries. Maps can even show you how many people live in an area, or how much rain falls there each year.

Sometimes you don't need a map to tell you where a place is. You may have a picture in your mind of where it is. A picture like that is called a mental map. Do you know how to get from your home to your school? Can you picture where your state is within the United States? If the answer to either of those questions is yes, you're using a mental map. As you learn more about where things are, your mental map grows.

Changes in the Land

The land is always changing. For instance, rivers change direction, or course. However, they may change very slowly. In other places the land changes more quickly. For example, many people who came to eastern North America about 300 years ago were farmers. They cut down trees to clear fields for farming. Those farmers changed the geography of their communities. Can you think of other ways people have changed the land?

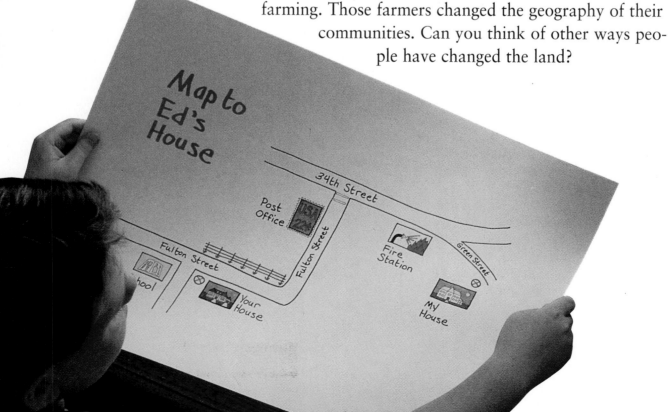

When land changes, the plants and animals that live on that land change too. What happens when a dam is built? Land that had been dry becomes covered with water. Plants and animals that lived there can no longer survive. They are replaced by plants and animals that live in water.

Changes in Living Things

Sometimes when the land changes slowly, certain kinds of animals and plants can **adapt**. This means that they change so that they can live in the new environment. The barrel cactus that grows in the southwestern United States is a good example of this. This kind of cactus has changed over many thousands of years to live in dry conditions. Once, it had leaves like most other plants. Today it has needles. Plants that have needles lose less water in the hot sun than do plants with leaves.

The study of geography covers a lot of ground! Geographers study the surface of the earth as it looks today. They also look at changes in the land over time. Geography itself helps us in many ways. It can help us in simple ways, like finding directions to unfamiliar places. It can also help us in complex ways, like understanding the way the land changes. Thinking geographically helps us see our world more clearly.

Needles help keep the barrel cactus from drying out in the desert. **Science:** *What other desert plants or animals do you know?*

Lesson Review: Geography

1 **Key Vocabulary:** Write a paragraph that tells where your hometown is, using the words **geography, environment,** and **hemisphere.**

2 **Focus:** What questions do geographers ask?

3 **Focus:** How could you describe where you live?

4 **Critical Thinking: Cause and Effect** How do you think you've changed your environment? Has your environment changed you?

5 **Theme: Our Land** Why is it important to know that living things change when the environment changes?

6 **Geography/Art Activity:** Answer this question: How many ways can you describe where you live? Then create a poster to illustrate your answer.

Skills Workshop

Using Latitude and Longitude

Your World Address Book

You can find where you live on a map even if your hometown, your state, or the United States is not marked on it. How? By using lines of **latitude** and **longitude.**

These lines form an imaginary grid around the earth's surface. Latitude lines run east and west. Longitude lines run north and south, between the North Pole and South Pole. Latitude and longitude help you find any place on the earth.

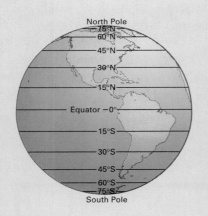

Latitude lines are also called **parallels** because they run parallel to one another. We start measuring latitude at the equator, which is the latitude line at 0 degrees, or 0°. Move your finger north and south of the equator. Notice that the latitude numbers get larger as they get closer to either the North Pole or the South Pole.

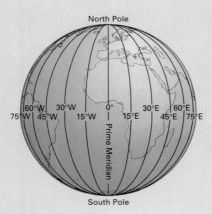

Longitude lines are also called **meridians**. We start counting longitude at the **prime meridian**, which is at longitude 0°. Find it on the map to the left. It runs through Europe and Africa. As you move either west or east, away from the prime meridian, the longitude numbers get larger.

① Here's How

Suppose you want to find the latitude and longitude of a place (for example, St. Louis).

- Find St. Louis on the map to the right.

- Run your finger above and below the place to find the nearest latitude line. Is this line north or south of the equator? The nearest latitude line to St. Louis is 40°N. That means St. Louis is located about 40 degrees north of the equator.

- Now run your finger to the left and right of the place to find the nearest longitude line. Is the line east or west of the prime meridian? The nearest longitude line to St. Louis is 90°W. That means St. Louis is located about 90 degrees west of the prime meridian.

- Now you can name St. Louis's location. First give the latitude, then the longitude. Be sure to include the degrees symbol and tell whether the location is east, west, north, or south. So, St. Louis's "address" is near 40°N, 90°W.

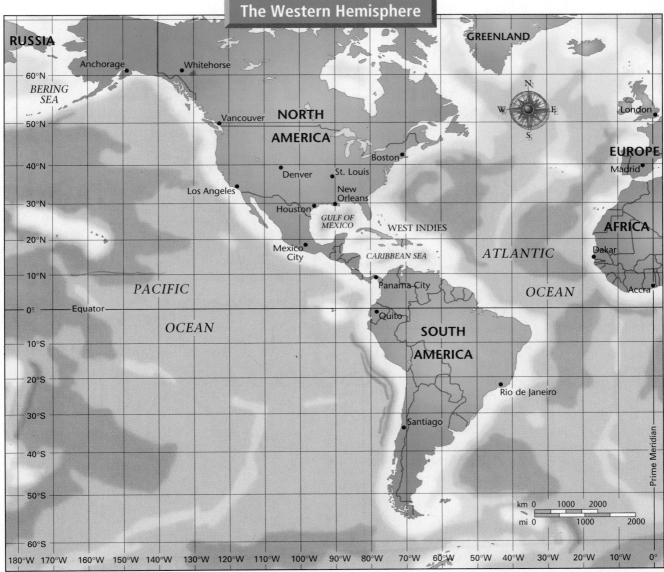

The Western Hemisphere

RUSSIA

GREENLAND

Anchorage   Whitehorse

60°N

BERING SEA

London

50°N   Vancouver   NORTH AMERICA

EUROPE

40°N   Boston   Madrid

Denver   St. Louis

30°N   Los Angeles   New Orleans

Houston   *GULF OF MEXICO*   WEST INDIES   AFRICA

20°N   Mexico City   Dakar

ATLANTIC

10°N   *CARIBBEAN SEA*   Accra

PACIFIC   Panama City   OCEAN

0°   Equator   Quito

OCEAN   SOUTH AMERICA

10°S

20°S   Rio de Janeiro

30°S   Santiago

40°S

50°S   km 0   1000   2000
mi 0   1000   2000

60°S

180°W 170°W 160°W 150°W 140°W 130°W 120°W 110°W 100°W 90°W 80°W 70°W 60°W 50°W 40°W 30°W 20°W 10°W 0°

What if you want to identify a place at a certain latitude and longitude (for example, the city located near 30°N, 90°W)?

- Look at the numbers on the edge of the map. Find the line of latitude labeled 30°N. Make sure this line is north of the equator.

- Next, move your finger along this latitude line until you reach the longitude line labeled 90°W.

- The place you're looking for is located on or near the point where the latitude and longitude lines meet. You'll find New Orleans, Louisiana, near the meeting place of these two lines.

❷ Think It Through

Why do you need both a latitude and a longitude line to pinpoint a location?

❸ Use It

1. Find the cities near these locations:
   50°N, 120°W   0°, 80°W
   30°S, 70°W   10°N, 80°W
   20°N, 100°W   50°N, 0°

2. Choose four places on the map and give their "addresses" in latitude and longitude.

The Global Positioning System is new technology that uses satellites to tell us latitude and longitude.

BLAST OFF TO EARTH!

BLAST OFF
TO EARTH!
A LOOK AT GEOGRAPHY
LOREEN LEEDY

NONFICTION

Here is a flat map showing the surface of the planet. There are seven continents and four oceans.

North is toward the top of the map, and South is toward the bottom. West is left, and East is right.

NORTH
AMERICA

ATLANTIC OCEAN

PACIFIC
OCEAN

SOUTH
AMERICA

NORTH

WEST   EAST

SOUTH

These outer space creatures are seeing the Earth for the first time. They have a lot to learn about geography, so they are starting with basic facts. If we look and listen, we can learn a few things, too.

A LOOK AT GEOGRAPHY

By Loreen Leedy

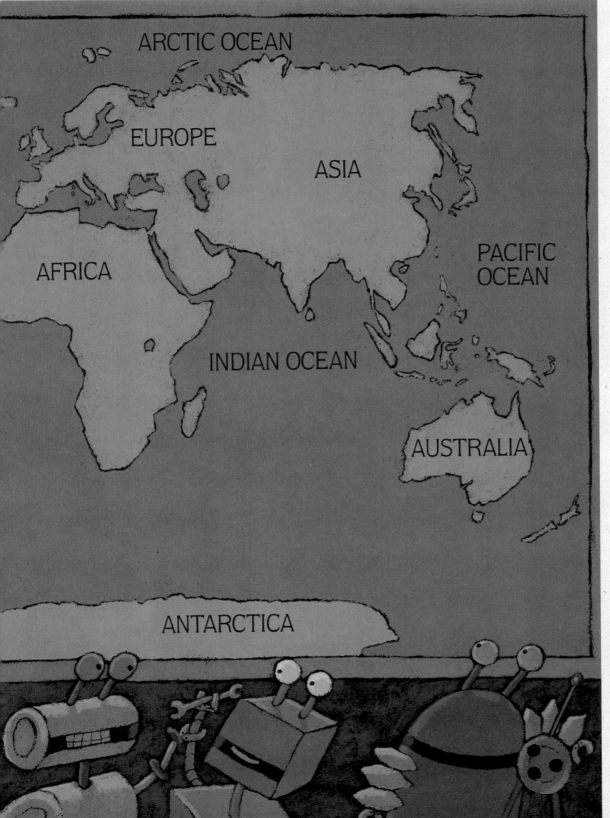

ARCTIC OCEAN

EUROPE

ASIA

AFRICA

PACIFIC OCEAN

INDIAN OCEAN

AUSTRALIA

ANTARCTICA

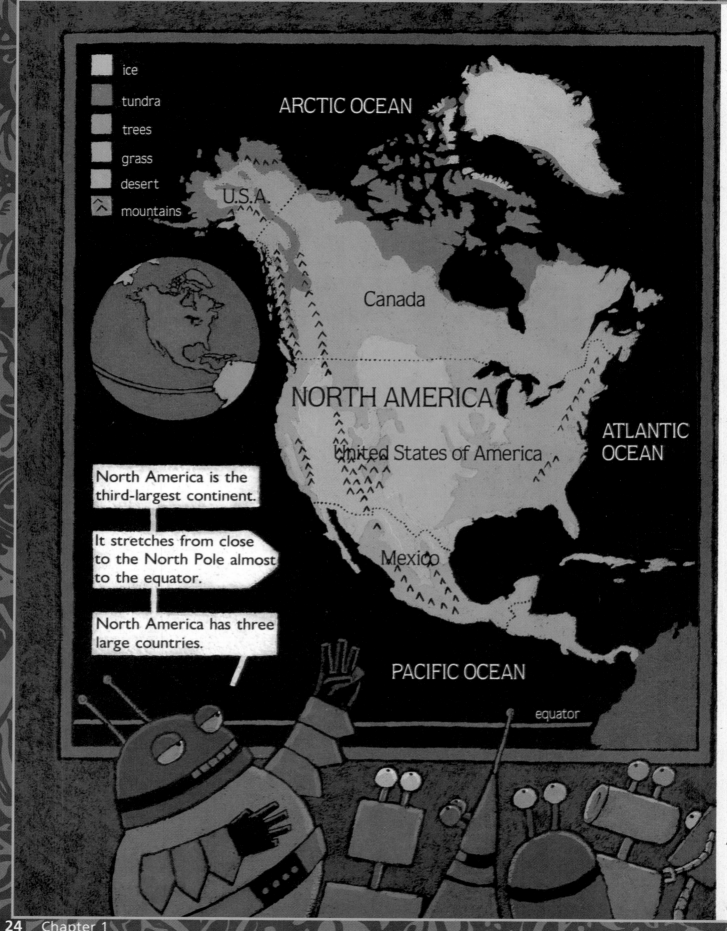

Meet the Author

Loreen Leedy likes to make books that teach in a fun way. Other books you might like are *Messages in the Mailbox: How to Write a Letter,* and *The Monster Money Book.*

Additional Books to Read

Maps: Getting from Here to There by Harvey Weiss
Explore the world of maps and mapmaking.

Where the River Begins by Thomas Locker
Read about a camping trip and a hike, all the way upstream.

Response Activities

1. **Classify Places** Name the continents and the oceans on the map. On which continent would animals have to adapt to the constant cold?

2. **Descriptive: Write a Poem** What would the outer space creatures see if they flew over a neighborhood park or your city zoo? Write a short poem that describes your community from the view of a spaceship flying over it.

3. **Geography: Plan a Quiz** Use a map of the world and the map of North America to come up with your own geography questions, like: "What ocean is east of North America?"

Geography Today

Main Idea Geographers use many tools and skills to explore the world.

All over the United States people face problems that geographers help solve. One city that faced a big challenge was Atlanta, Georgia. When Atlanta was chosen to host the Summer Olympics, the city had to decide where to hold the events. Where would the rowing events be held? What would be the best route for the marathon?

Geographers can help answer these kinds of questions. They could tell the city of Atlanta where to find a lake for the rowing events. They could also help plan the marathon route.

Geographers can solve many kinds of problems. They can help a business decide where to put a new store to attract the most customers. They can help cities plan in case of emergency. Thousands of geographers work in the United States. What problems do you think they help solve in your state?

A Geographer on the Job: Meet Kevin Scott

Focus *What problem does geographer Kevin Scott help people understand?*

Kevin Scott takes notes in the woods of Washington State.

Kevin Scott is a geographer. He works in Washington State. He helps people understand one danger of volcanoes. **Volcanoes** are places where melted rock underground squeezes through the earth's outer layer. When the rock reaches the surface, it piles up into a mountain. In 1980 Mount St. Helens, a volcano in Washington, **erupted**. That means that the melted rock inside the volcano burst out. Scott came to study the huge **avalanche**, or landslide, caused by the eruption. The eruption and avalanche gave him a chance to study an earth-shaping event.

The Eruption of Mount St. Helens

In 1980 Mount St. Helens was a 9,677-foot-tall volcano. In March of that year, the mountain started to shake. A small hole opened just below the top of the volcano. Steam and ash began to blow out. Scientists flocked to Mount St. Helens to study the changes. For weeks the mountain rumbled and spit ash. Then suddenly it exploded! The blast burst out sideways. The force was so strong it knocked down trees 17 miles away! When the eruption was over, Mount St. Helens was only 8,364 feet tall.

North Fork Toutle River

The huge mudflow swept down the North Fork Toutle River Valley. Mud and sand poured downstream. All that mud kept ships from moving on the Columbia River.

The Crater

The eruption left a huge crater, or hole, at the top of the mountain. The crater has a low north edge because the blast burst sideways.

Spirit Lake

The avalanche crashed into Spirit Lake. When the lake re-formed on top of the mudslide, it was over 200 feet higher than before. **Map Skill:** *Was Spirit Lake larger or smaller before the volcano erupted?*

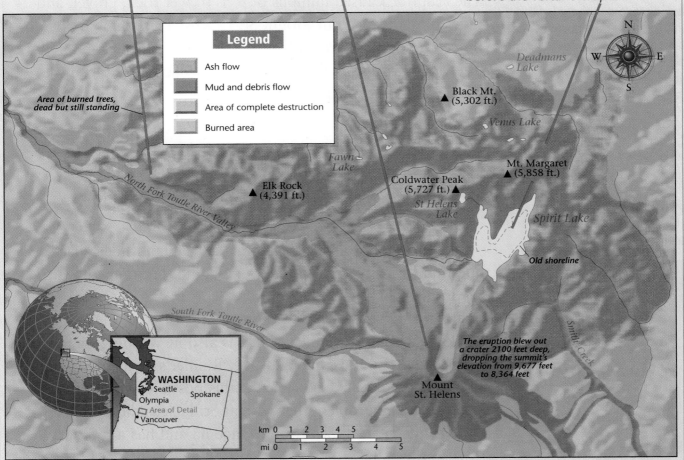

Legend

- Ash flow
- Mud and debris flow
- Area of complete destruction
- Burned area

Area of burned trees, dead but still standing

Deadmans Lake

Black Mt. (5,302 ft.)

Venus Lake

Fawn Lake

North Fork Toutle River Valley

Elk Rock (4,391 ft.)

Coldwater Peak (5,727 ft.)

St Helens Lake

Mt. Margaret (5,858 ft.)

Spirit Lake

Old shoreline

Smith Creek

South Fork Toutle River

The eruption blew out a crater 2100 feet deep, dropping the summit's elevation from 9,677 feet to 8,364 feet

Mount St. Helens

WASHINGTON
Seattle
Spokane
Olympia
Area of Detail
Vancouver

km 0 1 2 3 4 5
mi 0 1 2 3 4 5

These photos show Mount St. Helens after the eruption. The lake in the larger photo is filled with trees knocked down by the blast. **Geography:** *Why do you think the ground around the Mount St. Helens crater is gray?*

The city of Seattle, Washington, is near the volcano Mount Rainier.

A Dangerous Pattern

The eruption caused millions of tons of wet rock, gravel, and mud to fall away from Mount St. Helens. This soupy mix flowed down the north side of the mountain. Then it poured into the North Fork Toutle River Valley. Scott described the force of this avalanche:

> **"I**t was truly awe-inspiring. Houses were swept away on the flow along with thousands of trees. It was unstoppable.**"**

The Mount St. Helens eruption and its landslide caused a question for people in Washington: Could this happen again?

In the years since the eruption, Scott has studied nearby mountains to see how they compare to Mount St. Helens. He thinks that Mount Rainier, which is also in Washington, could be the site of another big landslide. Rainier's great size, steep slopes, and volcanic history make this possible. Mount Rainier also presents a problem that Mount St. Helens did not. It is close to the cities of Seattle and Tacoma and has a few small towns near its base.

Scientists like Kevin Scott have a good reason to look at the geography of Mount St. Helens and other mountains. Their studies help people understand the risks of volcanoes. This can help people protect their lives and homes.

The Geographer's Tool Kit

Focus *What are some tools geographers use to understand the world?*

When geographers study the land around them, they use special tools and skills. Kevin Scott used some of the most advanced tools available to study the avalanche at Mount St. Helens. He looked at photos of the area taken from an airplane. He also measured distances with the help of a special stream of light called a laser beam. This laser measures distances to within a fraction of an inch. Some of the newest tools in the geographer's tool kit are satellites. A **satellite** is a machine that flies around the earth in outer space. Satellites can pinpoint any location in the world. What tools would you use to study the land near your home?

No matter where geographers work, or what tools they use, their job remains the same. They study the earth and learn about how people live on this planet. What do you want to learn about the land around you?

This penguin carries a geographer's tool on its back. Instruments in the yellow backpack measure how the penguin is adapted to its home in Antarctica.

Lesson Review: Geography

1 Key Vocabulary: Write a short paragraph about a **volcano**, using **erupt** and **avalanche**.

2 Focus: What problem does geographer Kevin Scott help people understand?

3 Focus: What are some tools geographers use to understand the world?

4 Critical Thinking: Decision Making Would you move to a beautiful area if it was near a volcano? Explain.

5 Citizenship: Which people in your area help you prepare for natural disasters?

6 Geography/Science Activity: Volcanic rock starts out hot and melted. Then it cools and hardens. Design tools for taking rock samples at both stages.

GEOGRAPHER

The World in Spatial Terms

How Do Geographers Acquire and Use Information?

When geographers want to learn more about a place, they first ask questions. Where is it? What is it like there? Why is it there? Just asking questions, though, is not enough. The next step is to gather information about the physical and human characteristics of that place.

One way geographers find information about a place is to go there in person. While observing the place for a period of time, they record what they see in words, drawings, and photographs. Geographers also learn about places by reading books and studying maps.

After gathering information, geographers examine it carefully and draw conclusions. Then they find ways to organize and display this information for other people. Most geographers share their findings in reports. To support their ideas, they might use maps, drawings, photographs, graphs, tables, and diagrams.

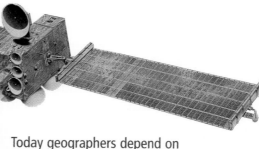

Today geographers depend on advanced tools. Satellites help geographers study large areas, as this photograph of the Grand Canyon shows.

After traveling through the Grand Canyon in 1869, John Wesley Powell spent 10 more years exploring and studying the Colorado Plateau. This 1873 photograph shows Powell talking with a Paiute Indian in the Grand Canyon.

The many maps Powell drew provided valuable information about the geography of the West. The map at far left shows part of the Green River region of Utah. Powell published the information he gathered in a book called *Exploration of the Colorado River of the West and Its Tributaries* (1875).

William H. Holmes drew this picture of the Grand Canyon in 1882. He served as an artist for several geographic expeditions through the West in the 1870s and 1880s.

Arts Connection

Paintings can provide useful information about the geography of a particular area. In the 1800s, a group of American artists painted many scenes of the Hudson River Valley. They became known as the Hudson River School. Why might their paintings of the Hudson River region still be of interest to geographers today?

Research Activity

Choose a nearby place that interests you.

1 Make a list of questions you might ask about the place. Then visit the place and gather information about it.

2 After examining the information you gathered, prepare a written report. Describe both the physical and human characteristics of the place you studied. Your report should contain maps, drawings, or photographs.

CHAPTER 1

Chapter Review

Summarizing the Main Idea

1 Copy the chart below. Then use what you have learned about geography to fill in the chart.

Things Geographers Use	How Geographers Use Them
Questions	*Geographers ask questions to learn about a place.*
Maps	
Tools	

Vocabulary

2 Think like a geographer! Use at least five of the following terms in a brief report about a place you would like to explore.

geography (p. 14)   **adapt (p. 19)**   **avalanche (p. 26)**
environment (p. 16)   **volcano (p. 26)**   **satellite (p. 29)**
hemisphere (p. 16)   **erupt (p. 26)**

Reviewing the Facts

3 How do geographers learn about places?

4 What are some ways that you can describe where you live?

5 What kind of information do maps show?

6 What can happen to plants and animals when the land changes?

7 What does Kevin Scott study?

8 How can Kevin Scott help the people who live near Mount St. Helens and other volcanoes?

9 What are some of the tools that geographers use?

10 Do latitude lines run north and south or east and west? What direction do longitude lines run?

11 Look at the map on page 21. What body of water lies between about 30°N and 20°N, and between 80°W and 110°W?

12 Why are degrees of latitude always labeled either N or S? Why are degrees of longitude always labeled E or W?

Geography Skills

13 Work with a partner. Choose a location on a globe, but don't tell your partner what it is. Describe the location. Then have your partner use your description to find the location.

14 Write a journal entry as if you were Kevin Scott. Describe what you saw at Mount St. Helens after the eruption.

Critical Thinking

15 **Generalize** Pick a location you'd like to learn about. Make a list of at least five questions that a geographer might ask about the location.

16 **Decision Making** Would you like to be a geographer? Why or why not? What is it about a geographer's work that appeals to you?

Writing: Citizenship and History

17 **Citizenship** Write a help-wanted ad for the position of geographer in your hometown. What features of your town might a geographer want to study?

18 **History** Write two or three questions about John Wesley Powell. Use a library to find the answers. As a group, put together a question-and-answer booklet about Powell.

Activities

Geography/Science Activity
Find out about a natural event that greatly affected the land and people where it occurred. Create a poster that tells about the event.

Citizenship/Literature Activity
How many ways can you describe where you live? Find and read a book or a magazine article about the people who live in your neighborhood, town, state, or country.

Internet Option

Check the
Internet Social Studies Center
for ideas on how to extend your theme project beyond your classroom.

THEME PROJECT CHECK-IN

Include the information from the chapter in your geographic dictionary.
• What questions would geographers want your dictionary to answer?
• How can you show the many ways to describe where you live?

Chapter Preview: *People, Places, and Events*

10,000 years ago

Bryce Canyon

How does water carve land into amazing shapes like this? *Lesson 1, Page 37*

The Appalachian Mountains

Where are some of the oldest mountains in the United States? *Lesson 1, Page 39*

Coal

What are some ways people use this resource? *Lesson 2, Page 45*

Our Nation's Landforms and Water

Main Idea The land we live in has many different features.

"America is a land of wonders . . . ."**"**

Alexis de Tocqueville (TOHK vihl) was a French visitor to the United States who said that more than 150 years ago. It's still true today. The land of the United States is filled with beauty. In some places you can find broad, rolling fields. Other parts of the United States are brightly colored, rocky deserts. Our country has jagged mountains sprinkled with snow. It has rounded hills covered with trees. It has giant lakes, powerful rivers, and dozens of other amazing sights. The United States is indeed a land of wonders.

◀ Wyoming's Yellowstone Canyon is one of this country's most striking landforms.

Key Vocabulary
- landform
- elevation
- sea level
- erosion
- Continental Divide

Key Places
- Pacific Ranges
- Basins and Ranges
- Rocky Mountains
- Great Plains
- Central Plains
- Appalachian Mtns.
- Coastal Plains

Today

Recycling

These people are working to conserve resources. Find out how.
Lesson 2, Page 46

Weathervane
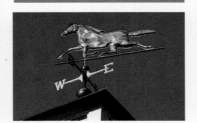
People use instruments like this weathervane to observe the weather.
Lesson 3, Page 48

Thunderstorm

Have you seen storms like this one? Find out about weather patterns near you. *Lesson 3, Page 49*

The Shapes of Land and Water

Focus *What are some of the landforms and bodies of water that make up the United States?*

The land of the United States is shaped into features called landforms. A **landform** is a feature of the earth's surface. The height of a landform is called its **elevation**.

Hills and mountains are landforms with high elevations. Elevation is measured in feet above sea level. **Sea level** is the level of the surface of the world's oceans. A hill is an area of land that rises above the land around it. Mountains are very large hills. Their steep slopes can rise thousands of feet above sea level. Mountains may seem permanent. In reality, they change all the time.

One process that changes mountains is erosion. Through **erosion**, rainwater, ice, and other forces wear away soil and rock. As you will read on the next page, erosion has shaped some very interesting landforms!

Low areas of land are called valleys. At the bottom of a valley you often find a river. Rivers are streams of fresh water that flow downhill. Other low areas are called basins. They lie below the land around them like shallow holes scooped out of the ground. Broad, smooth areas of land are called plains.

Valleys

The Snake River runs through a valley called Jackson Hole.

Rivers

This body of water is the Snake River.

Mountains

These mountains are the Teton (TEE tahn) Range in Wyoming.

Geography: *Which places in this photo are closest to sea level? Which places are farthest from sea level?*

Nature's Carver

Can water carve solid rock? Rainbow Bridge National Monument in Utah is proof that it can. Erosion has worn the rock there into arch shapes. How does this happen? Water soaks into cracks in the sandstone. Then it freezes. When water freezes, it expands. This makes the stone crack even more. After a while, chunks of rock break off. Eventually, the rock left behind forms a natural arch.

Erosion also affects things like these pebbles *(at right)*. It has smoothed their surfaces and rounded their edges. The earth everywhere is worn down by the slow, constant work of erosion.

Land Around Water, Water Around Land

Geographers define some landforms by their relation to water. A peninsula is a landform almost entirely surrounded by water. It reaches out into the water the way a finger reaches out from a hand. Islands are landforms completely surrounded by water. Lakes are the opposite of islands. They are large bodies of water surrounded by land.

The world is filled with many different landforms and bodies of water. You can find examples of all of them in the United States.

The Landscape of Our Country

Focus What are some of the major landform areas of the United States?

Have you ever taken a ride on a roller coaster? At first the coaster carries you slowly up a huge hill. When you reach the top, you speed down the other side. Then you race across a flat area until you reach another hill and start all over again.

Starting at the west coast, a trip across the United States at the 40th parallel (40°N latitude) can be like riding a roller coaster. Find that line of latitude on the map below. Your coaster first climbs hills and mountains called the Pacific Ranges. These mountains include the Coast Ranges, the Cascades, and the Sierra Nevada. The Pacific Ranges contain some of the youngest mountains in the country.

This map shows the major land-form areas of the United States.
Map Skill: *Where are the main mountain ranges in the United States?*

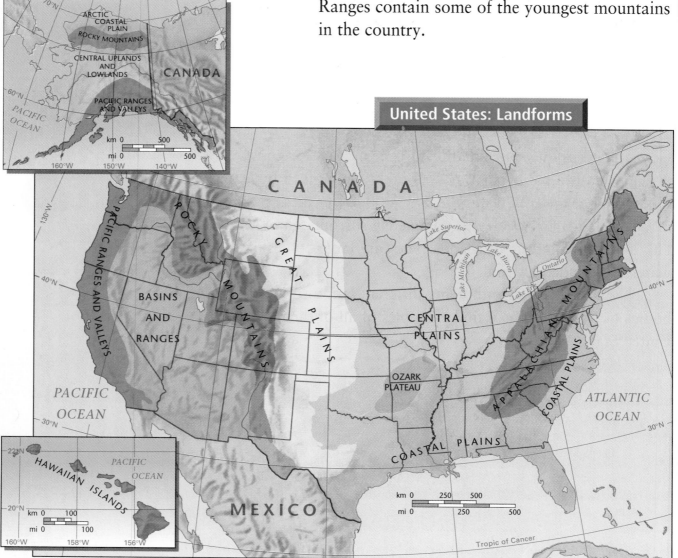

United States: Landforms

From the Pacific Ranges, your roller coaster slides into the Basins and Ranges. This area is also called the Great Basin. In that rocky country, you bounce over small mountain ranges. You also swoop into hundreds of basins.

As your coaster continues east, it starts uphill again. Now you're climbing the Rocky Mountains. The "Rockies" get their name from their sharp peaks. Many have elevations over 14,000 feet. A line called the **Continental Divide** runs along the top of the Rockies. Rivers that start west of the divide flow into the Pacific Ocean. Rivers that start east of it flow into the Atlantic Ocean, the Mississippi River, or the Gulf of Mexico.

The top photo shows the Rocky Mountains. The bottom photo shows the Great Plains.

From the Great Plains to the Atlantic Ocean

East of the Rockies, the coaster zooms across land that is mostly flat. Still racing from your descent down the mountains, you will first pass across the Great Plains. Then you will cross the Central Plains.

The Central Plains end at the Appalachian Mountains. There, your roller coaster climbs a final gentle hill. For millions of years, erosion has worn down the Appalachians. Their highest peaks are less than 7,000 feet above sea level.

From the Appalachians, the coaster crosses the Coastal Plains. This flat area is only slightly above sea level. Finally, the Coastal Plains end at the Atlantic Ocean. Your roller coaster has carried you all the way across the United States.

Lesson Review: Geography

1 Key Vocabulary: Use **landform, elevation, sea level, erosion,** and **Continental Divide** to describe a mountain range in the United States.

2 Focus: What are some of the landforms and bodies of water that make up the United States?

3 Focus: What are some of the major landform areas of the United States?

4 Critical Thinking: Conclude How do you think the Continental Divide got its name?

5 Geography: The Columbia River starts west of the Continental Divide. Into what ocean does it flow?

6 Citizenship/Writing Activity: With a partner, write a poem or a song. It should show your pride in the land in which you live.

Using Elevation Maps

High, Low, and In Between

If you go to Death Valley, you'll need to protect yourself against the sun and bring plenty of water. Just 100 miles away, on top of Mount Whitney, you'll need heavy boots, a parka, and a ski mask. As you change elevation — the height of land above or below sea level — the scenery and temperature change. **Elevation maps** can show you changes in height. Knowing a place's elevation helps you know what that place is like and what kinds of activities you can do there.

1 Here's How

Look at the elevation map on the next page.

- Read the legend. Different colors stand for different elevations. Find each of the color areas on the map. Find the lowest and highest elevations.

- Study what the map tells you about elevation. For example, notice that there are more orange areas in the west and more dark green areas in the east. What does this tell you about the elevation of different parts of the country?

- Use what you know about elevation to decide what activities you could do in different areas. Are there mountains for skiing near Chicago? Could you go snowboarding near Salt Lake City?

2 Think It Through

How could you use an elevation map to help you plan a camping vacation?

What activities can you do at sea level that you can't do at a high elevation?

The lowest elevation in North America is Death Valley, California. It is 282 feet below sea level.

3 Use It

1. Write down the approximate elevations of Chicago and Atlanta.

2. Name a city with an elevation of over 3,280 feet.

3. Name one place with a high elevation and one with a low elevation. List two differences in these places that might be caused by elevation.

4. Find Mt. Washington and New York City. How does elevation affect what people can do in each place?

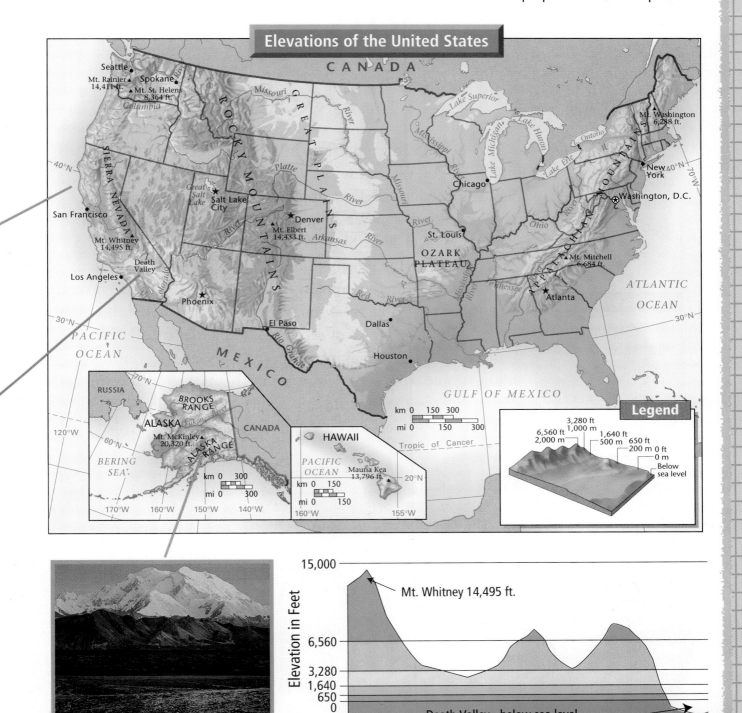

Elevations of the United States

CANADA

Seattle
Mt. Rainier 14,411 ft.
Spokane
Mt. St. Helens 8,364 ft.
Columbia
Missouri River
GREAT PLAINS
Lake Superior
Mt. Washington 6,288 ft.

SIERRA NEVADA
40°N
Great Salt Lake
Salt Lake City
Platte
ROCKY MOUNTAINS
Missouri
Lake Michigan
Lake Huron
Lake Ontario
New York
40°N
70°W

San Francisco
Denver
Mt. Elbert 14,433 ft.
Arkansas River
Chicago
Lake Erie
APPALACHIAN MOUNTAINS
Washington, D.C.

Mt. Whitney 14,495 ft.
Death Valley
Los Angeles
River
St. Louis
OZARK PLATEAU
Ohio
Mt. Mitchell 6,684 ft.

Phoenix
30°N
Red River
Tennessee
Atlanta
ATLANTIC OCEAN
30°N

PACIFIC OCEAN
El Paso
Rio Grande
Dallas
Houston

MEXICO
GULF OF MEXICO

RUSSIA
BROOKS RANGE
ALASKA
Yukon River
CANADA
Mt. McKinley 20,320 ft.
ALASKA RANGE
BERING SEA
70°N
60°N
120°W
170°W 160°W 150°W 140°W
km 0 300
mi 0 300

HAWAII
PACIFIC OCEAN
Mauna Kea 13,796 ft.
km 0 150
mi 0 150
160°W 155°W
20°N

km 0 150 300
mi 0 150 300
Tropic of Cancer

Legend
3,280 ft 1,000 m
6,560 ft 2,000 m
1,640 ft 500 m
650 ft
200 m 0 ft
0 m
Below sea level

At 20,320 feet, Mount McKinley, Alaska, is the highest peak in North America.

Mt. Whitney 14,495 ft.

Elevation in Feet
15,000
6,560
3,280
1,640
650
0
Death Valley - below sea level

The diagram above shows California's highest and lowest elevations.

A Land of Rich Resources

Main Idea The United States has many resources which we need to conserve for the future.

Key Vocabulary

resource
fossil fuel
mineral
conservation
recycling

Key Places

Gary, Indiana
Hutchinson, Kansas

Together, the farms of Washington grow more apples than the farms of any other state. **Economics:** *Hawaii grows more pineapples than any other state. What resources would a farmer in Hawaii need to grow and sell pineapples?*

The next time you shop in a supermarket, think about all the food you see on the shelves. What materials did people need to produce it? Take apples, for example. To produce apples, a farmer in Washington state needs apple trees, soil, water, and sunshine. She also needs a farm machine called a tractor. It is made mostly of metal and runs on a fuel called gasoline. To store her apples, the farmer needs wooden boxes.

All of these things — soil, water, sunshine, metal, fuel, and wood — are examples of resources. **Resources** are all of the things that go into making what people need. Most of those things come from the environment. They are natural resources. Everything in the supermarket comes from resources. People are resources, too. They are called human resources.

Natural Treasures

Focus *What are the different kinds of natural resources?*

Land, water, and air are the three most basic natural resources. Resources can be living things such as plants and animals. They can also be non-living things such as rocks, minerals, and even sunlight. All natural resources belong to one of three groups. They are renewable resources, nonrenewable resources, or flow resources.

Three Kinds of Natural Resources

Renewable resources are things like trees. They can be replaced. People cut down trees for wood. With time, trees can grow back. Nonrenewable resources such as petroleum (which is also called crude oil) cannot be replaced. Once people use petroleum, it is gone. Flow resources are neither renewable nor nonrenewable. They can only be used where and when they are found. Wind is a flow resource. It can be used as a source of energy only while it blows past a windmill. Putting up a windmill doesn't affect the amount of wind that will go by. People can't use up the wind, and they can't replace it, either.

People rely on resources every day of their lives. You are lucky to live in the United States! Within this country people can find a great variety of the resources they need.

Windmills can only capture the wind's energy where and when the wind blows.

Running water is a flow resource that people use to produce energy. One way to measure energy is in Btu. "Btu" stands for British thermal unit. **Chart Skill:** *Do you think the United States produces more energy from nonrenewable resources or from flow resources?*

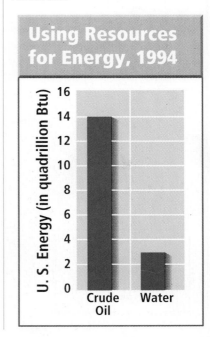

Using Resources for Energy, 1994

(Bar chart showing U. S. Energy (in quadrillion Btu) on vertical axis from 0 to 16. Crude Oil bar ≈ 14. Water bar ≈ 3.)

These car license plates show pictures of natural resources in these states. **Economics:** *What resources could you find in Oregon or Kansas?*

Map Skill: *What minerals or fossil fuels are found in your state?*

Using Our Natural Riches

Focus *How do people use some of the resources of the United States?*

You can find the natural riches of the United States in many places. The map below shows some of them. Two non-renewable resources are coal and petroleum. These are **fossil fuels.** They come from living things that died millions of years ago. People use fossil fuels for energy.

The map also shows resources called minerals. **Minerals** are nonrenewable resources that people dig from the earth. Copper, gold, and silver are minerals called metals. People use copper in pipes and in motors. Gold and silver can make electrical connections work well. So those two metals are used in computers. All three metals have been used as money. Minerals are some of the country's most important resources.

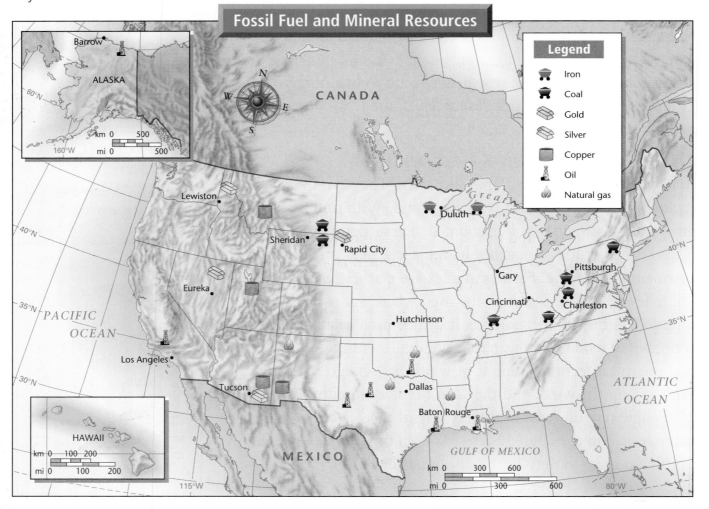

Fossil Fuel and Mineral Resources

Legend
- Iron
- Coal
- Gold
- Silver
- Copper
- Oil
- Natural gas

Iron and Coal Resources

Because people need resources, they often live in places where useful resources are found. One of the world's most useful minerals is a metal called iron. It can be combined with substances from coal to make steel. People use steel to make everything from boats to cars to skyscrapers to spoons.

The city of Gary, Indiana, was created to use iron and coal resources to make steel. A huge company called the United States Steel Corporation started building Gary in 1906. The company carefully picked a spot for their city on the southern tip of Lake Michigan. Find this place on the map on the left. You can see why they chose it. Iron resources lie north of Gary, between Lake Michigan and Lake Superior. South of Gary, coal is found. Railroads bring coal to the city. Boats bring iron. Workers in Gary's steel mills combine these two resources to create this important product: steel.

Soil and Wheat Resources

Not many cities were created the way Gary, Indiana, was. However, many cities and towns have grown up where resources are available. One such city is Hutchinson, Kansas. Its first resource is the rich Kansas soil. This resource attracted farmers. Thousands of them came from an area which is now the country of Ukraine. They settled near Hutchinson. The farmers brought something with them that became Hutchinson's second resource. It is a kind of wheat called Turkey Red. Turkey Red wheat grew amazingly well in the Kansas soil. Today, Kansas grows more wheat than any other state. Hutchinson is now proud to be the center of the most important wheat-growing area in Kansas.

Today, over 100,000 people live in Gary, Indiana *(above)*.

Workers in Gary's steel mills make steel products for many different uses. This man is working with a roll of sheet steel.

Ask Yourself

Think about the state and town that you live in. What role do resources play in your community?

?????????????

The shiny rectangular pieces on top of these houses are solar panels. They collect energy from sunlight. Then they turn that energy into electricity. *Science: What kind of resource — flow, renewable, or nonrenewable — is solar energy?*

These workers are digging bauxite out of the ground. The bauxite will be made into aluminum.

Using Resources Wisely

Focus *Why is it important to conserve resources?*

Resources are very precious. Not all of them will last forever. Many of the resources people depend on are nonrenewable. If people waste them or use them unwisely, these resources will run out quickly.

People can take many actions to keep resources from being used up. They can use renewable and flow resources. People in some parts of the country can create all the electricity they need with solar energy. Solar energy is energy that comes from sunshine. Using sunshine for energy saves nonrenewable resources like oil and gas. People still need these nonrenewable resources, however. They can make all their resources last longer by practicing conservation. **Conservation** is the careful use and protection of resources.

Recycling

The metal called aluminum is an important nonrenewable resource. You use it every time you drink a can of soda or ride in an airplane. People use more aluminum than any other metal except for iron and steel.

Aluminum is made from a rock called bauxite. There is enough bauxite in the world to make aluminum for hundreds of years. However, it takes a lot of energy to turn bauxite into aluminum. Also, even all that bauxite will run out someday.

One way to conserve aluminum is to use less of it. Yet aluminum is so useful that we use more of it every year. Fortunately, people can conserve aluminum — and other

The cans in the recycling center on the left have been crushed into blocks. Later, they will be made into new cans. The boy below is collecting steel cans. They can be recycled, too.

renewable and nonrenewable resources — another way. They can practice **recycling,** which means re-using things that have been thrown out. Today, over half of all aluminum cans sold in the United States are recycled. David Dougherty works for a recycling group called Clean Washington. He says that

> "**P**eople . . . *can recycle their waste every day of their lives.*"

Actions like recycling help people conserve resources. Conservation can help Americans make sure that this country will be as rich in resources tomorrow as it is today.

Lesson Review: Geography

1. **Key Vocabulary:** Use **resource, mineral, conservation,** and **recycling** in a paragraph about aluminum.

2. **Focus:** What are the different kinds of natural resources?

3. **Focus:** How do people use some of the resources of the United States?

4. **Focus:** Why is it important to conserve resources?

5. **Critical Thinking: Cause and Effect** Would many people live in a place that has few resources? Explain.

6. **Theme: Our Land** Why is recycling good for the environment?

7. **Citizenship/Math Activity:** Each day, a family throws out 17 pounds of trash and recycles three pounds of trash. Make a chart showing how much trash they throw out and recycle in one week.

A Land of Many Climates

Main Idea Weather and climate vary across the United States.

Key Vocabulary

weather
temperature
precipitation
climate

Key Places

Honolulu, Hawaii

Seattle, Washington

Williston, North
  Dakota

St. Louis, Missouri

Phoenix, Arizona

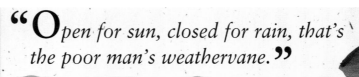

"**O**pen for sun, closed for rain, that's the poor man's weathervane."

This saying refers to the scarlet pimpernel plant. Before the days of television forecasters, people used things like pimpernel flowers to tell whether the next day would be sunny or stormy. On dry, sunny days, the pimpernel's flowers stay open. When the air gets damp — and rain is likely — its flowers close up. So, if you see a pimpernel with open flowers, expect clear skies. If you see them shut tight, watch out! It may rain soon.

Weather

Focus *What makes up the weather?*

Both television forecasters and scarlet pimpernels can predict the weather. What is weather, though? Scientists say **weather** is the condition of a layer of air around the earth. This layer is called the atmosphere. You can also say that weather is what it is like outside. Is it hot, cold, rainy, or windy? How would you describe the weather outside right now?

When scientists describe weather they measure many things. One thing is temperature. **Temperature** is a measurement of hotness or coldness.

Each glass ball in this old-fashioned thermometer is filled with a special liquid. The balls float at different heights depending on the temperature.

Another important part of weather is precipitation. **Precipitation** is moisture that falls from clouds. It can take the form of rain, snow, sleet, or hail.

Water and Weather

Have you ever watched rain fall? You might have wondered how all that water got up in the sky. The illustration below shows how that happens. Rain — and all other precipitation — is part of something called the water cycle.

Weather usually follows a cycle as well. Hot weather can turn cold. Sun can follow rain. Over the long run, every area has its own pattern of weather.

The weather affects people every day of their lives. **Science:** *How would you describe the weather in this photo? How do you think a scientist would describe it?*

The Water Cycle

In the water cycle, water moves from bodies of water to the air and then back again.

Sunshine heats water in oceans, rivers, and lakes until it evaporates. That means the water turns into a gas called water vapor. Plants also give off water vapor. The water vapor rises to form clouds.

Once it is high in the sky, the water vapor cools down. The cold makes it turn back into liquid water or ice. Then precipitation falls.

The precipitation collects in streams, rivers, lakes, and oceans. It also seeps underground in a process called infiltration. Then the cycle starts once again.

Map Skill: *What kind of climate do you live in?*

Climate

Focus *What affects climate?*

A **climate** is the usual weather pattern for an area of the world. To scientists, climate means the temperature and precipitation in an area over many years. Climate is affected by four things: latitude, elevation, distance from water, and winds.

Latitude and Elevation

Latitude has a big effect on climate. The sun's rays are most powerful at the equator. So, places at latitudes near the equator usually have warmer climates than places far away. Honolulu, Hawaii, is closer to the equator than Seattle, Washington. Which city do you think has a warmer climate? If you guessed Honolulu, you're right.

At high elevations, air cools. Places at high elevations are generally colder than those closer to sea level. The top of Hawaii's highest mountain is often cold. That's because its elevation is almost 14,000 feet above sea level!

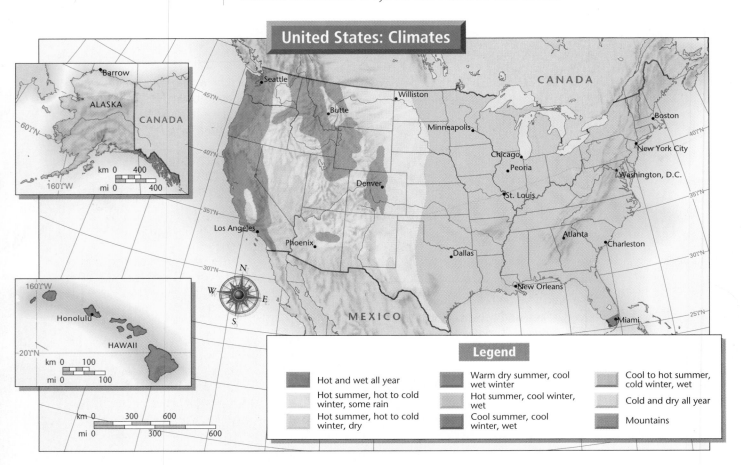

United States: Climates

Legend

- Hot and wet all year
- Hot summer, hot to cold winter, some rain
- Hot summer, hot to cold winter, dry
- Warm dry summer, cool wet winter
- Hot summer, cool winter, wet
- Cool summer, cool winter, wet
- Cool to hot summer, cold winter, wet
- Cold and dry all year
- Mountains

Water and Wind

Distance from water has two effects on climate. The temperature of water changes more slowly than the temperature of land. This keeps areas near oceans from getting as cold or as hot as areas far away from oceans. Places near water also tend to get more precipitation than places far from water. Look at the map. You can probably guess that Seattle, Washington, gets more rain than Williston, North Dakota. Seattle doesn't get as hot or as cold as Williston, either.

Winds can change the ocean's effects, though. Some places are like St. Louis, Missouri. They're far from the ocean, but winds bring them moist air. Those places get lots of precipitation. In other places, like Phoenix, Arizona, the winds are dry. Those areas get very little precipitation.

Together, latitude, elevation, distance from water, and winds create all the climates in the United States. Take one more look at the map. You live in one of the climates shown there. How do the four things you just read about affect you?

Mount Waialeale (WY ah lay AH lay), in Hawaii, can have 350 rainy days a year.

Parts of the Mojave (moh HAH vee) Desert, in California, have gone for a year without rain.

Lesson Review: Geography

1 **Key Vocabulary:** Write a weather report for your town using **weather, temperature, precipitation,** and **climate.**

2 **Focus:** What makes up the weather?

3 **Focus:** What affects climate?

4 **Critical Thinking: Cause and Effect** Why do you think Alaska is often cold and Florida is usually warm?

5 **Geography:** How would you go about learning about the climate of a new place? What measurements would you need to take?

6 **Theme: Our Land/Science Activity:** As a class, record the weather for a week on a chart. Make sure the chart includes the temperature and the precipitation. What kind of climate do you think your area has?

Chapter Review

Summarizing the Main Idea

1 Copy and complete the chart below. Fill in a key place and one
or two facts about its landforms, resources, or climate.

Key Place	Fact
Pacific Ranges	*They are made up of mountains and hills on or near the west coast.*
Gary, Indiana	
Phoenix, Arizona	

Vocabulary

2 Using at least eight of the following terms, write a letter
describing a place in the United States that you have visited.

landform (p. 36)	**resource (p. 42)**	**weather (p. 48)**
elevation (p. 36)	**fossil fuel (p. 44)**	**temperature (p. 48)**
sea level (p. 36)	**mineral (p. 44)**	**precipitation (p. 49)**
erosion (p. 36)	**conservation (p. 46)**	**climate (p. 50)**
Continental Divide (p. 39)	**recycling (p. 47)**	

Reviewing the Facts

3 What are some kinds of landforms
found in the United States?

4 What is a force that changes the shape
of the land? How?

5 How do people use resources?

6 What are the differences among renewable resources, nonrenewable
resources, and flow resources?

7 What are some nonrenewable resources
found in the United States?

8 What are some ways to keep nonrenewable resources from being used up?

9 What is the water cycle?

10 What different things affect climate?

Skill Review: Using Elevation Maps

11 Look at the map on page 41. What color represents the lowest elevation? What do you think the environment is like there?

12 Find your home state on the map on page 41. What are its highest and lowest elevations? Is most of it at a higher or lower elevation than the states around it?

Geography Skills

13 Look at the maps on pages 38 and 44. What resources might you find in the Great Basin?

14 Write a climate report for your state. Include information about what might affect the climate.

Critical Thinking

15 Predict Think about what you have learned about conservation. Describe what might happen in your community if you stopped conserving resources.

16 Decision Making What kind of weather do you like? Look at the climate map on page 50. Pick an area in which you would like to live and explain why you picked it.

Writing: Citizenship and Economics

17 Citizenship Write an advertisement urging people to visit your state. Include information about the land, resources, and climate.

18 Economics Find out about your state's resources. How are they used? Write a summary of what you have learned.

Activities

National Heritage/Art Activity
Work in a group of three or four. Design a banner describing a part of the land or resources of the United States that people cherish.

Geography/Research Activity
Select a specific landform in the United States. Prepare a brief oral presentation about the landform. Share the presentation with your classmates.

Internet Option

Check the **Internet Social Studies Center** for ideas on how to extend your theme project beyond your classroom.

THEME PROJECT CHECK-IN

Include what you have learned about in this chapter in your geographic dictionary.
- What are the major geographic features of the United States?
- How can you include resources mentioned and the products made from them?
- How can you show the impact of weather and climate?

Looking at Regions

Chapter Preview: *People, Places, and Events*

10,000 years ago

Jaguar

Find out about this jaguar's home and other regions. *Lesson 1, Page 57*

Four Corners

The edges of four states come together here. What are those edges called? *Lesson 1, Page 57*

The Oregon Trail

Start your journey across the regions of your country in Lesson 2. *Lesson 2, Page 60*

What Is a Region?

Main Idea Regions are areas with shared features. They are separated from other regions by lines called boundaries.

Key Vocabulary
region
boundary
border

Key Places
49th parallel
Rio Grande

You and your best friend are really hungry! You decide to order a pizza. You want mushrooms on it. Your friend wants only pepperoni. How can you decide what to get? "I know how we can both be happy," you say. "We'll get a pizza that has both."

Soon the doorbell rings. The pizza is here. Mmm! It smells good. It looks good, too. Juicy mushrooms cover one half. Crisp pepperoni covers the other.

You may not realize it, but you have divided your pizza into regions. A **region** is an area that shares one or more features. Those features make that area different from other areas. Mushrooms are a feature of one half of your pizza. They make it different from the other half. As you take a bite, think about this. Knowing about regions helps you understand your world.

◀ Boise, Idaho, is a city region within a region of hills.

Today

The Appalachian Mountains

How can this region overlap other regions? *Lesson 2, Page 62*

Writing Around the World

What writing system do people use in Russia? *Lesson 3, Page 69*

The Berlin Wall

Can people change the boundaries of regions? You bet they can! *Lesson 3, Page 70*

Regions

Focus *How and why do people divide the earth into regions?*

Regions are tools that help people understand the world around them. Many different features make up our world. People can use any of those features to divide the world into regions.

Human and Natural Regions

Some regions are based on human features. A city is that kind of region. It shares features made by people, such as buildings, roads, and telephone lines. Cities, states, and countries are also regions in which everyone follows the same set of laws.

Some regions are based on natural features. Climate, vegetation, and landforms are some natural features. You can see three regions based on other natural features on the map at right. Those regions are based on the areas in which certain animals live.

Some regions are based on both natural and human features. In Chapter 2 you learned about landform regions of the United States. Do you remember the states that include the Rocky Mountains? Those states make up a region called the Rocky Mountain states. That region is based on both a natural feature — the Rocky Mountains — and a human feature — states.

Boundaries

Focus *What is a boundary and how is it drawn?*

Think about a game of soccer. You race down the field toward the goal line. Then you kick the ball and it crosses the goal line. You score!

The goal line in soccer is a **boundary,** a line people draw to mark the edge of a region. The soccer field is the region. The goal line is one of its boundaries. The map at right

Some regions of a soccer field have special rules. If you're in the large rectangular region around your goal, be careful! That region is called the penalty area. If you break a rule in that region, the other team gets a special chance to kick the ball into your goal. **Cultures:** *What other games have regions where special rules apply?*

North American Animal Regions

Alaska

Hudson Bay

CANADA

NORTH

AMERICA

Lake Superior
Lake Huron
Lake Ontario
Lake Michigan
Lake Erie

PACIFIC OCEAN

ATLANTIC OCEAN

UNITED

STATES

Mississippi River

Rio Grande

The Everglades

MEXICO

Gulf of Mexico

N

Legend
Range of the polar bear
Range of the jaguar
Range of the crocodile

0   1500 km
0   1000 mi

shows boundaries of states and countries. Not all of the boundaries are alike. Some of them are curved or wavy. They follow natural features like rivers and coastlines. Other boundaries are straight lines. They follow features that people make. Those features are often lines of latitude and longitude.

The animals shown on this map eat mostly meat. Polar bears often eat seals. Jaguars like to eat piglike animals called peccaries (PEHK uh reez). Crocodiles swallow fish whole. **Map Skill:** *Compare this map to the climate map on page 50. In what climates do these animals live ?*

These photos show two of the United States' boundaries. **Geography:** *What other boundaries do you know?*

Can You Find the Boundary?

Finding a boundary on a map can be pretty easy. Finding boundaries in the real world is often hard to do. The photos on this page show special boundaries called **borders**. They are the boundaries of countries, states, and towns.

The photo on the top shows the border between the United States and Mexico. That border follows a river called the Rio Grande. Once you know that, the border is easy to see. Now look at the bottom photo. It shows the border between the United States and Canada. That border follows a line of latitude called the 49th parallel. You can't see lines of latitude. So, people have cut down trees to mark part of the border. If the trees had been left standing, you wouldn't see the border at all.

Other boundaries can be hard to find as well. Look back at the map on page 57. Suppose you travel around Florida. Do you think you could find the northern boundary of the region in which American crocodiles live? You probably couldn't. That's because the edge of the crocodile region is fuzzy. You won't find a line on the Florida soil that crocodiles won't cross. Instead, you'll see fewer and fewer crocodiles as you walk out of the region. The boundary line on the map marks the place where you're most likely to stop seeing crocodiles.

Like regions, boundaries are useful tools. Together, they can help you understand the world you live in.

Lesson Review: Geography

1 **Key Vocabulary:** Use **region**, **boundary**, and **border** to describe your town.

2 **Focus:** How and why do people divide the earth into regions?

3 **Focus:** What is a boundary and how is it drawn?

4 **Critical Thinking: Conclude:** Is your neighborhood a region? Why or why not?

5 **Geography:** Look at the map on page 57. Where in the United States do four state boundaries meet in one spot?

6 **Citizenship/Research Activity:** Choose a state. List the states and bodies of water that border it. Then trade lists with a partner and guess each other's states.

Regions of the United States

Main Idea The United States can be divided into many different kinds of regions. Some regions overlap one another.

I t was the end of a tiring day. Amelia Stewart Knight rested by the Platte River. In her diary she described what she saw.

> **"T**he road is covered with droves of cattle and wagons — no end to them.**"**

Amelia's family was traveling west along the Oregon Trail. During the mid-1800s, thousands of people made that journey. Many came all the way from the East Coast of the United States. These people started west through regions with many towns. They moved through regions of deep forests. Once on the Oregon Trail itself, they crossed dusty plains regions. They survived regions with snowy mountains and regions with hot deserts. The trip across the country could last nearly a year. It brought people through many regions of the United States.

Key Vocabulary

economy
goods
service
belt

Key Places

The Northeast
The South
The Midwest
The West

The Oregon Trail was about 2,000 miles long. **Map Skill:** *What mountains did the Knight family cross? What rivers did they follow?*

The Oregon Trail

Astoria
Oregon City
OREGON
Columbia River
Missouri River
Cascade Mountains
ROCKY
Snake River
Great Salt Lake
Mountains
Oregon Trail
Platte River
Independence, Mo.
Pacific Ocean

0 175 250 miles

N

Legend
— Oregon Trail
— Present-day state borders

If you traveled through all four regions of the United States, you would see beautiful scenery and exciting cities. You would also meet many friendly people.

Four Regions of Our Country

Focus *What kinds of features do the states in a region of the United States share?*

Unlike Amelia Stewart Knight, you could ride a bus across the whole country in less than a week. If you took a trip like that, you could pass through the four regions of the United States marked on the map at right. Those regions are the Northeast, the South, the Midwest, and the West.

An organization called the United States Bureau of the Census drew the boundaries of the four regions. The Census Bureau collects all kinds of information about the United States. It uses the four regions to sort that information. Then people can use the information to learn about this country.

The states in each region share many features. They may have the same kind of climate, natural resources, plants, animals, landforms, and bodies of water. The history of the states in a region may be much the same. The states in a region may also have the same kind of economy. The word **economy** refers to work that produces wealth. The economies of all regions depend on goods and services. **Goods** are things that people buy and sell, like books, clothes, or food. A **service** is work someone does for other people.

Census Regions of the United States

WASHINGTON

MONTANA

NORTH DAKOTA

OREGON

IDAHO

MINNESOTA

SOUTH DAKOTA

WISCONSIN

MICHIGAN

WYOMING

WEST

IOWA

NEBRASKA

MIDWEST

INDIANA

OHIO

NEVADA

UTAH

COLORADO

ILLINOIS

WEST VIRGINIA

D.C.

NORTHEAST

MAINE

VERMONT

NEW HAMPSHIRE

NEW YORK

MASS.

RHODE IS.

CONN.

PENNSYLVANIA

NEW JERSEY

DELAWARE

MARYLAND

CALIFORNIA

KANSAS

MISSOURI

KENTUCKY

VIRGINIA

ARIZONA

NEW MEXICO

OKLAHOMA

ARKANSAS

SOUTH

TENNESSEE

NORTH CAROLINA

SOUTH CAROLINA

GEORGIA

TEXAS

MISSISSIPPI

ALABAMA

LOUISIANA

FLORIDA

ALASKA

km 0 — 400
mi 0 — 200

HAWAII

km 0 — 200
mi 0 — 100

km 0 — 600
mi 0 — 300

Map Skill: *In which census region of the United States do you live?*

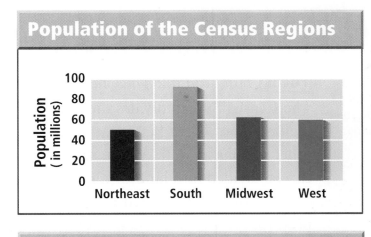

Population of the Census Regions

About 270 million people live in the United States today. **Chart Skill:** *Which census region has the most people?*

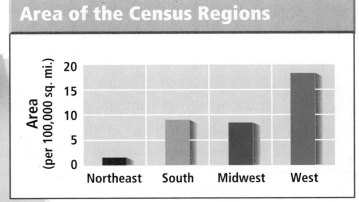

Area of the Census Regions

The area of the United States is close to four million square miles. **Chart Skill:** *What is the largest census region of the United States?*

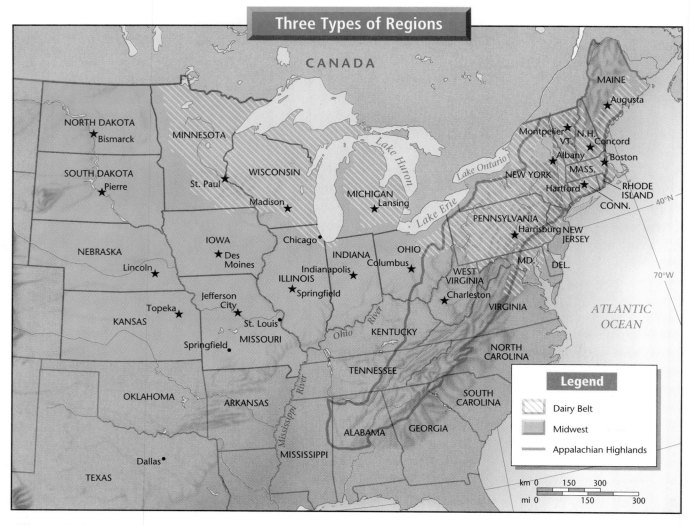

Different kinds of regions can overlap one another. This map shows a landform region, a census region, and a farming region. **Map Skill:** *From what you see on the map, why do you think people call some regions "belts"?*

Overlapping Regions

Focus *How can one place be part of many different regions?*
The Census Bureau divides the United States into four census regions. The United States can be divided into any number of other regions as well. As you saw in Chapter 2, your country can be divided into landform regions and climate regions. You can also divide the United States into regions where farmers produce certain foods. Look at the map above. It shows a region of the United States that produces a lot of milk. That region is called the Dairy Belt. A **belt** is a region that has a special feature. That feature sets it apart from other regions. The Dairy Belt is special because it produces so much milk.

The map shows something else about certain parts of the Dairy Belt, as well. Places that are in the Dairy Belt are also part of other regions. As you can see, regions can overlap.

These photos show the Dairy Belt and the Appalachian Highlands. Geography: *What other regions do you think these places are part of?*

One Place, Many Regions

Can you find Lansing, Michigan, on the map at left? It is part of the Dairy Belt. It is also in a census region called the Midwest. Now look for Harrisburg, Pennsylvania. It is part of the Dairy Belt, too. It is also in a landform region called the Appalachian Highlands.

Like Lansing and Harrisburg, any one place is part of many different regions at once. Many towns are part of farming regions, census regions, and landform regions. They are part of many other kinds of regions as well. The United States is full of different regions. You will learn about many of them as you read this book. Learning about those regions will help you understand your country.

Ask Yourself?

You have learned that a place can belong to many different regions. To what regions does your town or city belong?

? ? ? ? ? ? ? ? ? ? ? ? ? ? ?

Lesson Review: Geography

1. **Key Vocabulary:** Use **economy, goods, services,** and **belt** to describe a region you live in.

2. **Focus:** What kinds of features do the states in a region of the United States share?

3. **Focus:** How can one place be part of many different regions?

4. **Critical Thinking: Interpret** Why do you think the members of the Census Bureau drew the boundaries of the four regions the way they did?

5. **Theme: Our Land** What kinds of regions did the Knight family cross on the Oregon Trail?

6. **Geography/Arts Activity:** Make a simple map of your school. Divide it into regions and name each one.

★ CITIZENSHIP ★

Participating

What Is a State?

What state do you live in? What makes it a state? Read below to learn how Ohio, Indiana, Illinois, Michigan, Minnesota, and Wisconsin became states. They all started out as territories in the region known as the Old Northwest.

Case Study

The Northwest Ordinances

In 1776, the United States had 13 states and several large amounts of public, western lands. The laws for living in these lands were different from the laws in the states. In the 1780s, the U.S. government drew up some laws, or ordinances, so that land in the Old Northwest could become states.

These Northwest Ordinances said, first, that the U.S. government would choose someone to govern a territory until

it had 5,000 men. When it grew to 60,000 people, a territory could become a state. The Ordinances guaranteed rights to religious freedom, jury trials, and education. Slavery was not allowed.

Land in this area was divided into six-mile-square townships, and sold to settlers in one mile-square parcels. You can still see this rectangular pattern today.

Take Action

Have any of your classroom rules changed as you've gotten older? Have some stayed the same? Schools are like nations: as students move into new regions, some rules stay the same, some change. Try this to see how rules, like regions, overlap.

1 Think of your school as a country, and the rooms, halls, and playgrounds as states. Draw a map of all or part of your "country." Name this country and its "states."

2 Visitors coming to your state need to know your state laws. Write down your classroom rules. Visitors will also visit a classroom of younger or older children. Write down those state rules, too.

3 To move from one state to another, visitors need to pass through some shared spaces. What are the rules they should observe as they travel? Write them down.

4 Compare your lists of rules from these different states. How are they alike and different? Why are some the same and some different?

Tips for Participating

- Be open-minded about presenting and listening to ideas.
- Give everyone a chance to express an opinion.
- Tell other people what you like about their ideas.
- Try to use the word *and* more, and the word *but* less. This shows that you don't necessarily disagree but have something to add.

Research Activity

How did your state become part of the United States? Look for information in books and encyclopedias. Make a timeline that shows how your state came to be.

MILES
0   200   400   600

Writing Outlines

Put Your Ideas in Place

You can use regions to learn more about the world around you. There are animal regions, crop regions, climate regions, and many others. Dividing the world into smaller parts like regions can help you understand it better.

Dividing information into smaller parts can also help you understand it better. Suppose you have researched a report on the southern region of the United States. Making an **outline** can help. An outline divides your topic into smaller parts called main ideas and supporting details. Using an outline can help you write an interesting, easy-to-understand report.

Key Question #1:
What is the land in Arkansas like?

half the state is forest
rich in minerals
divided into eastern and
   southern lowlands and
   northwestern highlands
lots of plants and animals

① Here's How

- Choose a topic you want to write about. What key questions do you want your report to answer?

- Gather information to answer your key questions. Take notes. Group information according to the question it answers.

- Rewrite key questions into statements. These are now your main ideas. Use Roman numerals, such as I, II, and III, to order main ideas.

- Your notes are now called supporting details. Use capital letters, such as A, B, and C, to order them.

- Supporting details should be indented. Each Roman numeral and capital letter is followed by a period.

2 Think It Through

How does making an outline help you write a clear and organized report?

3 Use It

Start an outline of your own on a topic from this chapter, or use an encyclopedia to add to the outline shown on these pages.

I. The land of Arkansas is rich in natural resources.

  A. Half of Arkansas is covered by forests.

  B. Arkansas has many minerals.

  C. The Arkansas River Valley and the plains near the Mississippi River are good farmland.

II. Arkansas' land is important to its businesses.

  A. Farms, which raise mostly corn, soybeans, and rice, cover 16 million acres.

  B. The land is mined for valuable minerals.

  C. Forests, which cover half the state, are a rich source for timber.

Key Question #3

What is the climate like in Arkansas?

mild temperatures
good for farming and outdoor activities
long spring and autumn

Key Question #2

What is the economy like in Arkansas?

- Soybeans, rice, and corn are the most important crops.
- farms cover half the state
- timber was the first industry
- poultry and livestock are major farm products
- some mining

World Regions

Main Idea People can identify regions around the world. They can change what regions look like and where their boundaries are.

Do you remember learning to read? Your first step might have been to learn the alphabet. What if you had learned to read in Russia or Morocco? The alphabets people learn there are not the same as the one you learned in the United States. In China, people don't start with an alphabet at all.

Russia, Morocco, China, and the United States each use different **writing systems**. That means they each have a different way of writing down sounds or words. The map below shows regions of the world where people use these four systems. Learning about regions like these will help you understand how people around the world live.

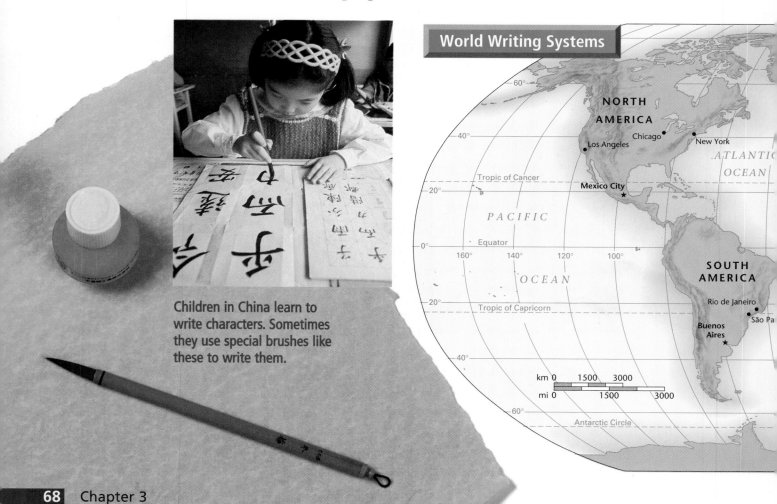

Children in China learn to write characters. Sometimes they use special brushes like these to write them.

World Writing Systems

NORTH AMERICA
Chicago
Los Angeles
New York
ATLANTIC OCEAN
Tropic of Cancer
Mexico City
PACIFIC
Equator
160°   140°   120°   100°
OCEAN
SOUTH AMERICA
Rio de Janeiro
São Pa
Buenos Aires
Tropic of Capricorn
km 0   1500   3000
mi 0   1500   3000
Antarctic Circle

Regions Around the World

Focus *How is the world divided into regions?*

As you read in Lesson 1, a region is an area that shares at least one feature. People divide the world into regions by seeing where certain features are. The map below shows four regions. Each region is an area where people use the same writing system.

In the region where you live, people write with the Latin alphabet. In Morocco, people use the Arabic alphabet. In Russia, people use the Cyrillic (suh RIHL ihk) alphabet. In China, people write with symbols called *zi* (DZUH). English speakers call *zi* "characters." Each character stands for an idea.

The map below shows more than where people use certain writing systems. It also shows how those regions overlap regions we call countries. However, there is something about regions that this map does not show. Regions can change.

Language	Word	Pronunciation
English	hello	heh LOH
Arabic	أهلاً.	AH lahn
Russian	здравствуйте!	ZDRAHST voot yeh
Chinese	你好	NEE HOW

How many ways can you say "hello"? Here are four ways.

This map shows four writing systems used throughout the world. It also shows the seven continents. **Map Skill:** *List the writing systems used on each continent.*

This sign is written in Arabic and in English.

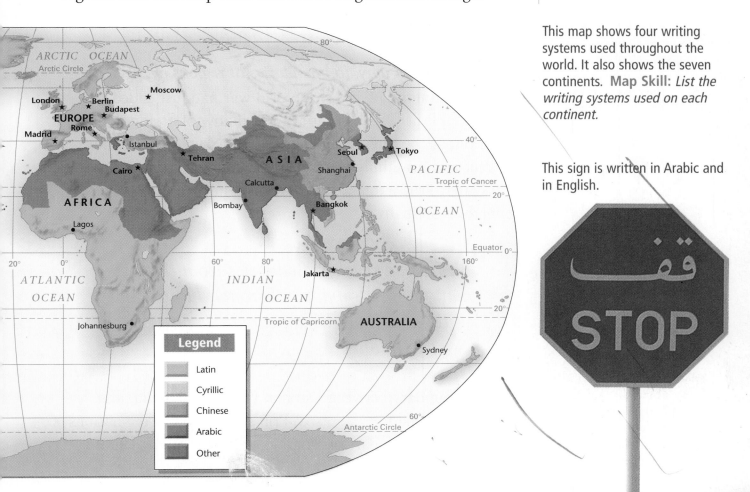

Legend

- Latin
- Cyrillic
- Chinese
- Arabic
- Other

European Borders, 1945

European Borders, 1995

Does it seem like the borders of countries never change? Look at these maps. Many of these borders changed in 50 years. **Map Skill:** *How many borders changed between 1945 and 1995?*

Curious Facts

Some people in the town of Estcourt Station, Maine, sleep in Canada and eat in the United States! The border between Canada and Maine was moved twice. Today, it runs right through the town. It even cuts through some people's homes.

Changing Boundaries

Focus *How and why do boundaries of regions change?*

It was the summer of 1945. A world war had just ended. A boy named Priit (PREET) sat at the window of an inn. He stared out at the town of Beilngries (BYLN grees), Germany.

Priit and his family were from the country of Estonia. Years later, Priit wrote about how his family came to Beilngries, Germany.

> **"W**e had reached Beilngries from the lost nation of Estonia. . . . Estonia, Latvia, and Lithuania [had] disappeared . . . into the Soviet Union.**"**

The boundary between Estonia, Latvia, Lithuania, and their neighbor had been erased. Priit's country and the nations near it had become part of a nation called the Soviet Union.

Drawing New Lines

People draw boundaries. People change boundaries, too. Look at the two maps at left. One shows the borders of countries in Eastern Europe in 1945. The other shows the same area 50 years later. During that time, people changed the borders greatly. You can read about one of these changes at the bottom of the page.

Why do people change boundaries? **Conflict** — fighting — is one reason. Countries that win wars often move the borders of countries that lose.

Just as people can change the boundaries of a region, they can also change the features within a region. In this way, people can turn one kind of region into another.

· **Tell Me More** ·

The Berlin Wall

Berlin, Germany, was once a single city. Then, in 1945, a group of countries divided it up. They drew boundaries that split the city into East Berlin and West Berlin. However, people kept trying to leave East Berlin. So the eastern government built a wall of concrete and barbed wire along the border in 1961.

Twenty-eight years later, the people of East Germany changed their government. On November 9, 1989, they decided to remove the boundary between East and West Berlin. That night, people cheered and shouted for joy. During the next few days, people began to tear the wall down. Berlin was a single city again.

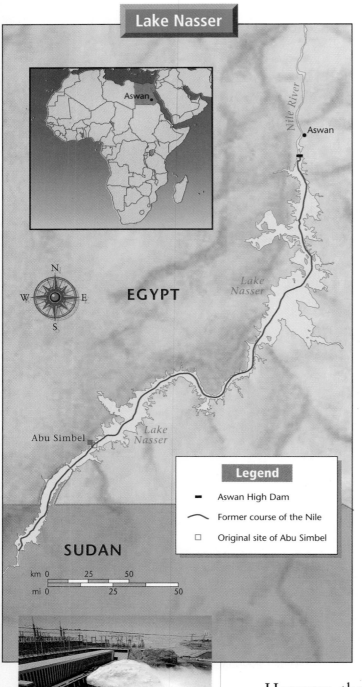

Nile River

Aswan

Lake Nasser

EGYPT

N
W   E
S

Abu Simbel

Lake Nasser

SUDAN

km 0   25   50
mi 0   25   50

Legend

— Aswan High Dam

⌒ Former course of the Nile

☐ Original site of Abu Simbel

The Aswan High Dam created Lake Nasser, one of the world's largest human-made lakes.
Map Skill: *What two countries were affected by the dam?*

Changing the Face of Regions

Focus *How do people change the features of regions?*

How do the features of a region change? Natural forces change the world around you all the time. In Chapter 2 you learned that erosion changed the Appalachian Mountains. They were once high peaks. Over millions of years, the force of erosion wore them down. Now they are lower, rounded mountains.

People can also change the features of a region. In the 1960s, people in Egypt built a dam on the Nile River. It is called the Aswan High Dam. You can find it on the map at left. The dam had a big effect on the land and people of Egypt.

Most of Egypt is desert. However, the area around the Nile is farmland. Before the dam was built, the Nile overflowed almost every year. Land near the Nile got fertile soil from those floods. **Fertile** soil is filled with things plants need to grow. Farmers planted crops in the soil. **Crops** are plants that people grow and gather.

However, the floods didn't always come. Without them, farmers couldn't grow enough food. At other times, the floods were too high. This also caused problems. People who lived near the river sometimes lost their homes.

The Effects of Change

The Nile valley was a region of floods and fertile soil for thousands of years. Then, in 1960, workers started building the Aswan High Dam. They finished it in 1971. The dam changed many features of the area around the Nile.

These photos show the temple of Abu Simbel. When the Aswan High Dam was built, the original site of the temple was flooded. To save the temple, workers cut it into huge blocks and moved it to higher ground.

Lake Nasser is one feature that the dam created. The lake is filled with water held back by the Aswan High Dam. Before the dam was built, that area was a region of dry land. People turned it into a region covered by water: a lake.

The dam has also changed the land downstream (north of the dam). It is no longer a region of floods. Without the floods, the soil is not as fertile as it used to be. The floods also used to wash salt out of the soil. Today, the soil is getting more and more salty.

People continue to change the features of regions. They also change the boundaries of regions. As you have read, these changes can turn one kind of region into another kind of region. People need to think hard before they make changes like this. The effects of these changes can last a long, long time.

Lesson Review: Geography

1. **Key Vocabulary:** Use **writing system, conflict, fertile,** and **crop** to explain how regions change.

2. **Focus:** How is the world divided into regions?

3. **Focus:** How and why do boundaries of regions change?

4. **Focus:** How do people change the features of regions?

5. **Critical Thinking: Generalize** What features other than writing could you use to divide the world into regions?

6. **Geography:** Besides Estonia, what countries on the 1995 map were part of the Soviet Union in 1945?

7. **Citizenship/Writing Activity:** Write a speech about how you would feel if your state joined with another state to become a bigger state.

Made in

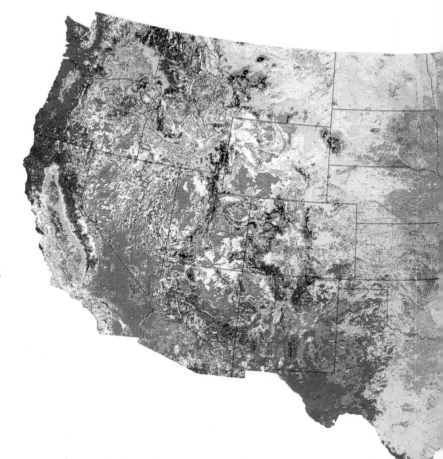

This map shows the U.S. in living color! Every color on the map stands for a different kind of plant life.

For example, purple shades show fir and pine forests in the west. Oranges stand for croplands. And yellow areas are grasslands. The map is helping scientists see how climate affects plant life.

Geologists combined satellite images and climate information to come up with 159 different regions. Then they chose 159 colors, one for each area's plant life. Talk about a "states-of-the-art" map!

Most people know that different kinds of plants grow in different parts of the United States. But did you know that scientists have found 159 different growing regions? Take a look!

the... USA

 SHRUBLAND/GRASSLAND
Greasewood, Sage,
Needlegrass, Wheatgrass,
Buffalograss

 CROPLAND
Wheat, Sorghum,
Corn, Alfalfa, Oats

 GRASSLANDS
Wheatgrass, Buffalograss,
Needlegrass

 IRRIGATED FARMLAND

 NORTHERN FOREST
Maple, Oak, Beech, Birch,
Jack Pine, Spruce

 COASTAL WETLANDS
Fresh/Saltwater Marsh

 BARREN
Desert

MAP KEY
Here are nine of the 159 color
codes. Each color represents a
different type of plant life:

 WESTERN CONIFER FOREST
Douglas Fir, Spruce,
Ponderosa Pine,
Western White Pine

 SHRUBLANDS
Creosote, Saltbush,
Sand Sage

Response Activities

1. Cause and Effect Look at the map
of United States climates in Chapter 2.
What connections can you make
between climate and plant regions in
the United States?

2. Geography: Draw a Picture
Pick a place on this map. Draw a
picture showing what you think the
landscape looks like in that place.

Chapter Review

Summarizing the Main Idea

1 Copy and complete the chart below, indicating what you have learned about regions.

	Natural Features	Human Features
The South	landforms, plants, and animals	economy, history
Polar bear region		
Estonia		
The Dairy Belt		
Johnny Appleseed's region		

Vocabulary

2 Describe a region in the United States, using at least eight of the following terms.

region (p. 55)	**goods (p. 60)**	**conflict (p. 71)**
boundary (p. 56)	**service (p. 60)**	**fertile (p. 72)**
border (p. 58)	**belt (p. 62)**	**crop (p. 72)**
economy (p. 60)	**writing system (p. 68)**	

Reviewing the Facts

3 List some regions based on natural features. List some regions based on human features.

4 Why are some boundaries hard to find?

5 What are the four census regions of the United States? What kinds of features do the states in each region share?

6 Is Minneapolis, Minnesota, in more than one region? How is that possible?

7 Why might it be difficult for a person from one writing-system region to understand a letter from a person from another writing-system region?

8 What is one reason why boundaries might change? What is one reason why the features of a region might change?

9 How did the Aswan High Dam change the area around the Nile River?

Skill Review: Writing Outlines

10 How do you label main ideas and supporting details in an outline?

11 Without writing an outline, write a paragraph about a region you live in. Read your work. How might it have been better if you had written an outline first?

Geography Skills

12 The map on page 57 shows the boundaries of many regions. Which boundaries do you think would be easy to see in the real world? Which ones would be hard to find?

13 If you worked for the U.S. Bureau of the Census, what information might you include in a report about the regions of the United States?

Critical Thinking

14 **Decision Making** Thanks to the Aswan High Dam, people in Egypt have a constant water supply. However, the dam has had other effects. Do you think building the Aswan High Dam was worthwhile?

15 **Compare Then and Now** What changes happened to the borders of Europe between 1945 and 1995?

Writing: Citizenship and History

16 **Citizenship** Write a plan for a trip to a region in the United States. Explain why you have chosen to go there and what you might see or do in that region.

17 **History** Learn more about the Berlin Wall. Write a journal entry as if you had seen the Berlin Wall being torn down. Describe what you saw and how you felt.

Activities

National Heritage/Research Activity
As a class, pick one national park or national monument in each census region. Then, in groups of four, create a short brochure about one of the parks or monuments.

Culture/Writing Activity
Find out more about one of the writing systems mentioned in the chapter. Write a brief description of how it is similar to or different from the Latin alphabet.

Internet Option

Check the **Internet Social Studies Center** for ideas on how to extend your theme project beyond your classroom.

THEME PROJECT CHECK-IN

Include information about regions in your geographic dictionary.
- What are some examples of regions you can show?
- What are the characteristics of each of the census regions of the United States?
- How can you show how regions can change?

A Nation of Many Peoples

"America is woven of many strands. . . ."

Ralph Ellison

·THEME·

Citizenship

"One thing that makes living in the United States special is freedom. There aren't very many countries that are free. We're one of the lucky ones."

**Matt Lyjak, Fourth Grade
Marietta, GA**

You probably know that every student in your class is different. You may dress differently and have different ideas, but you are all part of one group — your class. Many different people live in the United States. Together they make up one country. As you learn about the American people and government, you will see how people come together to form and to govern one nation.

Theme Project

Design a Museum

Create a museum that teaches visitors about the many people in the United States.

- Find pictures of many different people and the places they live.
- Write letters or stories describing different ways people live and work together.
- Create posters or charts to show what each part of the U.S. government does.

RESEARCH: Interview family members about your family history. Include the information in your museum.

◀ The President is sworn into office in Washington, D.C.

WHEN & WHERE ATLAS

Many different people work together to make the United States a good place to live. They come from many places and have settled all over the country. This map shows the boundaries of the 50 states of the United States and the 15 cities in this country where the most people live.

In this unit, you will learn more about the government and people of the United States. You will see how different people have moved and settled in the United States and made it their home. You will learn how the government is set up to help everyone. And you will see some ways you can help, too!

Unit 2 Chapters

Chapter 4   The American People

Chapter 5   Rights and Responsibilities

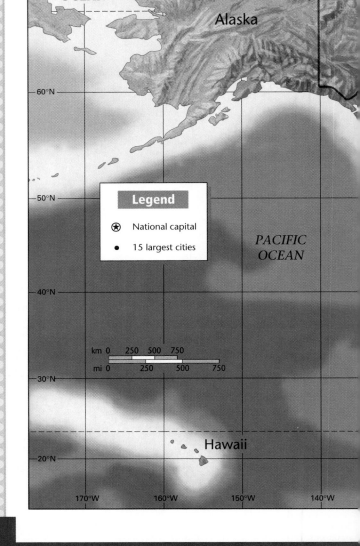

Legend

⊛   National capital

•   15 largest cities

ARCTIC OCEAN

Alaska

PACIFIC OCEAN

Hawaii

km 0   250   500   750
mi 0   250   500   750

Unit Timeline

1500   **1600**   **1700**

Immigration

People leave home and family to come to a new land. Find out why they move. *Chapter 4, Lesson 1*

Suburbs

What's the difference between living here and living in a city? *Chapter 4, Lesson 2*

CANADA

Missouri River

GREAT LAKES

Mississippi River

Detroit
Chicago
Indianapolis
New York
Philadelphia
Baltimore
Washington, D.C.

San Francisco
San Jose

Los Angeles
San Diego
Phoenix
Dallas
Houston
San Antonio
Rio Grande

MEXICO

Gulf of Mexico

Jacksonville

ATLANTIC OCEAN

Tropic of Cancer

N
W   E
S

30°W   120°W   110°W   100°W   80°W   70°W   60°W   50°W   40°W

1800   1900   **2000**

High-tech Industries

Would you like a job doing this? *Chapter 4, Lesson 3*

The Bill of Rights

These marchers are protected by the Bill of Rights. *Chapter 5, Lesson 2*

Samantha Smith

Samantha made a trip to Moscow. Find out why. *Chapter 5, Lesson 2*

The American People

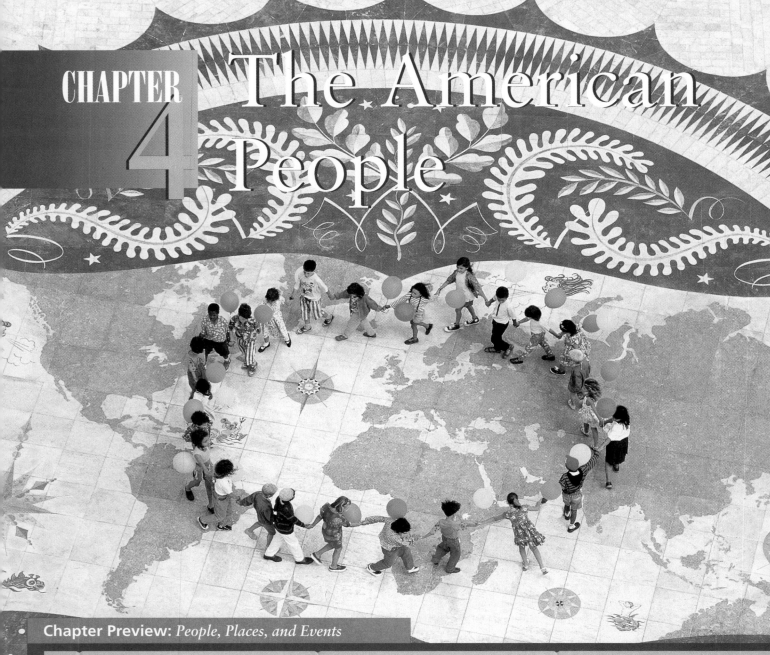

Chapter Preview: *People, Places, and Events*

1500	1600	1700

Coming to America

Read how people from many countries have come to the United States. *Lesson 1, Page 84*

We All Deserve a Chance

Meet this woman, who helps all children get a fair chance. *Lesson 1, Page 88*

St. Louis

St. Louis, Missouri, has been a transportation center for over 200 years. *Lesson 2, Page 98*

The Fabric of Our Nation

Main Idea The people of the United States live and work together, making our nation strong.

Key Vocabulary
enslaved
slavery
immigrant
opportunity

The next time you're holding a penny, look closely. See if you can find these Latin words in very tiny print: *E PLURIBUS UNUM.*
These words mean "out of many, one." From many states, there is one nation — the United States of America. The United States also has many people — around 260 million of them! You can't get to know every one of them in person. However, you may still want to learn as much as you can about them.

Who are these people called Americans? People have asked this question since before our nation began. Part of the answer lies in America's history. By learning who Americans have been, you can get a sense of who they are today, and how America might change in the future.

◀ **People from many places come together in the United States.**

1800   1900   **2000**

The Dust Bowl

Find out why people like this boy had to leave their farms. *Lesson 2, Page 100*

New Inventions

How did this machine make farming easier? *Lesson 3, Page 107*

Looking to the Future

Would you like to make the new movies these students are watching? *Lesson 3, Page 108*

Coming to America

Focus *How has immigration contributed to the diversity of the American people?*

Most Americans have ancestors who came to America during the last 500 years or so. An ancestor is a relative who lived some time ago, like a great-grandparent.

Native Americans were the first people to settle in what is now the United States. We know about some early cultures from the things they used and left behind. This bowl was made by the Mimbres people of the southwestern United States.

One group came much earlier. Native Americans have lived here for thousands of years. No one knows exactly how they got here. Many scientists believe that the first settlers walked across a narrow strip of land that once joined Asia and Alaska. Another theory is that they sailed from Asia by boat.

Native Americans were probably the only people who lived here, until about 1,000 years ago. That was when a group of northern Europeans — the Vikings — came by ship and lived for a short time in North America. The Vikings, however, didn't settle here permanently.

Settlements in America

Europeans first settled in the Americas in the late 1400s. Most of the early settlers were from Spain, Great Britain, France, the Netherlands, and Germany. Some came to find gold and silver. Others wanted to practice their religion freely. Many came for the abundant, fertile farmland.

Some people were forced to come to America. For over 200 years, Africans were brought as enslaved people to work in European settlements. An **enslaved** person is someone who is owned by another person and treated as property. The system in which people enslave other people is called **slavery**. Enslaved people could not own property. They were forced to work without being paid. In the 1860s, slavery was made illegal in the United States.

In the early 1900s, many people came to America from Southern, Central, and Eastern Europe. They came seeking a new life for themselves and their families. A person who moves to make a permanent home in another country is an **immigrant**. Many immigrants in the 1900s moved to the cities.

From the East and West

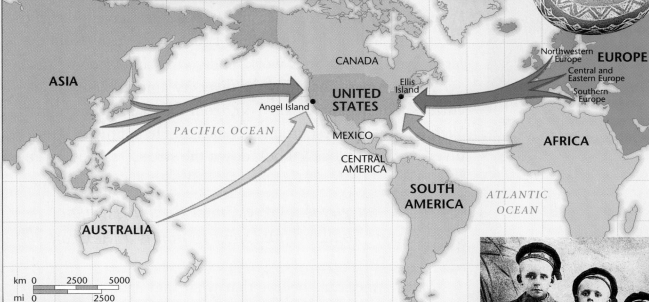

Immigration to the United States

EUROPE
- Northwestern Europe
- Central and Eastern Europe
- Southern Europe

CANADA

UNITED STATES

Ellis Island

Angel Island

PACIFIC OCEAN

ASIA

MEXICO

CENTRAL AMERICA

SOUTH AMERICA

ATLANTIC OCEAN

AFRICA

AUSTRALIA

km 0   2500   5000
mi 0   2500

Traveling to America

People came to the United States from many other places. Some came from Asia on ships that crossed the Pacific Ocean. They came to places like Seattle, Washington, and Angel Island in California.

Immigrants from Europe crossed the Atlantic Ocean in ships. Those ships stopped at places like Boston, Massachusetts, and New York City. Many people from Europe entered the United States through Ellis Island, in New York.

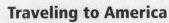

Wai Murata (above, left) immigrated to the United States from Japan in 1916. The baskets (left) were used by Chinese immigrants to carry things.

The eggs at the top of the page are from the Ukraine, in Eastern Europe. The brothers in the picture above came to New York from Austria-Hungary (*now separate countries*).

This African family came to the United States in 1985.

Together in America

People from all around the world make up the United States. Today, most new immigrants come from Latin America, the Middle East, the Caribbean, and Asia. The countries that Americans and their ancestors come from have different languages, different foods and clothing, and different ways of life. When people come together in America, they have to learn to accept one another's differences. Today, Americans from different backgrounds live, work, and go to school side by side.

Many Americans enjoy the diversity among their fellow citizens. For instance, Lam Ton, from the Asian country of Vietnam, owns a restaurant in Chicago. He appreciates the diversity of his block. "Look down the street," says Lam Ton.

> **"T**hat guy is a Greek, next to him is a man from Thailand, and next to him is a Mexican.**"**

Many Americans believe that what they share is very important too. Americans share the land that makes up the United States. They also share important ideas: the ideas of individual freedom and equality for all.

All these games came from different countries. **Cultures:** *What games from other countries do you play?*

Yo-yos *(left)* came from the Philippines.

The dreidel (DRAYD uhl) *(right)* originated in Israel.

Dominoes *(above)* were invented in China.

Mancala *(right)* is an African board game.

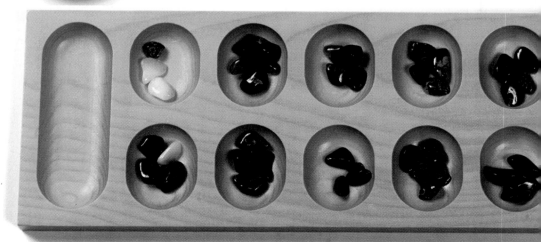

Bar chart: People (in thousands) vs. Home Countries of Immigrants

1850s
- Ireland: ~165
- Germany: ~78
- Great Britain: ~52
- Canada: ~10

1990s
- Mexico: ~213
- Vietnam: ~77
- Philippines: ~60
- Dominican Republic: ~42

Equal Opportunity for All

Focus *How does the belief in equal opportunity bring people together in the United States?*

Within a family, two children can be very different. They might look different and have different skills. When they grow up, they may choose different careers. Yet even though they are different, their parents try to give them the same opportunities. An **opportunity** is a good chance. It wouldn't seem fair any other way.

Most people in the United States agree that every American should have the opportunity to lead a fulfilling life. For example, they believe that all children should have the chance to learn to read, write, and understand arithmetic, science, and the history and geography of the world.

It is not easy to say what equal opportunity is. Yet many Americans know what it is not. If someone said, "You can't live in this neighborhood because of your religion," that wouldn't be equal opportunity. Or if someone said, "I won't give you a job because of the color of your skin," that wouldn't be equal opportunity either.

The charts above show from which countries the most immigrants came to the United States at two different times about 150 years apart.
Chart Skill: *About how many immigrants came from Ireland in the 1850s?*

A member of the Oneida nation, Norbert Hill *(above, left)* helps young Native Americans go to college. He encourages them to study science.

Marian Wright Edelman *(above, right)* founded the Children's Defense Fund in 1973. She works to give children a good education and health care. **Citizenship:** *What are some ways you can help everyone have good opportunities?*

A Fair Chance for Everyone

Every day, many Americans work to promote equal opportunity. Some speak out about issues they think are important. Others also take action to help their towns or cities. Norbert Hill, Marian Wright Edelman, and former President Jimmy Carter are examples of Americans who work to give everyone a fair chance.

Norbert Hill worked for an organization to help Native Americans get a better education. He has encouraged Native Americans to go to college and study science and engineering. He started programs that help Native American students of all ages, from elementary school through college. He says,

> "**P**eople can do anything if they have the belief they can do it."

Marian Wright Edelman remembers when there were separate schools for whites and African Americans. Usually, the schools for whites had better buildings and books, and teachers with better training. Her father told her, "Don't let anything get in the way of your education."

She didn't. She went to law school when very few African American women were lawyers. She joined Martin Luther King, Jr., to work for equality for all Americans. In 1973 she started an organization called the Children's Defense Fund. This organization helps children receive a good education and health care.

It's fun to watch a house being built. Look closely, and you might see former President Jimmy Carter! He and his wife Rosalynn help build homes through an organization called Habitat for Humanity. This organization has given many Americans the opportunity to own their own homes.

Helping other people have good opportunities is important to making a strong country. No one is ever too young to start thinking about how to help a community. Look around your neighborhood or town. Is there something that needs improving? Are there ways you can help? Talk to your friends, family, and teachers to find answers together.

Former President of the United States Jimmy Carter is a well-known supporter of Habitat for Humanity. He helps build houses for people who can't afford them.

Lesson Review

1 **Key Vocabulary:** Use the terms **enslaved, slavery, immigrant,** and **opportunity** in a story about people coming to the United States.

2 **Focus:** How has immigration contributed to the diversity of the American people?

3 **Focus:** How does the belief in equal opportunity bring people together in the United States?

4 **Critical Thinking: Conclude** Why is it important for all people to have equal opportunities?

5 **Geography:** How has the location of the United States between two oceans affected immigration?

6 **Citizenship/Research Activity:** Ask your family or friends where their ancestors came from. Mark the countries on a map of the world.

NONFICTION

...IF YOUR NAME WAS CHANGED
at Ellis Island

By Ellen Levine
Illustrated by Wayne Parmenter

***Ellis Island in New York Harbor was the first stop
for many newcomers to the United States. At least
12 million immigrants passed through the Ellis Island
immigration center between 1892 and 1924.***

America has always been a nation of immigrants — people
who have moved to the United States from other countries.
Even the first Americans, the Indians, are believed to
have crossed the Bering Strait over a strip of land that once
connected North America with Asia thousands and
thousands of years ago.

When the thirteen colonies were first settled, most
immigrants came from England, Holland, and France. Soon
there were Scandinavians, Welsh, Scots, Scotch-Irish, Irish,
and Germans. As early as 1643, a French priest visiting
New Amsterdam, which later became New York City, said
that eighteen different languages could be heard spoken in
the city streets.

By the end of the 1800s, Italians, Poles, Armenians,
Russians, and others from southern and eastern Europe began
to pour into America. On the west coast, Chinese and Japanese
immigrants arrived.

Why did people come to America?

Many people believed that America was a "Golden Land" — a place where you could get a decent job, go to a free school, and eat well. There was a saying in Polish that people came to America *za chlebem* — "for bread." One person added that they came "for bread, with butter."

In Russia, six-year-old Alec Bodanis was told that in America, "you'll become a millionaire in no time. Take a shovel with you because they shovel gold from the streets."

Some people came to look for work. Wages were higher in America than in their home countries. Until the late 1800s, businesses often sent agents overseas to encourage workers to migrate. If you agreed to work for their companies, they would pay your way to America.

Many people came because land was cheap and plentiful. In 1862, the U.S. government passed a law called the Homestead Act. Newcomers could stake a claim to 160 acres of land. After five years of living on and working the land, they'd pay a small amount of money, and the acres would be theirs. Railroad companies also owned a great deal of land in the west. They sent agents to foreign countries offering this land for sale at good prices.

Some governments of the new western states advertised in European newspapers about their growing towns and cheap farmland. They wanted new settlers. Often the advertisements were not true. They showed pictures of towns that didn't exist, and gave descriptions of farm fields where forests stood. But people came anyway. Searching, always searching, for a better life.

wages
money paid for work

agent
a person who represents a group

What contributions have immigrants made?

founding
the start of something

From the time of America's founding, new immigrants have played an important role. Eight of the fifty-five men who signed the Declaration of Independence were born in other countries. And when Thomas Jefferson wrote in the Declaration that "all men are created equal," he used the words of his Italian-born friend Philip Mazzei.

History books often list famous Americans who were immigrants. These lists usually include Albert Einstein, the German-Jewish scientist; Alexander Graham Bell, from Scotland, who invented the telephone; Elizabeth Blackwell, English-born, the first woman doctor in America; Knute Rockne, the Norwegian football player and coach; Marcus Garvey, from Jamaica, the leader of the Back-to-Africa movement; Greta Garbo, the Swedish movie star; Spyros Skouras, the Greek movie producer; Irving Berlin, the Russian-Jewish composer and songwriter; Enrico Fermi, the Italian scientist, and many others.

But millions of immigrants, not just the "famous" ones, created or started things that we think of as totally American. We take these things for granted, but they are the contributions of immigrants: — log cabins first built by Swedes; — symphony orchestras and glee clubs organized by Germans; — movies produced in America by Russian Jews and Greeks; — Santa Claus, bowling, and ice-skating from the Dutch.

Many people contributed to American English. "Yankee" is a Dutch word, and "alligator" is Spanish. "Phooey" is from German, and "prairie" is French. "Jukebox" is African, and "gung ho" is Chinese. And there are hundreds more words that were originally foreign and are now part of the English language.

As Abraham Lincoln said, immigrants have been "a source of national wealth and strength."

Meet the Author

Ellen Levine has written five books that start with the word "If." To learn about other times and places, look for her books like . . . *If You Lived at the Time of Martin Luther King* or . . . *If You Traveled West in a Covered Wagon.*

Additional Books to Read

My Fellow Americans by Alice Provenson Learn more about many famous Americans.

The Buck Stops Here: The Presidents of the United States by Alice Provenson Read about our Presidents.

Response Activities

1. **Cause and Effect** Name three reasons why immigrants came to the United States. Why do you think land was an important reason?

2. **Expressive: Write a Speech** What would you say at an awards ceremony for a famous American mentioned on page 92? Write a speech thanking this person for his or her contribution to the United States.

3. **Cultures: Research One Group** Give a report on an immigrant group that has moved to your state since 1700. Find places whose names or festivals show the group's influence.

Skills Workshop

Reading Circle Graphs

A Piece of the Pie

Americans have many different kinds of jobs. What kinds of jobs do people in each region have? Do more people in the Midwest work in factories or in shops? Are there fewer farmers in South Dakota than in North Carolina? A **circle graph** can help you answer questions like these.

Circle graphs, like those below, are also called pie graphs. Can you guess why? These graphs show how the parts of something are related to the whole. The size of each section tells which parts are largest and which are smallest.

Jobs in North Carolina

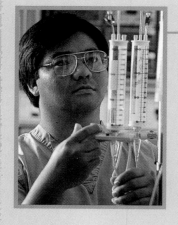

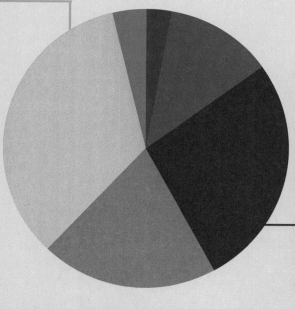

■ Agriculture   ■ Making Products   ■ Government
■ Banking/Health   ■ Buying and Selling Products   ■ Other

① Here's How

Study the two circle graphs comparing jobs in North Carolina and in South Dakota.

- Look at the title above each circle graph. What information does each graph show?

- Find the label for each section of the circle graphs. One section stands for the number of jobs in government. What do the other sections stand for?

- On each graph, compare the sizes of the sections. Is one section much smaller or larger than the other sections? What does that tell you?

- Study each graph and its parts in more detail. Compare the graphs. What differences and similarities between the two states do you see?

② Think It Through

How is gathering information from a circle graph different from reading a paragraph? What other information about these states could you show on a circle graph?

③ Use It

1. Which section of the graph is the largest for each state? Which sections are the smallest?

2. Compare the agriculture sections. One state has about four times as many agricultural workers as the other. Which state is it?

3. Find out what kinds of jobs your classmates want to have when they are adults. Make categories based on these jobs. Then make a circle graph to show your information.

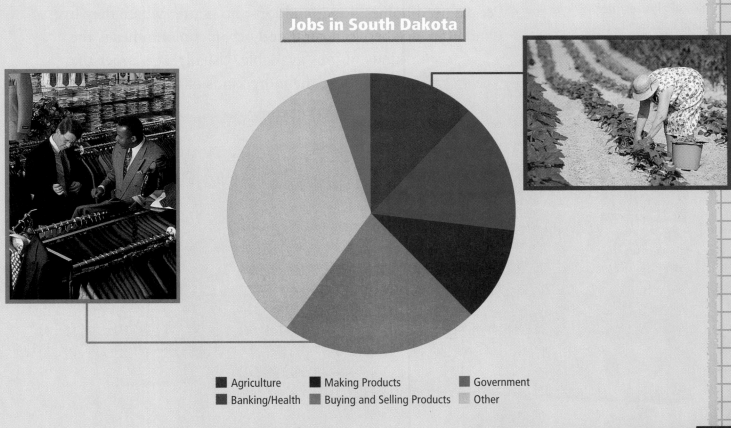

Jobs in South Dakota

- ■ Agriculture
- ■ Banking/Health
- ■ Making Products
- ■ Buying and Selling Products
- ■ Government
- ■ Other

Where Do People Live?

Main Idea Location and resources help to determine where people will choose to live.

Key Vocabulary
- urban
- rural
- suburb
- metropolitan area
- megalopolis
- migration

American communities come in all different sizes. If you ride along the highway in Michigan, you might see a sign that says, "Detroit, Population 1,203,339." You might see another sign that says, "Eagle River, Population 20." America is a land of bustling cities, quiet villages, and everything in between.

Our Communities

Focus *Where do Americans live?*

Cities are called **urban** communities. Those in the country are called **rural** communities. Some things are the same everywhere. People need homes, food, and jobs, no matter where they live. One difference between rural and urban communities is the kinds of jobs available. Usually, the larger the population, the more kinds of jobs there are.

The United States has communities of all sizes *(below, left)*. A rural community *(below, right)* is far away from cities.

You probably know that villages and towns are rural communities. Their populations range from 5,000 to around 10,000 people. Cities are larger communities. They have even more kinds of jobs and businesses than towns or villages.

Cities have different characteristics, just as people do. For instance, St. Paul, Minnesota, is famous for its winter festival and huge ice carvings. Detroit, Michigan, has many auto manufacturers. New Orleans is well known for its jazz and its Mardi Gras (MAHR dee grah) parades.

You may already know the word for communities around cities–suburbs. **Suburbs** are often less crowded than big cities. Many people who live in suburbs work in big cities nearby. A big city with its suburbs forms a **metropolitan area**.

If you drive from Boston to Washington, D.C., it's hard to tell where one city ends and another begins. This is called a **megalopolis** (mehg uh LAWP uh lihs). A megalopolis has more than 25 million people. One forms as cities expand. The map above shows Cascadia, an area in Oregon and Washington that is becoming a megalopolis.

Megalopolis "Cascadia"

As the cities in the Cascadia area grow, their suburbs will join to become a megalopolis. **Map Skill:** *What geographic features do all the cities share?*

Suburbs *(left)* are near cities. They usually have fewer people than cities.

Cities *(right)* are urban communities. Many people live and work there.

Growing Communities

Focus *How do people decide where to live?*

You won't find big cities in Death Valley, California, or on the tops of the Rocky Mountains. For most of America's history, communities grew fastest where there were two things nearby: good farmland and good transportation — especially good water transportation. Most of America's big cities are on the ocean or along a river.

The two largest rivers in the United States are the Missouri and the Mississippi. Can you find where they come together on a map? (Hint: Look along the border between the states of Missouri and Illinois.) Where the two mighty rivers meet, you won't be surprised to see that there is a big city nearby.

St. Louis

In 1764, French fur traders started a community where the two rivers met. They called it St. Louis. Rivers were the easiest way to transport people and things before there were good roads and railroads.

St. Louis in 1850

St. Louis had lots of river traffic in 1850. **Economics:** *How did transportation affect the economy of St. Louis?*

Trains connected St. Louis with many other places.

Steamboats and paddle-wheel boats like this one carried passengers up and down the Mississippi and Missouri Rivers.

Around 40 years later, the United States bought the land around St. Louis from France. It was part of an area called the Louisiana Territory that stretched to the Rocky Mountains. Settlers from many places farmed the land along the river valleys. The city provided an ideal place for business. *(See below.)*

Today, factories around St. Louis produce cars, airplane parts, chemicals, and food products. Railroads and highways provide an easy way to get to the city. Businesses can, however, still ship their goods down the Mississippi River. The city is one of America's busiest transportation centers.

Coming and Going

Focus *Why do people move?*

If you had to pick the most common reason that people move, what would you say? If you said jobs, you'd be right. People often move to find new and better jobs. Movement from one place to another is called **migration**. Americans have migrated for different reasons at different times in history.

St. Louis

At this dock, people loaded and unloaded goods from ships that traveled along the rivers.

Migration in the West

During the 1800s, many Americans migrated from east to west. They moved west with their families. They traveled with long wagon trains filled with all their possessions. These people were not settling empty lands. Many Native American peoples lived in the West. Because settlers took over much of the Native Americans' land, Native Americans were forced to move to lands called reservations. These lands were set aside by the United States government.

When gold was discovered in California in 1848, thousands of people joined the westward movement. They hoped to strike it rich in gold mining. If you hear of the "San Francisco '49-ers" football team, you'll know it is named after the people who rushed west in search of gold in 1849.

9192—Gold Miners and Packers on Dyea Trail, Alaska.

These people moved to Alaska to look for gold. Geography: *How would climate and geography have made the trip different?*

Migration During the 1900s

Another migration started in the early 1900s and continued through the 1920s. Thousands of African Americans moved from the South to the North. During this time, the United States fought in a major world war. The war, combined with growing industries, created new jobs in factories in the North. Many African American people moved North to take some of these jobs. This movement was called the Great Migration.

In the 1930s, some farmers who had settled in the Midwest and South had to leave their farms behind. Their farming techniques had dried and loosened the soil. Then strong winds blew, making huge dust storms in Texas, Oklahoma, and Kansas. Crops and cattle died. Thousands of families sadly packed up their belongings and headed toward California. This was called the Dust Bowl migration.

Fact File:

From St. Louis to San Francisco	
Form of Transportation	Time to Travel
Walking	3,340 hours (about 139 days)
Horseback	390 hours (about 16 days)
Train	58 hours (about 2 1/2 days)
Automobile	35–36 hours
Airplane	4 1/2 hours

Jacob Lawrence painted this picture to show African Americans migrating to the North during the Great Migration. **History:** *How did trains help make the Great Migration possible?*

Migration in America Today

Over time, people have moved from the country to the city. More recently, there have been two other big migrations. One has been from cities to suburbs. Cars and freeways make it easier to travel between the suburb and the city.

Today many Americans move to other parts of the country. Many people have moved from the Northeast and Midwest to the South and West. Some move to enjoy the weather. It's warmer and sunnier there. This has been called the Sunbelt migration.

Jobs are the main reason that Americans move. In the next lesson, you'll learn about the kinds of jobs Americans have had in the past, as well as some that may grow in the future.

Lesson Review

1 **Key Vocabulary:** Write sentences about where Americans live, using the terms **urban, rural, suburb, metropolitan area, megalopolis,** and **migration.**

2 **Focus:** Where do Americans live?

3 **Focus:** How do people decide where to live?

4 **Focus:** Why do people move?

5 **Critical Thinking: Cause and Effect** How have new kinds of transportation affected where people live?

6 **Theme: Citizenship** How is life in a city similar to life in a rural community? How is it different?

7 **Geography/Writing Activity:** Where would you move if you could? Write a short story about migrating there.

Human Systems

Why Are Many Americans Moving to Small Cities?

Americans have always been a people on the move. You might even say that the history of the United States is a history of migration: from different parts of the world to North America; from east to west; from farm to city; from city to suburb.

In recent years, many Americans living in large urban areas have decided to move to smaller cities. There are several reasons for this new wave of migration. Better job opportunities is probably the most important. Americans also seem drawn to small cities for their lower cost of living and slower pace of life. Whatever the reasons, the migration of Americans to small cities has increased steadily in the past decade.

1 Idaho

Boise
The population of Idaho's capital, Boise, has jumped from 103,000 to 140,000 in just four years. Newcomers are attracted by the many job opportunities, the low housing prices, and the beautiful scenery.

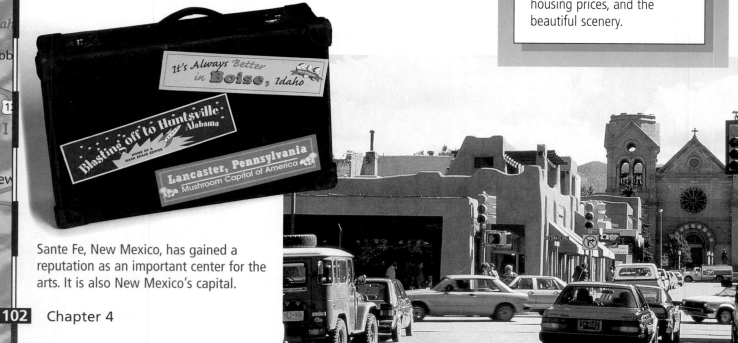

Sante Fe, New Mexico, has gained a reputation as an important center for the arts. It is also New Mexico's capital.

Music Connection

"Away, I'm bound away 'cross the wide Missouri," goes the refrain of "Shenandoah," a well-known folk song. "Shenandoah" is just one of many American folk songs that focus on the theme of migration. "Wanderin'," "Crossing the Plains," and "Alabama Bound" are three more examples of such songs. What are some other American folk songs that focus on this theme?

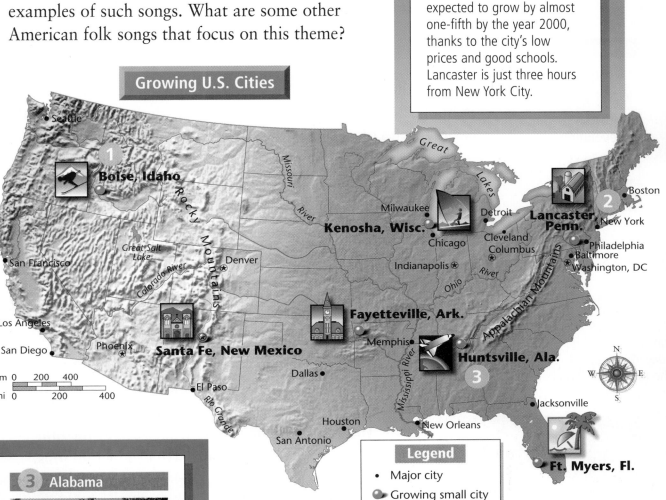

2 Pennsylvania

Lancaster

Lancaster's population is expected to grow by almost one-fifth by the year 2000, thanks to the city's low prices and good schools. Lancaster is just three hours from New York City.

Growing U.S. Cities

Legend
- Major city
- Growing small city

Map Skill: *In which region is each small city on the map located?*

3 Alabama

Huntsville

Huntsville, Alabama, has become a center for the computer and space industries over the years. Huntsville's low cost of living, well-paying jobs, and cultural resources have drawn people from all over the country.

Research Activity

Research your own family's history of migration.

1. Have you always lived in the same place? Where did your grandparents come from originally?

2. Create a timeline that shows the important moves family members have made from the time your grandparents were born to the present.

Working in America

Main Idea The kinds of jobs people do have changed and will continue to change in the future.

Key Vocabulary

craftsperson

industry

Industrial
  Revolution

assembly line

technology

software

Who made your lunch today? You? The cooks in your school cafeteria? If you had a sandwich, what about the farm worker who grew the wheat to make the bread? He or she helped to make your lunch. What about the people who work at the mill where the wheat was ground into flour? Or the person who brought the bread to the store? The more you think about it, the more you realize that hundreds of people helped to make your lunch today.

People and Jobs

Focus *What kinds of jobs do Americans have?*

The jobs that these people do can be divided into three groups. The farmer who grows the wheat for bread has a job in agriculture. Agricultural jobs include people who work on farms and ranches. The people who work at the mill that made the wheat into flour have production jobs. People in production jobs make things like cars, clothes, computers, or toys.

The clerks at the grocery store who sell the bread have service jobs. People with service jobs work in restaurants, post offices, fire departments, hospitals, offices, and stores, providing a service to other people.

Working by Hand

In the 1600s and 1700s, many things were made by craftspeople. A **craftsperson** is someone who is skilled in making things. Dressmakers, blacksmiths, and

Craftspeople still do some jobs today. This man is a woodworker who makes chairs and other furniture by hand.

wagonmakers were all craftspeople. When a farmer needed a wagon, he would go to a wagonmaker. The wagonmaker built it piece by piece, using wood, iron, and simple tools. Iron came from a blacksmith who shaped it by hand. The blacksmith might also make the wagonmaker's tools. A woodcutter who used a handsaw supplied the wood.

•Tell Me More•

A Nation Made by Hand

Women made butter in churns like this one.

Until the late 1800s, most people made everything they needed by hand. They sewed their own clothes with thread they spun themselves. They raised the animals and plants that became their food. Some of the pictures on this page show you the tools they used to make what they needed.

Men and women both worked hard. Children learned to help when they were very young. How do you help at home?

This family of settlers *(above)* made everything they needed, from their clothes and food to the house they lived in.

Women used the Saxony wheel *(left)*, from Germany, to spin flax.

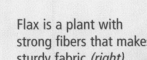

Flax is a plant with strong fibers that makes sturdy fabric *(right)*.

Thomas Edison was one of the people whose inventions made life easier. He invented the light bulb and the phonograph, among many other things.

Things people needed were made in much the same way for hundreds of years. Then, toward the end of the 1700s, new machines helped people make things more easily and quickly.

People started businesses which used machines to produce large amounts of goods. Another name for this kind of business is **industry**. The period when many new industries started is called the **Industrial Revolution**. In the United States, it started in the early 1800s. Many important inventions of the Industrial Revolution made it easier for people to clothe and feed themselves.

Making Life Easier

Cotton plants grew well in the South. Cotton made good cloth, but people had to remove the plant's seeds before it could be used. In 1793, Eli Whitney invented the cotton gin, a machine that did that job. It was a wooden box with little rows of teeth and brushes. There is a legend that Whitney got the idea from watching a cat. The cat tried to catch a chicken through a fence — and got a paw full of feathers! Whitney's machine combed out the seeds from the cotton, the way the cat's claws caught feathers. The cotton gin took seeds out faster than people could by hand. Cotton clothing became less expensive.

Major Inventions of the Industrial Revolution

1750

1800

1793 Eli Whitney's cotton gin made combing the seeds out of raw cotton much easier.

1831 Cyrus McCormick's reaper helped farmers harvest their crops faster using fewer farm workers.

Another inventor, Cyrus McCormick, made it easier to harvest grain. In 1831 he invented the "mechanical reaper." It cut grain much faster than people could. The Chicago Daily Journal of 1844 said that the reaper was "just the thing for our prairies, where more grain is sown than can possibly be gathered in the ordinary way . . . ." Now one man could harvest large fields of wheat. Fewer farm workers were needed. Many people moved to the cities to work in factories.

Most Americans today don't use the cotton gin or the mechanical reaper. Everyone can turn on a light, though, thanks to Thomas Alva Edison. In 1880, he discovered a way to channel electricity so a light bulb wouldn't catch fire when it was turned on. He also planned the world's first electric plant, which opened in New York in 1882. By the time he died in 1931, he had created 1,093 inventions.

Before the 1800s ended, another machine appeared — the automobile. It changed the way many people lived. Henry Ford didn't invent the automobile, but he invented a way to make it quickly and cheaply. It was called an **assembly line**. In the assembly line, each worker stayed in one place and added a part of the car. After the car passed all the workers, it was finished. In the early 1900s, Ford built millions of cars this way.

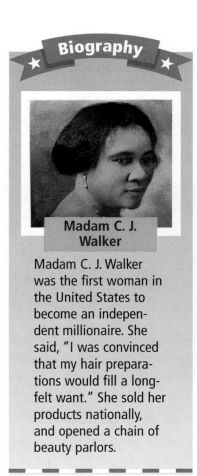

Biography

Madam C. J. Walker

Madam C. J. Walker was the first woman in the United States to become an independent millionaire. She said, "I was convinced that my hair preparations would fill a long-felt want." She sold her products nationally, and opened a chain of beauty parlors.

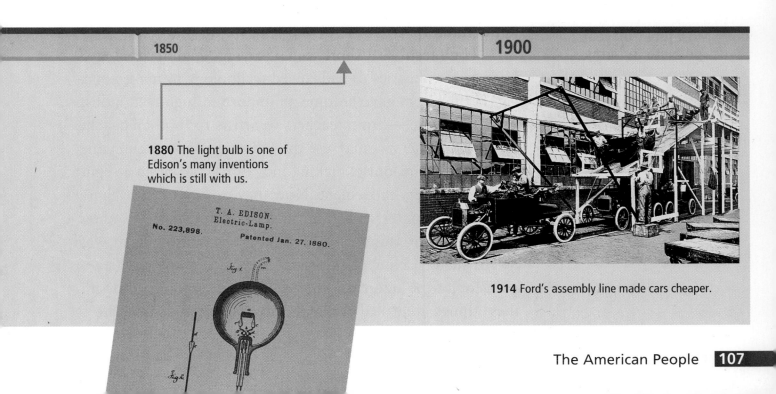

1850   1900

1880 The light bulb is one of Edison's many inventions which is still with us.

T. A. EDISON.
Electric-Lamp.
No. 223,898.
Patented Jan. 27, 1880.

1914 Ford's assembly line made cars cheaper.

Computers record the motions actors make *(right)*. Then they turn the motions into pictures in a movie. The people in the picture below are using special glasses to make the pictures in a movie look more real.

Technology and the Future

Focus *What kinds of knowledge will most jobs require in the future?*

New technologies have changed the way people live and work. **Technology** is the use of scientific knowledge in industry. Technology and industry will continue to influence each other in the future.

"High tech" is a short way of saying "high technology." High-tech industries use advanced technology to make products. Computers have become an important high-tech industry. Almost anyone — from teachers to artists to football coaches or fourth graders — may use them. Computers are changing many jobs. Cartoonists making movies used to draw a separate picture for every movement. Now they can move their characters on a computer screen. In the past, people in stores knew when they were running out of things by counting what was on the shelves. Now computers can keep track of supplies.

People who figure out how to "tell" computers to do all these things are called computer programmers. They write

Ask Yourself

Most jobs 100 years ago were in farms. Today, most jobs have to do with information. Where do you think jobs will be in the future?

? ? ? ? ? ? ? ? ? ? ? ? ? ?

instructions, or "programs," for computers, called **software**. Thousands of Americans have chosen a career in computers and creating the software programs that run them. In the future, America may need many more people who work with computers.

Though high-tech industries may keep growing, a strong country needs people in many fields. Medicine, education, architecture, and business will probably continue to offer important opportunities in the future. These fields often use technology. For example, Lloyd Hildebrand, an eye doctor in Oklahoma, uses computers to take pictures of his patients' eyes. With computers, teachers can link their classrooms to libraries or other schools. Architects can change a photo of a city block to show what the block will look like with a new building.

When you are an adult, America will need good workers in all kinds of jobs. Often people have found that what they learned when they were your age helps them every day when they grow up. Getting a good education in science, history, reading, geography, and mathematics is a great way to start. The things you study in school now can help prepare you for the job choices you have in the future.

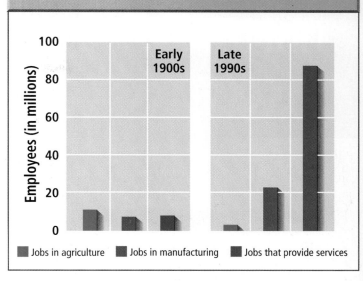

Jobs in the United States

Early 1900s

Late 1990s

Employees (in millions)

100
80
60
40
20
0

■ Jobs in agriculture ■ Jobs in manufacturing ■ Jobs that provide services

The kinds of jobs people do can change over time. Service jobs in the late 1990s included jobs in technology and health care.
Chart Skill: *About how many millions of jobs were there in agriculture in the early 1900s?*

Lesson Review

1. **Key Vocabulary:** Write a page about how Americans' jobs have changed. Use the words **craftsperson, industry, Industrial Revolution, assembly line, technology,** and **software.**

2. **Focus:** What kinds of jobs do Americans have?

3. **Focus:** What kinds of knowledge will most jobs require in the future?

4. **Critical Thinking: Interpret** How did the assembly line change how people made products?

5. **Geography** How does the geography of a place affect the jobs people do?

6. **Citizenship/Research Activity:** Choose a job you would like to do. Find out what education and skills you would need for that job. Present your information to your class.

Chapter Review

Summarizing the Main Idea

1 Complete the word web below. Then create a word web for each of the following phrases: Equal Opportunity, Jobs Americans Do.

Places Americans Live

Suburbs

Vocabulary

2 Using at least nine of the following terms, describe where people in the United States have lived and how they have worked.

enslaved (p. 84)
slavery (p. 84)
immigrant (p. 84)
opportunity (p. 87)
urban (p. 96)
rural (p. 96)

suburb (p. 97)
metropolitan area (p. 97)
megalopolis (p. 97)
migration (p. 99)
craftsperson (p. 104)
industry (p. 106)

Industrial Revolution (p. 106)
assembly line (p. 107)
technology (p. 108)
software (p. 109)

Reviewing the Facts

3 What were some of the reasons settlers came to America?

4 What is equal opportunity?

5 What are some ways people work for equal opportunity for all?

6 How are urban and rural communities different? How are they alike?

7 Why was St. Louis founded?

8 What are some reasons why people might move from one place to another?

9 What is the difference between a production job and a service job?

10 How did the Industrial Revolution change the way people lived?

11 How have new technologies changed the way people live and work?

Skill Review: Reading Circle Graphs

12 Look at the circle graphs on pages 94 and 95. Which state has more production jobs?

13 In the circle graphs on pages 94 and 95, what do you think the section "other" represents? Why is it so large? If you added new sections, how would the size of the section called "other" change?

Geography Skills

14 Look at the map of Cascadia on page 97. Which of the cities are located near bodies of water? How do you think that affected their growth?

15 Suppose you were in charge of a group of settlers. Make a list of the geographic features that would make an area a good location to start a new community.

Critical Thinking

16 **Compare** How were the Dust Bowl Migration and the Great Migration similar? How were they different?

17 **Predict** How do you think changes in technology will affect the skills needed for jobs in the future?

Writing: Citizenship and History

18 **Citizenship** Prepare a booklet for new immigrants moving to your area. What would they need to know for daily living? What would they need to know in an emergency?

19 **History** Suppose you were an African American who migrated north during the Great Migration. Write a letter to your friends in the South, telling them why you moved.

Activities

National Heritage/Arts Activity
Make a square for an "American People" quilt. On a square of paper, use a collage, drawings, or other art to show something you learned about the American people in this chapter. Put your square together with your classmates' to make a quilt.

Cultures/Music Activity
Use an encyclopedia or other books to learn about a musical instrument that came from another country. Make a poster or give a presentation for your class about the instrument you chose.

Internet Option

Check the **Internet Social Studies Center** for ideas on how to extend your theme project beyond your classroom.

THEME PROJECT CHECK-IN

Add what you have learned about the American people to your museum.
- Have you included people from many different cultures?
- What are some of the migration patterns in United States history?
- How can you show the kinds of jobs Americans have?

Rights and Responsibilities

Chapter Preview: *People, Places, and Events*

1750	1800	1850

James Madison

How did this man help to write the Constitution? *Lesson 1, Page 115*

Make Your Voice Heard

Find out how you can write to the President on a computer! *Lesson 1, Page 116*

Bill of Rights   1791

This stamp honors the Bill of Rights. Read about this document. *Lesson 2, Page 122*

Governing Ourselves

Main Idea The United States is a democratic nation with a government and laws based on the Constitution.

Have you ever voted? That's not such a silly question. Voting means expressing your opinion. You can vote to go for a bike ride instead of a swim. You can vote for a classmate to be president of your class. Now you can even vote for the President of the United States through a program called Kids Voting USA.

Students in Kids Voting USA participate in elections. In an **election,** a group makes a choice by voting. Before voting, students research the candidates and the issues. They discuss them with their families, teachers, and classmates. On election day, they "vote" along with their parents. The students' votes aren't counted officially, but they are reported to the local newspapers and radio and television stations.

◀ Election day for Kids Voting USA

Key Vocabulary
- election
- government
- democracy
- representative
- republic
- colony
- federalism

Key Events
1776 Declaration of Independence

1787 Constitutional Convention

1900   1950   2000

Fighting for Rights

What right did this woman fight for?
Lesson 2, Page 123

Working Together

Who helped build this playground?
A whole town!
Lesson 3, Page 132

Making a Difference

This student is helping herself and her community. Find out how.
Lesson 3, Page 134

The delegates to the Constitutional Convention signed the Constitution in Philadelphia, Pennsylvania. Today, you can see the Constitution they signed on display at the National Archives in Washington, D.C.

Fifty-six people signed the Declaration of Independence. **National Heritage:** *Why do you think it took courage to sign the Declaration?*

A Government for a New Nation

Focus *How was the government of the United States formed?*

Voting is how Americans choose the leaders of their government. **Government** is the system by which a group of people is ruled. The government makes laws, or rules, for people to follow. The government also provides services.

The United States' government is a **democracy,** a system in which the people rule. In such a large country, how can everyone rule? The United States has a representative democracy. A **representative** is someone who does something on your behalf. Americans vote for people to run the government. If they don't do what the voters want, then people can vote for new representatives. This system makes the United States a **republic.**

In the 1600s and early 1700s, Great Britain founded colonies in North America. A **colony** is a place controlled by another country. In 1776, leaders from the colonies decided they should be free from Britain. They signed a document called the Declaration of Independence. It said that the United States was a separate nation. For nearly seven years, the Americans and the British fought to decide who would rule.

The license plates spell out:

WE TH (Alabama) · P PUL (Alaska) · OF TH (Arizona) · U NI (Arkansas) · DIDD (California) · ST8S (Colorado)

INNOR (Connecticut) · DUR 2 (Delaware) · 4M A (Washington, D.C.) · MOR PUR (Florida) · FEC UNE (Georgia) · NONE (Hawaii)

S TAB (Idaho) · LISH (Illinois) · JUSTIZ (Indiana) · N SURE (Iowa) · DOME (Kansas)

ESTIK (Kentucky) · TRAN (Louisiana) · KWILI (Maine) · T PRO (Maryland) · VIDE 4 (Massachusetts) · TH COM (Michigan)

UN DE (Minnesota) · FENZ (Mississippi) · PRO MOT (Missouri) · TH JEN R (Montana) · L WEL (Nebraska)

FARE N (Nevada) · C CURE (New Hampshire) · TH BLES (New Jersey) · NGS OF (New Mexico) · LIBBER (New York) · T 2 R (North Carolina)

SELVS (North Dakota) · N R POS (Ohio) · TERI T (Oklahoma) · DO R (Oregon) · DANE N (Pennsylvania)

S-TAB (Rhode Island) · LISH (South Carolina) · THIS (South Dakota) · CON STI (Tennessee) · 2 10 (Texas) · 4 TH (Utah)

U NI (Vermont) · TID (Virginia) · ST8S (Washington) · OF AH (West Virginia) · MARE (Wisconsin) · E CUH (Wyoming)

In *Preamble,* artist Mike Wilkins used license plates from the 50 states to spell out the first words of the Constitution. The real document begins "WE THE PEOPLE of the United States, in Order to form a more perfect Union, establish Justice, insure domestic Tranquility, provide for the common defence, promote the general Welfare, and secure the Blessings of Liberty to ourselves and our Posterity, do ordain and establish this Constitution for the United States of America." **Language Arts:** *Look up the words you don't understand. Then state the Preamble in your own words.*

The Americans won the war and gained independence. Today we call that war the American Revolution.

The Americans had to decide how to govern the nation. At first they gave the national government little power. That system didn't work, so representatives met to find a new way. Their meeting was called the Constitutional Convention. From May to September 1787, they wrote the Constitution — a plan of government — in Philadelphia, Pennsylvania.

The Constitution

The men who wrote the Constitution discussed how many representatives states should have, and how much power the government should have. They wanted a government that was strong enough to keep order, but not so strong that it took away people's rights.

The delegates settled some issues. As James Madison, a leader of the convention, wrote, the Constitution,

James Madison *(below),* a leader of the Convention, was the United States' fourth President.

> " *. . . ought to be regarded [seen] as the work of many heads and many hands.* "

The delegates knew the Constitution wasn't perfect. Yet they thought the Constitution would serve the people. They were right. It has served the American people well for over 200 years, and it's still going strong.

Our Government

Focus *What do the different branches and levels of government in the United States do?*

To balance power between the states and the nation, the writers of the Constitution came up with a system that we call federalism. **Federalism** is a system of government in which the states share power with a national government. Each level of government has its own responsibilities. The different levels of government work together to serve the American people.

The federal government in Washington, D.C., serves the whole nation. Some of its responsibilities are the armed forces, the postal service, and printing money. The Constitution divides the federal government into three main parts, or branches. They are the executive, the legislative, and the judicial branches.

The President and Congress

The President of the United States heads the executive branch. The President's job is to see that the country's laws are carried out. The President has the power to choose people to help do this job. The President is also the leader of the armed forces.

Congress is the legislative branch. It is the part of government that makes laws. People elect representatives to the two houses of Congress: the House of Representatives and the Senate. In the Senate, each state has two senators. The number of representatives each state has in the

Would you like the President to know what you think? Write a letter!

By mail: You can send mail to the White House at:
The President

1600 Pennsylvania Avenue, Washington, DC, 20500.

By e-mail: You can send e-mail to the President at:
president@whitehouse.gov

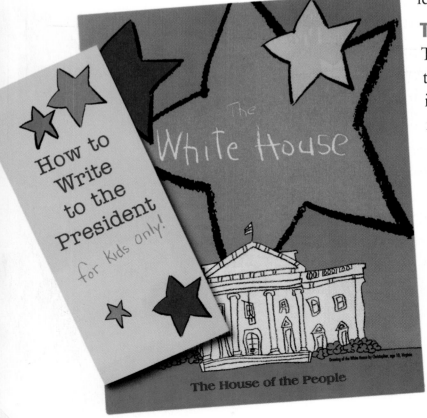

How to Write to the President for Kids only!

The White House

The House of the People

Branches of the Federal Government

Executive

The President enforces laws. The White House is where the President lives. The Oval Office inside the White House is the President's office.

Legislative

Congress makes the laws. The Congress meets in the Capitol Building in Washington, D.C. The Congress is made up of 100 senators and 435 representatives.

Judicial

The Supreme Court interprets laws. There are nine justices, or judges, on the Supreme Court. They meet in this building to decide cases.

House of Representatives depends on how many people live in that state. A state with more people has more representatives.

Congress passes laws by taking votes. It's important that people let Congress know what they think before representatives make laws. Then they can truly represent the people. Anyone can call representatives, write letters, or attend town meetings to voice their opinions.

The Courts

The judicial branch is made up of courts and judges. The highest court in the United States is the Supreme Court. The President chooses justices, who serve for life. The nine Supreme Court justices settle any conflicts that occur over a law or action taken by Congress, the President, or the states.

For example, in 1954, many states had laws that said African American children could not go to the same schools as white children. In a case called *Brown v. Board of Education of Topeka*, the Supreme Court decided that these laws didn't follow the Constitution. It ordered the states to change their school systems.

Our government's power comes from the people. Americans vote representatives into office. If they don't like what those representatives do, the voters can elect new representatives the next time they vote. It's that simple.

The diagram above shows the three branches of the federal government. **Citizenship:** *How are the responsibilities of government divided among the three branches?*

The case *Brown v. Board of Education* is named for Linda Brown *(below)*. Her parents argued that separate schools were unfair.

State Government

The United States began with 13 states. Others were added over time. Today the United States is made up of 50 states. States have power over things that aren't specifically mentioned in the Constitution. State government is responsible for schools, public welfare, holding elections, and licensing cars, for example. States also have authority over counties, cities, towns, and villages.

Most state governments are organized like the federal government, with three branches. The governor is the head of the executive branch. The legislature, which makes laws, is usually divided into two houses. Judges are appointed by the governor or elected by the people. State residents can also give their opinions to their governor and representatives.

• Tell Me More •

What's in a state?

Each state in the United States has some things in common — and many things that are unique to the state. Let's look at South Carolina.

South Carolina's capital is Columbia *(left)*. The governor and legislature meet there.

The oak tree below is the oldest tree east of the Mississippi River.

Each state has symbols. The state bird of South Carolina is the Carolina wren *(left)*.

Local government provides police for a city, county, or town. Police officers work with schools to teach safety. **Citizenship:** *What safety rules do you have in your school?*

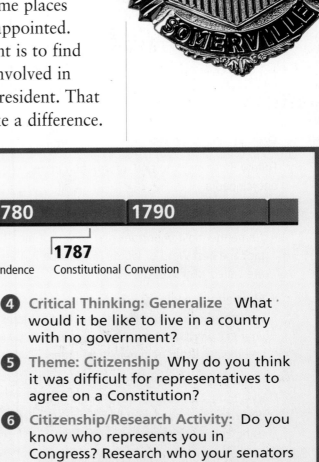

Local Government

Local government serves cities, towns, counties, townships, and villages. Police officers, firefighters, and public librarians all work for the local government.

Local governments are organized in many different ways. Some towns and cities elect a mayor who acts as a chief executive. Other towns have a small group of people known as a council or assembly that passes local laws. In some places council members are elected; in others they are appointed.

The best way to learn about local government is to find out how your community is governed. Getting involved in local government is as important as voting for President. That is where even a single person — you — can make a difference.

Lesson Review

1760	1770	1780	1790

1776
Declaration of Independence

1787
Constitutional Convention

1 **Key Vocabulary:** Write a paragraph about the Constitutional Convention using the words **government, republic, representative, democracy, colony,** and **federalism.**

2 **Focus:** How was the government of the United States formed?

3 **Focus:** What do the different branches and levels of government in the United States do?

4 **Critical Thinking: Generalize** What would it be like to live in a country with no government?

5 **Theme: Citizenship** Why do you think it was difficult for representatives to agree on a Constitution?

6 **Citizenship/Research Activity:** Do you know who represents you in Congress? Research who your senators and representatives are.

Skills Workshop

Using Encyclopedias

Straight to the Source

Your rights in this country are spelled out in the Bill of Rights, an important part of the Constitution. The Bill of Rights was based on the writings of George Mason. People don't know as much about Mason as they do about founding fathers like George Washington. To learn more about George Mason or the Bill of Rights, you can use an **encyclopedia**.

Encyclopedias are reference sources that can help you answer questions about anything from rights to satellites. They offer in-depth information and often include illustrations, charts, or maps.

George Mason

1 Here's How

Follow these steps to find information in an encyclopedia.

- Decide what you want to learn about.

- Name the most important part of your topic. Then pick the best word or words to describe it. These are called **key words**.

- Most encyclopedias are divided into many volumes (books). Find the volume that contains your key word or words. The topics in each volume are listed in alphabetical order.

- If your key word is not listed, think of a bigger idea to fit your subject into. For example, if *George Mason* was not listed, you could try using *constitution* as your key word.

- Look at the end of your subject entry. The encyclopedia may list other key words you can look up to find more information.

2 Think It Through

What kinds of information might an encyclopedia give you that you would not find in a dictionary?

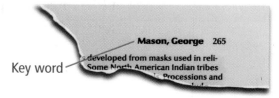

Key word

3 Use It

On a separate piece of paper, list the key words or subjects you would use to answer each question below in an encyclopedia. Then take the next step: Go to an encyclopedia and find the answers!

1. What state was George Mason from?

2. Was George Mason at the Constitutional Convention?

3. What rights are named in the Bill of Rights?

Our Heritage of Liberty

Main Idea The Constitution gives American citizens rights and responsibilities.

Key Vocabulary

right
amendment
militia
jury
responsibility
citizen

After the Constitutional Convention, the delegates sent the Constitution to each of the 13 states for approval. Newspapers published it. Americans read it and became alarmed. A storm of debate began. Many people spoke out against the Constitution. It seemed as though the Constitution might fail before it even got started.

We Have Rights

Key Events

1791 Bill of Rights

Focus *What are some rights guaranteed by the Bill of Rights?*
Americans were upset because the Constitution did not list their rights. **Rights** are basic freedoms that no one can take away. The Constitution called for a strong federal government — too strong, some thought. James Madison, a leader at the Convention, believed that simply having a democratic government would protect people's rights. He wrote to Thomas Jefferson, "What use . . . can a bill [list] of rights serve in popular Governments?" Jefferson replied:

> **"A** bill of rights is what the people are entitled [have a right] to . . . and what no just government should refuse. **"**

Jefferson believed a bill of rights had to be in the Constitution to make sure the government would respect people's rights.

Thomas Jefferson *(above)* believed that people needed a Bill of Rights. He was the third President of the United States.

This is the original text of the Bill of Rights. **National Heritage:** *Why is it important to protect historic American documents?*

The Bill of Rights

The states finally agreed to approve the Constitution. A bill of rights was added later. Madison himself wrote the first ten **amendments**, or changes, to the Constitution. These amendments became the Bill of Rights in 1791.

The Bill of Rights lists the basic freedoms of every American. Some of the most important are freedom of religion, freedom of speech, and freedom of the press. Freedom of speech and the press mean that Americans are free to give their opinions about the government — or anything else.

Another basic freedom is the right to hold peaceful public meetings. For example, in 1963, more than 200,000 Americans gathered in Washington, D.C., to call for laws that would guarantee the rights of African Americans. In some countries, a meeting this large wouldn't be allowed.

The right of groups to meet is one of the important guarantees in the Bill of Rights. This right is called freedom of assembly. It protects people like the peace protestors on the right. **Citizenship:** *Why is it important for people to be able to meet in groups?*

Other rights include the right to ask the government to change. People also have the right to own guns and to form state militias. A **militia** is an armed force. The National Guard is allowed by this amendment.

The Bill of Rights also states that you can't be arrested or have your home searched by the police, unless they have a reason and written permission from a judge. If you are accused of a crime, you have the right to a public trial by a jury. A **jury** is a group of people who listen to evidence in a court case and decide innocence or guilt. You also have the right to be defended by a lawyer, even if you can't pay for one.

These are just some of the freedoms guaranteed in the Bill of Rights. Over the years, more amendments have been added to protect the rights of all Americans. You can read about some amendments in the timeline at the bottom of this page.

The Bill of Rights says that Americans have rights that can't be taken away. Americans need to make sure that everyone pays attention to the Bill of Rights. If Americans don't stand up for their rights, who will?

Taking Part in Our Government

Focus | *What responsibilities do citizens have?*

Knowing your rights is one of the most important responsibilities you have. A **responsibility** is something you should do. American citizens have many responsibilities. An American **citizen** is someone who was born here or who comes here from another country and meets the requirements for citizenship. He or she has rights and responsibilities before the law.

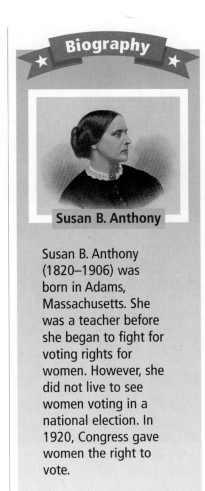

Susan B. Anthony

Susan B. Anthony (1820–1906) was born in Adams, Massachusetts. She was a teacher before she began to fight for voting rights for women. However, she did not live to see women voting in a national election. In 1920, Congress gave women the right to vote.

The timeline below shows some amendments. **Timeline Skill:** *Could African American women vote in 1900?*

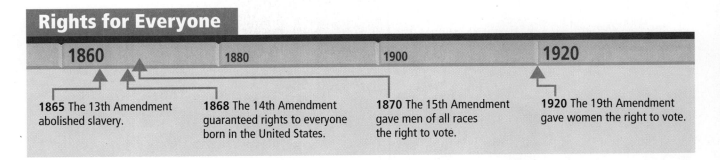

Rights for Everyone

| 1860 | 1880 | 1900 | 1920 |

1865 The 13th Amendment abolished slavery.

1868 The 14th Amendment guaranteed rights to everyone born in the United States.

1870 The 15th Amendment gave men of all races the right to vote.

1920 The 19th Amendment gave women the right to vote.

Before the 1960 presidential election, John F. Kennedy and Richard Nixon held a debate. It was the first time candidates for President had debated on television.

In the 2000 presidential primaries, candidates used the Internet as well as television to express their views. Yet the campaigns of candidates such as George W. Bush *(left)*, and Albert Gore, Jr. *(right),* still relied on public appearances to reach voters.

Our Responsibilities

For citizens in a democratic republic, rights and responsibilities go together. You already know that in a democracy people choose who they want to represent them in the government. Voting is the way Americans make this choice. So voting is one of the main responsibilities of citizens in the United States. If citizens don't vote, they shut themselves out of the democratic process.

Obeying the law is another responsibility Americans have. What would it be like if everyone in your class spoke at the same time? Or if drivers ignored red lights? You probably think it's important to obey rules so you don't get in trouble. It is also your responsibility to obey fair laws because they help people live together safely and peacefully.

Respecting other people's rights and property is another important responsibility. Rights apply to everyone in the United States. If you take away someone's rights or property, you may lose your own.

Staying Informed

It's important for all Americans to pay attention to what the government does. To make good choices when they vote, people have to understand what they are voting for. Staying informed about the world is another responsibility.

James Madison made this point when he said,

> **"A** *people who mean to be their own Governors must arm themselves with the power which knowledge gives . . .* **"**

Samantha Smith is holding the letter that Yuri Andropov sent her inviting her to visit the Soviet Union.

Madison meant that Americans need to be informed for democracy to work.

Going to school is one good way to stay informed. Writing to people who might be able to help is another. Samantha Smith, from Maine, was 11 years old when she read about nuclear weapons. In 1983, she wrote a letter to the leader of the Soviet Union, Yuri Andropov (ahn DROH puhv), telling him about her fear of nuclear war. He invited her to the Soviet Union for two weeks. Her visit led to greater efforts between the nations to understand each other.

Americans can't expect to enjoy their rights without exercising their responsibilities. Democracy won't work without the people's participation. Acting on your rights and responsibilities is an opportunity you should not miss.

Lesson Review

1770	1780	1790	

1791
Bill of Rights

1 **Key Vocabulary:** Write a paragraph about the Bill of Rights, using the terms **amendment**, **jury**, **citizen**, **right**, **responsibility**, and **militia**.

2 **Focus:** What are some rights guaranteed by the Bill of Rights?

3 **Focus:** What responsibilities do citizens have?

4 **Critical Thinking: Decision Making** The United States includes people of many different backgrounds, beliefs, and religions. Why is the Bill of Rights especially important in such a society?

5 **Citizenship:** Why should citizens have responsibilities in a democracy?

6 **Theme: Citizenship/Art Activity:** Make a collage to show the rights and responsibilities of an American citizen.

FROM THE PAGES OF Presidents

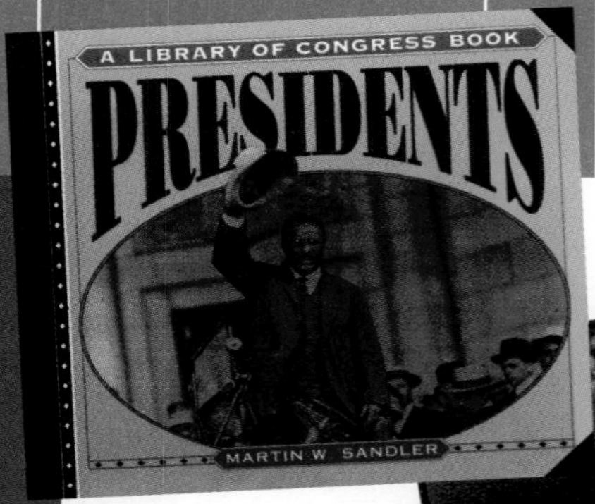
A LIBRARY OF CONGRESS BOOK
PRESIDENTS
MARTIN W SANDLER

ONE OFFICE, MANY DIFFERENT PEOPLE

By Martin W. Sandler

One of the most important responsibilities Americans have is to elect our president. Read on to learn some interesting facts about the people who have held this important office.

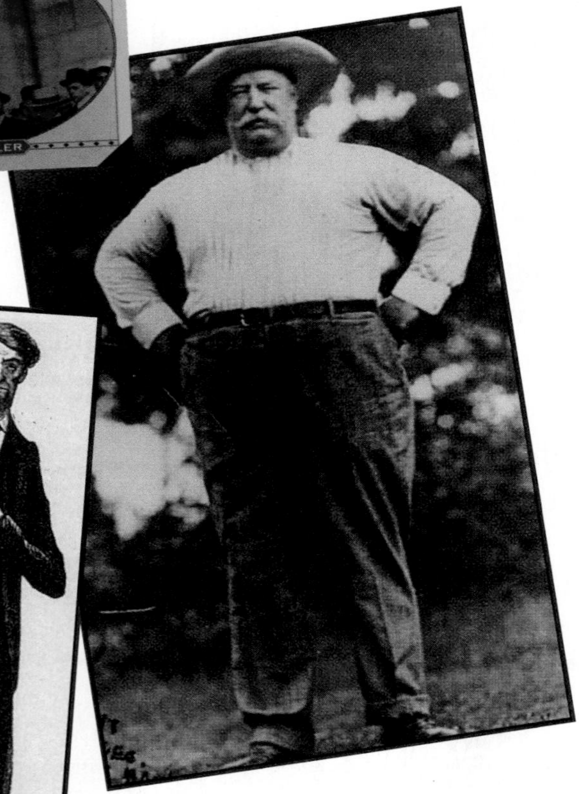

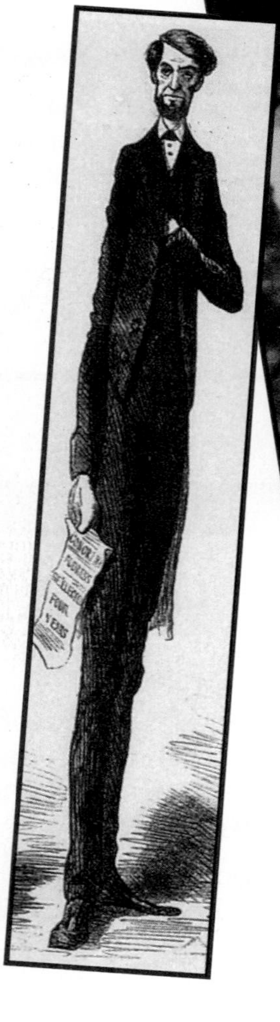

What we trust to the presidency we trust to a human being, and our presidents have differed in many human ways. The men who have led the nation have come in a variety of shapes and sizes, for example. Our smallest president was James Madison. He was only 5 feet, 4 inches tall and weighed less than a hundred pounds. William Howard Taft, on the other hand, was our biggest chief executive. He weighed about 340 pounds. The man who faced the nation's tallest challenges as president, during the Civil War, was also our tallest president. Abraham Lincoln stood 6 feet, 4 inches tall.

Our youngest elected chief executive was John F. Kennedy, who was 43 years and 236 days old when he won the presidency. Theodore Roosevelt was actually just short of 43 years old when he became president but as vice president he came to the office when President William McKinley was assassinated.

John F. Kennedy could read and understand 2,000 words a minute. Andrew Johnson was illiterate when, at age eighteen, he married Eliza McCardle. His sixteen-year-old bride taught the future president how to read and write.

Our oldest president was Ronald Reagan. The former governor of California was just sixteen days short of his seventieth birthday when he began his eight years in the White House.

Our longest-serving president was Franklin Delano Roosevelt. Before the Constitution limited a president's time in office, he served almost four full terms, from 1933 to 1945.

Since 1951, the Constitution has limited the president's length of time in office to no more than two full four-year terms. Many of our presidents have served for eight years. Others have been in office for a single four-year term. Eight presidents either died or were assassinated during their presidency. The shortest presidency was that of William Henry Harrison, who died in office in April 1841, only one month after being inaugurated.

The longest presidential inaugural speech was delivered by the person who served the shortest period of time. William Henry Harrison's inaugural address contained 8,443 words. The shortest inaugural speech was delivered by George Washington. His second inaugural address was only 133 words long.

William Henry Harrison

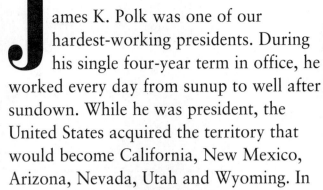

James K. Polk was one of our hardest-working presidents. During his single four-year term in office, he worked every day from sunup to well after sundown. While he was president, the United States acquired the territory that would become California, New Mexico, Arizona, Nevada, Utah and Wyoming. In addition, the Oregon boundary was established, and Texas, Iowa and Wisconsin were admitted as states. Worn out from overwork, Polk died only three months after leaving office. He was an ex-president for the shortest time of any of our presidents.

Herbert Hoover, who had the misfortune of being president during America's Great Depression, lived long enough after leaving office to earn a proud reputation by taking on a variety of humanitarian tasks around the world. Among the many awards he received were honorary degrees from over fifty American universities. Hoover lived for thirty-one years after leaving the White House, making him our longest-lived ex-president.

Response Activities

1. **Compare and Contrast** How are the responsibilities of the President like the responsibilities of everyday citizens? How are they different?

2. **Narrative: Write a Letter** Write a letter that one President in American history might have written to a close friend, describing his job and his feelings about it.

3. **Citizenship: Give a Speech** Learn more about one American President from history and then give a speech that he might have given when running for office.

★ CITIZENSHIP ★

Resolving Conflicts

How Do Laws Help You?

Does your teacher have a rule that says you must raise your hand if you want to talk in class? This rule prevents conflicts. It gives everyone an equal chance to speak. You can read below how Thurgood Marshall used laws to help equality, too.

Case Study

Thurgood Marshall and the Fourteenth Amendment

Thurgood Marshall was a Supreme Court justice from 1967 to 1991. He was also a courageous lawyer. Born in 1908, he grew up in Baltimore, Maryland. At that time, as an African American, he could not go to the same schools as white children. Marshall was determined to change that. All citizens, he believed, have the right to equal treatment under the law.

In an important 1954 Supreme Court case, *Brown v. Board of Education*, Marshall argued that African Americans have the right to the same education as whites. He based his argument on the Fourteenth Amendment to the Constitution, which states that all citizens of the United States have equal rights.

Marshall won his case. Now children of all races have the right to go to the same schools.

In 1958, Thurgood Marshall stands in front of the Supreme Court.

Take Action

By working to give everyone an equal opportunity at school, you can help stop conflicts before they happen. How do you and your school try to give this kind of equal opportunity? Follow these steps to find out.

1 In small groups, list what you think students in school need in order to learn and grow. Include all the needs students have, like extra help, ramps, or Braille materials.

2 Beside each need, write what you and your school do to meet the need. For instance, do you tutor someone?

3 Interview an adult in school to find out what he or she thinks the school does to make sure every student has an equal opportunity to an education.

4 Are any students or needs being overlooked? What could you and your school do better? Share your ideas. How do your actions help prevent conflicts?

Tips for Resolving Conflicts

- Consider other people's needs.
- Be prepared to do your part to make sure people's needs get met.
- Be open-minded.
- Be willing to compromise. Sometimes you can reach an agreement that helps several people at the same time.

Research Activity

Find out who the Supreme Court justices are today. Pick one and read about his or her life and beliefs. Create a poster about this justice to share with the class.

Strength in Unity

Main Idea People can improve life in their communities through cooperation.

How many different groups do you belong to? You are a member of your family. You're a member of your class in school. You probably have a group of friends. Maybe you play on a team or belong to some kind of club.

What about your parents? Depending on their jobs, one or both of them might be part of a team at work. They have their own groups of friends as well. A lot of adults belong to groups like church groups, school boards, or neighborhood groups.

The people in all these groups **cooperate**. That means they work together to achieve their goals — even when the goal is simply to have fun.

All the pictures on these two pages show how people worked together to build a playground. **Citizenship:** *What are some jobs you could volunteer to do?*

Students met with planners to design the playground.

Building Together

Focus *How do groups work together?*

John Ruggiero (ru gee EH roh) knows something about cooperation. John was in fourth grade when he entered a contest to see who could design the best symbol for Project Playground in his home town of Portsmouth, Ohio. Project Playground was a community effort that began in 1992. Its goal was to create a playground that kids designed and everyone in the community helped build. The town formed a committee called the Playground Committee. A **committee** is a group of people who work together.

John's playground design won. The Playground Committee used his design to decorate T-shirts. The money from T-shirt sales helped pay for the project. Raising money was just the beginning. Much more had to be done. The project needed materials and tools. The committee bought the materials. The tools would only be needed during construction, though. It did not make sense to buy tools. So the building committee asked local stores for help. The stores agreed to let Project Playground borrow the tools they needed.

From the beginning of the project, volunteers from the community planned to build the playground. A **volunteer** is a person who offers to do something without pay. These volunteers needed meals while they were building. Their young children needed care. The word went out. Soon, other volunteers were offering to provide food and daycare.

After more than a year of preparation, the volunteers began building. Children, college students, housewives, ministers, teachers, doctors, and many others joined together. The construction went on for five straight days.

Volunteers from the community worked together to build all the parts of the playground.

A nearby hospital uses the playground in some of their treatments for young patients *(left)*.

The playground *(below)* was named in honor of Maxine Levi. She came up with the idea of building a playground for local children.

Ask Yourself

What are some things that you would like to improve in your community?

? ? ? ? ? ? ? ? ? ? ? ? ?

The community felt united because of their accomplishment. Reverend C. Christopher Thompson, a volunteer, said,

> **"I**t happened! . . . Let us take note of what we can do when we . . . work for the entire community.**"**

Places that Need You

Focus *How can people contribute to their communities?*
The key to Project Playground's success was cooperation. Groups can achieve their goals only when everyone works together. When the people working together are there because they want to be there, then the chances of success are high.

In Los Angeles, a group of 40 high school students decided that they wanted to improve their neighborhood. The students worked with a teacher to turn an empty lot into a community garden. They planted herbs, flowers, and vegetables. The garden thrived. The students gave some vegetables to needy families. They sold the rest at local markets. They named their project Food from the 'Hood (short for *neighborhood*).

At Crenshaw High School in Los Angeles, students in the Food from the 'Hood project make a difference.

Students who work in the garden learn about science. They also learn about cooperation. Terie Smith, age 15, says about Food from the 'Hood,

> **"W**e *showed that a group of . . . kids can and did make a difference."*

Students make a difference in other places, too. In Evansville, Indiana, a group of teenagers called Teens Against Drug Abuse (TADA) uses puppet shows to teach children to stay away from drugs. You can also volunteer in groups that help the environment, the elderly, or others in the community.

Being a Good Citizen

The students who organized Food from the 'Hood and those who participate in crime prevention programs are giving something to their communities. That makes them good citizens. There are three parts to being a good citizen: Good citizens know their rights, they exercise their responsibilities, and they work together to build their communities.

You can be a good citizen too. If you have an idea for a way to improve your neighborhood, don't keep it to yourself. Share it with others. Ask an adult for help. Through cooperation, maybe you can turn your idea into a reality. It's up to each one of us to make the United States a better place to live.

TAKE A BITE OUT OF CRIME

The National Crime Prevention Council helps young volunteers fight crime. Their mascot is McGruff (above).

Lesson Review

1 **Key Vocabulary:** Write a paragraph about a project you would like to do, using the terms **cooperate, volunteer,** and **committee.**

2 **Focus:** How do groups work together?

3 **Focus:** How can people contribute to their communities?

4 **Critical Thinking: Cause and Effect** Do you think Project Playground could have succeeded without volunteers?

5 **Theme: Citizenship** Sometimes a project brings together people who may not get along. Why is cooperation important in this situation?

6 **Geography/Arts Activity:** Plan a garden for your community. Choose a place for the garden and draw a map of what you will grow where. How does geography affect your choices?

Chapter Review

Chapter Timeline

1760	1770	1780	1790

1787
Constitutional Convention

1776
Declaration of Independence

1791
Bill of Rights

Summarizing the Main Idea

1 Copy the chart below. Fill in the role each item plays in United States government.

Constitution	The plan that outlines the government of the United States.
President	
Supreme Court	
Congress	
Bill of Rights	

Vocabulary

2 Using at least twelve of the following terms, write a brief speech as if you were running for a position in the government.

election (p. 113)   colony (p. 114)   jury (p. 123)
government (p. 114)   federalism (p. 116)   responsibility (p. 123)
democracy (p. 114)   right (p. 121)   citizen (p. 123)
representative (p. 114) amendment (p. 122)   cooperate (p. 132)
republic (p. 114)   militia (p. 123)   committee (p. 132)
                                               volunteer (p. 133)

Reviewing the Facts

3 Describe the United States government.

4 What was the United States like before it had its own government?

5 What happened at the Constitutional Convention?

6 Describe the branches of the federal government.

7 How are state and local governments different?

8 What is the Bill of Rights' purpose?

9 Why is it important for citizens to exercise their responsibilities?

10 What key words could you use to look up information about James Madison in an encyclopedia?

11 Would you use an encyclopedia to find out what the Constitution is? Why or why not?

Geography Skills

12 Look at the map of South Carolina on page 118. Find Columbia, the capital. Is it a good place for the state government to be? Why or why not?

13 Design your own playground. Make a map to show the layout of your playground. Include symbols and a map key. Share your playground plans with a classmate.

Critical Thinking

14 **Cause and Effect** How do you think Project Playground affected the people in Portsmouth, Ohio? Do you think a similar project would be good for your community? Why?

15 **Interpret** Why do you think the United States divides the powers of the national government into three parts?

Writing: Citizenship and History

16 **Citizenship** Write a proposal for a community project. Include a step-by-step plan for the project. What materials and tools will you need? What jobs will volunteers have?

17 **History** You are a delegate at the Constitutional Convention. Write a speech you might give in favor of the Bill of Rights.

Activities

National Heritage/Music
Find and listen to "The Star-Spangled Banner," which is the national anthem of the United States. Then write an anthem for your community.

Citizenship/Research
Find out what people from other countries have to do to become citizens of the United States. Present your information to the class.

Internet Option

Check the **Internet Social Studies Center** for ideas on how to extend your theme project beyond your classroom.

THEME PROJECT CHECK-IN

Add what you've learned about rights and responsibilities to the materials you've collected for your museum.
- Have you included descriptions or quotations about good citizenship?
- How can you show what the different parts of the government do?
- What are some ways that people in the United States work together?

"The land may vary more;
But wherever the truth may be —
The water comes ashore,
And the people look at the sea."

Robert Frost

· T H E M E ·

Land and Sea

"In New Hampshire, we have lots of forests which give us lots of maple syrup and lumber and tourists, too."

**Amelia Kimball, Fourth Grade
Center Sandwich, NH**

The Northeast is the smallest of the four regions of the United States. Even though it is small, you will find many kinds of land, weather, plants, animals, and people there. The land and sea of the Northeast provide many resources for these people and animals. As you read more about the Northeast, think about how the geography of the region has affected the many people who live there.

Theme Project

Publish a Newspaper

Start your own newspaper called *Northeast News* to tell people in other regions about life in the Northeast.

- Write articles about living in the Northeast.
- Draw or find pictures of famous people and places in the Northeast.
- Create advertisements for products that are made in the Northeast.

RESEARCH: Read newspapers and magazines to find out about an important topic in the Northeast today. Write an article about that topic for your newspaper.

◀ A sailing ship is docked at a Connecticut port.

WHEN & WHERE
ATLAS

The Northeast has many different kinds of land and people. There are coasts battered by the ocean, forests full of animals, and green hills covered with farms. The region also has many resources. This map shows some of the physical features and resources of the Northeast.

In this unit, you will learn about the land and climate of the Northeast. You'll also see how the land and water of the region have affected the lives of Native Americans and settlers from other countries throughout history. Then you'll find out more about some of the ways people live and work in the Northeast today.

Unit 3 Chapters

Chapter 6 The Land and People of the Northeast

Chapter 7 The Northeast Today

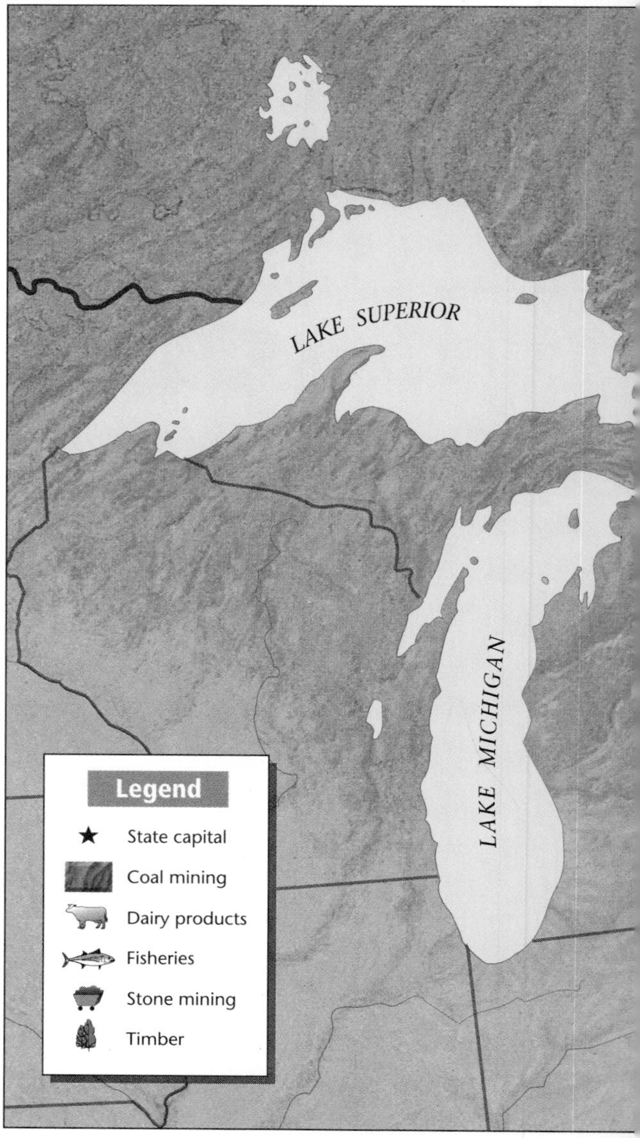

Legend

★ State capital

▨ Coal mining

🐄 Dairy products

🐟 Fisheries

⬚ Stone mining

🌲 Timber

LAKE SUPERIOR

LAKE MICHIGAN

Unit Timeline

1500	1600	1700

A Clambake

A clambake is a favorite tradition in the Northeast. *Chapter 6, Lesson 2*

The Stock Market

Find out what these people are buying and selling. *Chapter 6, Lesson 3*

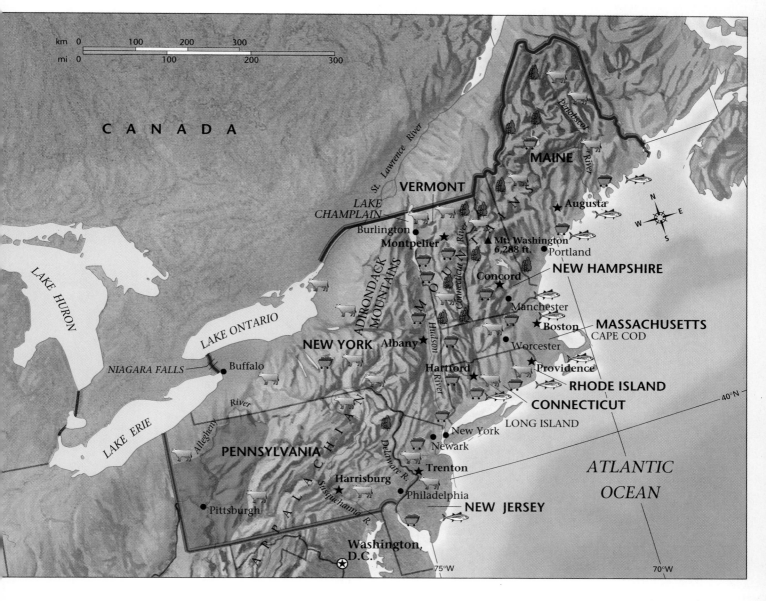

CANADA

LAKE HURON

LAKE ONTARIO

NIAGARA FALLS   Buffalo

LAKE ERIE

Allegheny River

PENNSYLVANIA

Pittsburgh

Harrisburg

Susquehanna R.

Washington, D.C.

ADIRONDACK MOUNTAINS

St. Lawrence River

VERMONT

LAKE CHAMPLAIN

Burlington
Montpelier

NEW YORK   Albany

Hudson River

Connecticut River

Hartford

Delaware R.

Trenton

Newark

New York

LONG ISLAND

Philadelphia

NEW JERSEY

MAINE

Penobscot River

Augusta

Mt. Washington
6,288 ft.   Portland

NEW HAMPSHIRE

Concord

Manchester

Boston   MASSACHUSETTS

Worcester   CAPE COD

Providence

RHODE ISLAND

CONNECTICUT

ATLANTIC OCEAN

40°N

75°W   70°W

APPALACHIAN   MOUNTAINS

km 0   100   200   300
mi 0   100   200   300

1800   1900   2000

Korean Celebration

What kinds of festivals are held in your community? *Chapter 7, Lesson 1*

Philadelphia

Find out how to get around in this city. *Chapter 7, Lesson 3*

Recycling

Are these toys or trash? *Chapter 7, Lesson 4*

The Land and People of the Northeast

Chapter Preview: *People, Places, and Events*

1500	1600	1700

Sledding in New York City

Sled rides and snowballs are part of winter in the Northeast. *Lesson 1, Page 144*

The Colors of Autumn

Orange, red, and yellow — in fall, leaves turn bright colors. *Lesson 1, Page 146*

The Fate of a Clam

Yesterday it lived in Cape Cod Bay. Today it will be someone's dinner. *Lesson 2, Page 148*

The Land

Main Idea The Northeast has many different kinds of weather, landforms, and wildlife.

High on New Hampshire's Mount Washington, the winter wind howls and shrieks. In winter, the wind can blow at speeds of over 100 miles per hour. It gets so strong that it can rip the buttons off your jacket. The temperature can drop to 30 degrees below zero!

Compared to some of the world's tallest mountains, Mount Washington, at about 6,300 feet, isn't very high. Still, it gets some of the worst storms in the world.

Workers in the weather station on Mount Washington know the power of those storms. Every day they record the wind speed, temperature, and amount of precipitation. Scientists use those records to learn about the region's climate.

Storms on Mount Washington can be scary. The Northeast has calm, peaceful weather, too. The Northeast is a region of rich differences and changing seasons.

◀ A man works on a tall building in New York City, around 1930.

LESSON 1

Key Vocabulary

temperate
blizzard
glacier
ecosystem

Key Places

Mount Washington, New Hampshire

1800   1900   2000

New Amsterdam

New York City, first called New Amsterdam, looked like this in colonial times. *Lesson 2, Page 150*

New York Stock Exchange

Find out what gets bought and sold here. *Lesson 3, Page 160*

A University in New Jersey

Princeton University is an old Northeastern school. *Lesson 3, Page 161*

Landforms and Climate

Focus *What landforms and climate does the Northeast have?*

Mount Washington is in New Hampshire's Presidential Range. This mountain range is part of the Appalachian Mountains. Besides mountain ranges, landforms in the Northeast include hills, fields, valleys, rivers, and lakes.

The Northeast's climate is **temperate** — neither very hot nor very cold. Its weather changes from season to season. It is warm in the summer and cold during winter.

Large bodies of water like lakes and oceans affect a region's climate. In the map below, notice that the Atlantic Ocean is on the eastern side of the Northeast. The Great Lakes border the western side. Northeast weather would be less temperate if not for the

Winter weather brings fun, as kids slide down a snow-covered hill. The maps on these two pages show average January and July temperatures in the Northeast.

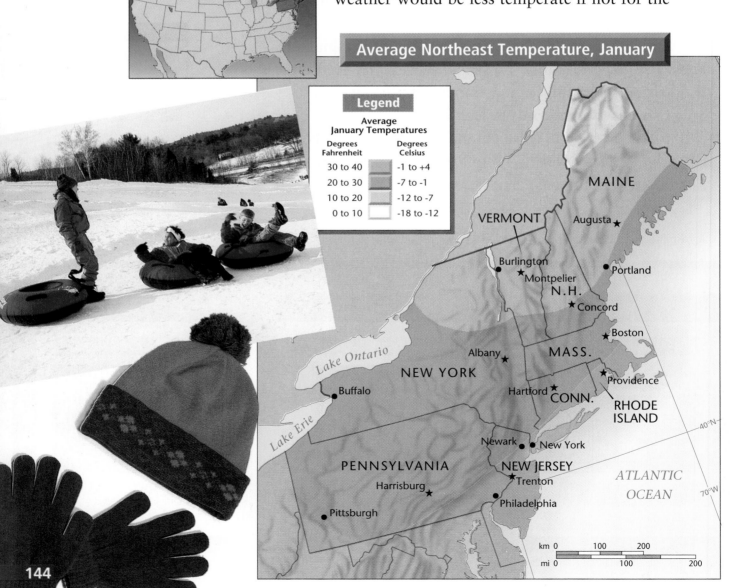

Average Northeast Temperature, January

Legend

Average January Temperatures

Degrees Fahrenheit	Degrees Celsius
30 to 40	-1 to +4
20 to 30	-7 to -1
10 to 20	-12 to -7
0 to 10	-18 to -12

MAINE

VERMONT — Augusta ★

Burlington ● ★ Montpelier — Portland ●

N.H.

★ Concord

★ Boston

Lake Ontario — Albany ★ — MASS.

NEW YORK — ★ Providence

Buffalo ● — Hartford ★ — CONN. — RHODE ISLAND

Lake Erie — 40°N

Newark ★ ● New York

PENNSYLVANIA — NEW JERSEY — ATLANTIC OCEAN — 70°W

Harrisburg ★ — ★ Trenton

● Pittsburgh — ● Philadelphia

km 0	100	200
mi 0	100	200

Atlantic Ocean and the Great Lakes. The ocean's warm currents heat the air and keep coastal areas warmer in winter. In summer, the ocean helps produce cooling winds and rainfall, which keep the heat down. Lakes affect the climate in the same way, but not as much as oceans.

Winter has a big effect on the Northeast. Heavy snowfall sometimes comes with high winds. A storm like this is known as a **blizzard**.

A region's climate can change over a very long time. For a long period ending about 10,000 years ago, the climate of North America was probably much colder than now. Glaciers covered much of the Northeast during that cold period. A **glacier** is a slow-moving sheet of ice that can be more than a mile thick. As glaciers moved, they pushed and scraped the land. They scooped out lakes and left rocky soil behind them.

Building sandcastles is a great way to spend a day at the beach. **Map Skill:** *In which state or states does it get hottest in July? Where does it get coldest in January?*

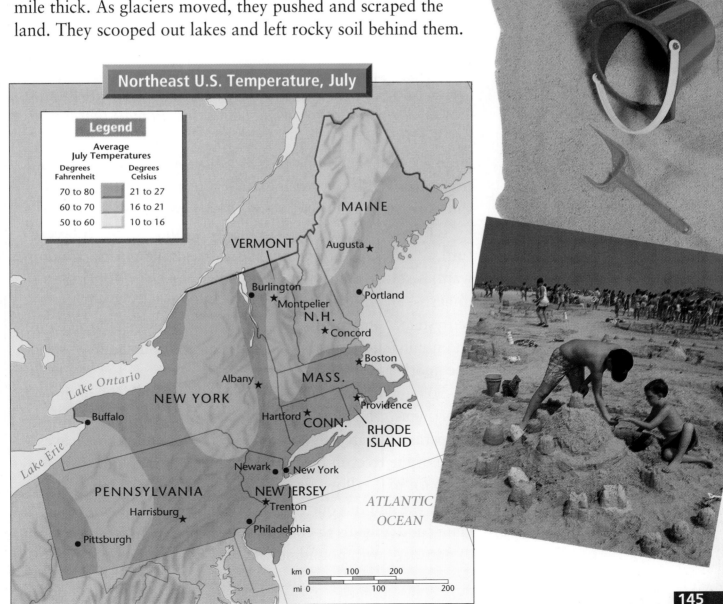

Northeast U.S. Temperature, July

Legend

Average July Temperatures

Degrees Fahrenheit	Degrees Celsius
70 to 80	21 to 27
60 to 70	16 to 21
50 to 60	10 to 16

MAINE

Augusta ★

VERMONT

Burlington ●
★ Montpelier

● Portland

N.H.

★ Concord

★ Boston

Lake Ontario

Albany ★

MASS.

NEW YORK

Buffalo ●

Hartford ★

★ Providence

CONN.

RHODE ISLAND

Lake Erie

Newark ● ● New York

PENNSYLVANIA

NEW JERSEY

★ Trenton

ATLANTIC OCEAN

Harrisburg ★

● Philadelphia

● Pittsburgh

km 0   100   200
mi 0   100   200

Animals of the Northeast

Different kinds of animals live near the streams and ocean of the Northeast. Large animals like the moose and the black bear live in the forests and swampy areas.

From Forest to Ocean

Focus *What are some of the plants and animals that live in the Northeast?*

Grab a paddle and hop aboard! You're about to take a canoe trip on a river in the Northeast. The picture on these pages shows some animals and plants you might see.

The river current helps move your canoe along. A breeze ruffles your hair. Trees line the riverbank. Be quiet! You don't want to startle the little deer nibbling on leaves. All those things — river, breeze, trees, deer — are part of the forest ecosystem. An **ecosystem** (EHK oh sihs tuhm) is all the living and nonliving things that make up an environment and affect one another.

Soil and climate help determine the kinds of living things in ecosystems. The Northeast's climate, with its high rainfall and temperate climate, is good for forests. In autumn, the leaves on some of the trees in the Northeast, such as maples, oaks, and ash, turn red, yellow, or orange. Then the leaves fall off.

At the end of your trip, your canoe reaches the ocean. Plants and animals in coastal ecosystems, such as seaweed and oysters, live with pounding waves and changing tides. They are

adapted to their environment. Seagulls and harbor seals search for food along the coastline. Farther out in the ocean, fish such as mackerel and cod swim in the cool waters. You might even spot a whale or some dolphins in the ocean.

As your journey has shown, the Northeast is home to many kinds of plants and animals. Just as those plants and animals depend on the land around them, people too have learned to use the resources of this region.

Coastal birds The black skimmer flies along the surface of the water, scooping up small fish. The herring gull cracks open clams by dropping them on rocks.

Ocean life Under the water you might find bluefish, jellyfish, squid, and lobster. Dolphin live in the waters off the coast.

Science: *How do streams and ocean provide food for the animals of the Northeast?*

Lesson Review: Geography

1 **Key Vocabulary:** Describe a hike you might take in the Northeast. Use the words **temperate, blizzard, glacier,** and **ecosystem.**

2 **Focus:** What landforms and climate does the Northeast have?

3 **Focus:** What are some of the plants and animals that live in the Northeast?

4 **Critical Thinking: Predict** Suppose the climate in the Northeast became much warmer. Predict what might happen to the plants and animals living there.

5 **Theme: Land and Sea** How does the ocean affect the climate in the Northeast?

6 **Geography/Science Activity:** Draw three pictures of a tree that loses its leaves in the fall. Show it in spring or summer, then fall, then winter.

Settling the Northeast

Main Idea Land in the Northeast provided different groups of people with the resources they needed to live and work.

Key Vocabulary
Pilgrim
waterway
canal
capital

Key Events
1620 Pilgrims found Plymouth Colony
1825 Erie Canal completed

Steven Peters, the boy shown below, is a Wampanoag (wahm puh NOH ag) Indian. Steven's grandfather is teaching him the Wampanoag way of holding a clambake. Clams, lobsters, corn, and other foods will be cooked over heated rocks. To the Wampanoag, a clambake is more than a delicious way of cooking food. It is a traditional ceremony that honors an important person or celebrates the changing seasons.

•Tell Me More•

Clambake

A Wampanoag clambake involves careful preparation. The food is cooked in a traditional way that's handed down from parents to children. The clambake shown in the pictures took place on Cape Cod in Massachusetts.

❶ Steven digs for clams in the sand at the edge of a bay.

❷ The clams and other food, such as lobsters and corn, will be cooked on a bed of rocks in a pit. The rocks come from the bay, too. They must be just the right size and shape.

Native Americans

Focus *How did Native Americans like the Wampanoag use their environment?*

Long before European settlers came to the Northeast, the Wampanoag lived in what is now eastern Massachusetts. They were a maritime people — they lived near the ocean. The Wampanoag traveled on the ocean in canoes. For food, Wampanoag men caught fish and shellfish such as herring and clams. They also hunted forest animals, such as deer and rabbits. The main source of the Wampanoag's food, however, was farming. The crops they grew included corn, beans, pumpkins, and squash. The women did most of the farming.

The Wampanoag are one of many Native American groups in the Northeast. Native Americans have lived in the Northeast and the rest of America for thousands of years. The Iroquois (IHR uh kwoy), Penobscot, and Pequot are a few of the many Native American groups in the Northeast.

3 After a wood fire has heated the rocks, Steven and a friend cover them with seaweed. Steam from the seaweed will help cook the food.

4 The food, wrapped in cloth, cooks on the heated rocks.

5 Hazel Oakley smiles as she gets ready to eat a delicious meal.

New Settlers

Focus *How did Europeans use the land they settled?*

In the early 1600s, settlers began to come from Europe to the Northeast. They came for many reasons. Some wanted better land to farm. Others were poor and looked for a richer life in the new land. Still others fled from governments that they thought were unfair. Many new settlers wanted freedom to live the life they chose.

The Pilgrims Come

In 1620 a group of settlers known as the **Pilgrims** founded Plymouth Colony in what is now Massachusetts. The Pilgrims wanted to be free to worship according to their beliefs in a way that they couldn't in Europe.

Geography affected the settlers' lives in their new land. At first, the Pilgrims did not know about the climate of their new home, or what crops would grow well there. Life was hard.

Luckily for the Pilgrims, local Native Americans helped them. The Wampanoag gave the Pilgrims food. They also gave them seeds for crops that grew well in the area. They taught the Pilgrims how to protect themselves against the bitterly cold winters. In the fall of 1621, the Pilgrims held a Thanksgiving feast to celebrate their first good harvest. Native Americans shared in the feast.

The Quakers in Pennsylvania

The Pilgrims were not the only group who came to the Northeast looking for freedom of worship. The Quakers, led by William Penn, settled in Pennsylvania starting in 1682. The colony of Pennsylvania gave religious freedom not only to Quakers but to people of other religions as well.

The Pilgrims and Quakers came from England. People from other countries settled in the Northeast, too, in the 1600s and 1700s. Germantown, Pennsylvania — as you might guess from its name — is one community that was settled by Germans. Dutch people settled in New York. Swedes came to Pennsylvania and New Jersey. People from

The children of settlers played with toys such as the doll shown here, made from corn husks. **Geography:** *How does this doll show the settlers' use of natural resources?*

France settled in New York, Massachusetts, and other places in the Northeast. During this time, Africans also came to the Northeast. Many of the Africans were enslaved and forced to come to the region. Most of the Africans came from western Africa.

The Importance of Water

Many early settlers had jobs that were tied to the sea. They fished, sailed, and shipped goods around the world. They also built ships. The huge forests of the Northeast provided the wood for these ships. Many of the tall trees of the Northeast became masts in these ships.

Model of a Colonial Sailing Ship

During colonial times, ships like this sailed from Salem, Massachusetts, and other ports.

Sailors climbed the ropes to raise and lower the sails.

Masts were usually made of pine. The wood was soaked in salt water to make it stronger.

A figurehead was carved on the front of the ship. Sailors thought that it protected the crew.

The ship carried spices, silks, and other fancy goods from places as far away as India and China.

From New York City to Buffalo in 1850

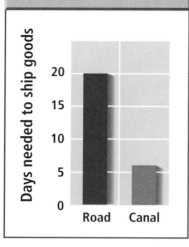

Days needed to ship goods

Road | Canal

The Erie Canal, shown in the painting, shortened the time it took to ship goods. **Chart Skill:** *How much longer did the trip take by road than by canal?*

During the 1600s, 1700s, and 1800s, settlers moved inland from the coast. They started farms in inland valleys. Forests now provided wood for buildings as well as for ships.

Before there were many good roads, water was a very important way of getting from one place to another. A **waterway** is a body of water, such as a river, on which boats and ships can travel. Many settlements grew up along waterways. The Hudson River, for example, linked the seacoast with inland areas. Albany, New York, grew up along the Hudson River. Buffalo, New York, developed on Lake Erie.

The Region Grows

As settlements spread farther west, people built canals for water transportation. A **canal** is a waterway that people dig, usually for shipping. The Erie Canal was completed in 1825. It went from Albany to Buffalo. It joined the Hudson River to

Lake Erie. The Hudson River flows into the Atlantic Ocean. Therefore, the Erie Canal linked the Atlantic Ocean to the Great Lakes. The canal gave settlers a way of moving from east to west. It also gave people a new route to ship goods.

In places where natural resources combine with good transportation, industry often develops. Both Buffalo and Albany became industrial centers after the Erie Canal opened. Both cities grew rapidly. Today Albany is the capital of New York State. A **capital** is the city where a state or country's government is located.

Like Albany and Buffalo, many Northeastern cities have grown because of their locations. People throughout this region have used its resources and waterways for hundreds of years. They continue to do so today.

Settlements grew around harbors, like the one at Boston, Massachusetts *(above left)*. Today, Boston Harbor *(above right)* continues to be a busy place. From there, goods are shipped all over the world.

Lesson Review

1600	1700	1800

1620
Pilgrims found Plymouth Colony

1825
Erie Canal completed

1. **Key Vocabulary:** Use these words in a story about settlers: **Pilgrim, waterway, canal, capital.**

2. **Focus:** How did Native Americans like the Wampanoag use their environment?

3. **Focus:** How did Europeans use the land they settled?

4. **Critical Thinking: Compare** Native Americans used the resources of their

land. How do people in your area use nearby resources?

5. **Citizenship:** The Wampanoag helped the Pilgrims. How do people in your area help newcomers?

6. **Geography/Writing Activity:** In the late 1800s, the Erie Canal became less important than before. Find out why this happened. Write an explanation.

GEOGRAPHER

Environment and Society

Why Did New England Become a Center for Mills?

For centuries people made yarn by hand. Then, in the late 1700s, the British invented machines that could spin yarn and weave cotton cloth. For a time the British tried to keep their inventions a secret. However, a young mill worker named Samuel Slater had other ideas.

In 1789 Slater memorized the plans for a cotton-spinning machine and sailed for America. The following year he built a small spinning mill next to the Blackstone River in Pawtucket, Rhode Island.

Slater's choice of New England for the nation's first spinning mill was no accident. Mills needed water power to run their machines. New England had many swift-moving rivers. Soon mills were springing up along rivers all around the region. By the 1830s, New England had become the manufacturing center of the United States.

1 Lowell

First Major Mill Town
A waterfall on the Merrimack River in Massachusetts became the site of a series of new spinning mills in the early 1820s. The city that grew up around these mills, Lowell, became one of the chief centers of the cotton industry in the United States.

The Amoskeag mills stretched along the Merrimack River for over a mile. Machines here produced 50 miles of cloth each hour.

Literature Connection

Lucy Larcom went to work in the Lowell mills in the 1830s. She soon began publishing stories and articles in the *Lowell Offering and Magazine*, which was written entirely by mill girls. Her book *A New England Girlhood* (1889) describes what it was like to work in the mills. Why have historians found this book useful?

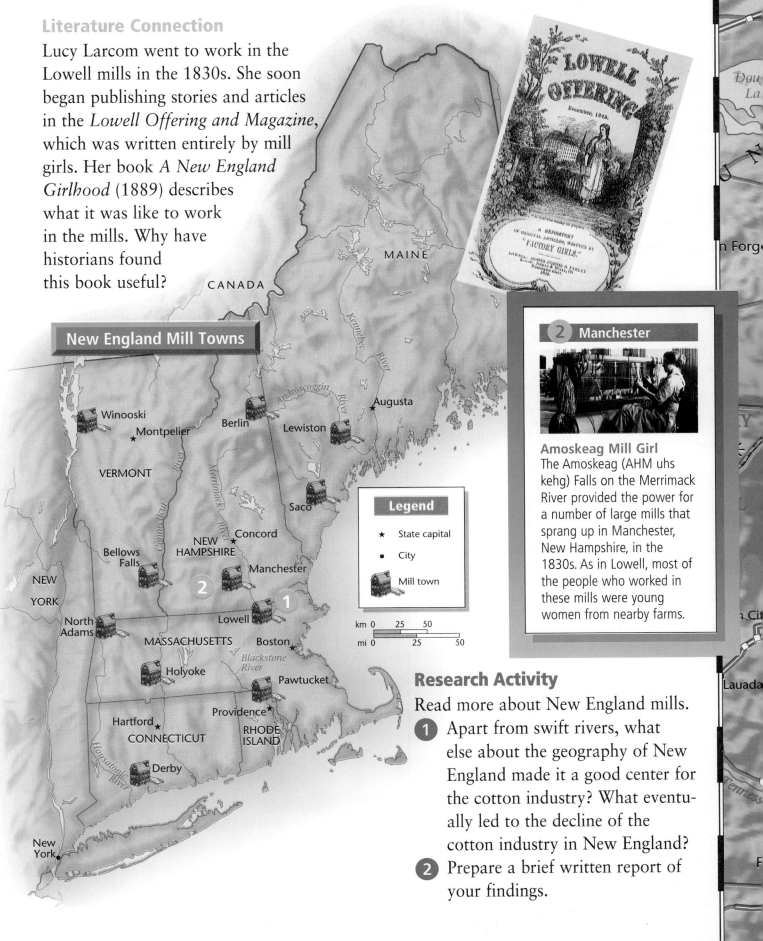

New England Mill Towns

Legend

★ State capital

• City

🏭 Mill town

km 0   25   50
mi 0   25   50

2 Manchester

Amoskeag Mill Girl
The Amoskeag (AHM uhs kehg) Falls on the Merrimack River provided the power for a number of large mills that sprang up in Manchester, New Hampshire, in the 1830s. As in Lowell, most of the people who worked in these mills were young women from nearby farms.

Research Activity

Read more about New England mills.

1. Apart from swift rivers, what else about the geography of New England made it a good center for the cotton industry? What eventually led to the decline of the cotton industry in New England?

2. Prepare a brief written report of your findings.

Reading Cut-Away Diagrams

An Inside View

Farming New England's rocky fields wasn't easy. In the 1800s, many people thought that working in a mill — a type of factory — promised them a better life. Sometimes entire families went to work in mills.

You can learn more about how these mills worked by studying a **cut-away diagram**. This type of diagram lets you see inside something you can't normally see into.

1 Here's How

Study the cut-away diagram of a New England mill on the next page.

- Gather information from the labels on the diagram. Find the water wheel, gears, belts, and spinning wheels.

- Study each part of the diagram. Study the different levels of the mill. Notice how the different parts of the mill work together.

- Look at the arrows. Directional arrows show how something moves. In this diagram, they show how the belts and pulleys move and how the water pushes the water wheel.

2 Think It Through

How does this cut-away diagram help you learn more about a New England mill? What are some other objects or ideas that a cut-away diagram might help explain?

3 Use It

Look at the diagram again.

1. Find the water wheel. Write an explanation of how water makes the water wheel move.

2. Locate the spinning wheels. Explain how belts make the spinning wheels work.

3. Create a cut-away diagram of something you know about, such as your school building or a piece of fruit.

Attic for storage

Spinning wheel

Belts

Gear

Water wheel

Northeast Living

Main Idea Today the Northeast is both urban and rural and is made up of people from many different backgrounds.

I t's breakfast time. You are about to dig into a stack of hot pancakes. So you reach for the maple syrup.

Pancakes, waffles, and French toast just wouldn't taste the same without sweet maple syrup. People in Vermont make maple syrup from the sap of maple trees. This syrup is then shipped all over the country. From rural Vermont comes maple syrup that people enjoy in urban areas such as Philadelphia, Pennsylvania.

Key Vocabulary

factory
wholesale
retail
finance
stock

Key Places

Wall Street
Princeton University
Rutgers University

Working in the Northeast

Focus *What are some kinds of work that people in the Northeast do?*

The maple syrup's journey from Vermont to Pennsylvania shows the different kinds of communities there are in the Northeast. People in this region live on farms and in small towns, as well as in suburbs and cities.

In all of these places, people have found ways of earning a living. Farms dot the countryside in states like Pennsylvania, New Jersey, New York, New Hampshire, and Maine. They produce dairy products, vegetables, and fruits. On the Atlantic coast, fishing is still important.

The Northeast was the first region of the United States to build factories.

Cranberries are an important crop in the Northeast.

Milk — from Cow to Customer

From the farm . . .

1 Dairy farmers raise cows for the milk they produce. Workers on the farm milk the cows. The milk then goes to a milk processor.

to the supermarket.

3 From the processor, the bottled milk travels in trucks to stores. When people buy milk in supermarkets or other stores, they are buying milk retail.

to the milk processor . . .

2 The processing company treats the milk to kill germs and then puts it in bottles. It sells the milk wholesale to stores.

A **factory** is a building or group of buildings in which goods are made. Factories are still very important in the Northeast. Industries there produce packaged foods, medicines, and machinery.

After products are made, they are sold. Many people in the Northeast work in wholesale and retail sales. **Wholesale** is the sale of large amounts of goods, usually to stores. Buyers of wholesale goods usually resell them in retail sales. **Retail** is the sale of goods directly to customers *(see above)*.

Wall Street

New York City is a major center of finance. **Finance** is the management of money, especially by businesses and banks. The heart of finance in the United States is a short — but very

Stocks are bought and sold on the busy floor of the New York Stock Exchange. **Economics:** *Few people own a whole company, but many people buy shares of stock. Why are shares more affordable?*

busy — street in New York City called Wall Street. On Wall Street and nearby, you can find many banks and other places where money is managed. One of these places is the New York Stock Exchange. That is where stocks are bought and sold.

Stock is a share in the ownership of a business. Most big companies are owned by a lot of people. The ownership of a company is divided into a certain number of shares — sort of the way a loaf of bread is divided into slices. When you buy a share of stock, you are actually buying a little "slice" of a business. Shares of businesses all over the country are sold in the New York Stock Exchange.

Lifelong Learning

Focus *What are some ways people get an education in the Northeast?*

Schools and education are an important part of life in every region of the country. Some of the oldest and most famous schools in the United States are in the Northeast. The first high school in the American colonies, for example, was the Boston Latin School, which opened in 1635.

Suwada Hinds goes to Boston Latin High School. She says,

"It's a real honor to be here. . . . We are reminded of our history all the time. We're very proud of our roots.**"**

There are many colleges and universities in the Northeast. Princeton, which was founded in 1746, is in New Jersey. Many of our country's leaders, including two Presidents, graduated from Princeton. Another old New Jersey college is Rutgers. Rutgers is a state university — a university that is partly supported by state taxes and is set up to educate the state's residents. All states in the United States have state universities.

Education doesn't have to stop with graduation. After people finish high school or college, they still want to learn. Adult education is education for men and women who are no longer full-time students.

Some adult education courses help people who have dropped out of school. By taking these courses, people can complete high school. Other courses teach people job-related skills, such as how to use a computer, fix a car, or speak a foreign language. Still others, such as dancing, are just for fun. Whether they are young or old, people in the Northeast have lots of opportunities to learn.

Curious Facts

A Connecticut baker named William Russell Frisbie sold pies and sugar cookies in tins. In the 1920s, students at Yale University began throwing those tins for fun, yelling, "Frisbie!" Later, a plastic disc-shaped toy was named in honor of those first flying Frisbie pie tins.

Lesson Review:

1. **Key Vocabulary:** Use these words in a paragraph about the economy of the Northeast: **factory, wholesale, retail, stock.**

2. **Focus:** What are some kinds of work that people in the Northeast do?

3. **Focus:** What are some ways people get an education in the Northeast?

4. **Critical Thinking: Interpret** When you buy a game or soccer ball in a toy store, what kind of sale is it — retail or wholesale? Explain why.

5. **Geography:** In general, the population of the Northeast is densest near the coast. Give a reason for this.

6. **Citizenship/Writing Activity:** Write a description of five courses that would be good in a community's adult education program. Some should be useful. Others should be fun.

CHAPTER 6

Chapter Review

Summarizing the Main Idea

1 Indicate what you have learned about the land and people of the Northeast by copying and filling in the chart below.

Northeast	
Climate	
Land	
Settlers	
Life Today	

Vocabulary

2 Using at least 10 of the following terms, write a script for a television commercial advertising the Northeast.

temperate (p. 144)   **waterway (p. 152)**   **retail (p. 159)**

blizzard (p. 145)   **canal (p. 152)**   **finance (p. 159)**

glacier (p. 145)   **capital (p. 153)**   **stock (p. 160)**

ecosystem (p. 146)   **factory (p. 159)**

Pilgrim (p. 150)   **wholesale (p. 159)**

Reviewing the Facts

3 What are some geographic features of the Northeast?

4 Describe the climate of the Northeast.

5 Name three ways that Native Americans and Pilgrims in the Northeast used their natural surroundings.

6 Why did the Quakers come to the Northeast, and where did they settle?

7 Why were waterways so important for settlers in the Northeast?

8 What happens at the New York Stock Exchange?

9 Look at the cut-away diagram on page 157. List three things that you can see that you couldn't see just by looking at the outside of the mill.

10 Draw a cut-away diagram of an apple, with the stem at the top. Label the stem, core, and seeds.

Geography Skills

11 Look at a map of the Northeast. Suppose you traveled from New Jersey to Pennsylvania and then went to Maine. In what direction would you be traveling as you left each state? About how far would you travel in all?

12 Plan a trip to the Northeast. Choose the season, the places you will visit, and the things you will do. What special items will you need to pack?

Critical Thinking

13 Conclude What are some reasons that people today might settle in the Northeast? What might be appealing about the region?

14 Cause and Effect How might northeastern winters be different if the region were not bordered by the Atlantic Ocean and Great Lakes?

Writing: Citizenship and History

15 Citizenship Think of something you would like to learn about your state, such as its history or how its government works. Then write a description of an adult-education course that would teach that subject.

16 History Start a diary as though you are one of the Pilgrims who have just arrived in the Northeast. What are your first impressions of your new home? Write an entry describing what you see, hear, and feel.

Activities

National Heritage/Research Activity
Research one of the Native American groups of the Northeast, such as the Wampanoag, the Iroquois, or the Penobscot. Create a visual display that tells about the group.

Geography/Art Activity
Make a collage that celebrates life in the Northeast. Focus on the land, the early settlers, or the Northeast today. Give your collage a title. Display it on a bulletin board with the other students' collages.

Internet Option

Check the **Internet Social Studies Center** for ideas on how to extend your theme project beyond your classroom.

THEME PROJECT CHECK-IN

Include what you've learned about the Northeast in your newspaper.
- Does your newspaper show the landforms, climate, and resources of the Northeast?
- How did the environment affect Native Americans and settlers in the Northeast?
- How can your newspaper show the kinds of work that northeasterners do?

CHAPTER 7

The Northeast Today

Chapter Preview: *People, Places, and Events*

1750	1800	1850

Celebrate St. Patrick's Day

The Irish community in New York City celebrates with a parade.
Lesson 1, Page 166

A Puerto Rican Community

These kids are about to shop in Pueblo store in Vineland, NJ.
Lesson 1, Page 168

He Invented the Telephone

Do you know who this is? Find out who invented the telephone.
Lesson 2, Page 170

A Region of Many Cultures

Main Idea The Northeast has a large population made up of many ethnic groups.

Key Vocabulary

port
ethnic group
value
tradition

Key Places

Vineland,
  New Jersey

It's a summer day in a northeastern city. On the way to the park to meet your friends, you pass a newsstand. You stop your bike to look at the newspapers and magazines on display.

At the newsstand, you find major daily newspapers in English. You might also see newspapers in many other languages, such as Russian, Chinese, and Arabic. One newspaper might give news about the country of Brazil. Other newspapers have stories of special interest to Chinese Americans. Still others might be written for Greek Americans or Italian Americans.

In large northeastern cities like Philadelphia or New York, you can read — and hear — many languages. People who live in the Northeast come from all over the world.

◀ At night in New York City, lights sparkle from streets, buildings, and bridges.

1900	1950	2000

A Dish but No Food?

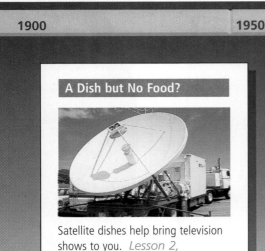

Satellite dishes help bring television shows to you. *Lesson 2, Page 173*

All Aboard the Train!

If you want to get from a suburb to Boston, you might ride a train. *Lesson 3, Page 174*

Just Barge In

Barges like this move trash in the Northeast. *Lesson 4, Page 186*

Immigration to New York State

Immigrants (in thousands)

30
25
20
15
10
5
0

Dominican Republic | Former Soviet Union | China | Jamaica

Sources of Immigration

Immigrants to New York State in 1993 came from some of the countries shown in the graph. **Chart Skill:** *From which country did most immigrants come?*

Chinese Americans hold a parade on Chinese New Year *(right)*. Irish Americans celebrate St. Patrick's Day *(far right)*.

Ethnic Communities

Focus *Why is the Northeast the home of many different ethnic groups?*

Until this century, most immigrants to the United States came from Europe. Because Europe is closer to the East Coast of the United States than to other parts of the country, many immigrants arrived at northeastern ports. A **port** is a place where ships can stop. There, passengers can get on or off, and goods can be loaded or unloaded. Many immigrants could not afford to travel far from the port where they landed. That's why they settled in the Northeast.

New immigrants often want to live in areas where there are other people of their ethnic group. An **ethnic group** is a group of people who share the same language, customs, and way of life. Members of the same ethnic group often share many of the same values. A **value** is an idea or belief that a person thinks is important. Honesty, for example, is an important value.

In the Northeast, some neighborhoods are made up of people who belong to the same ethnic group. Ethnic communities help immigrants in many ways. The stores sell foods and other goods that immigrants used in their home

countries. At places of worship, such as temples and churches, people practice their religion. Community organizations may help immigrants find jobs and learn about their new country. People in ethnic communities have fun together, too, as you can see from the pictures on this page.

Ethnic neighborhoods help keep traditions alive. A **tradition** is a practice that is handed down from parents to children. Eating turkey on Thanksgiving Day is a favorite tradition in the United States.

Some ethnic populations are larger in the Northeast than they are in the cities of their homeland. More than twice as many people with Italian ancestors live in New York City than in Venice, Italy. An ancestor is a family member from long ago, such as a great-great-grandparent.

In a parade in New York City *(top photo),* Korean American women wear brightly colored dresses. People with Caribbean roots celebrate at a festival in Boston *(bottom photo).* **Cultures:** *What are some festivals that ethnic groups in your state or community celebrate?*

With smiles and waves, Yeira and Carlos stand in front of Pueblo grocery store in Vineland, New Jersey. Inside the store, after examining the wide variety of fruits and vegetables, Carlos makes his choice.

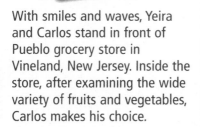

The Puerto Rican Community in Vineland

Focus *How can an ethnic community support the people who live there?*

Many people in Vineland, New Jersey, were born on the island of Puerto Rico (PWEHR tuh REE koh) — or their parents or grandparents were born there. Puerto Rico is part of the United States. However, it is not a state — it is a commonwealth that governs itself.

Vineland has a large Puerto Rican community. At Pueblo grocery store, people can buy Puerto Rican goods, such as vegetables grown and eaten in Puerto Rico. In the newspaper *El Veterano* (el veh teh RAH noh), many articles are in Spanish. Most Puerto Ricans speak Spanish.

The community keeps Puerto Rican traditions alive. One musical tradition is the *parranda* (pah RAHN duh). *Parrandas* take place between Thanksgiving and the New Year. A parranda starts when several people go to a neighbor's house. They play the guitar and sing, and the neighbor joins in. Then all the people, including the neighbor, move on to another house.

Jeselyn Matos is in the fourth grade in Vineland. She goes to an afterschool program held by Casa P.R.A.C. (P.R.A.C. stands for Puerto Rican Action Committee.) She speaks both Spanish and English. She enjoys Puerto Rican holidays, such as

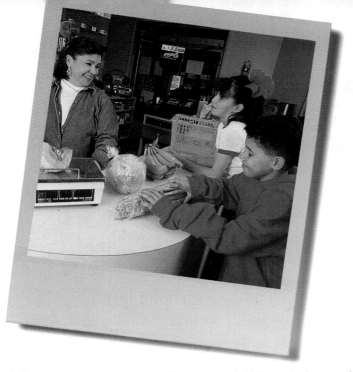

Three Kings' Day on January 6. Here is how she describes it:

> **"W**hen we wake up, there are presents. We have a little party that day. The whole family comes over.**"**

At the cash register, Mrs. Lopez helps Yeira and Carlos. Four children — Luis, Yolisbet, Angelica, and Jeselyn — stand in front of a mural, or wall painting. The mural is about Puerto Rico.

People who live in communities like Vineland share their culture with their neighbors. This sharing makes the Northeast a rich mix of traditions and cultures.

Lesson Review

1. **Key Vocabulary:** Define these key words: **port, ethnic group, value, tradition.**

2. **Focus:** Why is the Northeast the home of many different ethnic groups?

3. **Focus:** How can an ethnic community support the people who live there?

4. **Critical Thinking: Interpret** How can people in a community make new immigrants feel welcome?

5. **Citizenship:** What are some important traditions that all people in the United States should keep alive?

6. **Geography/Writing Activity:** Find out about a celebration held by an ethnic group that has immigrated to the United States. Create an advertisement for that celebration.

A Center for Communications

Main Idea The communications industry in the Northeast is making it easier for people to share information and ideas.

Key Vocabulary

- communications system
- media
- network
- telecommunications

Key Places

- Boston, Massachusetts
- New York, New York

The very first telephone call was a cry for help. In 1876, Alexander Graham Bell was trying to invent a telephone that would work. On March 10, as he was working on his invention, he spilled acid. Bell needed help — quickly. "Mr. Watson, come here. I want you!" Bell cried out to his assistant. Watson, in another room, heard Bell's words clearly, because they had traveled along a telephone wire.

The telephone changed communications systems forever. A **communications system** is a way of sending and receiving messages. The mail is a communications system, too, but it's a lot slower than the telephone.

In the years following Bell's invention, more and more people got telephones in their homes. The first telephone company, the Bell Telephone Company, began in 1877. Today the Northeast is home to many communications systems.

Communication Milestones in the Northeast

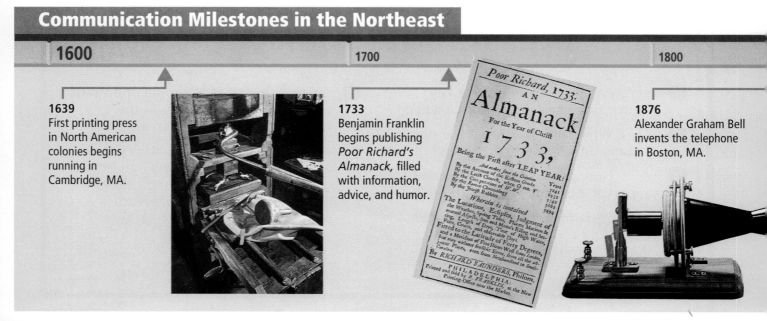

1600   1700   1800

1639
First printing press in North American colonies begins running in Cambridge, MA.

1733
Benjamin Franklin begins publishing *Poor Richard's Almanack*, filled with information, advice, and humor.

1876
Alexander Graham Bell invents the telephone in Boston, MA.

Words, Sounds, and Pictures

Focus *What types of communication are produced in the Northeast?*

Books, newspapers, radio, and television are ways of communicating with many people at the same time. They are called the **media.** Many northeasterners have jobs in the media.

Publishing, or the making of books, newspapers, and magazines, is an important industry in the Northeast. The cities of New York and Boston have many companies that publish books. When you curl up in a chair with a mystery or adventure story, you may have northeasterners to thank for editing that book. Many newspapers and magazines come from the region too. The *Wall Street Journal*, published in New York City, is a newspaper read by people all across the country.

People listen to the radio to hear music, news, the weather, and other things. Erik Nycklemoe is Executive Producer of New Hampshire Public Radio. He says this about radio news:

> **"R**adio *means you can have news any time, anywhere.***"**

Many television news programs are broadcast from the Northeast. ABC, CBS, and NBC — three companies that make TV shows — all have their headquarters in New York City.

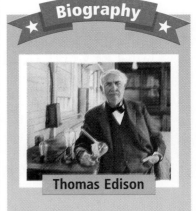
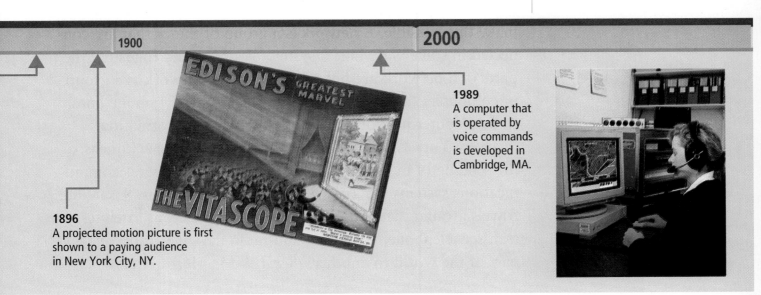

1900

2000

1896
A projected motion picture is first shown to a paying audience in New York City, NY.

1989
A computer that is operated by voice commands is developed in Cambridge, MA.

Broadcasting a Show

2 The show travels through the air as tiny, invisible waves. A series of transmitters *(right)* pass the waves along.

1 How does a show get from the TV station to your TV set? The show is filmed in a studio or somewhere else.

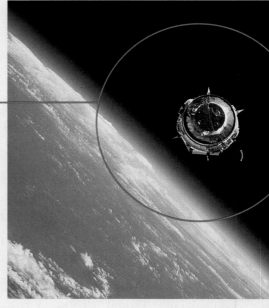

3 Transmitters may pass the waves on to a satellite. Satellites then send the waves to TV stations around the world.

Communications Networks

Focus *How do communications industries in the Northeast connect people around the world?*

The Northeast has played a big role in the development of computer technology. Today you can get information from around the globe in a matter of seconds. Computer networks make this possible. A **network** is a group of things that are connected in some way. Like a system of streets and roads, all the parts of a network are linked. A computer network is a group of computers that are connected to each other by phone lines. In a computer network, computers can share information.

New York City is a central point for **telecommunications,** or the sending of messages over long distances. Many telecommunications systems use satellites for sending messages. A satellite travels around the earth in space. Communications satellites transfer telephone, television, and radio messages from one part of the world to another. *(See Tell Me More above.)*

4 Waves from satellites are picked up by satellite dishes on earth.

5 Your television set receives signals through an antenna or through a cable.

ABC Cable Co.

News organizations in New York City depend on hundreds of satellites to get news from around the world. The diagram above shows how satellites can send messages. The people of the Northeast, in turn, help send out the world's information. They link the Northeast to other regions — and to the world.

Lesson Review

1 **Key Vocabulary:** Use the following words in a story about communication: **communications system, media, network, telecommunications.**

2 **Focus:** What types of communication are produced in the Northeast?

3 **Focus:** How do communications industries in the Northeast connect people around the world?

4 **Critical Thinking: Cause and Effect** Why are computer companies often found where there are a lot of colleges and universities?

5 **Citizenship:** Why are communications systems important to governments?

6 **Geography/Art Activity:** A computer message travels from New York City to Tokyo, Japan. Draw a map showing what its route might be.

Transportation in the Northeast

Main Idea People in the Northeast use different kinds of transportation to get to work and other places.

Key Vocabulary

commuter

public
  transportation

subway

tax

transportation
  system

Key Places

Philadelphia,
  Pennsylvania

It's a busy weekday morning, and you are flying in a helicopter over the city of Philadelphia, Pennsylvania. Looking down, you can see traffic moving from the countryside and suburbs to the city. Cars, trucks, and buses head for downtown Philadelphia. If you took your helicopter ride in the late afternoon, you'd see traffic moving in the opposite direction.

Many of the people in those cars, trucks, and buses are commuters. A **commuter** is someone who travels on most days to work or school. In the Northeast and throughout the country, many commuters travel from their homes in the suburbs to their jobs in the city.

Public Transportation

Focus *Why is public transportation so important in the Northeast?*

The two biggest cities in the United States are New York City in the Northeast and Los Angeles in the West. In Los Angeles, most people ride to work in cars. In New York City, it's very different. More than half of the people who commute to work there use **public transportation** — transportation such as buses, trains, and subways. A **subway** is an underground train.

Many big cities in the Northeast are old. They grew before cars were invented. A lot of their streets are narrow. There are traffic jams and few places to park. For many people, taking public transportation is easier and less expensive than driving a car. More people use public transportation in the Northeast than in any other region of the country.

Ask Yourself

If you could choose how to get to a friend's house, what would you choose? Would you bike, ride in a car, or ride public transportation?

? ? ? ? ? ? ? ? ? ? ? ? ? ? ? ?

Getting Around Philadelphia

Take a trip around the historic city of Philadelphia. You will use public transportation for part of the trip. **Map Skill:** *Are there places on the map you would like to visit that are not listed on your route?*

1. Arrive by train at 30th Street Station.

2. Take subway under Market Street to 6th Street. Walk one block to Independence Hall. See the Liberty Bell.

3. Walk through Independence Mall to the U.S. Mint and take a tour of it.

4. Then see Betsy Ross's house on Arch Street, where she may have made the first U.S. flag with stars and stripes.

5. Visit Elfreth's Alley, where there are 33 houses built in the 1700's.

6. Then walk to Market Street to catch the number 76 bus.

7. Visit the Philadelphia Museum of Art, then take a taxi back to the train station and head for home.

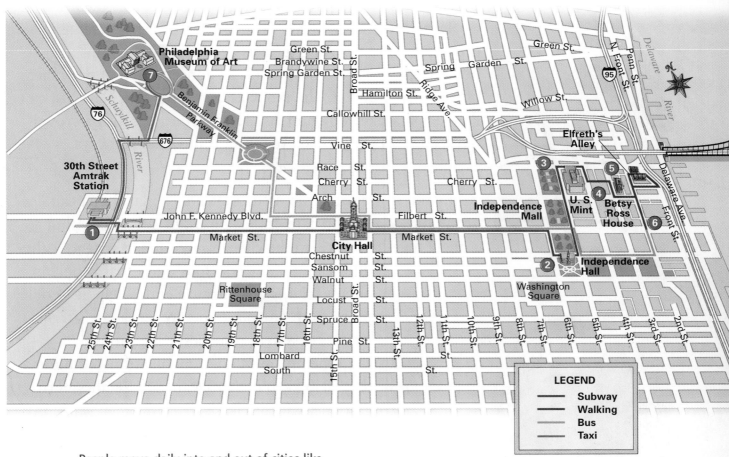

LEGEND
— Subway
— Walking
— Bus
— Taxi

People move daily into and out of cities like Philadelphia by bike, car, subway, and bus. **Map Skill:** *What forms of public transportation can you take along Market Street?*

The Northeast Today **175**

Acorn Street, in Boston, Massachusetts, was built for horses and people, not for cars.

Matthew Walker is a student at Temple University in Philadelphia. He says:

"I *enjoy riding the subway every day. It's much more relaxing than driving. I can read the paper. Sometimes I study on the subway.* **"**

Public transportation usually costs a lot to set up. Trains are expensive, and it costs millions of dollars to dig the tunnels for a subway. How do cities and states pay for this? People pay a fare when they use public transportation. Governments can also contribute money from taxes to public transportation projects. **Taxes** are money that people and businesses pay their government to help pay for the services it provides them.

It makes sense to spend this money when there are many people who are traveling to the same area. Public transportation works best when businesses are concentrated in one place, often called a downtown. Northeastern cities like New York or Philadelphia have downtowns. The Northeast is also a crowded region. Many people use buses, trains, and subways.

Choosing a Way to Travel

Commuters in northeastern cities such as Philadelphia can commute to work in cars, trains, buses, or subways. All of these together make up the city's **transportation system** — the different kinds of transportation that people in an area can choose from. Besides helping people move from one place to another, a city's transportation system provides many jobs.

When people choose public transportation, they help keep the air clean. Car engines burn gasoline, which releases harmful chemicals into the air. Buses burn gas, too. However, since many people ride on one bus, each commuter uses much less gas than if he or she drove a car.

Future Travel

Focus *What are some new ideas for transportation?*

Americans like their cars. It's very convenient to be able to drive wherever you want to go. However, cars can get caught in traffic. So, many people are thinking about new kinds of transportation that are safer, less expensive, and that use less gasoline.

Engineers are experimenting with different kinds of engines — for cars, buses, trains, and airplanes — that cause less pollution. Extremely fast trains, like ones used in Japan and Europe, are another way to travel. Those trains may be part of the transportation system in the Northeast when you grow up.

Some people are thinking about public transportation in a completely different way. One idea is called the "Skyway." If it is ever built, a Skyway would consist of a lot of big tubes, almost like roads, above a city. People could travel through the tubes in little cars that move by pedaling. It wouldn't pollute — and it sounds like fun!

SIDE VIEW
SKYWAY VEHICLE
CROSS SECTION OF TUBE

END
SKYWAY
CROSS SECT

DESIGNED BY: KOR
PROJECT: SKYWAY
SKYWAY — illustration

The Personal Rapid Transit for the Year 2000, or PRT2000, may be one system for the future. Like a personal train, it has small rail cars, designed to carry up to four people. **Economics:** *Do you think that PRT2000 would be expensive to build? Why or why not?*

Lesson Review

1. **Key Vocabulary:** Use these words to write a letter to an official about public transportation: commuter, subway, tax, transportation system.

2. **Focus:** Why is public transportation so important in the Northeast?

3. **Focus:** What are some new ideas for transportation?

4. **Critical Thinking: Conclude** Why do some people today live so far from where they work? Has public transportation made it easier or harder to live outside of a city?

5. **Citizenship:** Do you think governments should use taxes to pay for public transportation? Why or why not?

6. **Geography/Art Activity:** Make a map showing how you get to school or to a friend's home. Beneath the map, draw the different ways you have of getting there — walking, bus, car, and so on.

(handwritten margin notes) Maps · Writing outlines · Reading Graphs · Facts/Opinion · Using Atlases · Organizing Information

Drawing Conclusions from Maps

Getting Around

In New York City, the subway runs all night long. In some small towns, there is no public transportation at all. How can you tell which parts of the Northeast will have the most transportation choices? A **population map** can help. By studying the map's color patterns, you can see which areas have the most people. The more crowded the area, the more transportation choices you'll find. The map can help you draw conclusions about the transportation choices available in an area.

❶ Here's How

Look at the population map of the Northeast on the next page.

- Study the legend. Each color stands for a different number of people living in one square mile. A **square mile** is an area one mile long and one mile wide. Find the color area where there are fewer than 99 people living in a square mile. Then find the other population areas.

- Study the map to find out where most Northeasterners live. For example, many Northeasterners live along the coast. What other patterns do you see?

- Compare the populations on different parts of the map. How are the population patterns different throughout the Northeast? Why do you think fewer people live in northern Maine than in the city of Philadelphia? How would transportation be different in these two places?

❷ Think It Through

What conclusions can you draw from seeing a population map that you couldn't draw from seeing a list of places with their populations written next to them?

3 Use It

Use the map below to answer these questions:

1. How many people per square mile live in the purple area in New York state?

2. Are there more people in Harrisburg than in Buffalo?

3. What can you conclude about what transportation might be like in the following places: Portland, Maine; Springfield, Massachusetts; Philadelphia, Pennsylvania; Montpelier, Vermont; Newark, New Jersey; New Haven, Connecticut.

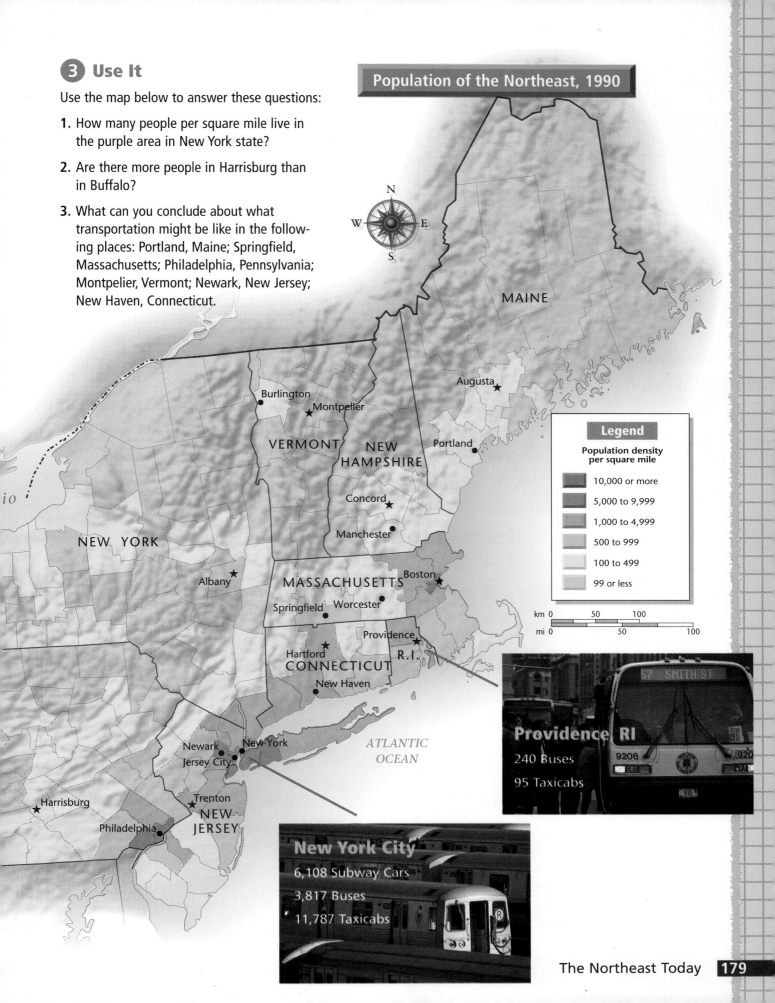

Population of the Northeast, 1990

Legend

Population density per square mile

- 10,000 or more
- 5,000 to 9,999
- 1,000 to 4,999
- 500 to 999
- 100 to 499
- 99 or less

Providence RI

240 Buses

95 Taxicabs

New York City

6,108 Subway Cars

3,817 Buses

11,787 Taxicabs

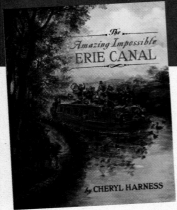

HISTORY

The Amazing Impossible ERIE CANAL

By Cheryl Harness

The early growth of the United States was from east to west. But there was a problem. Dense forests and the Appalachian mountain range made westward travel very difficult. Transporting people and goods by water was so much faster and easier, but only if the rivers went where travelers needed to go. It was a problem that needed to be solved.

It took nearly a month or more to get a barrel of flour from the shores of Lake Erie along the Mohawk Trail to the Hudson River. However difficult, this passage followed a

natural gap in the Appalachian range. Since ancient times, native peoples such as the Senecas and Onandagas had floated their light canoes along the Mohawk River, Wood Creek, and Oneida Lake on the way to Lakes Ontario and Erie. They carried the canoes around the rapids, over land, and through valleys where boats couldn't go.

gap,
*a break in
the mountains*

European colonists moved their heavy, flat-bottomed boats on the same waterways. They, too, had to work around the obstructions. Why not con-nect these rivers and lakes with man-made streams, as in the Old Country? they wondered. Smoothly floating boats could be pulled along by horses walking on the bank. After the War of Independence was over in 1783, George Washington himself championed the idea of such canals: Travel and trade made easy and cheap would hold a young country together.

to champion
to support an idea

If such a waterway was constructed between the Great Lakes and the Hudson, a person could float from Ohio clear to London! It seemed an impossible dream.

If only the millions of dollars could be raised . . . if only all the engineering problems could be solved . . . a ditch 40 feet wide carrying 4 feet of water could be made to go up and down 363 miles across the countryside . . . . *Impossible!*

Nevertheless, a politician named DeWitt Clinton argued that the canal was more than possible, it was necessary; not only for New York, but for America. It would be a pathway into the country's heartland. The people agreed, and Mr. Clinton became the governor.

politician
*person who runs for
political office*

On a long-awaited summer morning, gentlemen wearing tall silk hats gathered in a meadow near Rome, New York, in the level center of the state, where the digging was easy.

Turn
Page

The first ships on the Erie Canal sailed from the end of the canal in Buffalo down the Hudson River to New York City. When the ships reached New York Harbor and the Atlantic Ocean, fireworks were set off in celebration.

Romans wore their best clothes, and a band played a fanfare on shiny cornets as the ground was broken for the Erie Canal at dawn on the Fourth of July, 1817.

Five years later, the people were worried the project would never be paid for or finished. The governor lost his job. Mr. Clinton kept overseeing the work and making speeches anyway. His political enemies called the canal Clinton's Ditch.

But the voters felt better as they traveled more and more on the almost-finished waterway, which was already earning money in tolls. (For example, one penny for one ton of grain hauled one mile.) Mr. Clinton won the election of 1824. The following year, the impossible Erie Canal was done; *Clinton's Ditch* was said with pride. It was time to celebrate.

fanfare
a loud melody played by trumpets

Meet the Author

Cheryl Harness is an author and illustrator who likes to find exciting stories behind real events. Two of her other books, *Young John Quincy* and *Three Young Pilgrims* are also about people and events in American history.

Additional Books to Read

A River Ran Wild
by Lynne Cherry
Read about the cleanup of a polluted New England river.

A Year on Monhegan Island
by Julia Dean
Learn about life on an island off the Maine coast.

Response Activities

1. Identify Main Idea Why did Americans want to build a canal from the Great Lakes to the Hudson River? Who would use the canal?

2. Descriptive: Write an Invitation A celebration is to be held at the opening of the Erie Canal in 1825. Write an invitation to the event. Use descriptive words that show why this is such an important occasion.

3. History: Make a Report Use your school library to find out about the workers who built the canal and the many hardships they faced.

The Erie Canal

This popular folk song developed along the towpaths of the Erie Canal, the world's longest uninterrupted canal. If you listen to the rhythm, you can almost hear the clip-clop of the hooves.

I've got a mule, her name is Sal, Fif-teen years__ on the
We'd bet-ter get a-long, old gal, Fif-teen years__ on the

Er-ie Ca-nal.__ She's a good old work-er and a good old pal,
Er-ie Ca-nal.__ You can bet your life I'd nev-er part with Sal,

Fif-teen years__ on the Er-ie Ca-nal.__ We've hauled some bar-ges
Fif-teen years on the Er-ie Ca-nal.__ Git up there,__ mule,

in our day, Filled with lum-ber, coal, and hay, And
here comes a lock, We'll make Rome__ 'bout six o'-clock; Just

ev - 'ry inch of the way we know From Al - ba - ny to Buf - fa - lo.
one more trip, and then we'll go, Right back home to Buf - fa - lo.

Low bridge, ev - 'ry bo - dy down! Low bridge, for we're go - in' thro' a town. And you'll

al - ways know your neigh - bor, You'll al - ways know your pal, If you've

ev – er nav – i - gat – ed on the Er – ie Ca – nal.

Where would I be if I lost my pal?
Fifteen years on the Erie Canal.
Oh, I'd like to see a mule as good as Sal,
Fifteen years on the Erie Canal.
A friend of mine once got her sore,
Now he's got a broken jaw,
'Cause she let fly with her iron toe
And kicked him into Buffalo.

Low bridge, everybody down!
Low bridge, for we're comin' to a town!
You can always tell your neighbor,
Can always tell your pal,
If you've ever navigated on the Erie Canal.

Response Activities

1. **Interpret** Why would it be important for someone who moved goods along the canal to have a mule that was a dependable "good old pal"?

2. **Expressive: Write a Transportation Song** Think about the kinds of transportation that we use today. With a partner, write a song or a poem about one of them.

3. **Geography: Calculate Travel Distances** Find out more about other canals, such as the Panama or Suez canals. Look at travel routes before and after the canals were built. How have those routes changed?

The Recycling Industry

Main Idea Recycling helps the Northeast solve its garbage problems and provides new products and jobs.

Key Vocabulary

landfill

pollution

Key Places

Staten Island, New York

Rhode Island

Think of 19,000 football fields, each piled 10 feet high with garbage. That garbage would weigh about 200 million tons! (One ton is 2,000 pounds.) That's how much garbage Americans produce every year. Each day, the average person in the United States throws away four pounds of garbage.

The main problem with garbage is figuring out where to put it. This is true everywhere in the United States. In the Northeast, however, the problem is especially serious. The Northeast is the smallest region of the United States. It also has a very large population. People in the Northeast don't have much space for all the garbage they produce.

Recycling in the Northeast

Focus *Why is recycling important in the Northeast?*
Many communities get rid of their garbage by sending it to landfills. A **landfill** is a piece of ground in which garbage is buried. Communities can't put a landfill just anywhere. When rain falls on garbage, materials in the garbage wash into the soil. Some of those materials can get into ground water and pollute it. This **pollution** — making something dirty or impure — makes the water unhealthy. Landfills people create today must be well sealed so they don't cause water pollution. People also must carefully decide where to locate landfills.

In the spring of 1987, a barge called the *Mobro* wandered up and down the Atlantic coast, looking for a place to dump its garbage. The *Mobro* helped make people in the United States aware of their garbage problem.

Recycling Paper

Have you ever piled up your family's newspapers or other papers for recycling? The steps below show how paper is recycled.

1 → **2**

The newspaper you read may be printed on recycled paper. It can be recycled, too!

People like you pile up papers. The papers are picked up by recycling trucks.

7 **3**

After the paper dries out, it is ready to use again.

Recycling trucks dump used paper at a paper recycling plant.

6 **4**

Then the paper pulp is pumped through a machine that presses it out and dries it.

At the plant the paper is baled, or packed into cubes.

5

The paper passes through machines that wash it and turn it into useful paper pulp.

Glasphalt is a blend of glass and asphalt. It is used to pave many highways in the Northeast.

Presto — new shoes from old cloth! A company makes shoes from leftover cotton scraps.

This playground in Jamestown, Rhode Island, is made of recycled materials.

Overflowing Landfills

The biggest landfill in the country is in the Northeast, on New York City's Staten Island. It's called the Fresh Kills Landfill. (The word *kills,* as it's used here, comes from a Dutch word that means "tiny river" or "creek.") Fresh Kills Landfill is huge — it covers 3,000 acres. The garbage is 150 feet high in some places. Again and again, dump trucks bring New York City's garbage to Fresh Kills Landfill. Every day, the garbage pile grows about 75 feet longer.

Many landfills in the Northeast are filling up. However, if people recycle some of their garbage, landfills won't fill up so fast. As you learned in Chapter 2, when you recycle something, you use it over again. Paper, plastic milk jugs, and glass bottles are just a few things that can be recycled. Today, more and more people are helping to solve the Northeast's garbage problem by recycling.

New Steps Toward Recycling

When your parents were children, most people didn't think much about recycling. In 1986, Rhode Island passed the first state law requiring people to recycle some of their garbage. Three years later, Rhode Island opened a recycling plant to sort plastic, aluminum, newspaper, and other materials. This plant is called a materials-recovery facility [fah SILL uh tee] — MRF for short. Machines do most of the work there. With the help of six workers, these machines can sort about 80 tons of trash for recycling each day.

In the 1980s and 1990s, other states opened MRFs. Many communities across the country have passed recycling laws.

Products from Recyclables

Focus *What happens to recycled materials?*

Have you heard the expression, "from trash to treasure"? Trash can't be made into diamonds or gold, but people can make many useful things from it.

For instance, glass can be melted to make new bottles. Glass can also be mixed with asphalt, a sticky material like tar.

Together they make glasphalt. Glasphalt is good for paving highways. The glass in glasphalt is ground up so that it doesn't hurt tires or people's feet. Aluminum cans can be melted down to make new cans. Recycled plastic can be made into carpets, toys, and other products. Newspapers and other paper are made into new paper.

The recycling industry provides jobs for people. Recycling also helps cut down on our nation's garbage. The United States still produces more garbage than any other country, though. People need to keep looking for new ways to get rid of garbage.

At the Boston Schools Recycle Center in Boston, Massachusetts, children play with foam toys. Local industries donate the foam. It would otherwise be thrown out as scrap. **Economics:** *What other products do you think people could make from scrap materials?*

Lesson Review

1 **Key Vocabulary:** Write ideas for how your community can get rid of its garbage. Use the words **landfill** and **pollution**.

2 **Focus:** Why is recycling important in the Northeast?

3 **Focus:** What happens to recycled materials?

4 **Critical Thinking: Classify** Think of several products you throw away.

Which could you recycle?

5 **Theme: Land and Sea** Why shouldn't garbage be dumped in the ocean?

6 **Citizenship/Math Activity:** An average American throws out four pounds of trash each day. How much trash does an average family the size of yours throw away each day? How much does it throw away in a year? Make a chart to show this information.

★ CITIZENSHIP ★

Participating

Where Does Garbage Go?

What happens to your garbage once you throw it out? You know it doesn't just disappear! Here is how some people in the Northeast are turning garbage into something useful.

Case Study

Composting for a Better Earth

Recycling makes a difference. Just ask people in Pittsburgh, Pennsylvania. A company there — like companies and people across the country — is turning leaves, grass clippings, and branches into a rich soil material called compost.

Individuals and businesses bring their plant wastes, including food, to special centers. At these centers, the waste is allowed to decay, or break down naturally. This process is called composting.

Compost helps grass and plants grow. Pittsburgh used compost to grow thick ground cover at the zoo entrance. They also used compost to grow thick grass at Point State Park, pictured at right. Eight thousand people picnicked on this grass before the All-Star Baseball Game in 1994.

Take Action

Think about the ways you could help the environment by wasting less and recycling more. First you need to figure out what's in your garbage. Here's your chance.

1 For a day or a week, save the garbage you and your classmates normally throw out. Divide it into separate containers for each kind of garbage (food, paper, styrofoam, plastic, and so on).

2 Figure out how to measure each kind of garbage. Make a circle graph to show how much of the total garbage each kind is. Compare your graph to this national garbage circle graph.

3 Look over your garbage. Decide which items you and your classmates could waste less. Figure out how you could begin to recycle those items in your school.

4 Make a poster that convinces others to join in your efforts to waste less and recycle more.

Tips for Participating

- Think about ways that you contribute to the problem and to the solution.
- Be willing to help out.
- Keep others involved by expressing interest in their ideas.
- Remember that everyone's small efforts add up to something bigger.

Research Activity

What happens to your garbage after you throw it out? Choose a few items in your garbage. Find out from books, recycling specialists, or community leaders what happens once the items get in the garbage. Make a chart to show the process of decay, over days, weeks, and years. If the items you pick don't break down at all, represent that on your chart, too.

Chapter Review

Summarizing the Main Idea

1 Copy and complete the chart below, filling in one or more facts about the Northeast for each topic.

Topic	Facts
Ethnic communities	
Communication	
Transportation	
Recycling	

Vocabulary

2 Using at least eleven of the following terms, write a magazine article about the Northeast.

port (p. 166)

ethnic group (p. 166)

value (p. 166)

tradition (p. 167)

communications system (p. 170)

media (p. 171)

network (p. 172)

telecommunications (p. 172)

commuter (p. 174)

public transportation (p. 174)

subway (p. 174)

taxes (p. 176)

transportation system (p. 176)

landfill (p. 186)

pollution (p. 186)

Reviewing the Facts

3 Why are there so many different ethnic groups in the Northeast?

4 What are some ways in which ethnic neighborhoods help immigrants?

5 Name two traditions that Puerto Ricans in Vineland keep alive.

6 How do computer networks connect people all over the world?

7 What do communications satellites do?

8 What kinds of public transportation are available in the Northeast?

9 Describe what travel on Skyway might be like.

10 What is a landfill?

11 Why should people try to recycle their trash?

12 From the map on page 179, how does western Pennsylvania compare to eastern Pennsylvania in population?

13 Do you think many people in northern Maine use public transportation? Look at the map on page 179.

Geography Skills

14 Look at the map on page 175. From Independence Hall, can you walk to many historic places, or would you need to take a car or bus? Explain.

15 Create a brochure advertising what a person might see or do on a trip to the Northeast.

Critical Thinking

16 **Interpret** List three jobs in communications. Then list another job related to each of them. For example, paper-making is related to printing books.

17 **Problem Solving** Create a plan for improving recycling in your school. If you can, put your plan into action.

Writing: Citizenship and Economics

18 **Citizenship** Imagine you work for a radio station. Write an editorial about an issue in your community. Read your piece into a cassette recorder.

19 **Economics** Write an argument for or against using tax money to build a subway.

Activities

National Heritage/Art Activity
Cities are filled with ethnic neighborhoods such as Chinatown in New York and the North End (Italian) in Boston. Find out about one of these neighborhoods, or an ethnic neighborhood in your community or state. Make a collage that celebrates the neighborhood's interests and culture.

Economics/Math Activity
Compare the cost of communicating by mail and by phone. Choose 10 cities in different regions of the country. Find out how much it costs to make a 10-minute phone call to each of those cities during the day. Then find out how much a postage stamp costs. How much do you save by sending a letter? What things besides cost do you need to think of when communicating?

Internet Option

Check the **Internet Social Studies Center** for ideas on how to extend your theme project beyond your classroom.

THEME PROJECT CHECK-IN

Make sure your newspaper includes what you've learned about the Northeast.
- Do you show people from different cultures in the Northeast?
- What can you include to describe public transportation, communications, and industries in the Northeast?
- How can your newspaper help educate people about recycling in the Northeast?

"I've known rivers:
Ancient, dusky rivers.
My soul has grown deep like the rivers."

Langston Hughes

·THEME·

Rivers and Coasts

" *We live in West Virginia, surrounded by mountains. We can go snow skiing or water skiing.* **"**

Neil Patel, Fourth Grade
Vienna, WV

If you look at a map of the South, what do you see? Cities, farms, hills, and forests — and lots of water. Many Southern communities depend on rivers, the Atlantic Ocean, or the Gulf of Mexico. There are also dry places, far from water. Wherever Southerners live, they are affected by their geography. In this unit, you'll learn more about the land and people of the South.

Theme Project

Plan a Vacation
You are a travel agent. Create a fun vacation trip to show the important features of the South.

- Create a map of places to visit.
- Make brochures with pictures and descriptions of the places you chose.
- Give a speech to your classmates explaining why you think they should visit the South.
- Make a poster advertising your trip.

RESEARCH: Choose one place mentioned in this unit. Learn more about it. Make a brochure about that place.

◄ Bald cypress grow in Atchafalaya Basin, Louisiana.

4

WHEN & WHERE ATLAS

 The waterways of the South flow through many different landforms and environments. This map shows you some of the physical features of the region. It also shows you some of the South's important cities and resources.

In this unit, you will learn how the land and water of the region have made the South a home for many different plants, animals, and people. You'll find out why many people have moved to the South. You will also see some of the ways the people of this region make a living and how they have fun. Along the way, you'll learn how the South has changed over time.

Unit 4 Chapters

OKLAHOMA

Canadian River

Oklahoma City ★

Red River

Brazos River

Rio Conchos

El Paso

TEXAS

Austin ★

San Antonio ●

MEXICO

Rio Grande

Unit Timeline

1500	1600	1700

Red Wolf

Did you know that there are wolves in the South? *Chapter 8, Lesson 1*

Rural South

Many writers have loved the landscape of the South. *Chapter 8, Lesson 2*

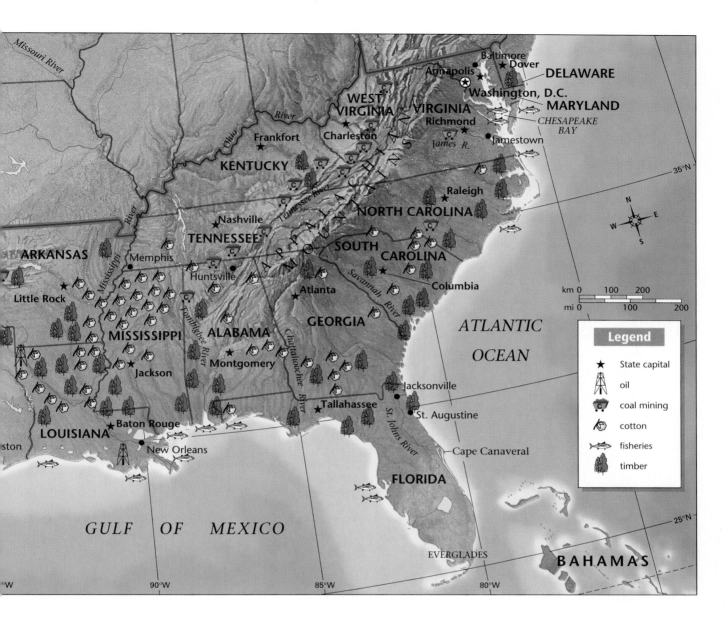

WEST VIRGINIA

VIRGINIA

Richmond ★

DELAWARE
Baltimore
Annapolis ★ Dover
Washington, D.C.
MARYLAND
CHESAPEAKE BAY

Jamestown
James R.

Frankfort ★
Charleston ★

KENTUCKY

Nashville ★
Memphis •

TENNESSEE

Huntsville •

Tennessee River

APPALACHIAN MOUNTAINS

35°N

Raleigh ★

NORTH CAROLINA

SOUTH CAROLINA

Columbia ★

ARKANSAS

Little Rock ★

Mississippi River

Atlanta ★

GEORGIA

Savannah River

MISSISSIPPI

ALABAMA

Tombigbee River

Chattahoochee River

Jackson ★

Montgomery ★

ATLANTIC OCEAN

km 0   100   200
mi 0   100   200

LOUISIANA

Baton Rouge ★

New Orleans •

Tallahassee ★

Jacksonville •

St. Augustine

Cape Canaveral

St. Johns River

Ohio River

Missouri River

GULF OF MEXICO

FLORIDA

EVERGLADES

BAHAMAS

25°N

90°W   85°W   80°W

N
W   E
S

Legend
★ State capital
⛏ oil
Ⓒ coal mining
cotton
🐟 fisheries
🌲 timber

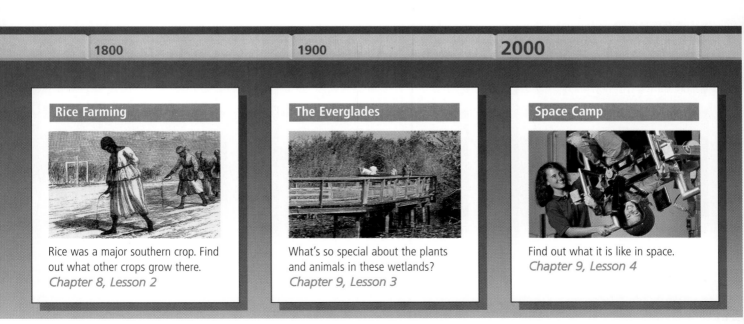

1800   1900   **2000**

Rice Farming

Rice was a major southern crop. Find out what other crops grow there.
Chapter 8, Lesson 2

The Everglades

What's so special about the plants and animals in these wetlands?
Chapter 9, Lesson 3

Space Camp

Find out what it is like in space.
Chapter 9, Lesson 4

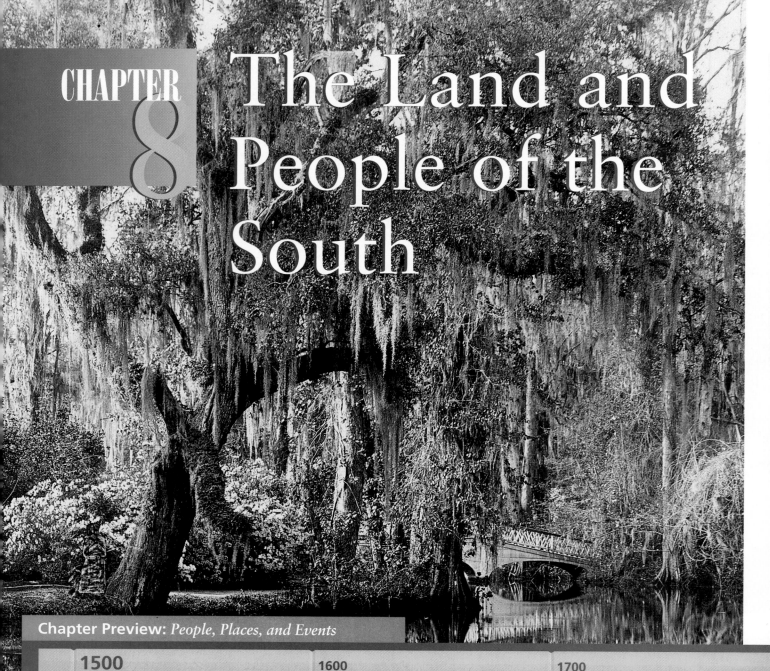

The Land and People of the South

Chapter Preview: *People, Places, and Events*

1500	1600	1700

Mississippi Paddle Boat

This giant wheel moves the boat along the Mississippi River. *Lesson I, Page 200*

Venus Flytrap

This plant catches insects and digests them. *Lesson I, Page 202*

An Ancient Mask

Long ago, Native Americans living in what is now Florida made this mask. *Lesson 2, Page 209*

COPR. DETROIT PHOTOGRAPHI

The Land

Main Idea The South has mountains, large waterways, and a climate that supports many different plants and animals.

> **"O**n *Ashe Mountain Nora Bonesteel . . . stood staring at the blue ripple of mountains that stretched away from the edge of her meadow. It was mid-September . . . woods glowing deep green, fields bronzed with hay, and orchards apple-laden on the hillsides."*

Key Vocabulary

hurricane
silt
delta
bay
bayou

Key Places

Mississippi River
Chesapeake Bay

Nora Bonesteel is a character in the novel *She Walks These Hills,* by Sharyn McCrumb. Like many southerners, she loves the beauty of the mountains. Nora has lived all her long life in the mountains of eastern Tennessee. She knows the history of the mountain people — stories that have been passed from parents to children for hundreds of years. When she was a child, her Grandma Flossie taught her the names of the trees she can see on her mountainside.

◀ Feathery Spanish moss hangs from trees in the South.

1800   1900   **2000**

Soldiers in a Terrible War

During the Civil War, the Southern states fought the Northern states. *Lesson 2, Page 214*

Water Power

Dams like this produce electricity for many southern communities. *Lesson 3, Page 219*

Which Horse Is Fastest?

The world-famous Kentucky Derby is held every spring. *Lesson 3, Page 220*

In the 1800s, many paddle-wheel steamboats traveled up and down the Mississippi, carrying cargo and passengers. Today there are still a few steamboats left, but ships and barges *(above left)* are usually used to carry cargo. **Economics:** *What kinds of jobs do boats and ships provide for people?*

Southern Landforms and Climate

Focus *What are the major landforms and waterways of the South, and what is the climate like there?*

The mountain that Nora Bonesteel lives on is part of the Appalachian (ap uh LAY chee uhn) Mountains, which stretch from the Northeast to Alabama. They are millions of years old. Flat coastal plains run along the Atlantic Ocean and the Gulf of Mexico. Between the coastal plains and the Appalachians is the Piedmont, an area of rolling hills. On the other side of the Appalachians are vast plains.

Much of the South is wetter than other parts of the United States. The map on the next page shows average precipitation in different parts of the South. Usually the weather in the South is calm and hot in summer and mild in winter. In August and September, fierce hurricanes can blow in from the ocean. A **hurricane** is a powerful storm with very strong winds and heavy rain.

The Mississippi and the Chesapeake

River valleys are one of the main landforms of the South. The Mississippi River doesn't start in the South, but it ends there. It forms the borders of five southern states. It empties into the Gulf of Mexico.

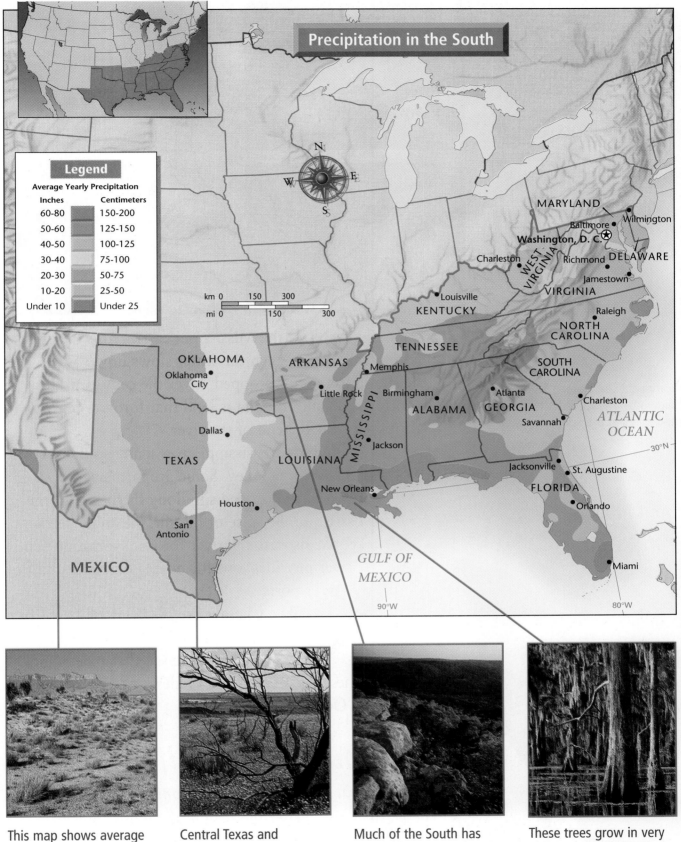

Precipitation in the South

Legend

Average Yearly Precipitation

Inches		Centimeters
60-80		150-200
50-60		125-150
40-50		100-125
30-40		75-100
20-30		50-75
10-20		25-50
Under 10		Under 25

km 0   150   300
mi 0   150   300

MARYLAND
Baltimore   Wilmington
Washington, D. C.   DELAWARE
Charleston   WEST VIRGINIA   Richmond
Jamestown
VIRGINIA
Louisville   KENTUCKY   Raleigh
NORTH CAROLINA
TENNESSEE
Memphis   SOUTH CAROLINA
OKLAHOMA   ARKANSAS
Oklahoma City   Little Rock   Birmingham   Atlanta   Charleston
Dallas   MISSISSIPPI   ALABAMA   GEORGIA   Savannah   ATLANTIC OCEAN
TEXAS   LOUISIANA   Jackson   30°N
Houston   New Orleans   Jacksonville   St. Augustine
San Antonio   FLORIDA   Orlando
MEXICO   GULF OF MEXICO   Miami
90°W   80°W

This map shows average precipitations in the South. In dry west Texas *(above),* few plants grow.

Central Texas and Oklahoma get more precipitation than west Texas. A greater variety of plants grow there.

Much of the South has average precipitation of 40 to 60 inches. With this much rain, the plant life there might look like this picture.

These trees grow in very wet areas. **Map Skill:** *Which states get over 60 inches of rain each year?*

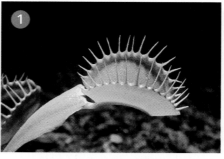

No, these pictures are not from a science-fiction movie. Venus fly-traps are real plants that grow in swampy areas in North Carolina.

1. The leaves of the plant are open.

2. An unsuspecting insect gets trapped in sticky goo.

3. Uh, oh! The leaves snap shut on the bug.

4. You can see the trapped insect inside the closed leaves.

You might see a green heron, shown below, around streams and rivers in the South.

The moving water of the Mississippi carries tons of sand and fine soil, called **silt**. When the water slows down at the Gulf, the silt and sand are dropped. Over the centuries, this process forms new land. A **delta** is land that forms when water drops silt near the end of the river.

The mighty Mississippi gives many southerners a way of earning money. Some are farmers. Floods in the past have dropped silt along the banks of the Mississippi. Because of the silt, the soil is fertile. People also use the river for transportation. The river provides jobs for people on boats and in river ports.

The Chesapeake (CHEHS uh peek) Bay is an important southern waterway too. A **bay** is a part of the sea that pushes into the land. The Chesapeake Bay is 200 miles long. It empties into the Atlantic Ocean.

Vegetation and Wildlife

[Focus] *What are some plants and animals in the South?*
The warmer and wetter the region, the more kinds of plants and animals you are likely to find there. The climate of the South is generally warm and wet. So it's not surprising that the South has many different plants and animals.

Pine forests cover large areas of the South. There are gum, live oak, and cypress trees, too. Hanging from some of those trees is Spanish moss, an unusual southern plant. Spanish moss has no roots. It absorbs water from the air.

In the warm spring, flowers bloom all over the South. Blossoms crown azalea and mountain laurel bushes. Fields and forest floors are blanketed with wildflowers such as morning glories and violets.

Fish fill the rivers and bayous. A **bayou** (BY oo) is a very slow-moving stream that flows through a swamp. Shrimp and clams are found along the coast, and Chesapeake Bay provides large oyster hauls. Bear, deer, and many smaller animals roam the forests and mountains.

The plant and animal life in bayous is very different from the living things in western Texas and Oklahoma. The climate in that western part of the South is very dry, as you can see in the map on page 201. The living things there, such as grasses and some cactuses, are adapted to the dry climate. Throughout the South, plants and animals have adapted to the climate of the region.

The endangered southern red wolf is found in forests across the region. Geography: *What might happen to the red wolf if forests are cut down?*

Lesson Review: Geography

1. **Key Vocabulary:** Use the following words in a description of the South: **hurricane, silt, delta, bay, bayou.**

2. **Focus:** What are the major landforms and waterways of the South, and what is the climate like there?

3. **Focus:** What are some plants and animals in the South?

4. **Critical Thinking: Compare** How does the climate of the South compare to the climate of the Northeast?

5. **Theme: Rivers and Coasts** How is the Mississippi River important to the economy of the South?

6. **Geography/Science Activity** Learn about the plants and animals of the South. Make a chart showing which ones live in a dry climate, in a wet climate, and in a climate that's in between wet and dry.

Skills Workshop

Using Maps to Find Cause and Effect

The Weather's Perfect

Have you heard the saying "That's like comparing apples and oranges"? It means that two things are very different. It's also true that a place that's good for growing apples can be very different from a place that's good for growing oranges. Knowing the climate of a place can help you know what kinds of crops might be grown there. Special maps called **climate maps** and **land use maps** can show you how climate and crops are related.

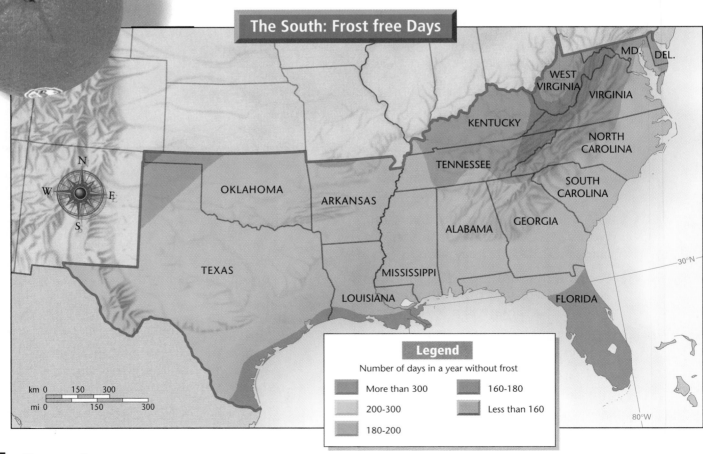

The South: Frost free Days

MD.
DEL.
WEST VIRGINIA
VIRGINIA
KENTUCKY
NORTH CAROLINA
TENNESSEE
SOUTH CAROLINA
OKLAHOMA
ARKANSAS
ALABAMA
GEORGIA
TEXAS
MISSISSIPPI
LOUISIANA
FLORIDA

—30°N

km 0   150   300
mi 0   150   300

Legend
Number of days in a year without frost

More than 300
200-300
180-200
160-180
Less than 160

80°W

1 Here's How

- Look at the frost free days map — a type of climate map — and study its legend. This map shows the number of days each year when there is no frost. The more days without frost, the longer the growing season.

- Now look at the land use map and study its legend. See what the map tells you about how people use the land in the South.

- Notice how the information on the two maps is related. For example, look at the state of Florida. What does the frost free days map tell about how long the growing season is in Florida? What does the land use map tell about the crops that are grown there?

- Think about the cause-and-effect relationship between the number of frost free days and land use. For example, Florida's long growing season makes it good for growing oranges.

2 Think It Through

In addition to land use, how else does climate affect a place and the people who live there?

3 Use It

Find the following places on both the frost free and land use maps. Then explain the cause-and-effect relationship between frost free days and land use.

1. Georgia   3. Maryland

2. Louisiana   4. Kentucky

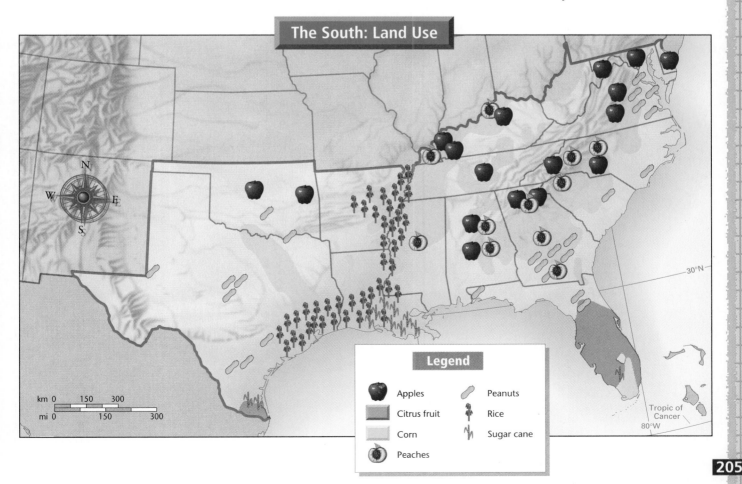

The South: Land Use

Legend

- Apples
- Citrus fruit
- Corn
- Peaches
- Peanuts
- Rice
- Sugar cane

N W E S

km 0   150   300
mi 0   150   300

30°N

Tropic of Cancer
80°W

Eye of the Tiger: How Hurricanes Work

B Strong upward wind increases the vortex's speed to 40 mph.

C Vortex now spins at 80 mph. Where it brushes against the hurricane winds, the vortex can blow at 200 mph—and destroy everything in its way.

In late August of 1992, Hurricane Andrew hit southern Florida. It was one of the most destructive hurricanes to ever hit the United States. Even with advance warning and storm preparations, Andrew caused tremendous damage and over 40 deaths. Hurricanes are a force to beware of.

Spin Cycle

While Andrew moved across Florida at 20 mph, warm, moist air was drawn to its calm center, or eye. As the air spiraled up the eye, vapor in the air quickly condensed, or changed into water. This action released heat, which kept the 25-mile-wide hurricane spinning. ☞

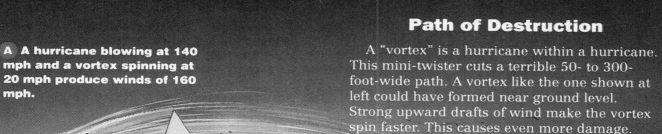

Path of Destruction

A "vortex" is a hurricane within a hurricane. This mini-twister cuts a terrible 50- to 300-foot-wide path. A vortex like the one shown at left could have formed near ground level. Strong upward drafts of wind make the vortex spin faster. This causes even more damage.

A A hurricane blowing at 140 mph and a vortex spinning at 20 mph produce winds of 160 mph.

140 MPH

STRONG
UPWARD
WIND

CENTER OF EYE

Response Activities

1. Cause and Effect Wind, heat, and moist air are necessary for hurricanes to form. Do you think the South is more or less likely than other regions to experience hurricanes? Why?

2. Citizenship: Give a Speech The Red Cross helps millions of people who are hurt by disasters such as hurricanes. Learn about the Red Cross and give a speech about what they do.

Settling the South

Main Idea Native Americans, Europeans, and Africans all contributed to the settling of the South.

Key Vocabulary

mission
descendant
plantation
secede
civil war

Key Events

1565 St. Augustine founded

1607 Jamestown founded

1861–1865 Civil War

1889 Oklahoma Land Rush

> "The paths made by deer and bear became roads and then highways, with towns in turn springing up along them and along the rivers. . . . "
>
> From the book *Go Down, Moses* by William Faulkner, a writer from Mississippi

William Faulkner wrote about the land he knew best — the South. He had a good sense of the region's history. In Faulkner's stories, the present world grows from the past, just as roads grew from what had once been animal paths.

Faulkner wrote about the Native Americans, Europeans, and Africans who settled the South. The first settlers of this region were Native Americans.

Giant trees hang over the carriage that travels down a peaceful country road.

Native Americans

Focus *How did the early Native Americans use the land of the South?*

Long before Europeans and Africans came, Native Americans lived in the southern forests. They hunted and fished. They cleared land to plant their crops. Many Native American groups have lived in the South — the Chickasaw, the Choctaw (CHOK taw), and the Creek, to name just a few. One of the larger groups is the Cherokee (CHEHR uh kee).

Before Europeans came, many Cherokee lived in what is now North Carolina, South Carolina, Georgia, Alabama, and Tennessee. They lived in small towns along the rivers. During the hot summer months, they built large, airy, rectangular shelters made of wood. When the winter winds came, they moved into small, round, wooden houses. They plastered their walls with mud to keep out the cold. A fire in the center of the house kept them warm.

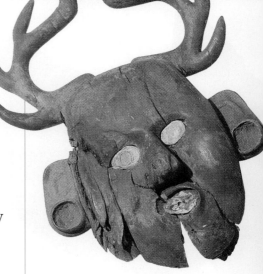

The branchlike structures on this very old Native American mask probably represent deer antlers. It was found in Oklahoma.

The map shows Native American groups in the South around 1700. **Map Skill:** *Which groups lived in the Southeastern part of the region?*

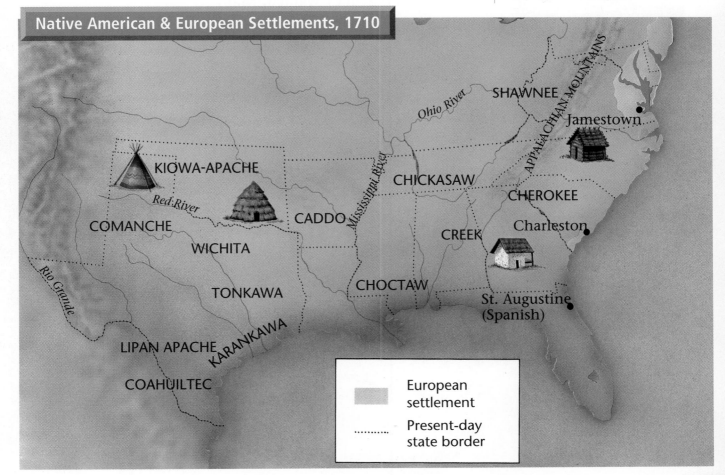

Native American & European Settlements, 1710

KIOWA-APACHE
COMANCHE
WICHITA
TONKAWA
LIPAN APACHE
KARANKAWA
COAHUILTEC
Red River
Rio Grande
CADDO
Mississippi River
CHOCTAW
Ohio River
SHAWNEE
CHICKASAW
CREEK
CHEROKEE
APPALACHIAN MOUNTAINS
Jamestown
Charleston
St. Augustine (Spanish)

European settlement

.... Present-day state border

Cherokee women were good farmers. They grew corn, beans, and squash. They cared for the children. They also carried water, gathered firewood, made clothing, and prepared meals. Their main food was corn.

Cherokee men hunted and fished. Sometimes they caught fish by putting a kind of nut — horse chestnuts — in the water. A chemical in the horse chestnuts paralyzed the fish. The fish were then easy to catch.

Europeans and Africans Arrive

Focus *When and how did Europeans and Africans come to the South?*

Native Americans had lived in America for thousands of years when Europeans came. The Europeans came from Spain, France, and England. Some Europeans came to search for gold and silver and to trade furs. Some wanted to teach Native Americans Christianity. Other settlers came for the freedom to worship God as they wanted. Many settlers came looking for good land for farming.

Tobacco, shown above, was grown by settlers in the South. The leaves are much bigger than the picture shows. Colonial farmers used tools such as the barley fork *(left)* and hay fork shown above.

The Spanish were the first Europeans to settle in the South. In 1565 they founded the settlement of St. Augustine in what is now Florida. Over the next 250 years, they established other settlements in the South, particularly in what is now Texas. An important one was San Antonio. The Spanish started a mission in San Antonio. A **mission** is a place set up for teaching a religion. The Spanish wanted to teach their Catholic religion to the Native Americans.

The largest group of Europeans to settle in the South was the English. Their first permanent settlement was Jamestown. That community was started in 1607 along the James River in what is now Virginia. Two-thirds of the settlers died from disease and hunger during their first year there.

Soon more settlers came. They learned how to farm in their new environment. The picture at the bottom of these pages shows what a settler's farm might have looked like.

A Southern Farm

1. In the 1750s, settlers built farmhouses like this.
2. Because of the danger of fire, the kitchen and small smokehouse were separate from the farmhouse.
3. Corn was used as food for people and animals.
4. Tobacco was grown in fields like this.
5. Tobacco was stored in the barn.

Economics: *What animals do you think settlers might have had on their farms and why?*

In the illustrations below, African Americans plant and harvest rice. The harvested rice was shaken in a shallow basket *(right)*; this separated the grains from other parts of the plant. Then the rice grains were pounded in the mortar and pestle *(above)* to remove the hull that covered the grain.

Over the next 170 years, more and more English, Scottish, and Scots-Irish settled in the South. First they settled along the coastal plain. Then they began moving westward across the Appalachian Mountains.

Not long after English people came to Jamestown, the first Africans arrived in the South. European traders brought them in 1619. Unlike most European settlers, who wanted to come to America, the Africans were forced to come. Most Africans came from western Africa, from areas such as present-day Nigeria and Angola.

At first, some Africans could become free after they worked for several years for European settlers. However, most Africans in the South were enslaved. They had to work for white settlers all their lives without pay. Their descendants were also enslaved. A **descendant** (dih SEHN duhnt) of someone is that person's child, grandchild, great-grandchild, and so on.

The French settled mainly in the Mississippi valley. New Orleans was founded in 1718. It became the capital of the French colony of Louisiana.

Some French settlers had lived in Acadia, in Canada, before they came to the South. English soldiers made them leave Acadia in 1755.

Many of the people from Acadia then moved to the bayous west of New Orleans. Their descendants live in that area and other parts of Louisiana and Texas today. They are known as Cajuns, which comes from the French word *Acadien.*

Growth and Conflict

Focus *What struggles took place in the 1700s and 1800s, and why did they happen?*

As the years passed, serious disagreements arose between the American colonists and the people in England who governed them. In 1776, the colonies declared that they were independent, or free, from England. To gain this independence, they fought the British army for eight long years in the American Revolution. The first President of the new nation was George Washington, a Virginian.

Westward Movement

After the war, many southern soldiers returned to their farms. Tobacco, sugar, and rice were important crops. Most southern farmers had small farms. Along the coastal plains there were some large farms called plantations. On a **plantation,** the planting and harvesting were done by enslaved African Americans.

About 10 years after the American Revolution ended, Eli Whitney invented the cotton gin, a machine that made it easier to clean harvested cotton. Cotton then became the South's biggest crop. It was sold to manufacturers in the Northern states and in Europe.

After a time, cotton and tobacco farming wore out much of the southern soil. So many southern farmers moved to new land farther and farther west toward the Mississippi River. The westward movement did not stop at the Mississippi, however. Settlers sometimes bought land from Native Americans. Other times they fought and drove the Native Americans farther west.

Then & Now

Scientists are looking for new ways to grow crops without wearing out the soil. One method of growing crops is hydroponics. With hydroponics, plants grow in a liquid rather than in soil. The liquid contains materials that the plants need to live and grow. The main advantage of the hydroponic system is that crops can grow where soils are no longer fertile.

Battles in the Civil War were fiercely fought, as the painting at the top of the page shows. Boys like this young Confederate soldier *(above)* fought on both sides in the Civil War.

In the winter of 1838–39, American soldiers forced about 15,000 Cherokee from their homes in Georgia. Most of the Cherokee walked for more than 1,000 miles to what is now Oklahoma. About 4,000 Cherokee died from disease and hunger along the way. This terrible journey became known as the Trail of Tears.

A Nation Divided

As settlers moved west, a conflict over slavery developed. The southern states said each state should decide for itself whether slavery was right or wrong. The northern states said that each state had to follow the laws of the national government, even if the state disagreed with those laws.

Finally, in 1860 and 1861, 11 southern states decided to **secede,** or leave the United States. They called themselves the Confederate States of America. The northern states, called the Union, were led by President Abraham Lincoln. They said the southern states couldn't secede. A terrible war began. It was a **civil war** — a war between two groups in the same country.

During the Civil War, southern Confederate soldiers fought northern Union soldiers. Many thousands of soldiers on both sides were killed.

The Union army had many more soldiers and weapons. In 1865 the Union won the war. Soon the national government outlawed slavery everywhere in the United States.

The South had lost more than a war. Most of the battles had been fought in the South. Farms, buildings, industries, and railroads had been destroyed in the bitter fighting. It took many years for the South to rebuild its economy.

A Move for More Land

After the Civil War, farmers again looked farther west for new land. Native Americans were driven into smaller and smaller areas of land.

Back in the early 1800s, much of present-day Oklahoma had been set aside for Native Americans. But in 1889, the United States government announced that on April 22 at noon, large areas of this Indian Territory would be open to other settlers. On that day, about 50,000 people lined up. At 12:00 sharp, the crowd eagerly rushed forward. Whoever arrived first on each 160-acre plot could claim it. That event came to be called the Oklahoma Land Rush.

The new settlers in Oklahoma were eager to obtain land. Today the land of the South is still a valuable resource.

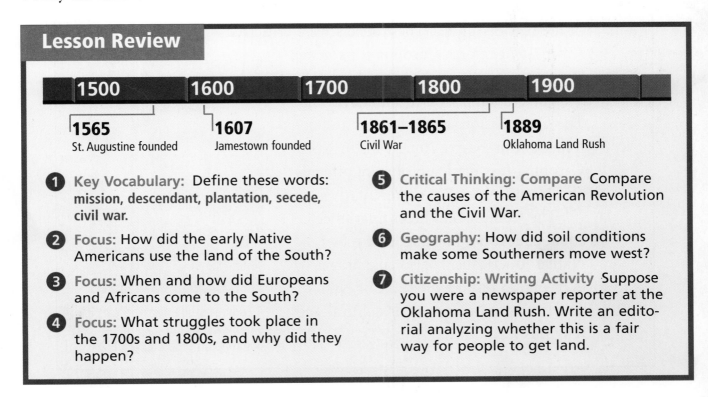

Lesson Review

1500	1600	1700	1800	1900

1565
St. Augustine founded

1607
Jamestown founded

1861–1865
Civil War

1889
Oklahoma Land Rush

1 Key Vocabulary: Define these words: mission, descendant, plantation, secede, civil war.

2 Focus: How did the early Native Americans use the land of the South?

3 Focus: When and how did Europeans and Africans come to the South?

4 Focus: What struggles took place in the 1700s and 1800s, and why did they happen?

5 Critical Thinking: Compare Compare the causes of the American Revolution and the Civil War.

6 Geography: How did soil conditions make some Southerners move west?

7 Citizenship: Writing Activity Suppose you were a newspaper reporter at the Oklahoma Land Rush. Write an editorial analyzing whether this is a fair way for people to get land.

Resolving Conflicts

Can You Change History?

When you've treated someone badly, can you do anything to make up for it afterward? Native Americans lost many rights when settlers came and pushed them off their land. Here is what one southern state is doing to give back those rights.

Case Study

Working for Native American Rights

North Carolina is home to about 80,000 Native Americans. They belong to tribes such as the Cherokee, Coharie, Haliwa-Saponi, Lumbee, Meherrin, and Waccamaw-Siouan. In the past, Native Americans were forced off their land. Their way of life was disrupted. Their beliefs were criticized.

In 1971, North Carolina took a step to change this. It formed the North Carolina Commission of Indian Affairs. The Commission works for fair and equal treatment of Native Americans in North Carolina. It is made up of state officials and Native American representatives.

The Commission helps guarantee equal education, housing, and jobs for Native Americans. It also encourages everyone to respect the right of Native Americans to practice their cultural and religious traditions.

A Lumbee student taking part in a project sponsored by the Commission of Indian Affairs.

Take Action

The Declaration of Independence talks of people's "inalienable rights." What are inalienable rights? Do such rights allow people to do whatever they feel like? What responsibilities go along with such rights, and how do they help prevent conflict? Try this to see.

1 Look up *inalienable*. Discuss what you think "inalienable rights" means.

2 Choose one of these activities: biking, music, hiking, fishing, soccer, or reading. Form a group with classmates who have chosen the same activity.

3 Suppose you had to get a license to do your activity. What rights would this license grant you? List them. Would you then be free to do this activity in whatever way you pleased, or are there also things you should and shouldn't do? List these responsibilities.

4 Make a poster to show the rights and responsibilities associated with your activity. As a class, discuss your posters. How do responsibilities help prevent conflict?

Tips for Resolving Conflicts

- Listen carefully to others.
- Keep everyone's needs in mind.
- Remember that you don't always need to agree on everything to be able to work together toward the same goals.

Research Activity

What Native American groups live or lived in your state? Use books and interviews to find out what their life is like today. Has any community or government group worked to guarantee their rights? Share your findings with your class.

Living in the South

Main Idea Southerners have many different occupations. Southerners enrich the culture of the United States.

Key Vocabulary

hydroelectric power
textile
mining

Key Places

Tennessee River

Do you wear T-shirts made of cotton? Much of the cotton used in the United States comes from the South. Maybe you like peanut butter and jelly sandwiches. More peanuts are grown in the South than in any other part of the country. If your apartment or house is heated with oil, that may come from the South too. No matter where you live, you probably use some products from the South every day.

Working in the South

Focus *How do southerners make a living?*

Rich soil and plenty of rain — this description fits much of the South's good farmland. Southern farmers grow crops such as oranges, peanuts, and rice.

Other southerners look to the sea for their jobs. Fishing boats head out into the Atlantic Ocean, the Gulf of Mexico, and the Chesapeake Bay.

Industries of the South

Did you ever think of rivers as a natural resource? Dams have been built in many places along southern rivers like the Tennessee River. Water from the dams turns giant wheels that help to produce electricity. Electricity produced by moving water is called **hydroelectric** (hy droh ih LEHK trihk) **power.** The supply of electricity along with cotton grown in the region lets the South produce a lot of **textiles,** or cloth.

Hydroelectric power

1 Water from behind the dam flows along the path shown by the arrows.

2 Water power makes the turbines turn. This spinning produces electricity.

3 Wires carry the electricity from the power substation to places where it is used.

The map below shows dams along the Tennessee River. **Map Skill:** *How many dams are near Nashville?*

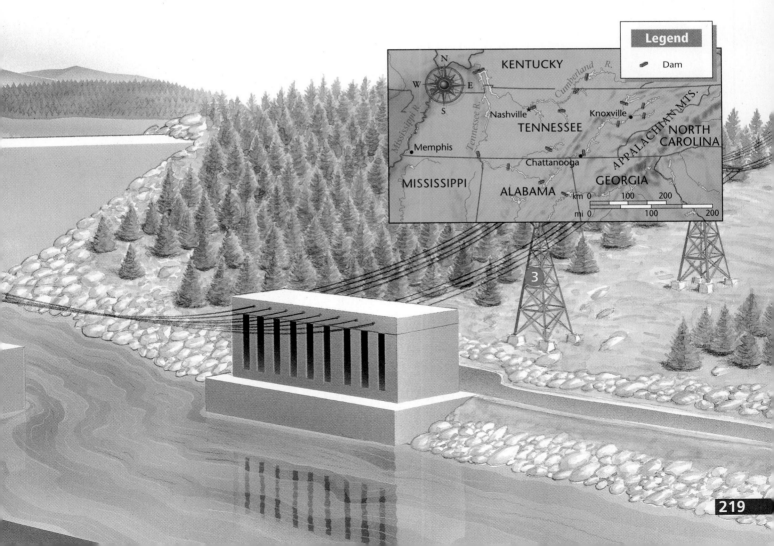

Legend
Dam

KENTUCKY

Cumberland R.

Nashville

Knoxville

TENNESSEE

APPALACHIAN MTS.

NORTH CAROLINA

Memphis

Tennessee R.

Mississippi R.

Chattanooga

MISSISSIPPI

ALABAMA

GEORGIA

km 0   100   200

mi 0   100   200

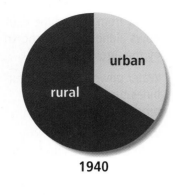

1940

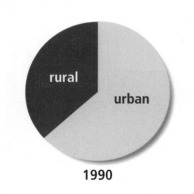

1960

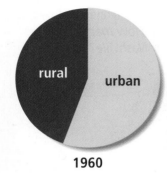

1990

The graphs show the urban and rural populations of Georgia in 1940, 1960, and 1990. **Chart Skill:** *In 1940, did more people live in urban or rural areas?*

And they're off! Hoofs pounding, the horses race swiftly around the track in the Kentucky Derby every year. **Culture:** *What are some other important events or celebrations that take place every year in the United States?*

The South also has natural resources that are under the ground. **Mining** is the removal of minerals from the ground. Much of the nation's coal comes from Kentucky and West Virginia.

Oil and natural gas are other important underground resources. Many people in Texas, Louisiana, and Oklahoma work in the oil industry. Oil is used to make gasoline, chemicals, paints, plastics, and other products.

Some southern cities are known for particular industries. In Newport News, Virginia, workers build and repair ships. Major centers of the space industry are located in Houston, Texas; Huntsville, Alabama; and Cape Canaveral, Florida.

Celebrating the Southern Way

Focus *What are some things that make life in the South enjoyable?*

Southerners celebrate at famous festivals and other events. At the Mardi Gras (MAHR dee GRAH) festival every February in New Orleans, you can hear lively music and watch colorful parades. If you like watching horses speed around a race track, you'll love the Kentucky Derby. This famous race has been run for about 125 years on the first Saturday of May in Louisville, Kentucky.

Every May and June, the city of Charleston, South Carolina, holds an arts festival — the Spoleto Festival U.S.A. Visitors to the festival look at art works, such as paintings. They also go to plays and listen to music.

Food — From Simple to Spicy

Celebrations usually involve food, and southerners have created wonderful foods. The region's cooking is a lot like southern geography — there is great variety. That's because the South has been influenced by many ethnic groups. Native Americans, English, French, Spanish, Africans, and Mexicans have given foods to the South.

Take gumbo, for example. Gumbo is a rich soup or stew that's a Louisiana dish. Gumbo usually contains the vegetable okra. Africans brought okra to the South. They also brought the word *gumbo,* which comes from a word in Luba, an African language. Gumbos have been influenced by Cajun cooking as well as African cooking.

Southern cooking, like most regional cooking, uses foods that can be found nearby. Catfish from southern rivers is a popular food. So are shrimps, crabs, and oysters from the ocean and bays. Corn is an important crop in the South, and many southern dishes contain corn.

Many people say there's something special about southern culture. They say that its people are as warm as its weather. Maybe that's one reason why the southern part of the United States is growing fast.

Cooks compete at the Memphis in May barbeque cook off.
Culture: *How many foods do you recognize in the photo at the top of the page?*

Lesson Review

1 **Key Vocabulary:** Use these key terms in a story about industry in the South: **hydroelectric power, textile, mining.**

2 **Focus:** How do southerners make a living?

3 **Focus:** What are some things that make life in the South enjoyable?

4 **Critical Thinking: Conclude** What natural resources does the textile industry use?

5 **Theme: Rivers and Coasts** Why are fish and shellfish used so often in southern cooking?

6 **Citizenship/Art Activity:** Create an advertisement to attract newcomers to the South. Your ad should show, in pictures and words, why the South is a good place to live.

Environment and Society

How Did the Boll Weevil Change Southern Farming?

It doesn't look like much — a one-quarter-inch-long beetle with a curved snout. Yet the boll weevil does more damage to American agriculture than any other insect. In fact, the boll weevil destroys almost one-third of the nation's cotton crop each year.

Boll weevils spread north into Texas in the early 1890s. At that time, many southern farmers depended entirely on cotton to earn a living. By reducing or ruining cotton harvests, boll weevils drove many farmers off the land. Oddly enough, this disaster had some positive effects. It forced farmers to grow a variety of crops and to use some land to raise cattle, hogs, and chickens. This system is called mixed farming. In many parts of the South, mixed farming has made the agriculture industry stronger.

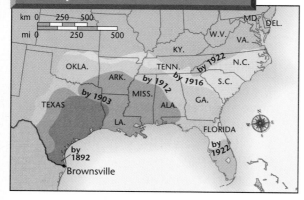

The Spread of the Boll Weevil

km 0 250 500
mi 0 250 500

MD.
DEL.
W.V.
VA.
KY.
OKLA.
TENN.
by 1922
N.C.
ARK.
by 1912
by 1916
S.C.
MISS.
GA.
TEXAS
ALA.
LA.
FLORIDA
by 1903
by 1892
Brownsville
by 1922

Boll weevils spread across the South in 30 years. **Map Skill:** *How far did they travel?*

The town of Enterprise, Alabama, built a monument *(right)* to the boll weevil in 1919 for encouraging the growth of mixed farming.

A female boll weevil *(far right)* deposits her eggs in a cotton bud.

Science Connection

Boll weevils spend the winter sleeping. When buds appear on cotton plants in spring, female boll weevils chew holes in them and lay from 100 to 300 eggs. Young insects from these eggs feed on the cotton buds for 7 to 14 days before becoming adults. Why is it significant that this cycle repeats from 5 to 10 times per year?

1 Brownsville

Texas Cotton Fields
The boll weevil invaded the Cotton Belt near Brownsville, Texas, in 1892. Half of Texas soon felt its destructive effects. The Texas legislature offered a $50,000 reward for a solution to the problem.

Mixed Farming in the South

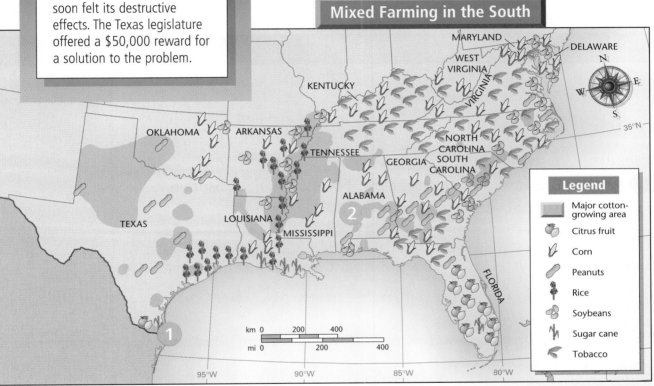

Legend

- Major cotton-growing area
- Citrus fruit
- Corn
- Peanuts
- Rice
- Soybeans
- Sugar cane
- Tobacco

Before the arrival of the boll weevil, southern farming depended mainly on cotton. Today the South grows a rich variety of crops.
Map Skill: *In which states is rice a major crop?*

Research Activity

Choose one southern state.
1. Do further research on the major crops grown in that state.
2. Make a chart that lists these crops from most important to least important, economically. Share your findings with the class.

2 Alabama

Soybean Fields
Cotton is still one of Alabama's major crops. Since the arrival of the boll weevil, however, Alabama farmers have started to grow more corn, soybeans, peanuts, and sweet potatoes.

Chapter Review

Chapter Review Timeline

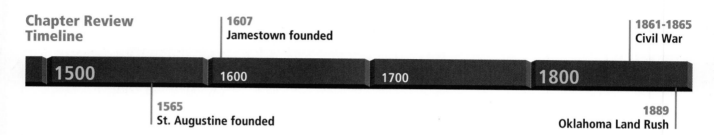

| 1500 | 1565
St. Augustine founded | 1600 | 1607
Jamestown founded | 1700 | 1800 | 1861-1865
Civil War | 1889
Oklahoma Land Rush |

Summarizing the Main Idea

1 Copy and complete the chart below. For each subject, list two or three facts about the South.

Subject	Fact
Landforms/Waterways	The Mississippi River is used for transportation.
Vegetation/Wildlife	
Settlers	
Industry	

Vocabulary

2 Using at least seven of the following terms, write a introduction for a television show about the South.

hurricane (p. 200)   mission (p. 211)   secede (p. 214)
delta (p. 202)   descendant (p. 212)   civil war (p. 214)
bayou (p. 203)   plantation (p. 213)   mining (p. 220)

Reviewing the Facts

3 Besides the Mississippi River, what other landforms and waterways are found in the South?

4 Describe the climate of the South.

5 Why are there so many different kinds of plants and animals in the South?

6 How did the Cherokee provide themselves with food, shelter, and clothing?

7 Which Europeans settled in the South? Where did they settle?

8 Explain how Africans came to the South.

9 What are some of the ways people earn a living in the South?

10 Look at the climate map on page 204. Which has more frost free days, Texas or North Carolina? Which crops are grown in each state?

11 In which states is rice grown? What kind of climate do these states have in common?

Geography Skills

12 Choose two things to show about the land and people of the South on an outline map of the southern states. Remember to use symbols and a key.

13 Which states border the Chesapeake Bay? How do people in these states use the Chesapeake Bay?

Critical Thinking

14 Problem Solving European settlers wanted to settle the land where Native Americans were living. How could settlers and Native Americans have compromised so they could share the land?

15 Decision Making Would you like to live in the South? Give reasons for your opinion.

Writing: History and Economics

16 History Write a diary entry that a settler in the South might have written. Describe something interesting that happened to the settler.

17 Economics Write a story about a family vacation in the South. Include the ways the family spends its money on items like food and entertainment.

Activities

Cultures/Arts Activity
Find out about the paddle-wheel steamboats that used to travel on the Mississippi River. Draw a picture of one of them.

Geography/Science Activity
Work with two other students. Put together a picture book about the different kinds of animals that live in the South. Illustrate each page and write two sentences describing the picture.

Internet Option

Check the **Internet Social Studies Center** for ideas on how to extend your theme project beyond your classroom.

THEME PROJECT CHECK-IN

Have you included what you've learned about the land and people of the South in your trip plans?
- Have you included pictures and descriptions of landforms in your brochures and posters?
- What Native American artifacts and places can you show?
- How does your trip reflect how people in the South earn a living?

Chapter Preview: *People, Places, and Events*

1800	1850	1900

Young Baseball Fans

What brings people to the South?
Lesson 1, Page 228

Manufacturing in the South

What kinds of businesses are there in the South? *Lesson 1, Page 229*

Jazz Music

Find out about the many styles of music that began in the South.
Lesson 2, Page 232

Moving South

Main Idea The climate, low cost of living, and high-technology industries have brought people to the South.

Fuad Faridi was just five years old when he moved to Georgia. He and his family came from Pakistan, a country in Asia. They didn't know much about the South.

The Faridis' new neighbors, though, made them feel right at home. They brought cake and flowers to welcome the family to the neighborhood. In Georgia, Fuad made many new friends. He describes his experience this way:

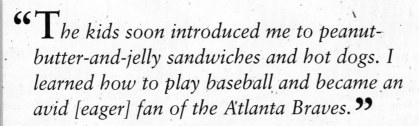

"The kids soon introduced me to peanut-butter-and-jelly sandwiches and hot dogs. I learned how to play baseball and became an avid [eager] fan of the Atlanta Braves."

Every year, thousands of families like the Faridis are happy to make the South their new home.

◀ A busy television newsroom in Atlanta, Georgia

Key Vocabulary
cost of living
manufacture
research

Key Places
Atlanta, Georgia
Research Triangle Park, North Carolina

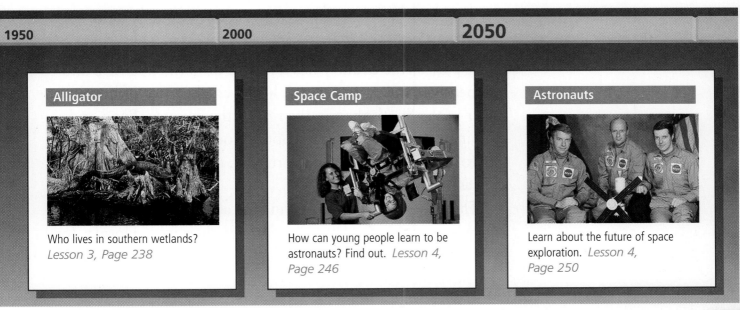

1950 2000 2050

Alligator
Who lives in southern wetlands?
Lesson 3, Page 238

Space Camp
How can young people learn to be astronauts? Find out. *Lesson 4, Page 246*

Astronauts
Learn about the future of space exploration. *Lesson 4, Page 250*

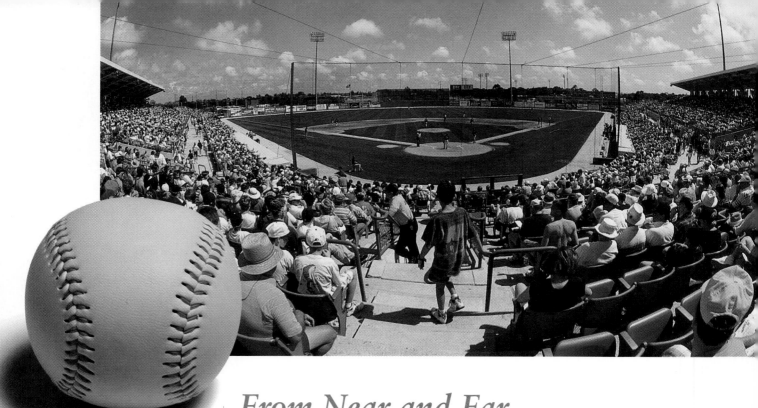

A crowd watches a baseball game during spring training in the South. Geography: *Why would baseball teams from the North have spring training in the South?*

From Near and Far

Focus *Why have many people moved to the South?*

More than one million people moved to the South from other parts of the United States between 1990 and 1993. Another 601,000 people came to the South from other countries.

People move to the South for many reasons. One reason is the weather. If you live in Buffalo, New York, you get about 90 inches of snow each winter. That's seven-and-a-half feet — taller than a basketball star! However, if you live in Atlanta, Georgia, you usually get only about two inches of snow each winter. Most of the South is a lot warmer than other regions.

The Cost of Living

Every part of the country has its share of both expensive and inexpensive houses. In general, however, the price of houses is lower in the South than in the rest of the country. Food and clothing often cost less in the South, too. The money people pay for food, clothing, transportation, and housing is called the **cost of living.**

The South's low cost of living attracts many people, including older people who have retired from their jobs. Florida, for instance, is well known for the large number of retired people who have moved there.

Lots of Jobs

Many people go to the South to work. Workers can find many new jobs available in southern states.

At one time, most African Americans in the United States lived in the South. Starting in the late 1800s and continuing until the 1970s, however, many African Americans moved north. They were looking for jobs in cities such as New York, Chicago, and Detroit. Recently, these patterns have changed. Now that the South has so many new jobs, many African Americans are moving there.

These women work in a textile factory in Waynesboro, Virginia.

Business Opportunities

Focus | *Why have many businesses moved to the South?*

Since the 1960s, the South has become a center for manufacturing. When you **manufacture** (man yoo FAK chur) something, you make it — usually with machines. Workers in the South manufacture things like computers and chemicals.

Businesses move to the South for some of the same reasons people do. The low cost of living makes it cheaper to do business there. Some materials that companies use to make things cost less in the South. Salaries tend to be lower there than in other parts of the country because the cost of living is low. Land is less expensive. Businesses pay less for the land on which they build their offices and factories. Many highways run between major cities. That helps businesses move goods to the people who buy them.

The chart below shows the difference in the cost of living in a northern and a southern city during 1995. **Chart Skill:** *Which items show the greatest difference in price?*

Cost of Living

Item	Birmingham, AL	Hartford, CT
house	$123,500	$188,000
gas, one gallon	$1.07	$1.26
haircut	$8.50	$11.17
man's shirt	$28.09	$28.79
eggs, one dozen	$.74	$.95
movie	$5.75	$6.50

Research Triangle Park in North Carolina

Southerners work hard to encourage companies to move to their region. One place they've done this is in North Carolina.

Have you ever done a research project for school? **Research** is the careful study of something. It can involve reading, asking questions, and doing scientific experiments. A lot of research goes into making new products, such as cars and computers.

Research Triangle Park (RTP for short) is an area in North Carolina between the cities of Raleigh (RAW lee), Durham (DUR uhm), and Chapel Hill. RTP is made up of about 70 companies and other organizations. Over 30,000 people work at RTP. Some of those workers do research. Other people use the information from the research to make new products.

Raleigh, Durham, and Chapel Hill all have universities. At the universities, students learn skills that some of them will use in jobs at RTP.

Many newcomers to the South find what they are looking for. They find jobs, a low cost of living, and a mild climate. As you will read in the next lesson, the rich culture of the South adds to the pleasure of living there.

North Carolina's Research Triangle Park is home to many high-tech companies. **Map Skill:** *What city is west of Research Triangle Park?*

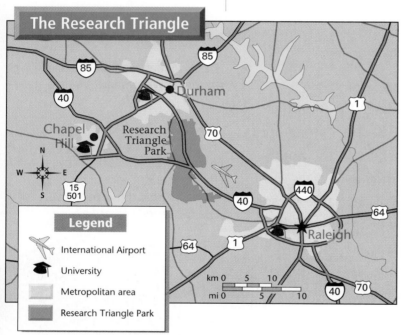

The Research Triangle

Legend

✈ International Airport

🎓 University

▢ Metropolitan area

▢ Research Triangle Park

Lesson Review

1 **Key Vocabulary:** Use each of these terms in a sentence about the South: **cost of living, manufacture, research.**

2 **Focus:** Why have many people moved to the South?

3 **Focus:** Why have many businesses moved to the South?

4 **Critical Thinking: Cause and Effect** What do you think brings more people to the South — the climate or jobs? Explain your answer.

5 **Citizenship:** If a family like Fuad's moved next door to you, what could you do to make them feel welcome?

6 **Geography/Research Activity:** If you were driving a truckload of Florida oranges to Chicago, Illinois, which roads would you follow? Look at a map and decide on your route. What states would you pass through?

The Music of the South

Main Idea Many kinds of popular music have their roots in the South.

These words ring out in churches in the South and other parts of the country:

> **"Y**ou got a right, I got a right,
> We all got a right, to the tree of life.**"**

The words come from an African American spiritual — a kind of religious song. Spirituals often contain powerful messages of hope. They give courage to people struggling with hardship. Many spirituals express a wish for freedom. The rhythms and singing style of these songs come partly from Africa.

People all over the world use music to express both joy and sorrow. More so than any other region of the United States, the South has been the birthplace of popular American music. People still sing spirituals — and not just in church. A lot of today's most popular music has grown out of the mix of cultures in the South.

Key Vocabulary

- jazz
- blues
- ragtime
- zydeco
- bluegrass
- country and western

Key Places

- New Orleans, LA
- Nashville, TN

THE STANLEY BROTHERS

CLINCH MOUNTAIN BLUEGRASS

Ralph Stanley, Jr., claps along with his dad, Ralph, Sr. The Stanley family travels all over the South playing bluegrass music.

No one really knows where the word jazz came from. Some people think it came from the French word jaser, which means "to gossip."

Jazz and Its Roots

Focus *How did jazz music develop in the South?*

Americans love music. Much of the music we like comes from the South. One kind of music the South is famous for is jazz.

Jazz is hard to pin down exactly. It can be soft and soothing. Other jazz tunes can really wake you up! Like a big pot of gumbo — Louisiana's special stew — **jazz** is music with a lot of different sounds and rhythms all mixed together.

The Roots of Jazz

Jazz began in the South, but some of its earliest roots are in the spirituals sung by enslaved West Africans. After slavery ended, many African Americans moved to cities like New Orleans. Even though they were free, most were poor, and life was hard. Many of the songs they made up were about the hardships they faced. They sang about how sad, or "blue," they felt. That's how blues music got its name. **Blues** are slow, usually sad, songs.

Other music was anything but sad. African American musicians played their trumpets, cornets (similar to trumpets), and

Jazz Through the Years

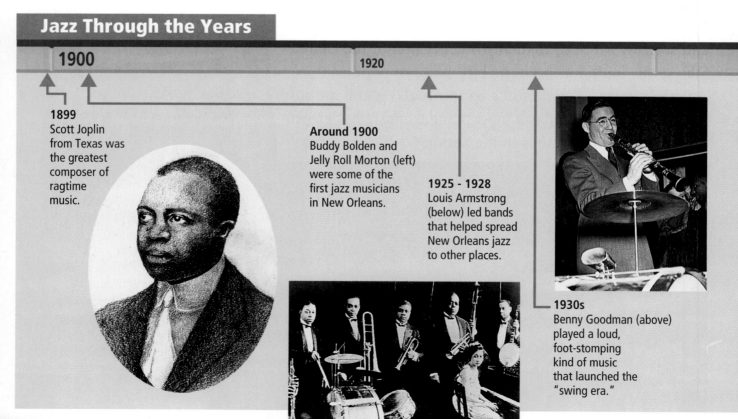

1900

1920

1899
Scott Joplin from Texas was the greatest composer of ragtime music.

Around 1900
Buddy Bolden and Jelly Roll Morton (left) were some of the first jazz musicians in New Orleans.

1925 - 1928
Louis Armstrong (below) led bands that helped spread New Orleans jazz to other places.

1930s
Benny Goodman (above) played a loud, foot-stomping kind of music that launched the "swing era."

trombones in marching bands. Some played the piano in dance halls. Musicians experimented with different rhythms on the piano. This music had an uneven, ragged beat, called syncopation (sihng kuh PAY shuhn). It was jumpy and lively. People called it **ragtime** music.

Mix all these kinds of music together, and what do you get? Jazz. It has the beat of ragtime, the cornets and trombones and saxophones of marching bands, the drums of Africa, and the deep feeling of spirituals and blues. Its audience grew — spreading to people of all backgrounds.

A Continuing Tradition

Jazz spread quickly from its New Orleans roots. Great jazz musicians like King Oliver and Louis Armstrong moved to Chicago and New York City and started jazz groups there.

Jazz was so popular in the 1920s that those years are sometimes called the "jazz age." On the timeline below, you can read about some of the most famous ragtime and jazz musicians from the past 100 years. Jazz is still popular today. You can play jazz on trumpet, guitar, saxophone, piano, and even flute. Jazz can also be heard in the rhythm and sounds of many other kinds of music that came out of the South.

1960

1980

1950s
Ella Fitzgerald (right) from Virginia was the most famous "scat" singer. "Scat" is singing made-up sounds.

1960s
John Coltrane (born in North Carolina) invented new kinds of jazz on his saxophone.

1980s and 1990s
Wynton Marsalis from New Orleans (right) is one of many musicians still creating jazz.

The Many Sounds of the South

Focus *What other kinds of music began in the South?*

Think of a big family reunion where there are hundreds of people, all related. Southern music is a little like that. Blues, ragtime, and jazz are musical cousins. So are many other types of music with southern roots.

Cajun and Zydeco

You read about the Cajuns in the last chapter. The Cajun culture has its own music. A lot of their songs are sad, like blues music. Many Cajun songs are in French. They are often accompanied by fiddle, accordion, and a metal instrument called the *frottoir* (frah TWAH). It makes a sound like "zhic-ka-zhicka" when you scrape it with your hands or a pair of spoons.

Like Cajuns, many African Americans live in the bayou country. Their music, called **zydeco** (ZEYE duh koh), is like Cajun music. It's bouncy, rhythmic, and joyful. They say that if you like what a zydeco band is playing, you don't clap. You dance!

Hank Williams, Sr., was a star of country and western music. The photograph below was taken during a square dance.

The harmonica is still a popular instrument for many southern musicians.

Clifton Chenier, a zydeco musician in Louisiana, plays his accordion.

Bluegrass

It's hard to keep your foot from tapping when you hear the fancy banjo playing bluegrass music. The musician's fingers just fly over the strings! If you go to a bluegrass concert, you'll hear plenty of stringed instruments. **Bluegrass** has its roots in fiddle music from England, Ireland, and Scotland.

Bill Monroe, from Kentucky, is called the "father of bluegrass." In 1939 he named his band the Blue Grass Boys — after a kind of grass that grows in Kentucky. That's how this music got its name.

Country and Western

Nashville, Tennessee, is the home of the Grand Ole Opry, which is famous for country and western music. **Country and western** songs often tell about people's concerns — about love and work, for example. Many are sad, but others are happy or funny. This music grew out of blues, popular songs of the 1800s, folk music from Great Britain, and religious music.

All of these different types of music have something in common. Southern musicians made up songs that expressed the difficulties they faced and how they felt — often using simple words. People all around the world like to listen to these songs. Maybe it's because people often face many of the same kinds of challenges no matter where they live.

Bill Monroe plays his mandolin at the Bluegrass Festival in Summersville, West Virginia.

Lesson Review

1. **Key Vocabulary:** Write a review of southern music, using these words: jazz, blues, ragtime, zydeco, bluegrass, and country and western.

2. **Focus:** How did jazz music develop in the South?

3. **Focus:** What other kinds of music began in the South?

4. **Critical Thinking: Predict** Popular songs are often about the concerns people have. What topics do you think songwriters will choose in 20 years?

5. **Geography:** St. Louis is the home of ragtime. New Orleans is the home of jazz. Which river connects these cities? How might a river help spread music?

6. **Citizenship/Music Activity:** Listen to a recording of one of the kinds of music in this lesson. Then write an advertisement for a band that plays this music.

Skills Workshop

Making Predictions Using Line Graphs

The More the Merrier

Where can you eat crawfish and alligator pie while listening to jazz, blues, country and western, Cajun, zydeco, and bluegrass music — all in one place? At the New Orleans Jazz and Heritage Festival, you can hear all the music the South is famous for. When the festival started in 1970, there were fewer than 200 people in the audience. Now there are thousands. You can easily show this kind of change on a **line graph**. Line graphs can also be used to predict what will happen in the future.

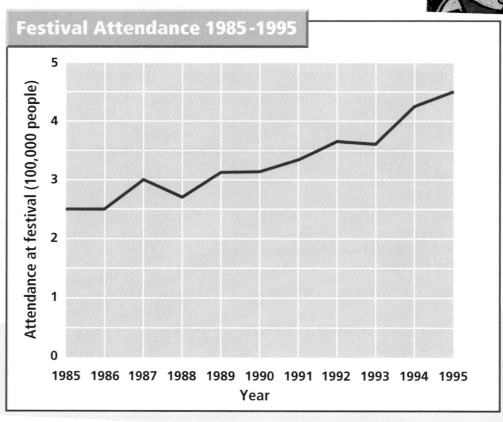

Festival Attendance 1985-1995

Attendance at festival (100,000 people) vs. Year

1 Here's How

- Read the graph's title. What do you expect to learn from this line graph?

- Find the label "Year" at the bottom of the graph. The line it labels is the horizontal axis. Look at the dates on this axis. Notice that they go forward in time, from 1985 to 1995.

- Find the label on the left side of the graph. The line on this side is the vertical axis. Study the numbers on the vertical axis, reading from bottom to top. What do they tell you?

- Combine information from the bottom and side. Follow the line above 1985 until you reach a point on the line graph. Then look to the left for the line until you reach the number. This graph shows that 250,000 people were at the festival in 1985.

- Find out more about changes in festival attendance by following the line that connects the points. Note how the line changes as it moves to the right.

2 Think It Through

Would a line graph be useful if the dates were not in order? Why do you need to know the sequence of events to make a prediction?

3 Use It

1. On your own paper, make a two-column chart. Label the left column "Date" and the right column "Attendance." Using the graph, write each year in the left column and the number of people at the festival that year in the right column.

2. Do you think the number of people attending the festival will grow or go down over the next 10 years? Explain your answer.

Wetlands: A Resource

Main Idea Wetlands are an important part of the natural environment.

Your boat slides quietly through the coffee-colored water of the swamp. Cypress trees grow crowded together along the water's edge. Their branches block most of the sunlight. Their roots stick up out of the water like bent knees. It's so quiet that you think you must be the only one around.

Suddenly you hear a rustle. A white and black bird that's taller than you rises from the grass with a fish in its mouth. It's a wood stork, and it has just caught its dinner in the Okefenokee National Wildlife Refuge in Georgia.

The Wetlands of the South

Focus *Why are the South's wetlands so important?*

The Okefenokee (oh kuh fuh NOH kee) Swamp is a large wetland in the South. A **wetland** is a place where the ground is soaked with water for at least part of the year. Swamps, marshes, and bogs are types of wetlands.

Wetlands are usually near lakes, rivers, or the ocean. Water from the Okefenokee Swamp, for example, flows into the St. Marys and Suwannee (suh WAH nee) rivers. Water in the Everglades, a large wetland in Florida, comes from Lake Okeechobee. From the Everglades, water flows into the Gulf of Mexico and Florida Bay.

Wetlands act like a gigantic sponge. They absorb water that falls as rain. This water then trickles underground and helps keep up the supply of ground water. **Ground water** is water beneath

Lily pads float around the base of cypress trees in Okefenokee Swamp, at the beginning of the Suwannee River.

the surface of the earth. Through wells, ground water supplies people with water for things like drinking and washing clothes.

The spongelike action of wetlands can help prevent floods, too. When a lot of rain falls, wetlands absorb the water. This keeps the water from flooding dry land. Wetlands can also act like filters, removing harmful chemicals from the water that passes through them.

Many plants and animals live in wetlands. The pictures on these pages show some of them. When wetlands are drained or polluted, some plants and animals may die. When a kind of plant or animal is in danger of dying out completely, it is an **endangered species**. The Florida panther and the wood stork are two endangered species that live in southern wetlands.

American alligators such as this one live in Okefenokee Swamp. A bird called a kite *(top)* eats a snail.

The Okefenokee Swamp is about 38 miles long and 25 miles wide. The Everglades cover about 4,000 square miles. Native American tribes, such as the Seminoles and the Creeks, once hunted in these wetlands. **Map Skill:** *What state boundary does the Okefenokee Swamp cross?*

The Everglades and the Okefenokee Swamp

Legend
- Wetlands
- Metropolitan areas
- Canal

People and Wetlands

Focus *How do people use and affect wetlands in the South?*

In the South and elsewhere in the United States, wetlands are disappearing. People have built farms, buildings, and shopping malls where the wetlands once were.

Just about everyone agrees that wetlands like the Everglades and Okefenokee Swamp need protecting. However, protecting wetlands can affect people's way of life. For instance, actions to save the Everglades might affect some farms. Years ago, parts of the Everglades were drained to make new farmland. Then wetland plants and animals became endangered. The government hopes to remove some dams and canals that had kept the water level low. This action might help endangered species, but it could flood farmland, too.

Paper companies use trees that grow in the Okefenokee Swamp. Those companies provide jobs for people in the area. However, papermaking produces chemicals that can pollute the water in the swamp and rivers. People disagree over how harmful these chemicals are to the wetlands.

Wetlands protection can help control floods and keep water pure. It can also help people economically. For example, people who catch fish for a living benefit from wetlands protection, because fish need clean water.

George Willson works to save wetlands near Okefenokee Swamp. He says,

> **"W**e're trying to show people that they can continue to fish, hunt, do some logging, that we're not locking up the land. **"**

People can have very different views of how a natural resource should be used. The more you learn about wetlands, the more you can help make good decisions about their future.

People walk across a boardwalk in Everglades National Park, Florida *(left)*. These red mangrove trees were cut to build houses *(above)*. **Economics:** *List the benefits and problems of building homes on a wetland. Then list the benefits and problems of protecting a wetland.*

Lesson Review

1. **Key Vocabulary:** Use these terms in a paragraph about the Everglades: wetlands, ground water, and endangered species.

2. **Focus:** Why are the South's wetlands so important?

3. **Focus:** How do people use and affect wetlands in the South?

4. **Critical Thinking: Decision Making** If you were thinking about building a house on a wetland, what would you consider in making your decision?

5. **Theme: Rivers and Coasts** Swamp water often flows into rivers. If swamp water becomes polluted, what might happen to the rivers? Explain.

6. **Citizenship/Writing Activity:** Learn about one of the endangered species mentioned in this lesson. Write a paragraph about how citizens can help save wetland plants and animals.

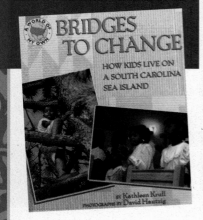

NONFICTION

BRIDGES TO CHANGE:

HOW KIDS LIVE ON A SOUTH CAROLINA SEA ISLAND

By Kathleen Krull
Photographed by David Hautzig

Many Americans visiting St. Helena Island might think it was like a dream vacation spot. But relatives of Travis Johnson and Martha Chisholm have lived in this southern coastal area for hundreds of years. For them, it's just home. It is also a good example of how life can be so different in different regions of our country.

St. Helena, where Travis and Martha live, is one of the Sea Islands off the coast of South Carolina and Georgia. The islands were once one of the most remote areas of the United

Bridges connect St. Helena to the South Carolina mainland.

States. Until this century, the only way to reach them was by boat. There were no bridges to St. Helena until the Depression, and some islands still don't have any.

In this isolation and tranquility, it can seem, even today, as though time has stood still. The islands remain a haven for numerous plant and animal species. Ancient oak trees lean into the roads, forming arches. Sunlight filters through the Spanish moss overhanging the branches, spotlighting the pink and red azaleas. Purple wisteria vines climb over anything they can. Peering into the dense forests, one can imagine the days when Cherokee and other tribes were the first residents on the islands, and when pirates such as the notorious Blackbeard and others used lonely Carolina beaches as hiding places. People then may have heard the same kinds of birdcalls and smelled the same things — the perfumy scent of yellow jessamine, the sweetness of tall pines, the salty tang of the Atlantic Ocean — that Travis and Martha do today.

The roads where Travis and Martha and other children live have no names. Dirt lanes wander across creeks, around palmetto trees, or through marshes. Even the language of the Sea Islands is unique. Longtime residents speak Gullah (pronounced *GULL-a*) — a distinctive blend of English (possibly Elizabethan English) with words and grammatical rules from West African languages. *Gullah* is also the word used to describe people from the Sea Islands, or the rural African-American culture that exists here. Relatively little is known about the Gullah people. Visitors will rarely even hear the language; speakers switch to English when talking to outsiders. Because the people are separated from

Away from the highway, roads are unpaved and unmarked.

tranquility
quiet

notorious
well known, but not in a favorable way

Drum music is one of the traditions brought from Africa.

the mainland by marshes and swamps, their language and culture have not become Americanized as rapidly as those of other groups that have come to this country.

Martha and Travis both spend their after-school hours at the Penn Center, a community service organization that began as the first school in the South for freed slaves. At the center, the children complete their homework, go for nature walks or hunt for fiddler crabs, and learn about Gullah history and culture. Sometimes Martha and Travis board a creaky old blue bus that takes them strawberry picking, for example.

Because of schoolwork, and her activities at the Penn Center, Martha's free time is very limited. Besides jumping double-dutch and riding into town to help her mother shop for household things, her favorite thing to do is watching the news. Her mother keeps the news on so Martha can become informed, but, says Martha, "My mother doesn't have to tell me to watch it because I think it's important."

In his free time, Travis plays basketball and baseball in the big park across the street from his school. At home, his

The Penn Center where Martha and Travis spend time after school.

mother is teaching him how to skip stones across the creek. He likes to draw and do lettering. Travis gets an allowance for doing chores, and he almost always saves it. Right now the money is going toward a mountain bike and a saxophone.

Martha sings in her church choir.

Travis plays the recorder at school and plans to learn saxophone.

Meet the Author

Writer Kathleen Krull and photographer David Hautzig have worked together on several books about children around the United States.

Additional Books to Read

Wetlands
by Ronald Rood
illustrated by Marlene Hill Donnelly
Learn about an important part of our environment.

Misty of Chincoteague
by Marguerite Henry
illustrated by Wesley Dennis
Read about this wild Chesapeake pony.

Response Activities

1. **Problem Solving:** How can wetland areas like the swamps on the Sea Islands be protected and at the same time be open to visitors?

2. **Informative: Write a Brochure** What do you think visitors to the island would like to see? Use the descriptions of the island in *Bridges to Change* to write a tourist brochure.

3. **Cultures: Make a Chart** Make a chart comparing and contrasting life on the Sea Islands and life in your community. Which plants do you have in common? Which things do you do after school that Travis or Martha also do?

Space Technology

LESSON 4

Key Vocabulary

aeronautics
space shuttle
astronaut
space station

Key Places

Kitty Hawk, NC
Cape Canaveral, FL
Houston, TX

Main Idea The South has many important centers for the technology that has made space travel possible.

> **"S**uccess. Four flights Thursday morning. All against twenty-one-mile wind . . . Longest fifty-nine seconds. . .**"**

With those words, Wilbur and Orville Wright sent their father the great news. On December 17, 1903, after years of experiments, their flying machine finally worked. Its two propellers spinning, the little airplane took off into the wind above a strip of sand near Kitty Hawk, North Carolina.

Those first flights at Kitty Hawk forever cut the bonds that tied people to Earth. Just 66 years later, a man would walk on the moon.

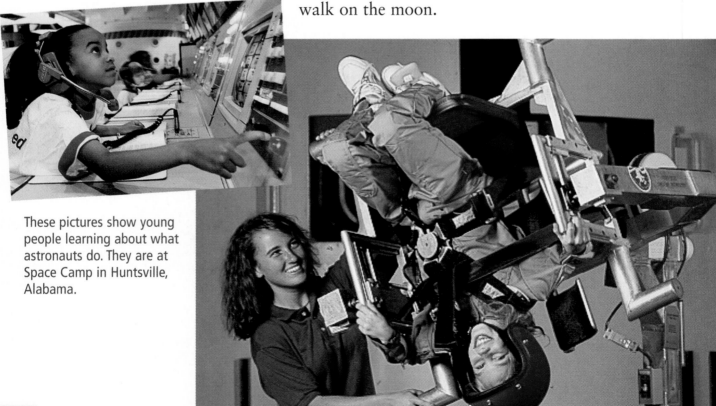

These pictures show young people learning about what astronauts do. They are at Space Camp in Huntsville, Alabama.

Space Centers in the South

Focus *Where are the centers for space technology in the South?*

The South has been a center for flight since the time of the Wright brothers. Today NASA, the part of government in charge of space exploration, has several major branches in the South — in Florida, Texas, Maryland, and Alabama. NASA stands for National Aeronautics and Space Administration. **Aeronautics** (air uh NAW tihks) is the science of building and operating aircraft.

One branch of NASA is the Goddard Space Flight Center in Greenbelt, Maryland. Workers there build some of NASA's satellites. Satellites orbit the earth but don't have any people on board. They are controlled entirely by computer.

The Space Shuttle

Cape Canaveral, Florida, is where space shuttles are launched. A **space shuttle** is a special kind of spacecraft that can be used again and again. **Astronauts,** people who are specially trained to travel in space, operate the space shuttles. The astronauts conduct scientific experiments in outer space. They take pictures of the earth and launch satellites.

Because of its location on the coast, Cape Canaveral is a good place for launching spacecraft. When a spacecraft takes

Astronauts are trained at the Lyndon B. Johnson Space Center in Houston, Texas. This is also the home of Mission Control, which helps operate spacecraft.

Then & Now

In 1640, a man named John Wilkins wrote about flying to the moon. He wrote that he thought it was "possible to make a flying chariot in which a man may sit." A chariot is a cart with wheels.

It took more than 300 years before John Wilkins's idea became a reality.

off, parts of the rocket fall back to Earth. Since the ocean is close, those rocket parts fall into the ocean, not on land.

The astronauts are trained at the Johnson Space Center in Houston, Texas. Many people besides astronauts work there. Some are instructors who teach the astronauts the skills and information they will need on space flights. For example, instructors teach astronauts how the machines on spacecraft work. Other people at the space center help design spacecraft. Workers test spacecraft to make sure they work properly. The Johnson Space Center provides jobs for about 13,000 people.

Support for a Shuttle Mission

The Johnson Space Center is also the home of Mission Control. That's where computers and other machines help people control the spacecraft during flight. If you visit Mission Control while the space shuttle is flying, what will you see?

You'll see many people watching television screens and working at computers that check the equipment on the shuttle.

The people on the ground help the astronauts do their jobs in space. Information from Mission Control helps astronauts fly the spacecraft and land it on Earth.

The space shuttle *Columbia* *(top)* lands in April 1981, after orbiting the earth. Scientists at NASA Mission Control Center in Houston *(bottom)* provide support for U.S. space flights.

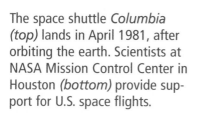

Mission Control workers talk to the astronauts about their work. Sometimes, they just talk. The astronauts like to hear a friendly voice. Mission Control even plays music to wake the astronauts up!

Space Suit

Fabric This suit, which was made for the Apollo moon-landing program, had a lining that kept astronauts cool. Rubber joints made it easier for astronauts to move.

First Moon Landing Astronaut Edwin E. "Buzz" Aldrin, Jr., steps off the lunar module onto the surface of the moon on July 20, 1969.

Helmets These were fastened to the suit. Astronauts could move their heads around inside the helmets.

Gloves These were made to protect the astronauts' hands but still allow them to use sensitive instruments.

Lunar Boots These boots were like a tall pair of overshoes. They slipped over the feet of the space suit to protect astronauts from jagged rocks on the surface of the moon.

The Future of the Space Program

Focus *What might the space program do in the future?*

Your parents or grandparents might remember the first moon landing. On July 20, 1969, Neil Armstrong and "Buzz" Aldrin became the first humans to walk on the moon. After that exciting day, people asked, "Where do we go from here?"

Some people think we should send astronauts to Mars. While it took four days for astronauts to get from Earth to the moon, it would take months to get to Mars. Many people think it would be too dangerous and cost too much.

Other people think we should build a space station. A **space station** is like a huge spaceship where people live and

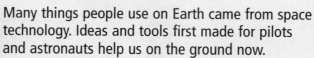
· Tell Me More ·

Space Comes Down to Earth

Many things people use on Earth came from space technology. Ideas and tools first made for pilots and astronauts help us on the ground now.

For example, NASA helped build the first voice synthesizer — a computer that speaks words aloud. Voice synthesizers were developed to help pilots. People who cannot talk can now use computers with voice synthesizers to communicate. They input the words they want to say into the computer. The computer says the words for them.

Solar-powered cars use space technology.

A voice synthesizer invented by NASA helps this boy communicate.

NASA research developed suits that protect people from fire.

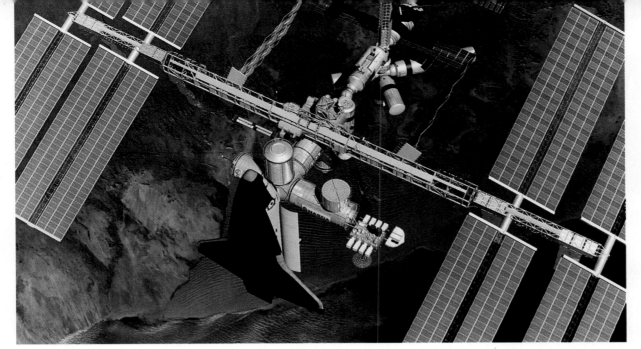

work while they orbit the Earth. The Russians have a space station called *Mir*.

People don't need to travel in space to learn about it. Scientists can learn a lot about the planets and other parts of space from satellites and other spacecraft that don't have humans in them. Computers control these spacecraft. It is much less expensive to send machines into space than it is to send people. So, some people think the space program should focus on building satellites.

Have you ever looked into the sky and wondered what is out there? There are many ways of exploring space. People in the South help make that exploration possible.

People have proposed building an international space station — one that many countries could use. A computer created this picture of how that space station might look. **Economics:** *Do you think the government will build many space stations? Why or why not?*

Lesson Review

1 **Key Vocabulary:** Use aeronautics, space shuttle, astronauts, and space station in a story about space travel.

2 **Focus:** Where are the centers for space technology in the South?

3 **Focus:** What might the space program do in the future?

4 **Critical Thinking: Decision Making** What kinds of space exploration should be done in the future? Give reasons for your choices.

5 **Citizenship:** Do you think it is important to have museums that let people know about the space program? Why or why not?

6 **Geography/Science Activity:** Learn about the physical geography of the moon. What is its surface like? What landforms are there?

Chapter Review

Summarizing the Main Idea

1 Copy and complete the chart below, listing one or two facts for each topic.

Topic	Important Facts
Moving south	
Southern music	
Wetlands	
Space industry	

Vocabulary

2 Using at least 10 of the following terms, write an introduction for a television show about the South today.

cost of living (p. 228)
manufacture (p. 229)
research (p. 230)
jazz (p. 232)
blues (p. 232)
ragtime (p. 233)

zydeco (p. 234)
bluegrass (p. 235)
country and western (p. 235)
wetland (p. 238)
ground water (p. 238)

endangered species (p. 239)
aeronautics (p. 247)
space shuttle (p. 247)
astronauts (p. 247)
space station (p. 250)

Reviewing the Facts

3 What are some reasons why people move to the South?

4 How is research part of the work done at Research Triangle Park?

5 How would you describe jazz?

6 Besides jazz, what other kinds of music come from the South?

7 Name two important wetlands in the South.

8 What are some of the problems affecting the wetlands?

9 Why is Cape Canaveral a good place for launching spacecraft?

10 What are some jobs that astronauts perform?

11 What projects might help people learn about space in the future?

12 Look at the graph on page 236. In what year was festival attendance less than the year before?

13 On a line graph that showed your height every year on your birthday, what would the line look like?

Geography Skills

14 Find the Everglades on the map on page 239. If water in the Everglades became polluted, what cities' water supplies would probably be affected?

15 A family is moving from Maine to Florida. Describe changes they might need to make in the clothes they wear.

Critical Thinking

16 **Interpret** If you were in a happy mood, what kinds of southern music might you want to listen to? What kinds appeal to a sad mood? Explain.

17 **Conclude** If you were to work at the Johnson Space Center, what kind of job would interest you? What special skills would you need for the job?

Writing: Citizenship and Economics

18 **Citizenship** Write a speech you might give in a town meeting about wetlands. Use arguments to support your point of view in favor of wetlands protection or in favor of building on wetlands.

19 **Economics** Create an ad to attract workers from all over the country to Research Triangle Park. Your ad should stress advantages of living in the South as well as the features of RTP.

Activities

National Heritage/Music Activity
Find out more about one of the great jazz musicians mentioned on the bottom of pages 232 and 233. Create a timeline that shows some of the key events in his or her life.

Economics/Math Activity
Create a third column for the Cost of Living chart on page 229. Find the prices of listed items in your community. How do these prices compare to those in Birmingham and Hartford?

Internet Option

Check the **Internet Social Studies Center** for ideas on how to extend your theme project beyond your classroom.

THEME PROJECT CHECK-IN

Look through your vacation plans. Did you include what you learned in this chapter?
• Why would people want to visit wetlands and a space center?
• Do your brochure and poster explain why people are moving to the South?
• How does your trip reflect the musical traditions of the South?

The Midwest

"*Plains, plains everywhere, plains generally level, but elsewhere rolling . . . like the waves of a sea which has fallen asleep . . . .*"

Isabella L. Bird

Prairies and Plains

" The climate affects the way we live in Wisconsin because there are different seasons. We get to do different things in each different season. "

Anthony Dixon, Fourth Grade
Milwaukee, WI

Do you know what prairies and plains are? They are part of the Midwest. The Midwest stretches across the middle of the United States. Some parts of the Midwest are covered with forests and farms. Elsewhere there are big cities and factories. In this unit, you will read about many things from the Midwest.

 Theme Project

Have a Fair

Celebrate the features of the Midwest in a fair. Plan booths that show something about life in this region.

- With your class, choose the displays and activities you want to show in your booths.
- Make posters and collages with pictures of different places and people.
- Write a short guide to your booth.
- Tape-record "interviews" with midwesterners.

RESEARCH: Find out about an industry in the Midwest. Include in your booth a diagram related to that industry.

◀ Sunflowers in full bloom in North Dakota

WHEN & WHERE
ATLAS

The wide lands of the Midwest are rich in resources that are important to the rest of the world. This map shows you the flat plains and rolling hills of the Midwest, as well as some of the region's major cities. The map also shows some resources and farm products of the Midwest.

In this unit, you'll learn about the prairies, plains, and hills of the Midwest. You'll see how Native Americans built cities there and how people spread over all the Midwest. You'll also learn the different ways that people make a living in the Midwest today.

Unit 5 Chapters

Chapter 10 The Land and People of the Midwest

Chapter 11 The Midwest Today

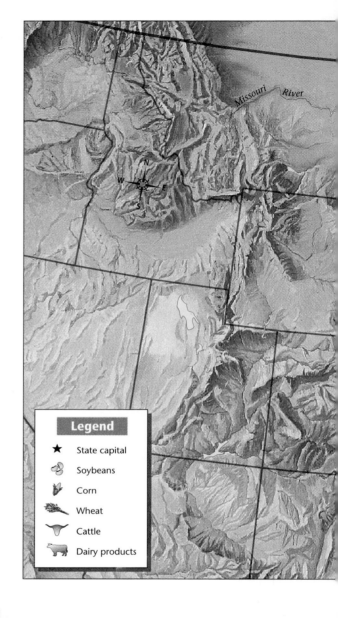

Missouri River

Legend	
★	State capital
	Soybeans
	Corn
	Wheat
	Cattle
	Dairy products

Unit Timeline

1500	1600	1700

South Dakota Prairie

What are the major landforms of the Midwest? *Chapter 10, Lesson 1*

Ice Sculptures

Find out how midwesterners enjoy winter. *Chapter 10, Lesson 3*

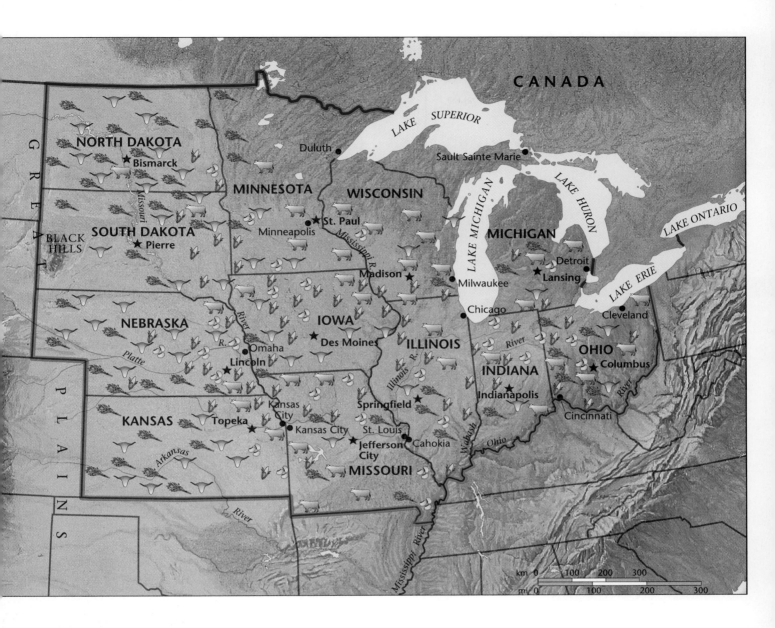

CANADA

GREAT PLAINS

NORTH DAKOTA
★ Bismarck

SOUTH DAKOTA
★ Pierre

BLACK HILLS

Missouri

Duluth

LAKE SUPERIOR

Sault Sainte Marie

MINNESOTA

Minneapolis
★ St. Paul

WISCONSIN

LAKE MICHIGAN

LAKE HURON

MICHIGAN
Detroit
★ Lansing

LAKE ONTARIO

Milwaukee

Chicago

LAKE ERIE

Cleveland

Madison ★

Mississippi R.

NEBRASKA

River

Omaha
Lincoln ★

Platte R.

IOWA
★ Des Moines

ILLINOIS

Illinois R.

River

OHIO
★ Columbus

INDIANA
Indianapolis ★

River

Cincinnati

KANSAS
Topeka ★

Arkansas

Kansas City
Kansas City

Springfield ★

St. Louis
Jefferson City
Cahokia

Wabash

Ohio

MISSOURI

River

Mississippi River

km 0   100   200   300
mi 0   100   200   300

1800   1900   2000

Making Steel

What industry do steel factories depend on? *Chapter 11, Lesson 2*

A Farming Family

What happens during a day on a farm? *Chapter 11, Lesson 3*

Stained Glass Window

How did the prairies inspire an architect? *Chapter 11, Lesson 4*

The Land and People of the Midwest

Chapter Preview: *People, Places, and Events*

1500	1600	1700

Lake Superior

Which states touch the edges of this lake? *Lesson 1, Page 260*

Bison in South Dakota

What does this animal like to eat? *Lesson 1, Page 262*

Native American Mounds

Who built these mounds of dirt along the Mississippi River? *Lesson 2, Page 268*

The Land

Main Idea The Midwest is covered with plains and grasslands and has many important lakes and rivers.

On July 12, 1804, William Clark stood on a Nebraska hill. He looked out over land he had never seen before. Later, he wrote in his journal about what he saw that day:

> **"A** *leavel [level] and extensive meadow, as far as I could See. . . .* **"**

Clark was describing the Great Plains — a huge area of land that had just been made part of the United States.

The Great Plains are in the western part of what we now call the Midwest. By 1804, eastern parts of the Midwest had already been settled. The Great Plains, however, were almost unknown. Clark called the plains one of the most beautiful sights he had ever seen. From Nebraska, he and Meriwether Lewis continued on their journey westward, mapping new territory for the United States.

Key Vocabulary
aquifer
tornado
prairie

Key Places
Tornado Alley

◀ Mules pull wheat harvesting machines during the 1890s.

1800   1900   2000

Sod House in Nebraska

How did settlers on the Great Plains build their homes? *Lesson 2, Page 272*

Iron Mining in the Midwest

Find out about different ways Midwesterners earn a living. *Lesson 3, Page 277*

Fairs and Festivals

What do people in the Midwest do for fun? *Lesson 3, Page 278*

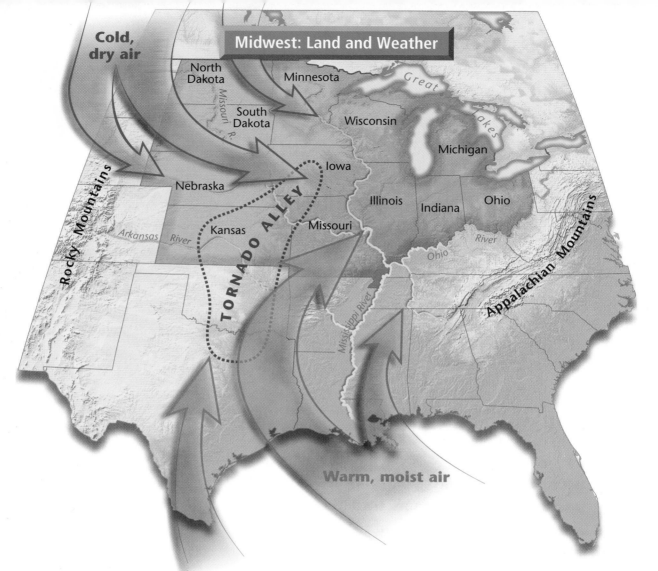

Midwest: Land and Weather

Cold, dry air

North Dakota

Minnesota

Great Lakes

South Dakota

Wisconsin

Michigan

Missouri R.

Iowa

Rocky Mountains

Nebraska

Illinois

Indiana

Ohio

TORNADO ALLEY

Kansas

Missouri

Ohio River

Arkansas River

Mississippi River

Appalachian Mountains

Warm, moist air

Winds play a big part in this region's weather. When cold, dry winds from Canada mix with warm, moist winds from the Gulf of Mexico, big storms can form on the plains and prairies of the Midwest. **Map Skill:** *Why do you think "Tornado Alley" is located where it is?*

Landforms and Weather Patterns

Focus *What are the landforms and climate of the Midwest?*

Picture a dinner plate. It's wide and flat in the middle and slopes upward at the edges so your food doesn't fall off. The middle of the United States is shaped like that plate. Its eastern edge is the Appalachian Mountains. Its western edge is the Rocky Mountains. The wide center of the plate is the Midwest.

The Midwest isn't really as flat as a plate. However, it is one of the flattest parts of the United States. Look at the map above. Two kinds of flat land make up the major landforms of the Midwest. The Central Plains are in the eastern part of this region. The Great Plains are in the west.

The map shows that water also shapes the Midwest. Some of the largest rivers in the United States run through this region.

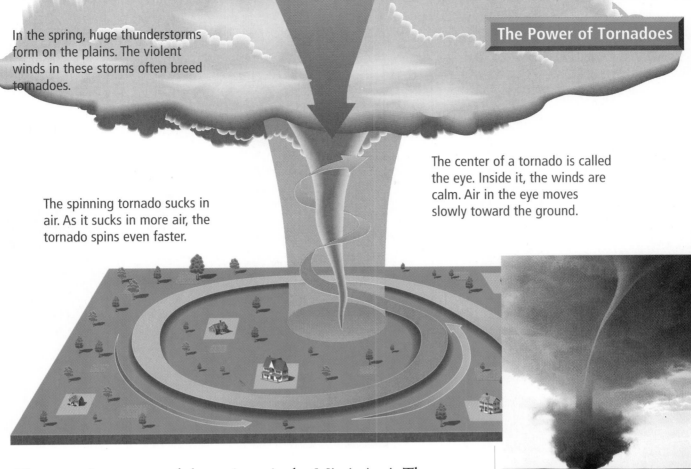

In the spring, huge thunderstorms form on the plains. The violent winds in these storms often breed tornadoes.

The spinning tornado sucks in air. As it sucks in more air, the tornado spins even faster.

The center of a tornado is called the eye. Inside it, the winds are calm. Air in the eye moves slowly toward the ground.

Winds in a tornado can reach 250 miles per hour! When a tornado hits the ground, or "touches down," it sucks up dirt and other loose objects. It can pick up cars and take the roofs off buildings. **Science:** *What happens to crops in the path of a tornado?*

The most important of these rivers is the Mississippi. The Midwest also has water that you can't see on the map. A huge underground collection of water called an **aquifer** (AK wuh fur) lies under part of the Midwest. Its water is trapped in gravel and rocks under the earth's surface.

The largest bodies of water in this region are the Great Lakes. (See pages 264–265 to find out how glaciers created these lakes.) The Midwest has thousands of smaller lakes, too. There are more than 15,000 lakes in Minnesota alone.

Temperatures in the Midwest can be extreme. There is no ocean nearby to cool the land in summer and warm it in winter. So summers in much of the region are very hot and winters very cold. Places near the Great Lakes are an exception. The lakes affect the weather the way an ocean does. Areas around them stay warmer in winter and cooler in summer.

Midwestern weather can be harsh. As you can see in the diagram above, huge, swirling windstorms called **tornadoes** often strike this region. Take a look at the area called "Tornado Alley" on the map. As many as 300 tornadoes strike this region every year.

Bison As many as 60 million bison once lived on the plains. Today, bison often gather around prairie-dog "towns" because the grass there is better to eat.

Prairie Dogs These animals dig different rooms, called chambers, for different purposes. They dig listening chambers near the surface, so they can listen for enemies. Flood chambers are places that stay dry during floods. They also dig nest chambers to make room for baby prairie dogs.

Wild Plants and Animals

Focus *What kinds of plants and animals live in the Midwest?*
In the early 1800s, the Great Plains and much of the Central Plains were covered by grasslands. These grasslands are called **prairies.** Today, these areas are mostly covered with corn and wheat farms. However, prairies still exist. The illustration above shows plants and animals that can live in those areas.

The land around the Great Lakes is very different from the prairies. In 1855, a man named Henry Wadsworth Longfellow wrote a poem called "The Song of Hiawatha" (HY uh WAH thuh). In it, he described the beauty of the Great Lakes area:

> "**D**ark behind it rose the forest . . .
> Rose the firs with cones upon them,
> Bright before it beat the water,
> Beat the clear and sunny water."

Predators Four-legged predators, such as foxes and coyotes, depend on prairie dogs for food. Winged hunters, such as falcons and eagles, also eat prairie dogs.

Deer White-tailed deer feed on prairie grasses across the plains.

The plants and animals that live around the Great Lakes have adapted to an environment very different from that of the prairie. Forests cover much of Minnesota, Wisconsin, and Michigan. Deer and moose hide among the trees. In the north, wolves howl. Ducks nest near lakes. Many kinds of fish, such as trout and bass, swim in lakes and streams.

The Midwest has rich soil and thick forests. It has broad waterways and wide open spaces. All these features have made it a good home for many plants and animals. They have also made it a good home for people.

Prairie Grass Out of every four prairie plants, three are wildflowers! The blossoms of these flowers attract many kinds of butterflies. **Science:** *Which animals do you think need prairie grasses to survive? Which might be able to live around farmland?*

Lesson Review: Geography

1. **Key Vocabulary:** Write a paragraph about the plains, using these words: **aquifer, tornado, prairie.**

2. **Focus:** What are the landforms and climate of the Midwest?

3. **Focus:** What kinds of plants and animals live in the Midwest?

4. **Critical Thinking: Cause and Effect** How do plants influence the kinds of animals that live in the Midwest?

5. **Theme: Prairies and Plains** Look at the map on page 260. How do you think landforms in the Midwest affect the weather?

6. **Geography/Research Activity:** Look in an encyclopedia or a book about wildlife. Find out what bison, deer, and beaver eat. Draw a picture showing where they live. Write a paragraph describing their food and their home.

Physical Systems

How Did Glaciers Shape the Great Lakes Region?

To a geographer, the Great Lakes are very young. In fact, these giant lakes reached their present form at the end of the last Ice Age, roughly 10,000 years ago. Other lakes in the world are close to 25 million years old.

Chicago, Illinois, is a large city that grew up on the shore of Lake Michigan.

Only 20,000 years ago, great sheets of ice covered much of Canada and the northern United States. These huge glaciers, one to two miles thick, shaped the land of the Great Lakes region. They pushed soil and loose rocks into large ridges and scooped out deep basins in the earth. Later, when the glaciers melted, water gradually filled these basins to form thousands of lakes. The largest of these lakes — Superior, Michigan, Huron, Erie, and Ontario — became the five Great Lakes. Today the Great Lakes contain nearly one-fifth of the world's aboveground fresh water.

Science Connection

A Swiss scientist named Louis Agassiz (AG uh see) was the first person to claim that glaciers dug the basins for the Great Lakes. On an expedition to Lake Superior in 1848, Agassiz found rock formations that had been cut by glaciers and boulders that glaciers had carried from Canada. How did this evidence prove his ideas?

The Great Lakes: 17,000 Years Ago

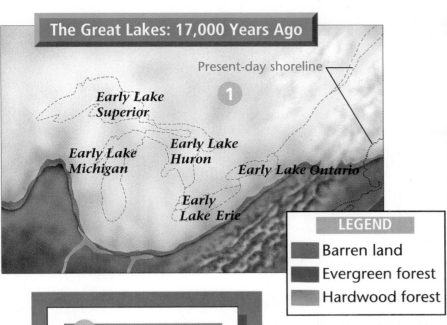

Present-day shoreline

1

Early Lake Superior

Early Lake Michigan

Early Lake Huron

Early Lake Ontario

Early Lake Erie

LEGEND

- Barren land
- Evergreen forest
- Hardwood forest

1 Canada

Continental Glaciers
During the last Ice Age, continental glaciers, or icecaps, spread out from Hudson Bay. Today this type of glacier is found only in Greenland and Antarctica.

2 Minnesota

Land of Lakes
Glaciers have left their mark on every part of the Great Lakes region. The state of Minnesota, which borders on Lake Superior, has thousands of glacial lakes.

The Great Lakes: 11,000 Years Ago

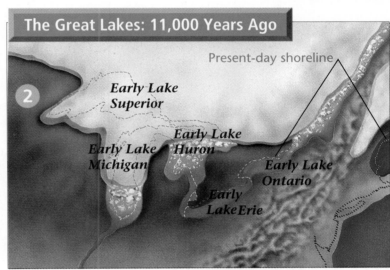

Present-day shoreline

2

Early Lake Superior

Early Lake Michigan

Early Lake Huron

Early Lake Ontario

Early Lake Erie

The Great Lakes: 3,500 Years Ago

St. Lawrence River

Lake Superior

Lake Huron

Lake Michigan

Lake Ontario

Lake Erie

As the glaciers gradually retreated northward, the Great Lakes emerged in their present form.

Research Activity

The glaciers that covered the Great Lakes region shaped the physical features of this area in many ways.

1 Read more about how Ice Age glaciers shaped the land they once covered.

2 Make a model that illustrates some of the physical features created by glaciers. Label each of these features carefully. Share your model with your class.

Illustrated by
Jack Unruh

Written by
Michael E. Long

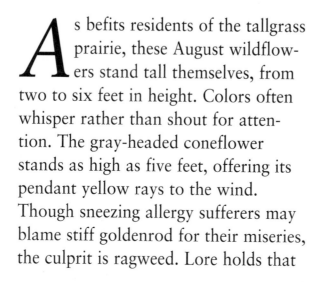

Wildflowers Across America
Tallgrass Prairie

As befits residents of the tallgrass prairie, these August wildflowers stand tall themselves, from two to six feet in height. Colors often whisper rather than shout for attention. The gray-headed coneflower stands as high as five feet, offering its pendant yellow rays to the wind. Though sneezing allergy sufferers may blame stiff goldenrod for their miseries, the culprit is ragweed. Lore holds that whoever carries a goldenrod will find treasure and good fortune.

Monarch butterflies head for a favorite nectar in flowers of the rough blazing star. Maximilian's sunflower likes to migrate from roadside ditches into planted fields, causing farmers to fret. To the right of the sunflowers stands a sheaf of bluestem, the native grass reaching six feet in height that once dominated the prairie.

Leaves of the smooth aster are almost waxy. Preferring wet sites in undisturbed prairie, the swamp thistle grows to six feet and offers magenta blossoms. Tall blazing star also prefers a moist habitat. In recent years the flower has achieved increasing popularity with florists.

Meanwhile, meadowlarks throng among the flowers to eat insects and sing melodious and loud thanks.

Response Activities

1. Conclude Why do you think many midwesterners today want to protect the wildflowers that grow there?

2. Descriptive: Write About Wildflowers Find out about wildflowers or other plants that grow in your region, and write a paragraph describing them for someone who has never seen them.

3. Cultures: Share Flower Traditions People used to say that whoever carried a goldenrod would find good fortune. Learn about other traditions or sayings related to flowers, and share them with your class.

Settling the Midwest

Main Idea The land of the Midwest supported many different groups of people.

Key Vocabulary

artifact
archaeology
pioneer
sod

Key Events

1812 Settlers enter Louisiana Purchase

1930s Drought creates the "Dust Bowl"

A thousand years ago, Cahokia (cah HOH kee uh), Illinois, was the biggest city in what is now the United States. That was long before Europeans, Africans, and Asians arrived in North America. The people of Cahokia were part of the Mississippian culture. These Native Americans lived near the Mississippi, Missouri, and Ohio rivers.

By 1600, the Mississippians had disappeared from the Midwest. Today, people know about them from huge mounds they built in Cahokia and other places. People also know about the Mississippians from artifacts. **Artifacts** are things people made, used, and left behind. Studying artifacts to learn about how people lived is called **archaeology**.

Native Americans in the Midwest

Focus *How did Native Americans in the Midwest use their resources?*

Through archaeology, people know that the Mississippians farmed the rich Midwestern soil. Like the Mississippians, Native American groups across the Midwest also took advantage of the resources that their land offered them.

The northern and eastern parts of the Midwest

This statue is an artifact from a group of Native Americans called Mississippians.

were home to woodland peoples like the Kickapoo and Ojibway (oh JIHB way). They made their houses, called wigwams, from the bark of trees. For food, they hunted and farmed.

The people who lived on the prairies were once mostly farmers. They lived in villages along the Missouri River. In the 1500s, Spanish explorers brought horses to North America. Horses changed the Native Americans' way of life. A new culture grew on the Great Plains. Look at the illustration below to learn more.

Tepees These were made of tree trunks and bison hides. It took 12 to 14 hides to make one tepee.

Life on the Great Plains

With horses, Native Americans on the plains could move quickly and carry many things. This allowed them to start a new way of life. They hunted bison, following these animals as they moved in herds across the plains.

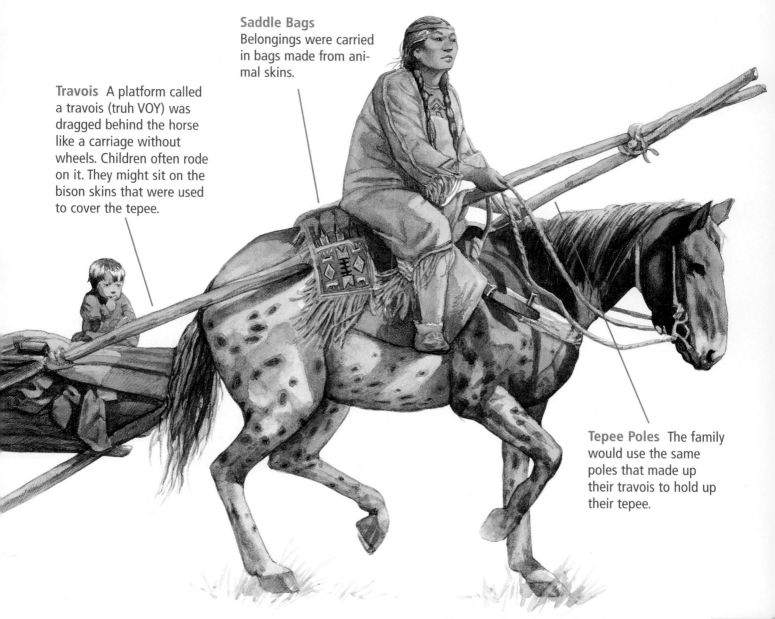

Saddle Bags Belongings were carried in bags made from animal skins.

Travois A platform called a travois (truh VOY) was dragged behind the horse like a carriage without wheels. Children often rode on it. They might sit on the bison skins that were used to cover the tepee.

Tepee Poles The family would use the same poles that made up their travois to hold up their tepee.

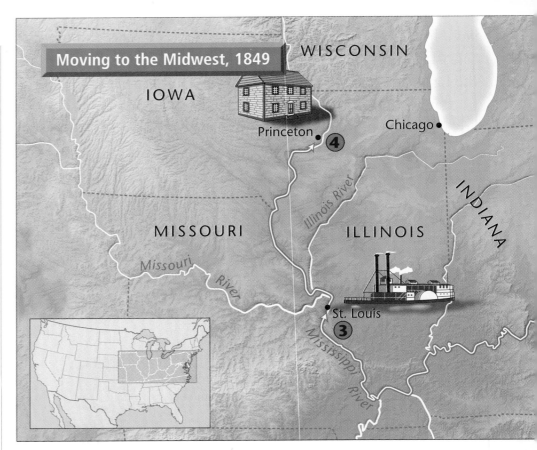

Moving to the Midwest, 1849

WISCONSIN
IOWA
Princeton ④
Chicago •
Illinois River
MISSOURI
ILLINOIS
INDIANA
Missouri River
St. Louis ③
Mississippi River

European Settlers

Focus *How did Europeans come to the Midwest?*

The first Europeans who lived in the Midwest came from
France in the 1600s. They wanted to trap animals for their fur.
These French trappers lived on the land around the Great
Lakes. British trappers arrived soon afterwards.

In the mid-1700s, Britain and France fought a war over
many issues, including this land. Both countries wanted what is
now Ohio, Indiana, Illinois, Michigan, and Wisconsin. In
1763, Britain took the area from France. In 1783, the United
States won independence from Britain and gained control of it.

Native Americans who lived in the area fought, too. They
didn't want Europeans to take their land from them. However,
United States soldiers defeated the Native American forces.

By 1812, thousands of European settlers had started to
arrive in the area around the Great Lakes. Others were settling
in the Ohio River Valley and other parts of the Central Plains.
Like most people who would come to the Midwest during the
next 100 years, these settlers wanted land for farms.

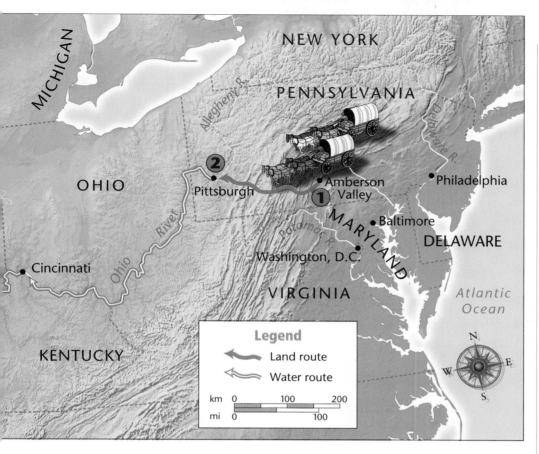

1. In the fall of 1849, John Culbertson's family packed their belongings into two covered wagons. They headed west.

2. John and his family boarded a steamboat in Pittsburgh, Pennsylvania. The boat carried farm animals as well as people.

3. In St. Louis, Missouri, the Culbertson family boarded a steamboat headed for St. Paul, Minnesota.

4. The Culbertsons got off the steamboat in Princeton, Iowa. On the way from Princeton to their new home, they stopped at a neighbor's house. They arrived at their new farm in October, 1849. **Map Skill:** *What mountains did the Culbertsons cross? On what rivers did they travel?*

Pioneers Cross the Mississippi

Desire for land brought settlers farther west. In 1803, the United States bought a large area of land from France. Called the Louisiana Purchase, it began just west of the Mississippi. It included what is now Iowa, Missouri, Kansas, and Nebraska. It also held much of Minnesota and North and South Dakota.

During the 1800s, European pioneers began moving into this area. **Pioneers** are people who take on new challenges, such as settling a new area. They forced Native Americans to move out. Conflicts over land soon broke out. The result was the same as it had been in the eastern part of the Midwest. U.S. soldiers made Native American groups give up their land.

Settlers continued moving west. They entered Missouri in 1812. In the 1830s, pioneer families like the one on the map above started moving into Iowa and Minnesota.

There was one part of this new area that the pioneers did not settle, at least at first. This was the Great Plains. The settlers were used to forests, and they didn't know how to live on plains. So, in the 1840s and 1850s most settlers headed farther west, to Oregon and California.

Pioneers brought along many things they needed, including candlesticks.

The Land and People of the Midwest   **271**

Settling the Great Plains

It was not until the 1860s that pioneers finally began to settle the Great Plains. Unlike forests, the plains had no wood and very little rain. Settlers had to learn new skills to survive.

To make a living on the plains, settlers learned new ways of farming. They planted crops that grew in winter, when more water fell on the plains. They kept the top layer of soil loose. That way, it would hold water. They also left fields empty in the summer, so water in the soil wouldn't evaporate.

The settlers also needed places to live. So they cut sod into shapes like bricks. **Sod** is earth held together by the roots of prairie grasses. They stacked the sod bricks on top of each other to make their houses.

· Tell Me More ·

Living on the Treeless Plains

Pioneers on the plains could not cut wood to build houses. There were hardly any trees! They used sod instead. Farmers who could afford lumber bought planks to make roofs. Others made roofs by weaving together brush and grass and then covering it all with sod. These roofs leaked in the rain.

Settlers pose in front of a sod house in Nebraska in 1887. Pioneers on the plains used plows to work their fields and build their homes.

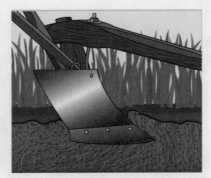

Prairie grass wove a strong tangle of roots into the soil. This made it difficult to cut through the sod with a plow.

In 1837, John Deere invented a plow that could cut through prairie sod.

This picture was taken in Kansas in 1935. The cloud of dust hanging over this farm is soil blown by the wind. **Geography:** *Do you think dust storms could have happened in other parts of the country? Why or why not?*

Soil: The Heart of the Heartland

Soil has always been the Midwest's greatest resource. Settlers, however, didn't always know how to keep the soil in good condition. They plowed up the sod and planted crops. Without the prairie grasses' strong, tangled roots, the soil eroded. In the 1930s, a long dry period added to the problem. Crops failed across the Midwest. In part of Kansas, the soil turned to dust. Strong winds created dust storms. These storms gave a name to this area: the "Dust Bowl." Many farmers lost their land.

Today, people are working to bring back the prairie grasses. Others are learning new ways to farm without hurting the soil. Finding solutions to the problems early settlers faced is still important to life in the Midwest.

Ask Yourself

What would it feel like to be in a dust storm? Would it be different from a rain storm? How would it be the same?

? ? ? ? ? ? ? ? ? ? ? ? ?

Lesson Review

1800	1850	1900	1950

1812
Settlers enter Louisiana Purchase.

1930s
Drought creates "Dust Bowl."

1. **Key Vocabulary:** Use these words to write a paragraph about the Midwest: artifact, archaeology, pioneer, sod.

2. **Focus:** How did Native Americans in the Midwest use their resources?

3. **Focus:** How did Europeans come to the Midwest?

4. **Critical Thinking: Cause and Effect** What effects did farming have on the land of the Midwest? Were these effects good, bad, or both? Explain.

5. **Geography:** How did the climate and plants affect pioneers on the plains?

6. **Citizenship/Writing Activity:** Write an article that tells about how people deal with the challenges of the climate in your state.

LESSON 3

Living and Working in the Midwest

Key Vocabulary

irrigation
raw materials
livestock

Key Places

Springfield, Illinois
St. Paul, Minnesota

Traders work in the Minneapolis Grain Exchange. One of the purposes of these exchanges is to help farmers get the best price for their crops.
Economics: *Why might grain exchanges be in the Midwest?*

Main Idea People in the Midwest use the great natural and human resources of their land in farming and manufacturing.

In a big room in Minneapolis, Minnesota, people are shouting at the top of their lungs. They're waving their arms. Some people are giving hand signals to one another. Others are nodding or shaking their heads. What's happening here? Is this a big party? No! It's the Minneapolis Grain Exchange.

The Minneapolis Grain Exchange is a place where people buy and sell shipments of grain. The people in this room are traders. Their job is to buy and sell crops such as wheat, barley, oats, rye, and corn.

Shouting and arm-waving is just part of the business. The traders use calls and hand signals to ask about prices and make sales. The big room they work in is called a "pit." In the pit of the Minneapolis Grain Exchange, traders buy and sell about a million bushels of grain every day!

Grain and other agricultural products are a huge part of the Midwest's economy. Farmers all over the region send their grain to Minneapolis. With the help of the Grain Exchange, people then turn those products into foods you eat every day.

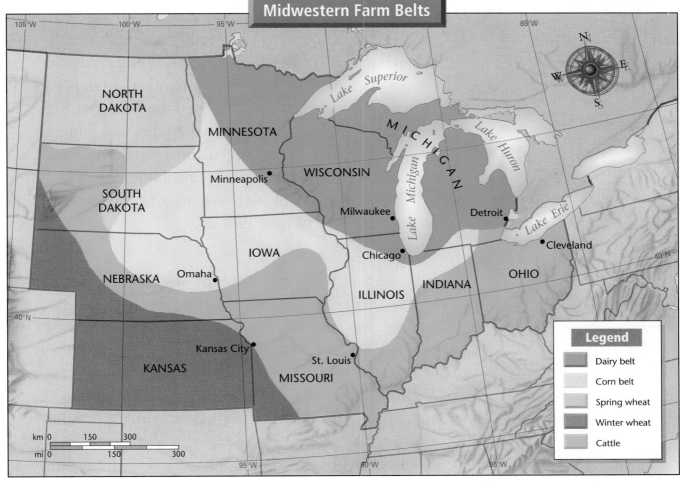

NORTH DAKOTA

MINNESOTA

SOUTH DAKOTA

Minneapolis

WISCONSIN

MICHIGAN

Lake Superior

Lake Huron

Lake Michigan

Milwaukee

Detroit

Lake Erie

Cleveland

IOWA

Chicago

NEBRASKA

Omaha

ILLINOIS

INDIANA

OHIO

Kansas City

St. Louis

KANSAS

MISSOURI

km 0 150 300
mi 0 150 300

Legend
- Dairy belt
- Corn belt
- Spring wheat
- Winter wheat
- Cattle

The map above shows how people farm the land in the Midwest. **Map Skill:** *Identify the Corn Belt, the Dairy Belt, and the Wheat Belts on the map. What do the states in each belt have in common?*

Working in the Midwest

Focus *How do people in the Midwest earn a living?*

Much of the corn, wheat, milk, beef, and pork that people eat in the United States comes from the Midwest. So do many of the cars people drive, as well as other machines. Airplanes and tractors are made here. In the Midwest, growing food or manufacturing useful things is how many people earn their living.

Different Crops, Different Belts

The map above shows major farming areas, or belts, in the Midwest. Which states grow the most corn? They're part of a region called the "Corn Belt." The hot, moist summers and rich soil of this belt make it perfect for growing corn. Most of this corn is used to feed animals.

Cows in the Midwest's Dairy Belt produce almost one-third of the milk in the United States. Milk from these states goes into dairy products such as cheese and ice cream.

Land Use in the Midwest

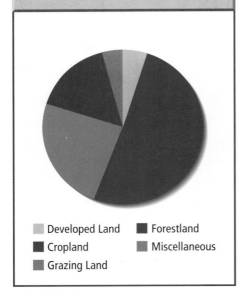

Legend:
- Developed Land
- Cropland
- Grazing Land
- Forestland
- Miscellaneous

This chart shows how land is used in the Midwest.
Chart Skill: *How much land is used for farming?*

Curious Facts

What happens to a mine when no one mines it anymore? Sometimes it is used for storage. One Kansas salt mine is now a home for stamp collections, original Hollywood films, and other valuable things people want to save.

Farmers in the Wheat Belt grow wheat for bread, baked goods, pasta, and other foods. Wheat feeds more people in the United States than any other grain.

Like the early settlers, farmers in the Midwest today need to water their plants. They use pipes and pumps to bring water from creeks, rivers, and aquifers. The process of watering a field artificially is called **irrigation**. Without irrigation, Midwestern farmers couldn't produce the amazing amount of food they do.

Mining and Manufacturing

Farming isn't the only way people in the Midwest make a living. Thousands of people work to mine the region's rich mineral resources. Minnesota and Michigan are centers for iron mining, as described on the next page. Ohio, Illinois, and other states produce coal. Iron and coal are the raw materials for steel. **Raw materials** are resources in their natural form.

Trucks, trains, and ships carry the iron and coal to Illinois, Indiana, and Ohio. Those states are centers of the steel industry. People there turn the raw materials into steel. Then they ship much of the steel to factories.

These mineral resources have helped factories and other industries grow. Many Midwesterners work in these businesses. Around Detroit, Michigan, people use steel to make cars. In Wichita, Kansas, and St. Louis, Missouri, they make airplanes.

Recovering Industries

In the 1970s, manufacturing industries had problems. Not enough people were buying what they made. So companies closed many factories. Workers lost their jobs. People began to call the area around the Great Lakes the "Rust Belt" because machines were rusting in closed factories.

Today, old and new industries are helping the Midwest recover. Cars made in the region are selling well again. People in Indiana cut limestone that is used in many buildings. Ohio sells more automobile tires than any other state. Minnesota and Wisconsin use wood from their forests to supply the paper industry there. People in the Midwest are working hard to keep their region strong both in agriculture and in industry.

Iron Mining in the Midwest

Most of the iron mined in the United States is taken from states around Lake Superior. Mining in this area first began in 1844, when mines were opened in Michigan's Marquette Range.

Today, iron ore is mined from large open pits. Once the iron ore has been taken from the ground, it is separated from unwanted rocks and other minerals. Then it is heated in blast furnaces and turned into iron. Most iron is then made into steel, which is used to make cars and trucks, stoves and refrigerators, and many other things.

The machinery used in iron mining is huge! The bucket on this machine is 10 feet tall and 13 feet wide.

Iron ore is carried away in specially designed railroad cars.

When all the iron ore has been taken from the ground, open-pit mines can leave ugly scars on the landscape. Modern mining companies reclaim, or fix up, the land. This old mine is now home to beavers, deer, ducks, and geese.

Machines dig an open-pit mine in Minnesota.

Celebrating the Midwest

Focus *How do fairs and festivals reflect life in the Midwest?*
The people of the Midwest work hard all year, but they also know how to enjoy themselves. Whether they live in the country or the city, Midwesterners gather to celebrate their region — its businesses, its culture, and even its weather.

Country Fairs

Have you ever been to a country fair? From up on top of the Ferris wheel, you get a great view. Over by the big striped tent, you might see people twirling batons. Down in the stables, a girl is shearing a sheep. Her brother is washing his prize calf.

Welcome to the Illinois State Fair in Springfield, Illinois.

At the Illinois State Fair, people from all over the state show off their best work. One important part of state fairs in the Midwest is livestock judging. **Livestock** are animals people raise on farms. Judges look at them to decide which one is the best example of that kind of animal. People also show off crops such as fruits and vegetables. They display the latest manufacturing products, too. Competing at a fair is a lot of work, but as one woman explains: "We do this for pride."

Other people come to the Illinois State Fair just to have fun. Exciting rides attract many people. Others enjoy the food sold there. They can also watch car races and other events.

It takes a long time to get an animal ready for a livestock show. Would you do it? Here are some steps to follow:

❶ Give your animal good, nutritious food.

❷ Wash and brush it carefully.

❸ Hope for the best when you lead your animal into the ring!

T.J. Pierceall, of New Berlin, Illinois, raises chickens. His chickens won the Junior Grand Champion prize at the Illinois State Fair two years in a row.

City Festivals

Have you ever seen a castle? Maybe you've seen one made of stone. What about a castle made of ice? You'd see an ice castle if you went to the Winter Carnival in St. Paul, Minnesota.

A high point of the festival every year is the ice sculptures. One year sculptors made an ice castle that was 128 feet tall! People also carve dragons and other creatures. On the last night of the Winter Carnival, fireworks fill the sky around the sculptures.

Fairs and festivals are one way midwesterners celebrate the things that make their region special. These gatherings help everyone enjoy living in the Midwest.

How do people in St. Paul, Minnesota, make ice sculptures? They carve them out of blocks of ice *(above right)*. Castles are made with many blocks of ice, some weighing as much as 700 pounds. The blocks are carved and fastened together with "slush cement." Then the castles *(above left)* are lit up with multicolored lights.

Lesson Review

1. **Key Vocabulary:** Use irrigation , raw materials, and livestock in a paragraph about making a living in the Midwest.

2. **Focus:** How do people in the Midwest earn a living?

3. **Focus:** How do fairs and festivals reflect life in the Midwest?

4. **Critical Thinking: Generalize** Which do you think contributes more to the Midwest — farming, mining, or manufacturing? Explain your reasons.

5. **Citizenship:** What kinds of things do you think make people at the Illinois State Fair proud of their state?

6. **Geography/Arts Activity:** Find out about agriculture and industry in your state. Then design a state fair booth to display one of your state's products.

Skills Workshop

Making Special Purpose Maps

Find the Animals

On a clear day in the Midwest, you might see hawks flying overhead, prairie dogs running for cover, or a deer listening to your footsteps in the cool shade of the woods. At night, if you're lucky, you can hear the eerie howl of a coyote. The animals you see will vary, depending on which part of the Midwest you're in.

The map on the next page uses symbols to show where different plants grow in the Midwest. Because the map shows special information, it is called a **special purpose map**. You can show where the animals of the Midwest live by making your own special purpose map.

1 Here's How

- Think about the kind of map you will make. What will it show? Who will use it?

- Find the information to put on your map.

- Trace or sketch the outline of your map on a sheet of paper.

- Create a map legend. Draw symbols that stand for the data on your map. For your map of animals in the Midwest, for example, you might design a symbol for each different animal.

- Draw the symbols on your map in the correct locations.

- Write a title for your map.

Prairie
Butterflies, burrowing owls, prairie dogs

Northern Midwest
Bears, deer, skunks

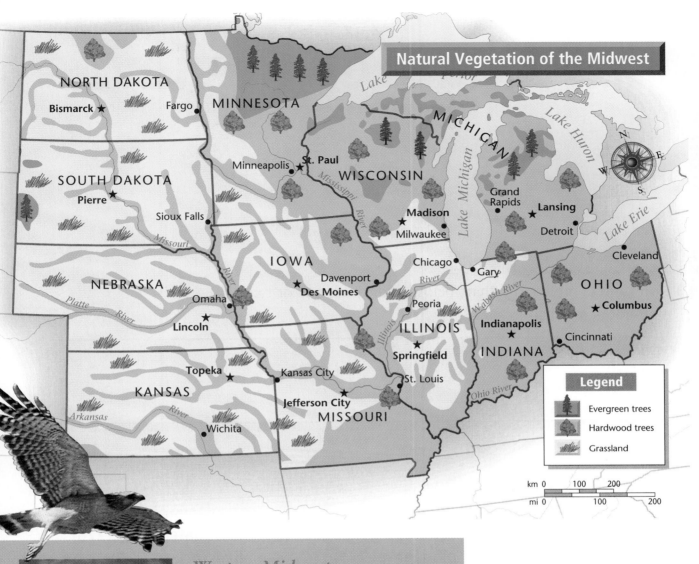

Natural Vegetation of the Midwest

NORTH DAKOTA
Bismarck ★   Fargo ●

MINNESOTA

SOUTH DAKOTA
Pierre ★

Sioux Falls ●
Minneapolis ●   St. Paul ★

WISCONSIN
Madison ★
Milwaukee ●

MICHIGAN
Grand Rapids ●   Lansing ★
Detroit ●

Lake Michigan

Lake Huron

Lake Erie

Cleveland ●

NEBRASKA
Omaha ●
Lincoln ★

IOWA
Davenport ●
Des Moines ★

Chicago ●   Gary ●

OHIO
Columbus ★
Cincinnati ●

Peoria ●

ILLINOIS
Springfield ★

INDIANA
Indianapolis ★

Missouri River
Platte River

KANSAS
Topeka ★
Wichita ●

Kansas City ●
Jefferson City ★
MISSOURI

St. Louis ●

Arkansas River

Mississippi River

Wabash River

Ohio River

Legend
- Evergreen trees
- Hardwood trees
- Grassland

km 0   100   200
mi 0   100   200

Western Midwest
Hawks, jackrabbits, coyotes

Northern Lakes
Beaver, walleye, pike

❷ Think It Through

What would happen if your map had no legend? How would that change how people understand it?

❸ Use It

Draw a map that shows where different animals live in the Midwest. Use the map above to trace your map's boundaries. Use the information on the left for your map.

Chapter Review

Summarizing the Main Idea

1 Copy and complete the chart below, indicating one or two main ideas for each lesson.

Lesson	Main Idea	
Lesson 1		
Lesson 2		
Lesson 3		

Vocabulary

2 Using at least seven of the following words, write a letter encouraging someone to move to the Midwest.

aquifer (p. 261)   archaeology (p. 268)   raw materials (p. 276)

tornado (p. 261)   pioneer (p. 271)   livestock (p. 278)

prairie (p. 262)   sod (p. 272)

artifact (p. 268)   irrigation (p. 276)

Reviewing the Facts

3 What are some of the major landforms and waterways in the Midwest?

4 How does the geography of the Midwest affect the climate there?

5 Who were some of the groups living in the Midwest before the Europeans?

6 Why did European settlers come to the Midwest?

7 Why didn't pioneers settle in the Great Plains at first? Why did they change their minds?

8 What was the "Dust Bowl"? Why did it develop?

9 What kinds of food and other products come from the Midwest?

10 What might you see at a fair or festival in the Midwest?

11 Look at the map on page 281. Where do forests grow? Where are the grasslands? Which states have both?

12 Research industries in one midwestern state. Make a special-purpose map of businesses there. Include a legend.

Geography Skills

13 Look at the map on pages 270–271. How did settlers travel west by water? Why do you think they did this?

14 On an outline map of the Midwest, show some of the areas where Native Americans and European settlers lived.

Critical Thinking

15 Conclude What might have happened if settlers in the 1840s and 1850s knew how to live on the Great Plains? Would they have gone on to Oregon or California or stopped there?

16 Cause and Effect What kinds of businesses buy what iron mines produce? What do you think happened to iron mines when people stopped buying certain products during the 1970s?

Writing: Citizenship and History

17 Citizenship Write a brief essay about job opportunities available to someone moving to the Midwest.

18 History The year is 1870. Your family is moving to Nebraska. Write a letter to someone who already lives there, asking what it is like.

Activities

Economics/Science Activity
Choose an animal that might be shown at a fair in the Midwest. Find out about how this animal is raised. Draw a picture of the animal you have chosen and display what you have learned.

History/Literature Activity
Choose a book about settling the Great Plains. Find some descriptions of what it was like to live there as a pioneer. Read two of these passages aloud to the class.

Internet Option

Check the **Internet Social Studies Center** for ideas on how to extend your theme project beyond your classroom.

THEME PROJECT CHECK-IN

As you plan your booth, make sure you've included what you've learned about the Midwest.
- Which landforms, plants, and animals do you want to show?
- How can you celebrate the people who have lived in the Midwest?
- What can you include to show the jobs midwesterners do?

Chapter Preview: *People, Places, and Events*

1500	1600	1700

Shipping on the Great Lakes

Find out how this ship might travel through the Great Lakes.
Lesson 1, Page 286

The First Cars

Americans loved this new way of getting around. *Lesson 2, Page 290*

Hard at Work

This person works in one of the biggest industries in the Midwest.
Lesson 2, Page 291

The Great Lakes

Main Idea The Great Lakes are a valuable resource that people in the Midwest continue to use as they learn to protect it.

It's 10 o'clock at night. Six miles out on Lake Ontario, two ships move over the dark waters. Aboard one of the ships, people haul in wet, heavy nets. Water sprays and fish scales fly. About 100 pounds of silvery fish land wriggling on the deck. On the second ship, a scientist watches a sonar screen intently. **Sonar** is a machine that finds objects under water by bouncing sound off them. Right now, the scientist is studying an enormous school of alewives, a kind of tiny fish.

These two ships are counting the fish that live in the Great Lakes. If there are too many fish or too few, it upsets the natural balance of the lakes. That can affect other animals and plants — and people's lives.

The Great Lakes offer many natural resources, including fish. Millions of people live near the lakes to use those resources. How do the lakes and the people affect one another?

Key Vocabulary
sonar
recreation

◄ A view of Chicago, Illinois, and Lake Michigan.

1800	1900	2000

Midwestern Dairy Farm

Meet Alyssa Raess and her family on their dairy farm in Wisconsin.
Lesson 3, Page 300

A New Start

Learn how a terrible fire changed Chicago forever.
Lesson 4, Page 308

Midwestern Architecture

People in the Midwest have built some beautiful and unusual buildings. *Lesson 4, Page 310*

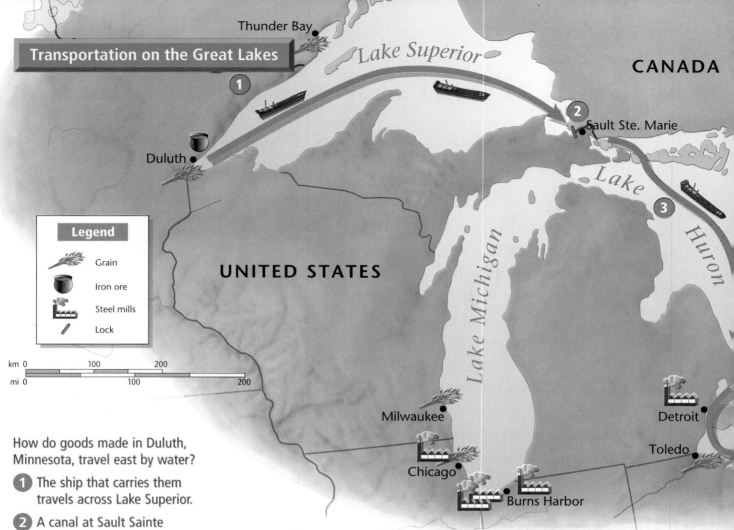

Legend

Grain

Iron ore

Steel mills

Lock

km 0   100   200
mi 0   100   200

How do goods made in Duluth, Minnesota, travel east by water?

1 The ship that carries them travels across Lake Superior.

2 A canal at Sault Sainte Marie (soo saynt muh REE) takes the ship out of Lake Superior.

3 The ship travels across Lake Huron to Detroit, Michigan.

4 The ship goes through Lake Erie and across Lake Ontario.

5 Lake Ontario connects to the St. Lawrence Seaway, which carries the ship to the Atlantic Ocean.

Map Skill: *How might goods travel by water from Detroit to Chicago?*

Cities on the Great Lakes

Focus *Why did major cities develop on the Great Lakes?*

The Great Lakes are the largest lakes in the United States. One-fifth of all the fresh water in the world is contained in lakes Huron, Ontario, Michigan, Erie, and Superior. Some of the biggest cities in the country, such as Chicago and Detroit, have been built on their shores.

Why do so many people live around the Great Lakes? The Midwest has many natural resources. Factories need these resources to make their products. Businesses came to this region partly because the lakes gave them a way to move those natural resources to their factories. The lakes also allowed them to move finished goods to people who might buy them.

One of the most important resources that the Great Lakes offer to businesses in the Midwest is a transportation system. *(See map above.)* As businesses grew, cities grew around them.

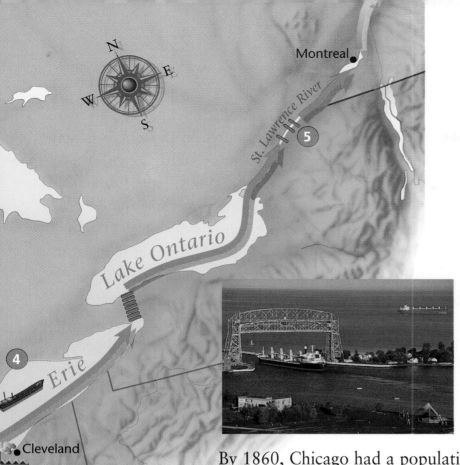

An ocean-going vessel sails under an aerial bridge on the Great Lakes. *(left)*

Because of canals, boats on the Great Lakes can reach the Atlantic Ocean from the Great Lakes. *(above)* The St. Lawrence Seaway is the most important of these waterways. Smaller boats can still use the Erie Canal. Another canal begins in Chicago and connects to the Mississippi.

By 1860, Chicago had a population of 100,000. The number of people grew to 300,000 by 1866 and one million by 1890.

The Great Lakes are a transportation system, however, that people have improved. Originally, large boats could not move between all the lakes. Canals were built to connect Lake Superior with Lake Huron and Lake Ontario with Lake Erie. Canals and rivers connect the lakes with the Atlantic Ocean. The Great Lakes tie the Midwest to the world.

The Changing Lakes

Focus *How has pollution affected the ways people use the Great Lakes?*

Transportation helped industries grow. Growing industries gave people many different ways to earn a living, so more people made their homes near the lakes. Yet these people also wanted to enjoy themselves. They wanted to be able to use the lakes for **recreation** — fun activities like swimming and fishing.

Transportation and industry, however, made it harder to use the Great Lakes for recreation. Boats leaked oil and other

substances into the water. Chemicals from factories poisoned the lakes. Harmful wastes such as these are called pollution.

Pollution spread through the lakes. It hurt plants and fish in the water, as well as birds and animals on shore. For people who fished in the lakes, there was less to catch. The fish they caught were not healthy to eat. By the 1960s, Lake Erie had become so filthy that people who swam in it came out covered in a strange slime that dried to a green powder on their skin.

The United States and Canada passed laws that made companies stop using some of the chemicals that were ending up in the lakes. Industries also had to be more careful about how they dumped their wastes. Today, the lakes are cleaner.

Fish are healthier. Their numbers are growing, and people are fishing on the lakes again. Wally Joe Carlson, a guide who leads fishing trips, is excited about recreation on Lake Erie.

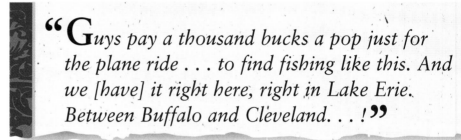

"Guys pay a thousand bucks a pop just for the plane ride . . . to find fishing like this. And we [have] it right here, right in Lake Erie. Between Buffalo and Cleveland. . . !"

Businesses and individuals are still learning to keep the Great Lakes clean. Yet, like other resources in the Midwest, people now believe it is possible both to use the lakes and enjoy them.

Lesson Review

1. **Key Vocabulary:** Use these words in a paragraph about the Great Lakes: **sonar** and **recreation**.

2. **Focus:** Why did major cities develop on the Great Lakes?

3. **Focus:** How has pollution affected the ways people use the Great Lakes?

4. **Critical Thinking: Predict** What would happen if people did nothing about pollution in the Great Lakes?

5. **Citizenship:** Which way of using the Great Lakes is more important, transportation or recreation? Why do you think so?

6. **Geography/Research Activity:** Find out more about one of the waterways that connects the Great Lakes to the Atlantic Ocean. How long is it? What states, cities, or countries does it pass through? Make a map showing what you have learned.

The Automobile Industry

Main Idea The automobile industry developed in the Midwest, and it is still important to the region.

Key Vocabulary
mass production
interchangeable parts
labor force

It's a rainy summer afternoon in Michigan in 1916. All you want to do is go for a ride in your brand-new car, but you can't just run outside and jump in it. Your car doesn't have a roof, and you're going to get wet. So you put on a cap and pull on a long coat called a duster. Most of the roads are just dirt, and you'll also need goggles to protect your eyes.

The roads are dirt except when it's raining. Then they're mud. You'll be lucky if you don't get stuck. So bring tools to get your car out of a mudhole: a jack, tire chains, a tow rope, and a pulley. In 1916, motoring may be fun, but it isn't easy.

The First Cars off the Line

Focus *How did the auto industry grow in the Midwest?*
The Midwest wasn't the home of the first car ever made. Europe was. It wasn't the home of the first car built in the United States. That was Massachusetts. The Midwest, however, was home to the industry that put a car in almost everyone's garage.

When cars were first invented, only rich people could afford them. Highly skilled workers assembled — put together — the entire car themselves. One person did all the work for each car before starting on the next one. It took a long time to make cars this way, which was why cars were so expensive.

A woman wears some of the clothes people needed to drive in the first cars.
History: *Why did drivers in the early 1900s need special clothes?*

Henry Ford and his son, Edsel, sit in an early Model T.

An Affordable Automobile

In Detroit, Michigan, a man named Henry Ford believed ordinary people should be able to buy cars. To produce cars everyone could afford, he had to find a way to make them quickly.

Other industries were using a process called mass production. **Mass production** is a system for making large amounts of a product in a short time. It uses **interchangeable parts,** pieces made to fit into each car without being changed.

Ford improved on this system. He introduced the assembly line. An assembly line uses many people to make one car. Each worker has a small job to do. They stand still and the car moves toward them. They each do their job when the car gets to them — adding a door, for example — and then the car moves on to the next worker. This continues until all the parts are added and the car is finished. *(See diagram below.)*

A Car on the Assembly Line

Starting the Body In today's factories, people work with robots. A robot welds pieces of the body into place — the floor, roof, and sides.

Attaching a Transponder A worker attaches a radio that helps keep track of the car as it moves through the factory.

Painting the Car Paint is sprayed on the body. The transponder tells workers and robots what colors to use.

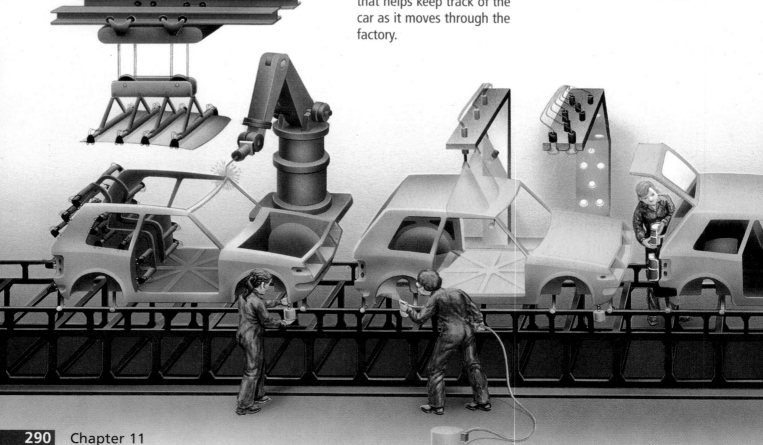

In 1908, Ford began selling the Model T, for $850. By 1927, he had brought the price down to $290. Suddenly many people could afford cars.

Other companies started using Ford's ideas. By 1920, there were over 8 million cars on the road. These cars were easier to use and more comfortable than before. They had roofs, so no one had to wear special clothes. Roads also improved. Cars changed how people lived. They could shop far from home. They could live in the country and drive to work in the city.

Effects of the Auto Industry

Focus *How has the auto industry affected the Midwest?*

As the auto industry grew, so did Detroit. The assembly lines needed workers. Word of new jobs spread. During the 1920s, people flocked to the city from all over the United States. Many people migrated from the South, including African Americans.

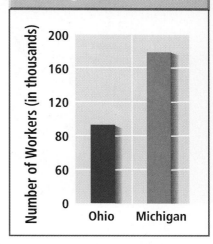

Auto Workers in Michigan and Ohio

This chart shows the number of auto workers in two midwestern states. **Chart Skill:** *Which of these states depends most on the auto industry?*

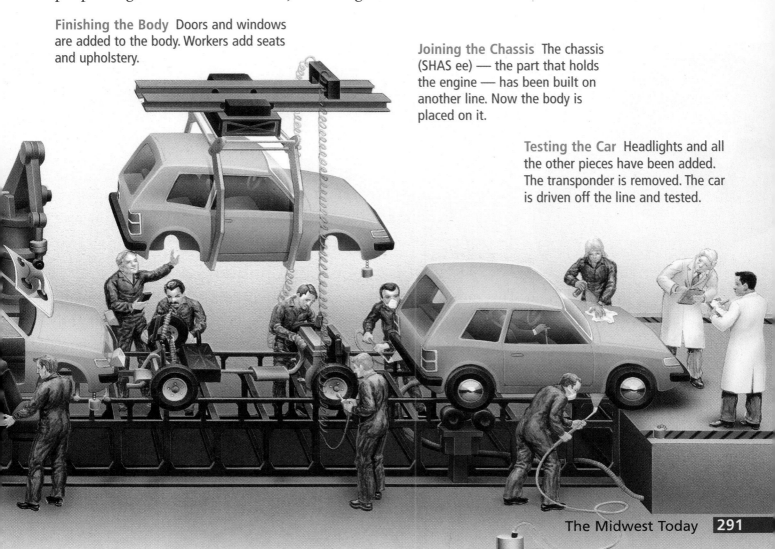

Finishing the Body Doors and windows are added to the body. Workers add seats and upholstery.

Joining the Chassis The chassis (SHAS ee) — the part that holds the engine — has been built on another line. Now the body is placed on it.

Testing the Car Headlights and all the other pieces have been added. The transponder is removed. The car is driven off the line and tested.

The Detroit Sound

In 1959, a man named Berry Gordy, Jr., started a record company in Detroit. Born and raised there, Gordy once worked on the assembly line in a Ford factory. He called his company "Motown," after the nickname for Detroit.

Motown had big hits in the 1960s and 1970s, with groups such as the Supremes and the Jackson Five. When asked to describe his company and the musicians who recorded with him, Gordy said: "We haven't forgotten where we came from. . . . It's not just climbing up out of poverty, escaping from it — it's being young, creating, doing things with dignity. It's pride."

Berry Gordy, Jr., and Mary Wilson, one of the Supremes, posed together on the Hollywood Walk of Fame in 1994. *(above)*

The Temptations were one of the groups that recorded hits with Motown Records. *(right)*

By 1930, there were almost five times as many people in Detroit as there had been in 1900. It became a large, flourishing city. In honor of the industry that supported it, Detroit was nicknamed "Motor City" or "Motor Town."

The Auto Industry Faces Challenges

This industry was important not only to Michigan but to many midwestern states. This is still true today. Most of the iron and steel from Ohio and Illinois goes into cars. The jobs of the people who work in these businesses depend on the auto industry.

Changes in the auto industry affect the economy of the entire Midwest. In the 1970s and early 1980s, fewer cars were produced because Americans bought more cars made in other countries. Auto makers closed factories. Companies that made products used in cars also closed. Many people lost their jobs.

Then, in the 1980s, American auto manufacturers changed the way they designed and sold their cars. So more Americans wanted to buy them, and the industry recovered somewhat. Today, auto plants in the area around Detroit are busy. These factories are now producing as many as 400,000 brand-new automobiles a year — 60 to 80 an hour.

It takes engineers, designers, computer experts, mechanics, assembly-line workers, and others to make a car. This supply of workers is called a **labor force.** The auto industry has helped create a labor force that is well trained and educated. Dennis Donovan, a business expert, talks about midwestern workers:

> **"T**he Great Lakes states have a lot to offer. The region's number one asset [advantage] is its quality labor force."

Auto companies from other countries have built factories in the Midwest to make use of the skills these workers have. These workers also draw high-technology companies and other manufacturing businesses to the Midwest.

The Midwest is less dependent on auto making today than it has been. Yet as midwesterners look ahead, they know their region would not be the same without the industry that first made cars affordable. Neither would the rest of the country!

Biography

Elijah McCoy

Elijah McCoy (1844–1929) invented a "lubricating cup" for adding oil to large engines. In 1920, he started his own company in the Detroit area. Devices based on his lubricating cup are still used in machinery today. "The real McCoy" is an expression based on his invention.

Lesson Review

1 **Key Vocabulary:** Write about the auto industry, using these terms: mass production, interchangeable parts.

2 **Focus:** How did the auto industry grow in the Midwest?

3 **Focus:** How has the auto industry affected the Midwest?

4 **Critical Thinking: Predict** What if cars had never been invented? How would your life be different?

5 **Geography:** List three places that are connected to your town or city by major roads. What would your area be like without these roads?

6 **Citizenship/Research Activity:** Find one business in your community that depends on the auto industry. Interview someone who works there about his or her job, and write a report about what that person does.

★ CITIZENSHIP ★

Making Decisions

What Is Good Business?

Have you ever wondered what it takes to own and run a successful business? Our economic system of free enterprise means that everyone has a chance to run a business. Here's how one midwestern woman used her skills to run a trucking company.

Case Study

A Successful Trucking Company

Edith Gorter never expected to run a trucking company. She designed dresses and ran a fabric shop for six years. When her husband's father died, she took over his trucking business.

Edith had to borrow money from banks and people to buy more trucks. She bought good trucks. "If you spend a little bit more, you'll save in the long run," her father-in-law always said. Edith spends money carefully and wisely. She makes sure her drivers deliver on time. She treats her drivers and customers well.

Today Edith has hundreds of customers and owns almost 2 million dollars' worth of trucks and equipment. She pats herself on the back sometimes. "If you really want to do something, you can," she says. "Hard work, careful planning, and good personal relations are important. Some of work should be fun, too."

Take Action

What would you do? You own your own business. Your business has just won the U.S. Business of the Year award. A television station wants to interview you on its morning news program. You need to get ready!

1 In small groups, decide what your business is. Do you make something? Do you provide a service? Give your business a name. Decide who your customers are and where they live.

2 Decide why your business has been awarded this prize. What do you do especially well? Make up a motto for your business.

3 Write down what you think are the three most important qualities a business can have. Be ready to explain how your company shows each of these qualities.

4 Prepare and present a television interview for the class. If you can, videotape it.

Tips for Making Decisions

- Make sure you know what your goals are.
- Think about the steps you need to reach those goals.
- Come up with several ideas and then decide which works best.
- Avoid taking unnecessary risks.
- Remember that hurrying often leads to mistakes.

Research Activity

Learn more about what it takes for a business to succeed. Find a relative, friend, neighbor, or business person in your community who runs his or her own business. Ask that person how the business works. What is that person especially proud of in the business? Write a list presenting that person's guidelines for success.

Life on a Farm in the Midwest

Main Idea Farmers in the Midwest use science, technology, and business knowledge to make a living from the land.

Tromp through the muddy soil. Reach up, push the leaves aside, find the tassel on top of the cornstalk. A quick pull and it's off. Throw it away and move on.

For thousands of midwestern kids, this is their summer job. They spend eight hours pulling the tassels off cornstalks. "It was dirty work," said Bret Czys, age 15. "If you didn't want to get cut up by the corn you had to wear long sleeves. I always took a long shower after I got home."

Companies that grow corn to sell for seed try to develop new kinds of corn. In order to do this, tassels on some of the corn must be taken off. So they pay young people to do it. These kids learn at least one thing about farming. Running a farm is hard work.

On some farms, students walk between the rows to take off the tassles on the top of corn plants. On farms like the one shown below, people are carried in baskets attached to tractors.

Modern Farming

Focus *How do people make a living on midwestern farms?*
In the last chapter, you read that different parts of the Midwest are good for different kinds of farms. Depending on the climate and soil of their area, farmers might grow corn,

soybeans, or wheat. They also grow more unusual crops, such as the spearmint that is used in chewing gum. Other farmers raise livestock, such as cattle, pigs, or sheep. The crops they grow, such as hay or corn, are harvested to feed their animals.

On all of these farms, one thing is the same. Whether they raise crops or animals, farmers have to earn money from what they produce. Farming is a kind of business.

Growing Crops and Raising Livestock

Just like other business people, farmers first need a product to sell. They have to know how to grow crops or raise animals.

Livestock farmers know how to feed their animals a balanced diet. They can also help prevent diseases. Other farmers have the same kind of knowledge about crops. Crops take their food from the soil. This food is called **nutrients**, and farmers often add fertilizer to the soil. Fertilizer contains the nutrients plants need. Because certain insects harm crops, some farmers use **pesticides**, or chemicals that kill insects.

Farmers also know a lot about machinery. Modern farming often involves large, complicated machines, such as tractors and harvesting machines called **combines**. Many farmers have computers to keep track of what their crops need to grow. Some have computers in their combines to record how much they harvest from each part of their farm.

Curious Facts

Did you ever wonder why school lasts only nine months a year? It's because back in the days when most people were farmers, children had to work in the fields during the summer months.

Planting and Harvesting Corn

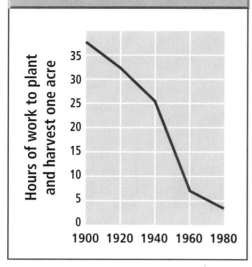

Machines have made farming easier and faster. This chart shows how farmers today have less work to do on each acre of their farm than they once did. **Chart Skill:** *When did the amount of hours decrease the most? Why do you think this happened?*

Below are some of the crops that are grown on farms in the Midwest. Do any look familiar?

The Economics of Farming

After harvesting their fields, farmers often wait for the best price before they sell their crop. Corn, wheat, soybeans, and other crops are sold in grain exchanges in cities such as Minneapolis or Chicago. Farmers keep track of the prices in these markets by reading the newspaper or listening to the radio. They sell their crops when the price is right. Some farmers use computers to help them make these decisions, too.

All this machinery farmers use costs a lot. Farmland can also be very expensive. Do you know how much money the average farmer has put into his farming operation? Around a million dollars! Many farmers borrow money from banks, just like other business people, to buy land and machinery. This is another reason that modern midwestern farmers have to be good at managing their money.

Agricultural Companies Change Farming

In recent years, farming has become even more of a business in the Midwest. Many small farms have been bought by large agricultural companies called **agribusinesses**.

Agribusiness is one reason why the average size of farms is growing and the number of farms is shrinking. In 1940, there were six million small farms in the United States. Now there are two million large farms. These changes have made fewer farms available in the Midwest. This makes it harder for individuals and their families to run their own farms.

Rye

Wheat

Millet

A Farming Season

What happens on a farm between spring and autumn? For farmers growing most crops, the season starts in April or May, once the snow is gone and the fields are dry enough to drive machinery over them. It ends in October or November.

1 Plowing The first job is preparing the soil. Farmers use a plow to loosen it so plants can grow more easily.

2 Planting Planting is done with a machine called a seed drill. It makes holes in the soil, drops in seeds, and covers them back up again.

3 Spraying A sprayer adds fertilizer to feed the plants and pesticides to protect them from certain insects.

4 Harvesting A combine cuts and processes the grain and then sends it pouring into wagons or trucks.

5 Storage The crop is stored in a grain elevator until the farmer is ready to sell it.

Milking Alyssa's father, Robert, has to wake up very early to milk the cows.

Feeding Feeding the animals is one of Alyssa's jobs after school.

This is the schedule Alyssa and her family keep. **Economics:** *How is it like yours? How is it different?*

Alyssa feeds one of her family's sheep *(below)*.

The Farm Family

Focus *What is life like for farm families in the Midwest?*

Many families in the Midwest have been farming the land for generations. Because they do different work, families on these farms live differently from one another. Yet whatever a farm family needs to do, just about everyone helps out. There are crops to harvest, weeds to pull, animals to feed, or fences to repair. Even small children, younger than you, can help. Let's see how one family in Wisconsin takes care of their farm.

A Wisconsin Dairy Farm

Alyssa Raess lives on a dairy farm in Platteville, Wisconsin. She is 11 years old, and she lives with her mother, father, and her younger brother, Trevor.

The family has about 40 cows. They also have pigs, sheep, chickens, cats, and a dog. It takes a lot of work to take care of all those animals! Alyssa and Trevor help feed them. They also give them water and help clean the places where they sleep.

Alyssa's father, Robert, wakes up at 5:00 every morning to milk the cows. "Sometimes I'll go up and help," Alyssa says. At 7:30, Alyssa catches her school bus. She helps feed the animals when she gets home from school at 4:00.

End of the Day Alyssa walks home with her father when their chores are done.

Homework Alyssa helps her brother, Trevor, do his homework.

> **"T**here's a lot of kids in my class who haven't lived on a farm, ever. It's fun! You get to help out a lot. You get to pet animals all the time. It's really quiet.**"**

All farm families have to work together to get everything done. Still, it is not easy for family farms to succeed. "Small family farms are worth saving," says Ronald L. Rosmann, an Iowa farmer. Alyssa and her family agree with him, as do many people in the Midwest and throughout the country.

Lesson Review

1 **Key Vocabulary:** Use the following words to write a paragraph about farming: **nutrient, pesticide, combine, agribusiness.**

2 **Focus:** How do people make a living on midwestern farms?

3 **Focus:** What is life like for farm families in the Midwest?

4 **Critical Thinking: Conclude** Do you agree that small family farms are worth saving? Explain your answer.

5 **Theme: Prairies and Plains** What geographic features of the Midwest make the region good for farming? What might make it difficult?

6 **Citizenship/Writing Activity:** What if you lived on a farm? What kind of farm would it be? Write a journal entry describing all the things you might do in one day.

NONFICTION

CORN BELT HARVEST

By Raymond Bial

After rice and wheat, corn is the third most important grain crop in the world. Half of all the corn in the world is grown in the United States, and three-fourths of that is grown in the region called the Corn Belt. The Corn Belt stretches across the Midwest. Each fall the golden harvest is ready to be gathered and stored.

During the autumn harvest, ripe corn fills the plains. As you travel up and down the roads, you can see ears nodding on the stalks or being snatched by the teeth of the combines. You can see the shelled corn pouring out of the combines in a steady stream of bright yellow or heaped up on the backs of trucks lumbering down the country roads.

Fitted onto the front of the combine, cornheads guide the stalks into rollers, which gather, shuck, and shell the corn.

Late in the afternoon, the light of the setting sun gleams on the stalks.

The combine quickly fills with shelled corn, leaving crushed stalks and leaves scattered on the ground behind it.

Usually, the operator is able to make one "pass," or trip, down the rows and back again before the combine is filled with corn. The combine is then drawn alongside a truck or a wagon, its unloading auger rotated over the wagon, and the load of corn transferred.

It takes only a few minutes to transfer corn from the combine to a truck or wagon. Then the operator steers the combine down the rows again.

The combining continues until the trucks and wagons are heaped with shelled corn. Then the corn is transported to a grain elevator, where it will be stored.

Always located beside railroad tracks, modern grain elevators rise up in many small towns throughout the Midwest. With their strong, vertical lines, they appear out of place on the plains, where most everything, notably the distant horizon, tends toward the horizontal. You can ride in a small cage to the top of the elevators, where you can see for miles across the flat land.

This combine harvests eight rows of corn at a time. Others may harvest as few as four or as many as twelve.

auger
a piece of equipment shaped like a drill

Standing at the edge of the field, these wagons will soon be on their way to the elevator.

accelerate:
to speed up

Elevators are groups of cylinders made of poured concrete. When they are constructed, the work continues nonstop until all the concrete is poured to avoid any seams or cracks in each cylinder.

Most elevators are part of large companies which may own four or five to as many as thirty or forty elevators in a particular region.

As the harvest accelerates, trucks begin to line up at the elevator office. Each of the loaded vehicles is weighed at the scale in front of the office. The weight of the wagon or truck is subtracted from the total weight to determine the weight of the load of corn.

While the trucks are on the scales, an arm is dipped into the corn and a small sample vacuumed through a pipe and into a small box inside the elevator office.

The sample of incoming corn is dropped into a pan. It is then weighed and its moisture content determined. If the moisture content is 20 percent or higher, the farmer will be charged a drying fee to bring it down to 15.5 percent.

The concrete bins at the elevator stand ready to receive the harvest of corn.

After the corn is weighed and a moisture sample is taken, the trucks move down the road to the elevator storage area.

At the elevator storage areas, the corn is dumped into a pit covered with a grate. It is then drawn into the tall elevators by augers through a complex system of pipes.

Throughout the day, one load of corn after another is dumped into the pits. Trucks and wagons often must line up to wait their turn. There is barely enough time for workers to sweep up around the pit before the next truck pulls up.

As the truck bed is tilted backward, the corn spills into a pit. In just a minute or two, the truck is empty and heading back to the fields for more corn.

Meet the Author

Raymond Bial has created many photographic books for children. Two of his other books, *Portrait of a Farm Family* and *County Fair,* are also about rural life in America.

Additional Books to Read

**Prairie Songs
by Pam Conrad
This is a story about the trials and
joys of homesteading.**

**Heartland, by Diane Siebert
illustrated by Wendell Minor
Read poetry and see paintings about the Midwest.**

Response Activities

1. Sequence Events: List the steps that are part of the corn harvest by answering questions such as the following: How does the corn travel from the farm to the railroad? Where is corn stored after it leaves the farm?

2. Informative: Write a Grocery List Write a shopping list of foods that are made from corn or that include corn.

3. History: Illustrate Farming Then and Now: Use what you learned in Chapter 10, Lesson 2 (p. 272) to draw a picture of an early settler's farm. Use *Corn Belt Harvest* to draw a picture of farming today.

The Architecture of the Midwest

Main Idea Midwestern architecture has influenced the way people design buildings throughout the country and the world.

Have you ever walked through a neighborhood and noticed how the houses don't all look the same? Have you ever noticed the same thing about offices in a city? Buildings look different because people use them differently. They also look different because people have different ideas about what makes a building beautiful. Sometimes, all this variety can tell you something about your region.

The art of designing beautiful and useful buildings is called **architecture.** Months before the first worker starts constructing a home or office, an architect draws sketches and makes a model of the building. Like artists, architects have visions of how buildings should look. These architects' ideas can be shaped by the geography and history of their region.

Frank Lloyd Wright *(right)* was an architect famous for houses he designed to fit in with the midwestern prairie. *(below)*

Prairie Houses

Focus *How did the geography of the Midwest shape a style of architecture?*

One of America's greatest architects was Frank Lloyd Wright. Born in Wisconsin, he spent much of his life in the Midwest.

When Wright was a young child, his mother believed he would be a famous architect. So she taught him things she thought an architect needed to know. She gave him blocks in simple shapes such as triangles, rectangles, squares, and circles. Then she showed him how to use these blocks to make buildings. By doing this, his mother taught him to see architecture in a special way: as combinations of simple shapes.

When Wright was older, he worked on a Wisconsin farm and admired what he saw — trees and flowers, flat fields and rolling hills. He used to look for the simple shapes in these natural things and wonder how they might fit into a building.

As an adult, Wright wanted the shapes of the buildings he created to match the shapes he found in nature. He believed that architecture should be connected to the land around it.

Wright used long, level lines to design prairie houses such as the Robie House in Chicago. *(below)* This was so his houses looked like the flat prairies. Also, he planned them so they spread out across the ground, rather than rise up, and he added gently sloping roofs. This low, sweeping shape matched the shape of the land.

Wright also loved the prairies: "We of the Middle West are living on the prairie. The prairie has a beauty of its own and we should recognize and accentuate [emphasize] this natural beauty, its quiet level." Wright created many kinds of buildings, but he is most famous for his houses. To some people, his houses seemed to grow out of the land around them. He called them "prairie houses." Other architects liked his ideas. They built their own prairie houses. The suburbs around Chicago and across the country filled with houses built in this same low, flat style.

Wright designed many of the decorations for his homes, including rugs, furniture, and windows. He based the patterns for many of his stained glass windows on plants that grew on the prairie.

Lakeside Skyscrapers

Focus *How did architects in Chicago change the way people around the world built tall buildings?*

On October 8, 1871, a terrible fire broke out in Chicago. The fire roared through the city. Once it was over, as many as 18,000 buildings were destroyed. Chicago was in ruins.

The fire was a disaster, but it was also an opportunity. Many architects from the East came to help rebuild the city. Louis Sullivan was one of these architects. When he stepped off the train in 1873, he could see the ruined city. All those empty spaces that had to be filled with new buildings! He became so excited that he shouted, "This is the place for me!" Like Sullivan, many architects saw a great future for themselves in Chicago. The fire gave them a chance to try new ideas.

To Reach the Sky

One new idea architects tried in Chicago was the skyscraper. A **skyscraper** is a very tall building. In the 1880s, "very tall" meant 10 floors. (See the illustration on the next page.) Before that, almost no buildings had more than five. Why did buildings start to grow? Chicago needed more space for people. Yet the downtown area was surrounded on three sides by water. There was not much land for buildings. Skyscrapers allowed architects to put more people on smaller pieces of land.

The Reliance Building

Finished in 1895, the Reliance Building was designed by two different architects — John Root and Charles B. Atwood. It was one of the most important early skyscrapers built in Chicago, and it still stands today.

Outside Walls Walls attached to the building's steel skeleton are called "curtain walls."

Elevators Tall buildings wouldn't have been much use if people couldn't get to the floors at the top. A man named Elisha Otis built a safe elevator, so no one had to climb all those stairs.

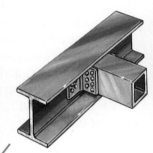

Steel Framework New methods of joining steel beams made it possible to support tall buildings with a skeleton of steel.

Chicago Windows Windows like this, with glass in three parts, let in lots of light along crowded city streets.

Lake Point Tower This building was completed in 1968. The architects were G.D. Schipporeit and J.C. Heinrich.

John Hancock Center This skyscraper has 100 floors. Completed in 1970, it was designed by Bruce Graham and Fazlur Khan.

Chicago Skyline

Important skyscrapers have been built in Chicago throughout the 20th century. Above are some of the skyscrapers that are a part of the city's architecture today. **Arts:** *Which building do you think is most beautiful? Which is most useful?*

New methods of construction and new inventions helped people make buildings taller. Large buildings are very heavy, and for hundreds of years they had been designed so all this weight was supported by their walls. This meant that the walls at the bottom had to be extremely thick. This was expensive. It also used up the space skyscrapers were supposed to save.

In the 1860s, Henry Bessemer invented a process for making steel cheaply. Engineers learned to design buildings supported by steel beams. These beams became the skeleton of the structure. Walls were fastened to them like a skin. The Home and Insurance Building in Chicago used this new method. Finished in 1884, it is considered the first modern skyscraper.

Making Tall Buildings Beautiful

Sullivan wanted to do more than make skyscrapers people could use. He wanted to make them beautiful, too — like "the branching oak" and "the drifting clouds," as he once wrote.

Sullivan was the first architect to create a distinct kind of beauty for skyscrapers. He planned the **facade**, or front walls, of his tall buildings to emphasize their sweeping height. He used large windows to make the inside brighter, and he decorated the buildings with designs based on the shapes of plants.

Marina City Bertrand Goldberg designed these unusual towers. They were completed in 1962.

Sears Tower The tallest building in the world, this was also designed by Graham and Khan. It was completed in 1974.

Then & Now

In 1882, the tallest building in Chicago was the Montauk Block. It was 10 floors and 130 feet tall.

Today, the tallest building there is the Sears Tower. It's 110 floors — 1,454 feet tall. Ten Montauk Blocks wouldn't stack up that high!

The history and geography of the Midwest moved architecture in new directions. A modern architect named Cesar Pelli has said that the development of skyscrapers in Chicago was "The first time that an American architecture led the world." Do you know who Sullivan's most famous student was? Frank Lloyd Wright, whose designs for houses changed the way people thought about their homes. The open spaces and fast-growing cities of the Midwest inspired architects like these to try new designs. Their ideas spread throughout the world.

Lesson Review: Geography

1. **Key Vocabulary:** Write a post card from Chicago using these words: **architecture, skyscraper, facade.**

2. **Focus:** How did the geography of the Midwest shape a style of architecture?

3. **Focus:** How did architects in Chicago change the way people around the world built tall buildings?

4. **Critical Thinking: Cause and Effect** Which was more important to the development of skyscrapers: steel or elevators? Explain your answer.

5. **Citizenship:** Describe the architecture of your school. How do people use the building? What parts are beautiful?

6. **Geography/Art Activity:** What geographic features is your region known for? Hills? Forests? Design a house that looks like one of these features. Explain how it fits your region.

Skills Workshop

Organizing Information in Interviews

Asking Questions

Architect Bertrand Goldberg designed Chicago's Marina Towers like two giant corncobs.

How can a building look like a giant corncob or blend with the prairie? Who designed the buildings that you see every day? Where did they get their ideas? If you want to learn more about architecture, you can read books and magazines or visit some buildings. You can also interview an architect. In an **interview**, you can ask questions to learn information. When you interview someone, don't count on just sitting down and chatting. Before you begin, you'll need to get organized.

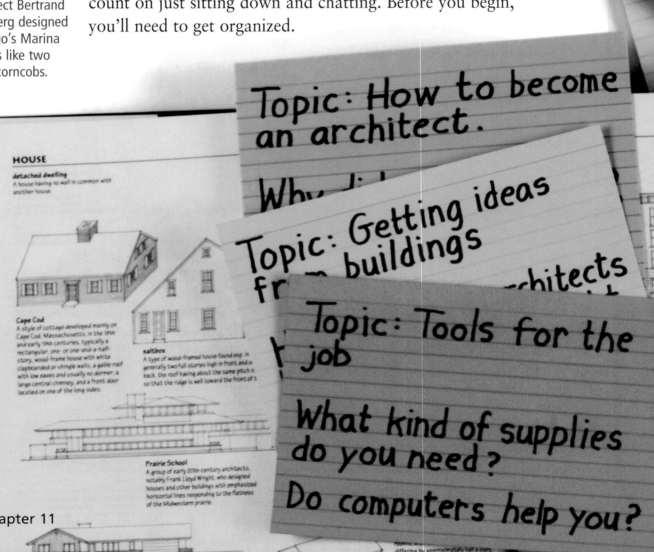

HOUSE

detached dwelling
A house having no wall in common with another house.

Cape Cod
A style of cottage developed mainly on Cape Cod, Massachusetts, in the 18th and early 19th centuries, typically a rectangular, one- or one-and-a-half-story, wood-frame house with white clapboarded or shingle walls, a gable roof with low eaves and usually no dormer, a large central chimney, and a front door located on one of the long sides.

saltbox
A type of wood-framed house found mainly in New England, generally two full stories high in front and one in back, the roof having about the same pitch in both directions so that the ridge is well toward the front of the house.

Prairie School
A group of early 20th-century architects, notably Frank Lloyd Wright, who designed houses and other buildings with emphasized horizontal lines responding to the flatness of the Midwestern prairie.

Topic: How to become an architect.

Why di...

Topic: Getting ideas from buildings

...chitects...

Topic: Tools for the job

What kind of supplies do you need?

Do computers help you?

1 Here's How

Before the Interview

- Decide the purpose of your interview. What do you want to find out?

- Think of a topic, for example, *How to become an architect.*

- Write each topic on several note cards.

- On each card, write a question that is related to that topic: for example, *Where do you get your ideas for a design?*

- Contact the person you want to interview. Ask if he or she would like to be interviewed. Explain the kinds of questions you will ask. Arrange for a convenient time to meet with that person.

- Plan to bring a pen, a note pad, and your note cards. If you can, and that person agrees, bring a tape recorder and tapes.

During the Interview

- Think of new questions to ask about each topic. Listen carefully to the answers.

- Repeat the answers in your own words to be sure you have understood correctly.

- Take notes on your cards.

After the Interview

- Write a thank-you note to the person you interviewed.

- Review your notes. If you used a tape recorder, listen to the tapes and write down important quotes.

- Write a summary of your interview, using your notes.

2 Think It Through

How does organizing your questions ahead of time help you conduct a better interview?

3 Use It

Choose someone whom you would like to interview about the kind of work that he or she does.

1. Plan the interview, writing down the questions you will ask.

2. Interview the person, taking careful notes.

3. Write a summary of the important things you have learned from the interview.

mew
A street having small apartments converted from stables. Also, **mews.**

row house
One of a row of houses having at least one sidewall in common with a neighboring dwelling, and usually uniform or nearly uniform plans, fenestration, and architectural treatment.

penthouse
An apartment or residence on the top floor or roof of a building, often set back from the outer walls and opening onto a terrace.

duplex apartment
An apartment with rooms on two connected floors. Also called **duplex.**

flat
An apartment or suite of rooms on one floor forming a residence.

walk-up
An apartment above the ground floor in a building that has no elevator.

Chapter Review

Summarizing the Main Idea

1 Copy and complete the chart below, indicating a main idea and one or two facts about it.

Lesson	Main Idea	Facts
Lesson 1	*The Great Lakes are a valuable resource.*	*They are used for transportation and recreation.*
Lesson 2		
Lesson 3		
Lesson 4		

Vocabulary

2 Using at least 10 of the following terms, write a magazine article about the Midwest today.

sonar (p. 285)

recreation (p. 287)

mass production (p. 290)

interchangeable parts (p. 290)

labor force (p. 293)

nutrient (p. 297)

pesticide (p. 297)

combine (p. 297)

agribusiness (p. 298)

architecture (p. 306)

skyscraper (p. 308)

facade (p. 310)

Reviewing the Facts

3 Why do so many people live around the Great Lakes?

4 How are people working to keep the Great Lakes clean?

5 How did the assembly line help make cars available to more people?

6 Why is Detroit called "Motor City"?

7 How is the auto industry part of the economy of the Midwest?

8 What are some of the things about business that a farmer must know?

9 What kinds of tasks do people in farm families do?

10 What kind of houses did Frank Lloyd Wright build?

11 How did architects rebuild Chicago after the fire of 1871?

12 What should you do before interviewing someone? Why is it so important to be organized?

13 Talk to someone who has been to several parts of the Midwest. Interview them about the region. What states and cities did they see? How do people make a living there?

Geography Skills

14 Look at the map on pages 286–287. How do you think the Great Lakes have helped the auto industry grow?

15 Write a description of what you might see if you were flying over the Midwest in an airplane. What do you find the most interesting?

Critical Thinking

16 **Conclude** What are the benefits of an assembly line? What are the disadvantages? Would you like working on an assembly line? Why or why not?

17 **Predict** What if the Chicago fire had never happened? Do you think skyscrapers would have developed in that city? Explain your answer.

Writing: Citizenship and History

18 **Citizenship** What natural resources are in your area? Interview someone who uses these resource for business or recreation. Write a summary of the interview.

19 **History** Write a journal entry as if you were an architect coming to Chicago after the fire of 1871. What plans do you have for the city? What new ideas will you try?

Activities

Cultures/Music Activity
Listen to some songs recorded on Motown Records. What do the words tell you about the singer who recorded each song? Choose two songs and play them for the class. Describe what you have learned about the people singing.

Economics/Science Activity
Get together with a group and decide on something you all want to make. Gather the materials you need. Then create an assembly line to produce it. How many can you make? How quickly can you make them?

Internet Option

Check the **Internet Social Studies Center** for ideas on how to extend your theme project beyond your classroom.

THEME PROJECT CHECK-IN

Look over your booths. Make sure you have included what you have learned about life in the Midwest today.
- What do you want visitors to the fair to know about the Great Lakes?
- How can you show all of the things that happen on a farm?
- What can you include to reflect the automobile industry?
- Did you show any important buildings? Which ones?

*"The West is color. . . .
the colors of earth
and sunlight and
ripeness. . . ."*

Jessamyn West

· THEME ·

From Desert to Tropics

> **The Willamette Valley is between two mountain ranges. Our crops grow because of the rain and rich soil.**
>
> **Amber Holifield, Fourth Grade**
> **Albany, OR**

The West is the largest region of the United States. It stretches from the Great Plains into the Pacific Ocean, and includes Alaska and Hawaii. What are the land and climate of the West like? That depends on where you are! The West's environments range from desert to tropics — and nearly everything in between. As you will read, the West is a place of beauty and variety.

Theme Project

Make a Guidebook

Write a guidebook to help people visit all the different environments and unusual places in the West.

- Describe the climates and landforms of the West and the places where people live and work in the region.
- Find photographs and draw pictures of the places you describe.
- Include quotes from westerners about their region.

RESEARCH: Choose one of the climate regions of the West. Include information about its plants and animals in your guidebook.

◄ A rainbow follows a storm in Ecola State Park, Oregon.

UNIT 6

WHEN & WHERE
ATLAS

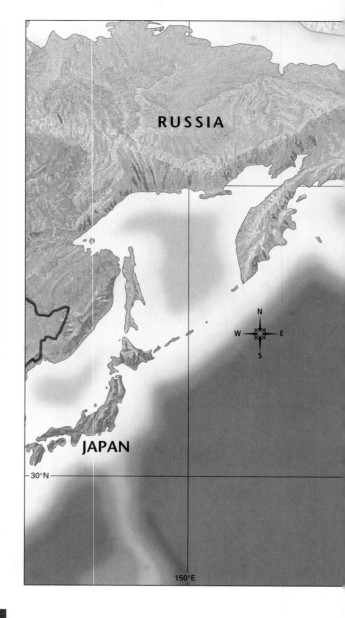

RUSSIA

JAPAN

30°N

150°E

N
W · E
S

The West's many environments mean that people in this region live and work in many different ways. This map shows some of the geographic features and resources of the West.

In this unit, you will learn how the many different kinds of land and climate make the West a land of extremes. You will also read about how the West's geography has affected its people, from the early Native Americans to modern immigrants from around the world. Then you'll read how these people solve problems, share resources, and make a living today.

Unit 6 Chapters

Unit Timeline

1500	1600	1700

Earthquake!

Sometimes the ground shakes and rolls. Find out why. *Chapter 12, Lesson 1*

Gold and Silver Strikes

Thousands of people came West to strike it rich. *Chapter 12, Lesson 2*

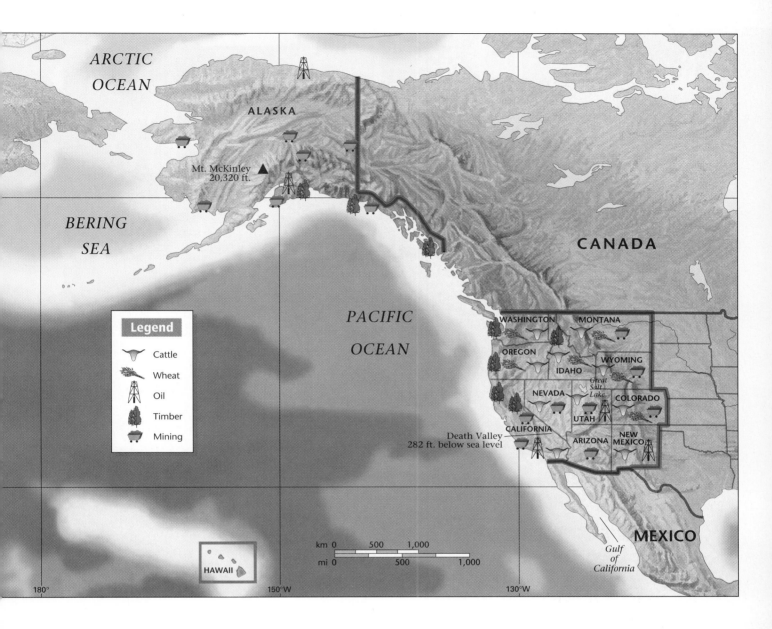

ARCTIC
OCEAN

ALASKA

Mt. McKinley
20,320 ft.

BERING
SEA

CANADA

PACIFIC
OCEAN

Legend

- Cattle
- Wheat
- Oil
- Timber
- Mining

WASHINGTON   MONTANA

OREGON

IDAHO   WYOMING

NEVADA   Great Salt Lake

UTAH   COLORADO

CALIFORNIA

Death Valley
282 ft. below sea level

ARIZONA   NEW MEXICO

MEXICO

Gulf
of
California

km 0   500   1,000

mi 0   500   1,000

HAWAII

180°   150°W   130°W

| 1800 | 1900 | **2000** |

The Aerospace Industry

If you have flown in a plane, it may have been made in the West.
Chapter 12, Lesson 3

Farming in the West

Tomatoes, potatoes, strawberries and onions. What do they have in common? *Chapter 13, Lesson 3*

Computer Technology

Find out which California valley is famous for computer chips.
Chapter 13, Lesson 4

CHAPTER 12

The Land and People of the West

Chapter Preview: *People, Places, and Events*

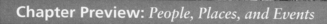

| 1500 | 1600 | 1700 |

Volcano

Find out about volcanoes and other earth-shaping events in the West! *Lesson 1, Page 322*

Redwood Trees

Did you know that the tallest trees in the world grow in the West? *Lesson 1, Page 327*

Hopi Pottery

Some of the first people to live in the West made beautiful pottery like this. *Lesson 2, Page 331*

The Land

Main Idea The changing landforms of the West help create climates where many different plants and animals live.

A mountain reaches into the cold, blue sky. Its two peaks rise up through snow and ice. The southern peak is 20,320 feet above sea level. It is the highest point in North America. The Athabascan people who live here in Alaska call the mountain *Denali*. That means "great one." Many people in the United States call it Mount McKinley.

More than 2,000 miles southeast of this mountain lies a dry valley. It sizzles in the bright, hot sun. The bottom of this valley is 282 feet below sea level. It is the lowest point in North America. It is Death Valley, in California.

You can find both of these places in the same region of the United States: the West. It is a region of contrasts, in climate as well as land. The West has dry deserts. It has rainy tropics. It has nearly every other kind of climate as well. The West is filled with some of the most exciting land in the world.

◀ This cowhand herded cattle across the Nevada range.

Key Vocabulary
- fault
- rain shadow
- habitat
- rain forest

Key Places
- Denali/Mount McKinley
- Death Valley
- The Arctic

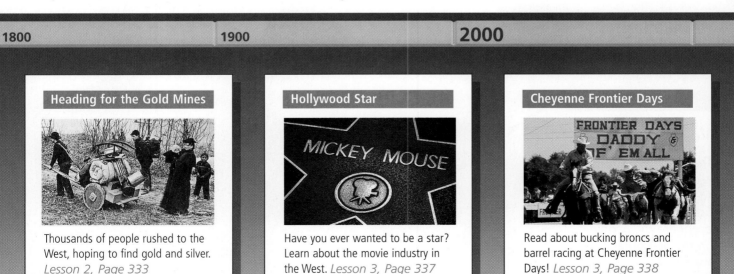

1800   1900   **2000**

Heading for the Gold Mines

Thousands of people rushed to the West, hoping to find gold and silver. *Lesson 2, Page 333*

Hollywood Star

MICKEY MOUSE

Have you ever wanted to be a star? Learn about the movie industry in the West. *Lesson 3, Page 337*

Cheyenne Frontier Days

FRONTIER DAYS
DADDY OF' EM ALL

Read about bucking broncs and barrel racing at Cheyenne Frontier Days! *Lesson 3, Page 338*

Landforms and Climate

Focus *How were the landforms of the West created, and how do they affect the West's climates?*

What could have created the great differences in land and climate in the West? The answer begins right under your feet.

Though you may not know it, the ground you stand on is moving all the time. How does this happen? Think of the outer layer of the earth as the shell of a cracked hard-boiled egg. It is broken into pieces called plates. The plates move slowly and constantly. The cracks in the earth where plates meet and move are called **faults.** The rugged western land is the result of these movements.

Consider the Rocky Mountains. To understand how they grew, think about what happens when your foot slips under a rug. The rug bunches up as it slides over your shoe. The North American plate crashed into other plates this way. Those crashes made the land bunch up to form the Rockies.

The movement of plates made other landforms in the West, too. Some of the most exciting are volcanoes. Several mountains in the West's Cascade Range are volcanoes. Like many volcanoes, they rise near where plates meet.

Volcanoes

The volcano in this photo is called Kilauea (KIH loo AY ah). It is in Hawaii.
Science: *What volcanic event are the people in the helicopter watching?*

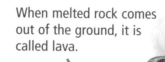

When melted rock comes out of the ground, it is called lava.

The mountain is made of lava that has cooled and hardened.

Melted rock inside the earth is called magma.

Other volcanoes rise up in the middle of plates. These volcanoes sit on top of very strong flows of melted rock. Scientists call those flows "hot spots." The volcanoes of Hawaii grew this way. They sit on top of a hot spot in the middle of the Pacific plate.

Earthquakes

The movement of plates sometimes has a violent effect on the West. It makes the ground shake in events called earthquakes. Most earthquakes happen where plates meet.

The strongest earthquake in the history of the United States happened near Anchorage, Alaska. A woman named Betzi Woodman was there when it hit, on March 27, 1964. She later remembered that the earthquake sounded like

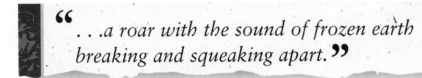

" . . .a roar with the sound of frozen earth breaking and squeaking apart. "

Most earthquakes aren't as strong as the one that shook Anchorage. However, those that are can cause terrible damage. The danger of earthquakes is a part of life in the West.

The Anchorage, Alaska, earthquake made the ground crack open like this.

Faults

This photo shows the San Andreas Fault, in California. It is a place where the Pacific plate meets the North American plate. The two plates move past each other as shown below.

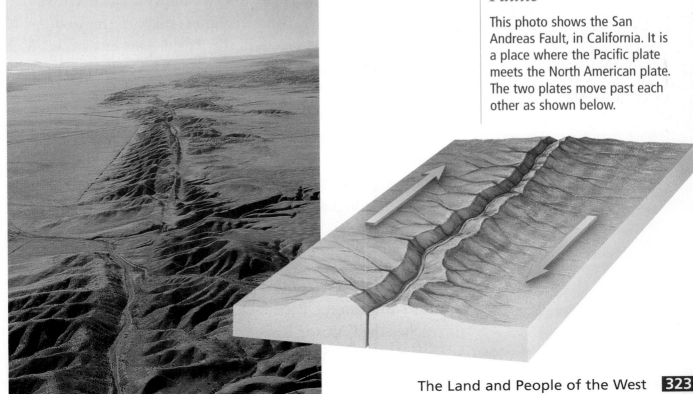

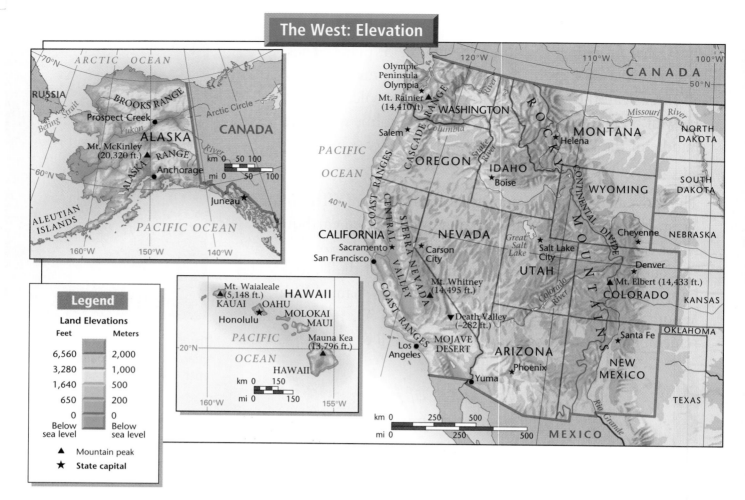

The West: Elevation

Legend

Land Elevations

Feet	Meters
6,560	2,000
3,280	1,000
1,640	500
650	200
0	0
Below sea level	Below sea level

▲ Mountain peak
★ State capital

Climate records in the West are:
Prospect Creek, Alaska: Lowest temperature
Death Valley, California: Highest temperature and driest place
Mount Waialeale, Hawaii: Most rainy days in a year
Yuma, Arizona: Most sunshine in a year
Mount Rainier: Most snow in a year.

Map Skill: *In which mountain range is Mt. Rainier?*

Western Climates

Weather in the West can be as varied as the western land. This region boasts the highest and lowest temperatures ever recorded in the United States. It has the driest place in the country. It has one of the wettest places in the world. One city in the West usually sees more sun in a year than anywhere else on earth. One mountain got the most snow ever measured in one year. You can find all these places on the map above.

The map also helps explain the West's climates. Look at the lines of latitude. The climates closer to the equator are generally warmer than ones farther away. Now look at the elevation. The higher the elevation is, the cooler the climate becomes.

Mountains and Climate

The mountains have another effect on climate as well. When air blows in from the Pacific Ocean, it carries moisture. As the air reaches the Cascade Range and the Sierra Nevada, it rises. At high elevations, the air gets colder. Cold air can't hold as much moisture as warm air. So the air drops its water on the western side of the mountains as rain and snow. That side of the mountains is often cloudy and damp. When the air gets to the other side of the mountains, it doesn't have much moisture left. This keeps the side of the mountains away from the ocean sunnier and drier than the side near the ocean. This effect that mountains have on weather is called **rain shadow**. In the "shadow" of the mountains, the land receives less rain.

The photos below show how different parts of Washington state are affected by this weather pattern. In the west, forests on the Olympic Peninsula can get 150 inches of rain a year. In the "shadow" of the mountains, the plains of Washington may only get seven inches a year. Together, latitude and elevation cause many different kinds of weather in the West.

Rain Shadow in Washington State

This illustration shows rain shadow, the effect that mountains can have on weather. The blue arrow is moist air from the ocean. The red arrow is dry air. It blows over the mountains after it has lost its moisture.

Mosses, ferns, and other plants thrive in the moist forests on the Olympic peninsula.

Air cools as it passes over the high Cascade mountains.

The hills east of the Cascades receive little rain. These fields near Yakima, Washington, grow with the help of irrigation.

Western Vegetation and Wildlife

Focus *What are some of the plants and animals in the West?*

You have read that the West has many different climates and kinds of land. That means the West has places for many different kinds of plants and animals to live. A place where a certain kind of plant or animal lives is called a **habitat**.

The birds below all live in the West. Yet they have very different habitats. One bird lives in Hawaii's rain forests. A **rain forest** is a thick evergreen forest. It is wet all year long. Another lives in northern Alaska. It is in a region called the Arctic, which is dry and cold. The West includes both of these habitats. It also has nearly every kind of habitat in between.

• Tell Me More •

Birds of the West

All animals are adapted to their environment. The West has many different environments. That helps explain its wide variety of plants and animals. The birds below are just a small example of the variety of living things in the West.

The **snowy owl** is found in northern Alaska. The owl's white feathers blend in with the snow that often blankets the Alaskan landscape. The snowy owl even has white feathers on its feet!

You can find **Hawaiian honeycreepers** in Hawaii's rain forests. This kind of Hawaiian honeycreeper has a long, curved bill. The bill lets it sip nectar from tube-shaped flowers.

Brandt's cormorants flock on the Pacific Coast. They dive in the water to catch fish. However, their feathers aren't waterproof. They perch on shore and hold their wings out to dry.

Roadrunners thrive in the hot, dry desert. They eat snakes, lizards, scorpions, and other small animals. Roadrunners get their name from the way they move. Often, instead of flying, they run!

Well-Adapted Plants

Plants in the West are well adapted to their habitats. One of the best examples of this is the saguaro (suh GWAHR oh) cactus. It is the largest type of cactus in the country. Most saguaros live in the Sonoran Desert in Arizona. That area can get less than six inches of rain a year. To stay alive, saguaros store water. They keep it in the pointed ridges you can see in the illustration. Saguaros also have a waxy coating. That keeps them from losing water on hot, dry days.

The days are rarely hot or dry on the coasts of Oregon and northern California. That's a good thing for the redwood trees that grow there. Winter rain and summer fog give them the water they need to grow. Redwoods are the tallest trees in the world. They can be almost 400 feet high!

The West is filled with all different kinds of plants and animals. Their habitats range from the wet warmth of the tropics to the dry cold of the Arctic. The West has enough variety for all of them. They help make this region a very special place.

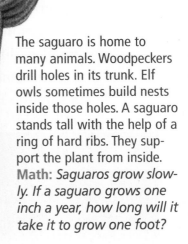

The saguaro is home to many animals. Woodpeckers drill holes in its trunk. Elf owls sometimes build nests inside those holes. A saguaro stands tall with the help of a ring of hard ribs. They support the plant from inside.
Math: *Saguaros grow slowly. If a saguaro grows one inch a year, how long will it take it to grow one foot?*

Lesson Review: Geography

1. **Key Vocabulary:** Use **fault, rain shadow, habitat,** and **rain forest** to describe some of the landforms and climates of the West.

2. **Focus:** How were the landforms of the West created, and how do they affect the West's climates?

3. **Focus:** What are some of the plants and animals in the West?

4. **Critical Thinking: Conclude** Do you think a saguaro or a redwood could live in your area? Why or why not?

5. **Geography:** The climate in Nevada is very dry. Why do you think that is the case?

6. **Citizenship/Science Activity:** Invite a local weather forecaster to speak to your class. Find out how the landforms in your area affect the climate.

Reading a Satellite Image

A View from Space

Hundreds of miles above us, satellites are circling the earth. Some satellites send radio and television signals around the world. Others are busy making pictures of our planet. Satellites called *earth observation satellites* are an important tool for geographers. Over time, images from these satellites show changes in features like deserts and rain forests. In satellite images, different features on the ground show up as different colors. Once you know what the colors mean, you can read a satellite image.

Making Satellite Maps

Satellites use instruments to measure light waves that are reflected from Earth. A computer then turns those measurements into an image. Satellite maps of large areas of land are made up of many smaller images, as shown by the small white boxes below.

1 Here's How

On the next page is a satellite image of the area around San Francisco, California.

- Look at the image. Find the major landforms. Do you see mountainous areas? Did you know that San Francisco is surrounded by water on three sides? Do you see any islands?

- Look for signs of human use of the land. In this satellite image there are two large bridges. The airport runways show up as a big X. You can also see major roads and highways.

- Notice the major color areas on the image. This satellite image uses mostly red, blue, and yellow.

- Find the red areas. In this image, areas with a lot of vegetation, like forests and city parks, show up as red. San Francisco has many large parks. The color red can help you find them.

- Find the yellow areas. In this image, land with higher elevations, like mountains, is yellow.

- Look at the blue areas. Blue shows the areas that are most populated or have less vegetation.

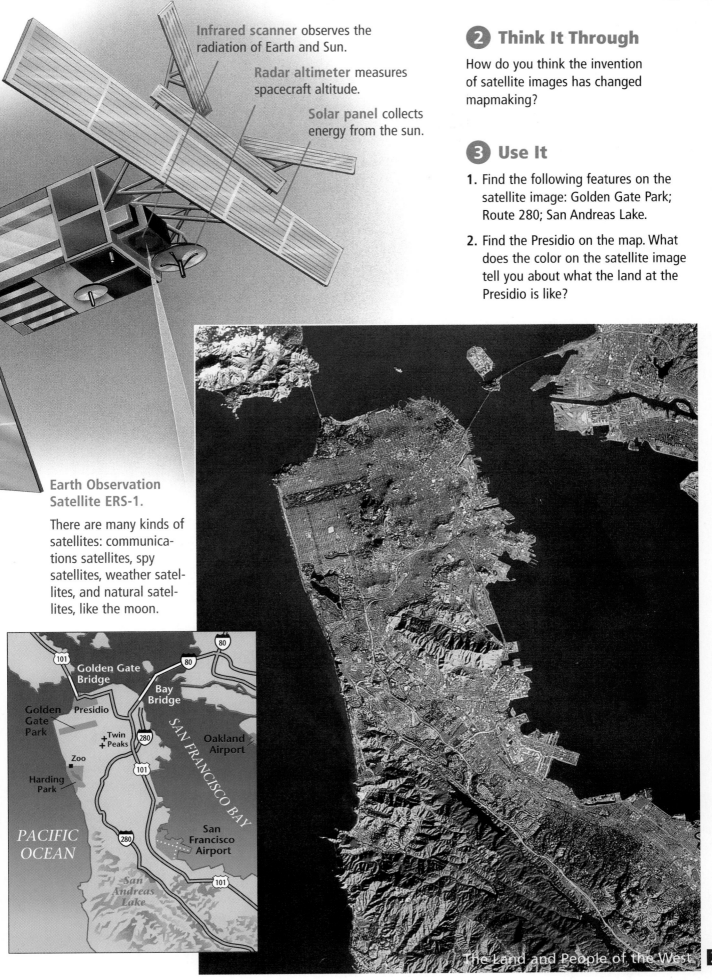

Infrared scanner observes the radiation of Earth and Sun.

Radar altimeter measures spacecraft altitude.

Solar panel collects energy from the sun.

Earth Observation Satellite ERS-1.

There are many kinds of satellites: communications satellites, spy satellites, weather satellites, and natural satellites, like the moon.

2 Think It Through

How do you think the invention of satellite images has changed mapmaking?

3 Use It

1. Find the following features on the satellite image: Golden Gate Park; Route 280; San Andreas Lake.

2. Find the Presidio on the map. What does the color on the satellite image tell you about what the land at the Presidio is like?

Settling the West

Main Idea People have been drawn to the land of the West for many reasons.

> "There were many colors on the hills, and the plain was bright with different-colored clays and sands . . . there was a dark wilderness on the mountains beyond. The land was still and strong. It was beautiful all around."
>
> N. Scott Momaday

The land of the West is indeed beautiful. People have been drawn to it for thousands of years. People have also come to the West for a different kind of beauty. For these people, the West was beautiful because it gave them what they wanted. Some wanted food and shelter. Others wanted gold or silver. Still others wanted to own land, or to find jobs. Many of these people stayed in the West and made this region their home.

Early Westerners

Focus *How did the West's first settlers live?*

The first people in the West were Native Americans. They came to North America thousands of years ago. The West's many resources provided Native Americans with a variety of ways to live.

Salmon were the Haida's most important food. The Haida dried much of their salmon in the wind or over a fire so it would keep for a long time.

The Haida

Haida canoes were known for their beautiful carvings.

The Inuit (IH noo iht) are one group of people who live in northern Alaska and Canada. In the past, the Inuit got what they needed from the animals there. They ate seals, fish, and other animals. They made clothes and tents from skins. The Inuit also carved walrus and whale tusks into beautiful shapes.

The Hopi live in the Southwest. They once got much of what they needed from the earth. The Hopi grew corn, squash, and other crops. They used clay to make pottery. The Hopi also built houses with materials from the earth. They used stone and adobe (uh DOH bee), a mixture of earth and straw. Their traditional houses were built on top of one another. Towns made up of these buildings are called **pueblos.**

The Haida (HY duh) live on the coast of Alaska and Canada. The illustration below shows you what their villages were once like. The Inuit, Hopi, and Haida are only three Native American groups in the West. Hundreds of cultures have existed there, from the Crow of Montana to the Polynesian people of Hawaii. Today, some Native Americans still live the way their ancestors did. Most now follow a different way of life. This change was caused by a new group of settlers. They first came to the West about 500 years ago.

The tall, carved pole in front of the house is called a totem pole. Carvings on the totem pole told the families' story.

The Haida lived in longhouses made of cedar wood. Each longhouse was home to several related families.

The mission on the right is in Taos (TAH ohs), New Mexico. Inside it you can find beautiful artwork, including the painting shown below.

European Settlers

Focus *Why did Europeans and other settlers come to what is now the West?*

Explorers from Spain first came to North America in the early 1500s. Most of them were looking for gold. The explorers also wanted to take the land for Spain, even though Native Americans already lived there. Priests from Spain came too. They wanted to convince Native Americans to accept their Christian religion. To do this, the priests built missions. By 1800, Spain claimed land from what is now the West through what is now Mexico. They called that land New Spain.

In 1821, New Spain became the independent nation of Mexico. Later, in 1848, the United States won a war against Mexico. As a result, Mexico had to give most of what is now the West to the United States.

For Farms and Freedom

In the 1840s, people in the United States thought of the land west of the Mississippi River as the frontier. A **frontier** is a place where few people live. It is also any area that people are just starting to explore.

Land on the frontier was cheaper than it was in the East. Also, more of it was for sale. A lot of people in the United States moved to the frontier to get land for farms. Native Americans had lived on that land for thousands of years. Many settlers ignored that fact. They considered the land to be theirs.

In the 1840s, farmers moved to places like Oregon, California, and Utah. Then, in 1848, something happened that brought another kind of settler to the West.

Rushing to the Land

John Sutter's California farm was a quiet place. That changed on January 28, 1848. A worker found gold at a sawmill on Sutter's land. That find changed the history of the West.

About 80,000 people rushed to California to look for gold in 1849. They became known as **forty-niners**. Thousands more soon joined them. "Gold fever" had hit the country. As Sutter's gardener said,

> **"P**eace and quiet vanished. To all appearances men seemed to have gone insane. **"**

Sutter's Mill wasn't the only place in the West where people found treasure like the gold nugget above. The map below shows several places in this region where people found gold or silver. **Map Skill:** *Where and when did people find silver in the West?*

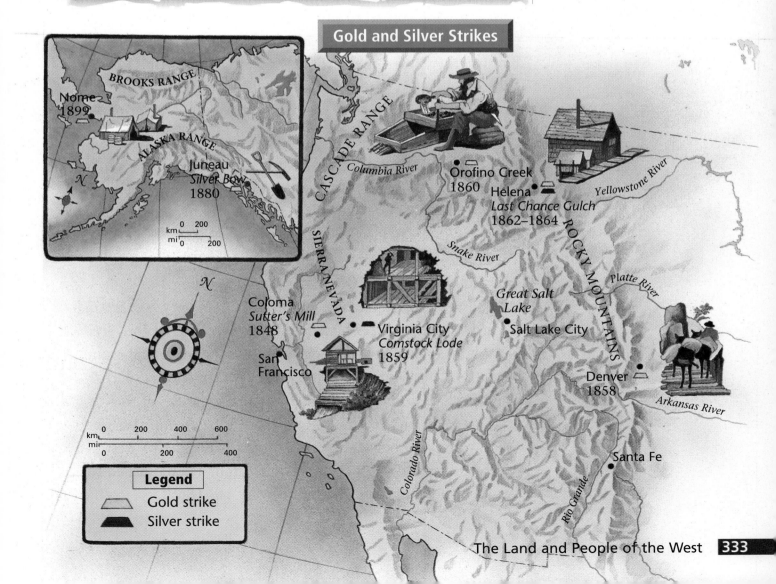

Gold and Silver Strikes

Nome 1899

BROOKS RANGE

ALASKA RANGE

Juneau
Silver Bow
1880

km 0 200
mi 0 200

CASCADE RANGE

Columbia River

Orofino Creek
1860

Helena
Last Chance Gulch
1862–1864

Yellowstone River

Snake River

ROCKY MOUNTAINS

Platte River

SIERRA NEVADA

Coloma
Sutter's Mill
1848

Virginia City
Comstock Lode
1859

San
Francisco

Great Salt
Lake

Salt Lake City

Denver
1858

Arkansas River

Colorado River

Santa Fe

Rio Grande

Legend
Gold strike
Silver strike

The railroad bridge above is called a trestle (TREHS uhl). The men at right built structures like that trestle. Without the hard work they and other men did, the railroad would never have been finished.

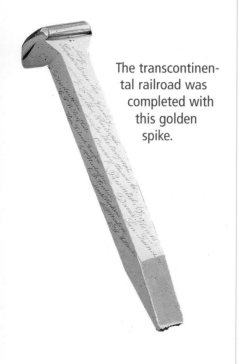

The transcontinental railroad was completed with this golden spike.

Arrivals from China

Focus *Why did people come to the West from China?*

News of the California gold rush raced across the United States. It soon spread to other countries. In 1852, it crossed the Pacific Ocean and reached China. China had just lost a war. Bad weather had ruined crops. People could not find jobs. When they heard about the gold rush, many Chinese men came to the United States. Some mined gold. Others ran businesses in mining towns. Still others worked to build the railroads.

The Transcontinental Railroad

United States railroad companies took on an enormous project in the 1860s. They began America's first **transcontinental** railroad. That means the first railroad across the continent.

Thousands of Chinese men and other workers built this railroad. The Chinese workers did some of the most dangerous jobs on the project. They also worked under very harsh conditions. Chinese workers had to blast away pieces of the Sierra Nevada to make way for the tracks. They braved frightening blizzards. One winter, the snow was 60 feet deep in places! The men had to dig tunnels through the snow to get to work.

One team of workers laid railroad tracks from west to east. Meanwhile, another team was working from east to west. The two teams met at Promontory Point, Utah. They finished the transcontinental railroad there on May 10, 1869.

The Western Melting Pot

Between 1852 and 1882, about 250,000 Chinese men came to the United States. Most wanted only to make enough money to take care of their families. Then they planned to go home to China. However, many ended up staying. They added the Chinese culture to the growing mix of cultures in the West.

Today, people continue to come to the West from other countries. People from other regions of the United States also continue to make homes in this region. Together, these people have helped make the West a diverse part of the United States.

This poster advertises the opening of the transcontinental railroad. Above, you can see the kind of train that traveled on that railroad. **Geography:** *What two cities were joined by the railroad line described on the poster?*

Lesson Review

1840	1850	1860	

1848
United States wins war with Mexico

1849
California Gold Rush

1869
Transcontinental railroad completed

1. **Key Vocabulary:** Use **pueblo, frontier,** and **forty-niner** to write about people who settled in the West.

2. **Focus:** How did the West's first settlers live?

3. **Focus:** Why did Europeans and other settlers come to what is now the West?

4. **Focus:** Why did people come to the West from China?

5. **Critical Thinking: Predict** How do you think the transcontinental railroad affected Western settlement?

6. **Citizenship:** How did settlers in the West want to improve their lives?

7. **Geography/Arts Activity:** Learn about the artwork of one group of people in the lesson. What does it tell you about the place those people live or lived?

Living and Working in the West

Key Vocabulary

- motion picture
- aerospace
- ranch
- rangeland
- rodeo

Key Places

Hollywood, California

Cheyenne, Wyoming

Main Idea Ways of life in the West are as varied as the Western land.

Rex! Rex! Where are you?" the shopkeeper cries.

Lights turn on in the apartments next to the shop. People open their windows. A crowd starts to gather in the street. Just then, a police car pulls up. A tall young woman gets out.

"Detective Williams!" the shopkeeper cries. "I'm so glad you're here! My dog, Rex, has disappeared!"

"Don't worry, sir," Detective Williams says. "Just tell me what happened. I'll solve this mystery as soon as I can."

"Cut!" someone yells. Detective Williams stops talking. She, the shopkeeper, and the people in the crowd are actors. They have just performed a scene in a movie. The word "cut" is a signal that the scene is over. It's time to film another part of the movie.

The people shown here are filming movies. **Technology:** *What equipment are these people using to do their work?*

Making a Living in the West

Focus *What are some ways people make a living in the West?*
Scenes like the one with Detective Williams are part of one of the most famous industries in the West. It's the **motion picture** industry. You know it as the movies. The motion picture industry is centered in Hollywood, California. Hollywood is a district of the West's largest city: Los Angeles, California. Look at the chart below. It shows you how many people live in the three largest cities in this region.

Urban and Rural Industries

Much of the West's business is based in urban areas. Cities in Washington, California, and Arizona are centers of the **aerospace** (AIR oh spays) industry. People in that industry make airplanes. Other urban businesses in the West make different kinds of machines. Some make special machines or parts for the high-technology industry. You will learn more about them in Chapter 13.

Rural areas are also important to this region's economy. Two of the industries in the rural West are mining and logging. They bring a lot of money to the region. However, the West's largest rural industry is agriculture. Growing crops is a big part of this industry. Another important part of agriculture is raising livestock. In the West, that happens at ranches.

Los Angeles is much larger than any other city in the West.
Chart Skill: *How many more people live in Los Angeles than in San Francisco or Seattle?*

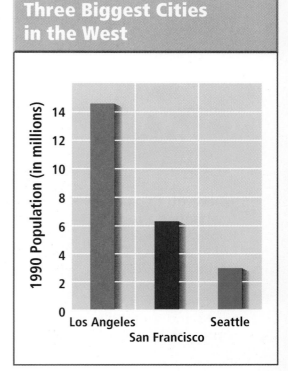

Three Biggest Cities in the West

1990 Population (in millions)

Los Angeles · San Francisco · Seattle

The photo at right shows a ranch in Montana. Above you can see some of the clothing and equipment they use. **Economics:** *How do these clothes and equipment help cowhands do their work?*

Then & Now

When you think of a cowhand, do you think of someone riding a horse? Think again! Today, cowhands still ride horses, but they also use trucks and even helicopters to herd cattle.

Ranching in the West

A **ranch** is a farm where people raise cattle, sheep, or horses. It is also the place where people do one of the most famous jobs in the West. These people are cowhands who herd cattle.

Ranch livestock need plenty of grass to eat. Some ranchers keep them on grassy land called **rangeland,** or the range. Rangeland can't be used for other agriculture. It is too dry, too wet, or too cold. Rangeland often isn't fenced in. Ranchers can hire cowhands to guard their livestock and move them across the range.

People on ranches work hard together. They make sure the animals have plenty of food and water, especially in winter. They keep the ranch's fences and farm machines working. Finally, they round up the livestock to be sold.

A Western Festival

Focus *What is one way to have fun in the West?*

To see how much fun the West can be, check out Cheyenne Frontier Days! People from all over the country enjoy this festival of Western life. One of the most exciting parts of Cheyenne Frontier Days is the rodeo. In **rodeos,** cowhands show off their skills and compete for prizes.

Most rodeo events come from ranch tasks. Barrel racing tests speed and horseback riding. The winner is the rider who circles three barrels in the least amount of time. Both bareback bronc riding and saddle bronc riding come from the job of

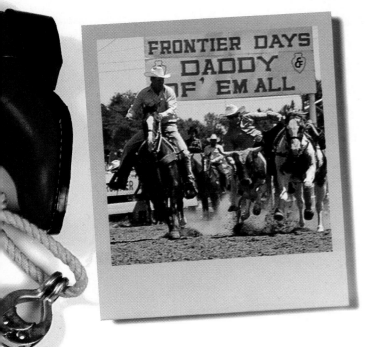

training a horse to carry a rider. In those events, a rider tries to stay on a bucking horse — a bronc — for eight seconds. In bull riding, the rider tries to stay on a bucking bull for eight seconds. Other events come from the need to catch runaway livestock. In calf roping, steer roping, and steer wrestling, the cowhand who catches a calf or steer fastest is the winner.

The rodeo is just part of Cheyenne Frontier Days. This festival also celebrates Native American traditions. Dance, storytelling, and music are some traditions people share.

Cheyenne's citizens and visitors also enjoy parades and many more activities. Cheyenne Frontier Days is a lot of fun. It is a celebration of the West of yesterday and today.

The cowhands on the left are trying to catch a steer. The cowhand above is a bull rider.

Lesson Review

1. **Key Vocabulary:** Use **motion picture, aerospace, ranch, rangeland,** and **rodeo** in a paragraph inviting people to visit the West.

2. **Focus:** What are some ways people make a living in the West?

3. **Focus:** What is one way to have fun in the West?

4. **Critical Thinking: Conclude** Do you think the motion picture industry and the ranching industry would have succeeded in a different region of the country? Why or why not?

5. **Theme: From Desert to Tropics** How do the climates of the West affect the industries discussed in this lesson?

6. **Citizenship/Music Activity:** The songs cowhands sang are part of the West's heritage. Research some of those songs and have a class sing-along.

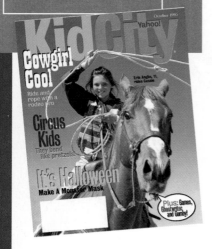

Rodeo got its start before 1900, during the days of the big cattle drives. Rodeos began as contests between cowboys to see who was best at some work-related skill like taming a wild horse. When crowds of ordinary Americans started lining up to see a little of the Wild West in action, modern rodeo was born.

The Cowgirl Way!

By Susan Brody
Photos by Martha Cooper

Meet Erin Anglin, rodeo star.

If 11-year-old Erin Anglin got her wish, she'd go everywhere on horseback!

Erin has ridden horses by herself since she was five. Erin, who lives in Windsor, Colorado, has three horses. "Their names are Floyd, Santa Fe, and Ready," Erin told KC. "Ready got his name because he always looked ready to go!"

Let's Rodeo

Erin has competed against other kid riders in rodeos since she was eight. When she grows up, she wants to be a professional rider.

A rodeo is like a track

Erin gets the goat

① Erin gets off her horse . . .

② Heads for the goat . . . (Whoops! Her hat!)

③ Lassoes the goat . . .

meet, except the athletes are on horses. Each event tests a different skill. Erin rides in six events. Her favorite is breakaway calf roping. The rider has to chase after a calf, lasso it, and bring her horse to a full stop. The rider who does it fastest wins. (None of this hurts the calf.) At a recent rodeo in Las Vegas, Nevada, Erin was the only girl in her age group to rope all five calves!

Horse Homework

Erin has worked hard to get so good at rodeo events. "It takes a lot of practice," she says. "But I like to practice, because that's the only way to get better. I try to improve every time I compete."

Erin rides every day. The only part she doesn't like is saddling up the horses. "It takes a long time," she says. But once she's on one of her horses, it's tough to get her down. For Erin, life is one great ride!

GIDDY YAP!

The **National Little Britches Rodeo Association** sponsors rodeos for kids ages eight to 18. To find out more, write to:

National Little Britches
Rodeo Association
1045 W. Rio Grande
Colorado Springs, CO 80906

GOT YOUR NUMBER Erin's dad helps her get ready to ride.

PONY EXPRESS Erin puts mail in a mailbox as part of the trail course event.

5 Ties three of its legs together. Then the goat is let go — unhurt and fine.

4 Picks up the goat, and . . .

Response Activities

1. **Conclude** Write a paragraph explaining how Erin's rodeo skills might help her if she were working on a ranch in the West. Use "breakaway calf roping" as an example.

2. **Write a Set of Rules:** Make up your own events or competition based on the work you do at school or at home.

3. **History: Learn About Cowhands** Find out about famous cowhands who rode on the cattle drives and used the skills that are tested in rodeos today.

Environment and Society

How Has Arizona Avoided Water Shortages?

On Mount Waialeale (WAH ee AH lee AH lee), Hawaii, it is almost always raining. Mount Waialeale is the wettest spot in the West — and in the country. Yet in large sections of the West, annual rainfall is low and water is a precious resource.

Much of Arizona, for example, is a desert. For decades the state depended on underground supplies of water for its farms, factories, and cities. By 1962, however, Arizona farmers were pumping far more water out of the ground than could be replaced by rainfall. As a result, the state's political and business leaders looked for new ways to bring water into the state.

Thanks to their efforts, the U.S. Congress agreed in 1968 to loan Arizona the money to build the Central Arizona Project (CAP). This huge network of pumping stations, tunnels, and canals was finally completed in the mid-1990s. The CAP's 336-mile-long canal moves water from the Colorado River (on the California-Arizona border) to farms and cities in central Arizona.

Like a huge blue snake, the Central Arizona Project's canal *(right)* stretches across western Arizona. In addition to bringing water for homes and industries, the CAP also carries water for crop irrigation *(above).*

Mathematics Connection

In 1963 the U.S. Supreme Court ruled that Arizona has the right to use 2,800,000 acre-feet of water from the Colorado River annually. (One acre-foot equals 325,851 gallons.) The Central Arizona Project can pump 1,500,000 acre-feet of water into Arizona each year. How much more water from the Colorado River could Arizona use each year if the CAP could pump it?

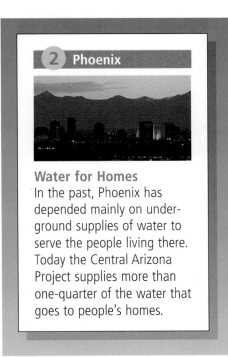

1 Little Harquahala

Pumping Station
The Central Arizona Project depends on a series of pumping stations to keep water moving in its canal. In some places, water has to be lifted almost 2,900 feet in elevation.

2 Phoenix

Water for Homes
In the past, Phoenix has depended mainly on underground supplies of water to serve the people living there. Today the Central Arizona Project supplies more than one-quarter of the water that goes to people's homes.

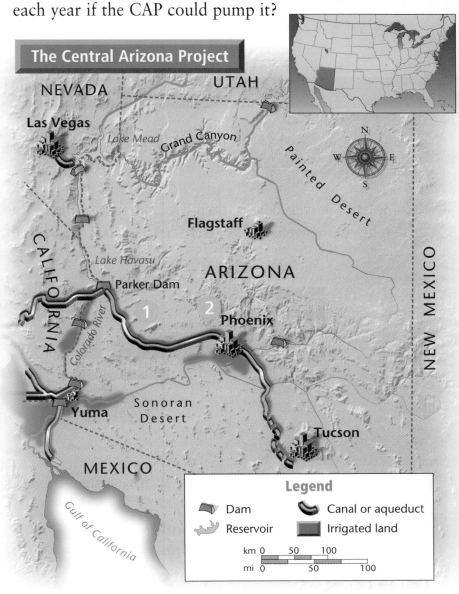

The Central Arizona Project

Legend
- Dam
- Reservoir
- Canal or aqueduct
- Irrigated land

km 0 50 100
mi 0 50 100

Research Activity

The Central Arizona Project has created problems that no one expected. For example, many farmers cannot afford the price of CAP water.

1. Do further reading about a large dam or other major water project.
2. Prepare a brief oral report about the results of building this particular dam or project.

The Central Arizona Project carries water 336 miles from Lake Havasu to Tucson. **Map Skill:** *Why do you think this huge water project is called the Central Arizona Project rather than just the Arizona Project?*

CHAPTER 12

Chapter Review

Chapter Timeline

1849
California Gold Rush

| 1840 | 1850 | 1860 |

1848
United States wins war with Mexico

1869
Transcontinental railroad completed

Summarizing the Main Idea

1 Complete the web below, then use information from the chapter to create word webs for Western Settlers and Western Industries.

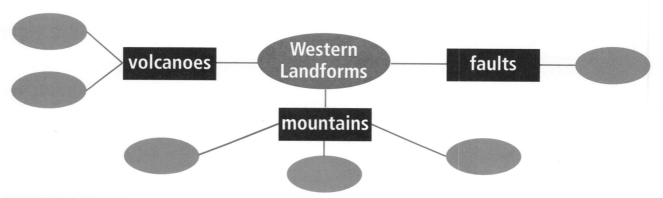

volcanoes — Western Landforms — faults

mountains

Vocabulary

2 Using at least six of the following terms, write a travel plan for a trip to the West.

fault (p. 322)   **frontier (p. 332)**   **ranch (p. 338)**
rain forest (p. 326)   **forty-niner (p. 333)**   **rangeland (p. 338)**
pueblo (p. 331)   **motion picture (p. 337)**   **rodeo (p. 338)**

Reviewing the Facts

3 How does the movement of plates affect landforms in the West?

4 What are some reasons why the West has so many different climates?

5 Why is the plant and animal life in the West so varied?

6 Who were some of the people who settled in the West?

7 What are some of the West's important industries?

8 Look at the satellite image on page 329. What do the colors red, yellow, and blue stand for?

9 How is reading a satellite image like reading a map? How is it different?

Geography Skills

10 Look at the maps on pages 324 and 333. What can you tell about the land where people found gold and silver in the West?

11 What might it be like to see the West for the first time? Write a friendly letter describing plants and animals you might see. Include information about landforms and climate.

Critical Thinking

12 **Compare** Many different groups of people settled in the West. How were their reasons for settling there alike? How were they different?

13 **Decision Making** Think about the West's economy. Would you rather live in an urban area or a rural area in the West? Explain your answer.

Writing: Citizenship and Culture

14 **Citizenship** Cheyenne Frontier Days is a celebration of the West. Write a plan for another celebration of life in the West.

15 **Culture** Find out what kinds of houses the people who settled the West lived in. Write a description of the kind of house you would most like to live in.

Activities

Cultures/Literature
Each group of people who settled in the West created folktales about the land they found there. Find some of those folktales. Then read them aloud in a class storytelling session.

History/Science
Find out more about historic earthquakes in the West. In a small group, give a presentation about one of those earthquakes. You may want to include photographs and first-person accounts in your presentation.

Internet Option

Check the **Internet Social Studies Center** for ideas on how to extend your theme project beyond your classroom.

THEME PROJECT CHECK-IN

Make sure you include what you have learned about the West in your guidebook.
- Have you listed and shown landforms and climates in the West that are very different from one another?
- What are some of the reasons people have settled in the West?
- How can your brochure reflect how people work in the West?

Chapter Preview: *People, Places, and Events*

1900	1925	1950

Immigrants in the West

People have come to the West from countries all over the world. Find out why. *Lesson 1, Page 349*

The Lumber Industry

This is how people in the West relax. See how they work! *Lesson 2, Page 359*

Old-Growth Forests

Find out who lives in and around these ancient trees. *Lesson 2, Page 360*

Coming to the West

Main Idea People from all over the world have made new lives in the West.

Key Vocabulary

refugee
employee
self-employed
chamber of
   commerce

Key Places

Denver, Colorado

During the 1970s, a man named Thao Chau (tow choh) lived in Vietnam. Thao Chau had just fought in a war, and his side had lost. That meant he and his family were in danger. Years later, Thao Chau's son, Hoang Anh (wahng ahn), told his family's story:

"My *parents planned secretly to escape from Vietnam and seek a new life of safety and freedom in the United States.* **"**

The Chaus are one of many families who came here from Vietnam. They are some of the people living in the West today.

◀ Sequoia trees in Sequoia National Park, California.

1975   2000   **2025**

Irrigation

How do people in the West turn deserts into fruitful farms? *Lesson 3, Page 366*

Computer Chip

This tiny invention changed the world. Read about the valley it made famous. *Lesson 4, Page 370*

Computer Animation

How have computers changed what we see in the movies? *Lesson 4, Page 372*

Arrivals in the West

This photograph shows immigrants arriving at Angel Island, in California, during the 1800s.

Focus *Why have people come to the West during the 1900s?*

A writer named Horace Greeley gave Americans a famous piece of advice in the mid-1800s:

> "**G**o west, young man, and grow up with the country. "

For more than 150 years, thousands of Americans have moved west from other regions of the country. They have helped the population in the West grow faster than in any other region.

For people from other countries, coming to the West might not mean traveling west. Look at the map below. It shows where some of the people who have moved to this region since 1900 came from. Many people who have come to the West actually traveled north, or even east, to get there!

People who are born in one country but come to spend their lives in another are called immigrants. Between 1980 and 1990, more immigrants came to the West from Mexico, the Philippines, and Vietnam than from any other nations.

This map shows how people came to the West from some of the countries around the Pacific Ocean. **Map Skill:** *If you lived in South Korea and wanted to move to Colorado, in what direction would you travel?*

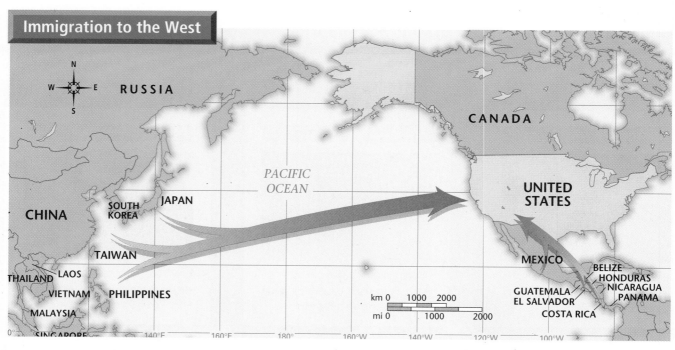

Immigration to the West

Both immigrants and non-immigrants can find high-paying jobs at technology companies in the West. Here, a worker assembles computers in a Colorado factory. Computers use chips such as the one below.

Hoping to Make a Better Living

Many immigrants came to the West so they could make a better living. Some of them had special skills. They were doctors, scientists, or business people. They believed the West was a good place for them to use their knowledge.

Other people came to this region without this kind of special training. They believed they could find better jobs in the West than they could at home. The promise of better jobs also drew people from other regions of the United States.

Looking for Safety and Freedom

Many people came to the West for another reason. Like the Chaus, they wanted safety and freedom.

These people came from places like Vietnam, Laos, Guatemala, and El Salvador. Those countries had wars, unfair governments, or other troubles. The individuals and families who fled from these dangers are called refugees. **Refugees** are people who are forced to leave their homes to find safety. It takes a lot of courage for people to leave the country where they were born, no matter what the reason.

These immigrants carried parts of their old lives with them. Today, the cultures that people brought from other countries have become part of the culture of the West.

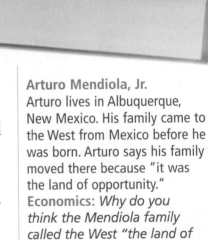

Arturo Mendiola, Jr.
Arturo lives in Albuquerque, New Mexico. His family came to the West from Mexico before he was born. Arturo says his family moved there because "it was the land of opportunity." **Economics:** *Why do you think the Mendiola family called the West "the land of opportunity"?*

A Denver Community

Focus *How have immigrants started new lives in Denver, Colorado?*

Many different kinds of immigrants have come to the West over the last 150 years. One chapter of this history is still being written today. Denver, Colorado, is a good example of what is happening in many cities around this region. Almost 500,000 people lived in Denver in 1990. Nearly 36,000 of them were born outside the United States.

Angel Chi gives people advice about money. Her clients include doctors, engineers, and business people.

Success Stories

A family named Chinsomboon (CHIHN sohm boon) moved to Denver from Thailand (TY land) in 1970. Once they arrived, the Chinsomboons worked for other people. By 1975, they had saved enough money to start their own business. They opened a grocery store and made it successful.

Denver is full of success stories like this one. When many immigrants first arrived in Denver, they worked as **employees**. That means they were paid to work for other people. These people worked very hard and saved money, like the Chinsomboons. Today, thousands of immigrants in Denver own their own businesses. They are **self-employed**. That means they work for themselves, not someone else.

Wendy Chao looks over her newspaper, the *Colorado Chinese News.* Her paper provides information to Colorado's Asian community.

A Varied Business Community

People starting their own companies often need help. Many look to a chamber of commerce for advice and support. A **chamber of commerce** is a group of business people working together to make all their companies more successful.

Denver has different chambers of commerce for people of different backgrounds. One is made up of Asian business owners. Another is made up of Hispanics, which means they or their ancestors came from Spain, Mexico, Central America, or South America. In addition to helping their members, these different chambers of commerce also work together.

Wendy Chao works in Denver. She runs a newspaper there called the *Colorado Chinese News.* Wendy sees the ethnic groups of Denver working together each day. She is proud to be part of a varied business community. As she says:

Wendy Chao came to Denver from Taiwan in 1984. When she started her business, she worked 12 to 14 hours a day — sometimes until 3:00 in the morning!

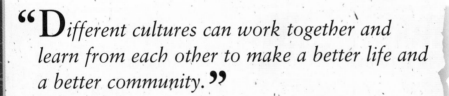

> "**D**ifferent cultures can work together and learn from each other to make a better life and a better community."

Many people in the West agree with Wendy about how valuable these different cultures have been to this region.

Lesson Review

1. **Key Vocabulary:** Use the following words in a paragraph about Denver: **refugee, employee, self-employed, chamber of commerce.**

2. **Focus:** Why have people come to the West during the 1900s?

3. **Focus:** How have immigrants started new lives in Denver, Colorado?

4. **Critical Thinking: Problem Solving** Suppose your family moved to another country. How would you adjust to your new home? What steps would you take?

5. **Citizenship:** Why do you think people in Denver are proud of their city?

6. **Geography/Research Activity:** Are there any immigrants in your town or city? Find out where these immigrant groups are from. Locate those places on a map. Draw arrows to show how they came to this country.

NONFICTION

THE OTHER SIDE

How Kids Live in a California Latino Neighborhood

By Kathleen Krull
Photographs by David Hautzig

The promise of a better life that has always made people want to come to America still attracts newcomers today. Here is a look at the true story of two families who have recently come to the United States from Mexico.

When Cinthya Guzman (pronounced *SIN-thi-a GOOZ-man*) moved to the United States at age eight, her terror nearly got the best of her.

"Every morning I cried hard, because I didn't want to go to school," she says. The idea of a new school, where she understood so little of what was going on, was overwhelming. Her family was worried; her father became so concerned that he offered to move the family back to Tijuana, Mexico. After all, it was only a matter of seven miles.

overwhelming
very difficult

Cinthya had to reassure him that her misery would pass. And, in fact, after about a month she stopped crying.

At first she was in classes mostly taught in Spanish. Now, at age twelve, she gets straight A's in most of her all-English classes and is completely fluent in both languages. She can't wait for next year, when she will study a third language, French. "I really like languages!" she says.

Francisco Tapia (*fran-SIS-co TAH-pia*), age eight, also has language concerns. He, too, is bilingual. But lately, especially when he gets angry, he has noticed that he forgets words in Spanish. For instance, when recently trying to say "turkey" in Spanish to one of his Mexican cousins, he couldn't recall the word until after she had left.

This bothers him. His biggest concern is a practical one: "My whole family speaks Spanish, and if I'm not going to be able to communicate with them, my grandma will ask, 'What are you saying?'" This seems to him like a bad dream.

Francisco and Cinthya, both born in Mexico, now live in southern California. Their neighborhood, Castle Park, is within a small city called Chula Vista, which means "beautiful view." This is halfway between two tourist destinations, the large city of San Diego and its sister city, Tijuana, or TJ, which is across the border.

Living only seven miles from Tijuana means that kids like Francisco and Cinthya don't leave their old world behind when they move to the new world. The border between the two countries becomes *el otro lado*, simply "the other side" of their lives.

Reading at the Castle Park Library.

destination
*the place someone
wants to reach*

Castle Park looks like many southern California neighborhoods, which are, in fact, heavily Spanish-influenced. As in Mexico, palm trees are everywhere. Purple jacarandas and orange trees thrive in warm weather under sunny blue skies. This is a suburban, not an urban area — you need a car to get around. License plates frequently read "BC," for Baja California, a part of Mexico. Churches have Spanish names, as do many streets. San Diego and Chula Vista are Spanish names, as are the names of most of the surrounding towns, from El Cajon to La Jolla. Latino kids make use of the Castle Park Library, nearby playgrounds, and parks.

Pedro and Francisco Tapia go bodysurfing.

The words *Latino* (a Spanish word) or *Hispanic* (an English word) can refer to people from various countries besides Mexico, such as Cuba, Puerto Rico, countries in Central or South America, and Spain. People from these countries may feel they have little in common besides the Spanish language. In Castle Park, the majority of Spanish speakers are Mexican or Mexican-American.

The Tapia and Guzman families moved to the United States for the same reason as most other immigrants, to have a better life. Jobs are more plentiful here than on *el otro lado*, and they pay much better.

Francisco's father got a job here and at first commuted to Tijuana. Then he moved the family to Castle Park, bought a house, and now owns his own glass installation business. Cinthya's father was studying to become a doctor in Mexico, but he dropped out of school to support his family. He assembles planes in the United States. He moved here not so much for himself as for his three children.

"He wanted us kids to have better chances for success," Cinthya explains.

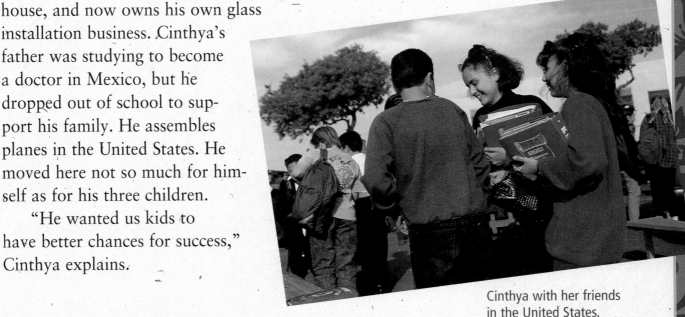
Cinthya with her friends in the United States.

Meet the Author

Writer Kathleen Krull and photographer David Hautzig enjoy getting to know the people they tell about in their books. They have a whole series of nonfiction books about how kids around the United States live, work, and play.

Additional Books to Read

Radio Man by Arthur Dorros Find out about migrant farm workers.

A Brand Is Forever by Ann Herbert Scott illustrated by Ronald Himler Read about life on a modern cattle ranch.

Response Activities

1. **Generalize:** What do you think are the biggest challenges for immigrant students coming to a new school?

2. **Expressive: Write a Welcome Letter** What would you write in a letter to Cinthya or Francisco to make them feel welcome in your community or school?

3. **Citizenship: Research Immigration Facts** Use your school library to find out how many immigrants became U.S. citizens last year. From which continent did most of the new citizens come?

Participating

What Makes You Special?

Sometimes we find out only by accident that a friend can do something special, like throw a lasso or cook chili. We each have special talents. Here is how people in one western city celebrate these talents and bring the community together.

Case Study

Tucson Heritage Experience

Every October, people in Tucson, Arizona, hold a special celebration. For three days, people representing all groups of the city come together to share their hobbies and talents. People have a chance to see Tohono O'odham Indian dances, hear Scottish bagpipers and West African drumming, make Mexican paper flowers, eat Middle Eastern *falafel*, and more.

This festival, called the "Tucson Heritage Experience," began in 1974. The organizers wanted to create a time for everyone to appreciate the different heritages and skills of the people in that city.

The festival has helped unite the people of Tucson. They have learned about one another and continue to take pride in who they all are.

The Redhouse Family Intertribal Dancers, from eastern Arizona, perform Apache and Navajo dances and songs at the Tucson festival.

Take Action

When the Tucson festival first began, it was called "Tucson Meet Yourself." Now you, too, can "meet yourselves." Create a festival in your classroom that lets you and your classmates learn about one anothers' different heritages, arts, and skills.

1 As a class, think about and write down the different heritages you represent or are interested in learning more about.

2 Write down the special traditions, arts, talents, or objects connected to each heritage.

3 Which of these would you like to share with your classmates? Plan a presentation.

4 Come up with a plan and date for a classroom festival. Invite another class or your family to the festival. Afterward, talk about the things you learned about one another.

Tips for Participating

- Listen to other people's ideas as carefully as you want them to listen to yours.
- Pick a job or activity that makes good use of your talents.
- Learn more about your subject so you have more to offer the group.
- Try to think of many possibilities before you pick one.

Research Activity

Is there a cultural group or activity that you've been interested in or wish you could find in your community? What is it? Do some research to find out more about it. Share your findings with the class.

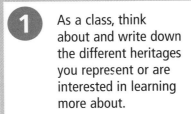

The Northwest's Forests

Main Idea The forests of the Northwest are a valuable resource for industry and an environmental treasure.

Key Vocabulary
- timber
- lumber
- old-growth forest
- clear-cutting
- contour

What does it mean to be rich? To some people, it means having a lot of money in the bank. Yet there are other ways to be rich. You can be rich in talent or in happiness. You can also have many friends. Then you are rich in friendship.

To countries, being rich sometimes means having many natural resources. These resources can be sold to other countries for money, or they can be used by a country's own citizens. The United States is a fortunate country. It is rich in resources. Many of these can be found in the West.

A Precious Resource

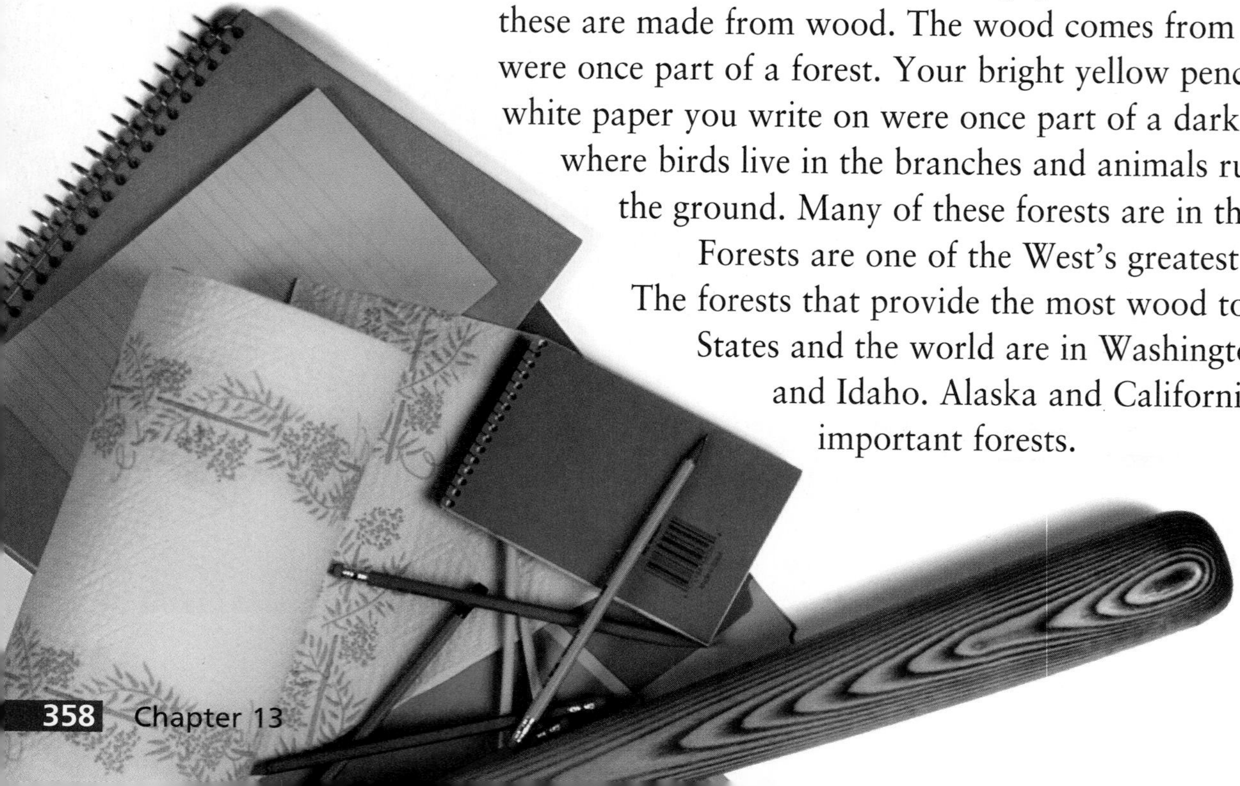

Many of the products we use every day are made from wood. Some of them are shown here.

Focus *What makes the Northwest's forests valuable?*

Think about pencils. Think about paper or cardboard. All of these are made from wood. The wood comes from trees that were once part of a forest. Your bright yellow pencil and the white paper you write on were once part of a dark forest, where birds live in the branches and animals run across the ground. Many of these forests are in the West.

Forests are one of the West's greatest resources. The forests that provide the most wood to the United States and the world are in Washington, Oregon, and Idaho. Alaska and California also have important forests.

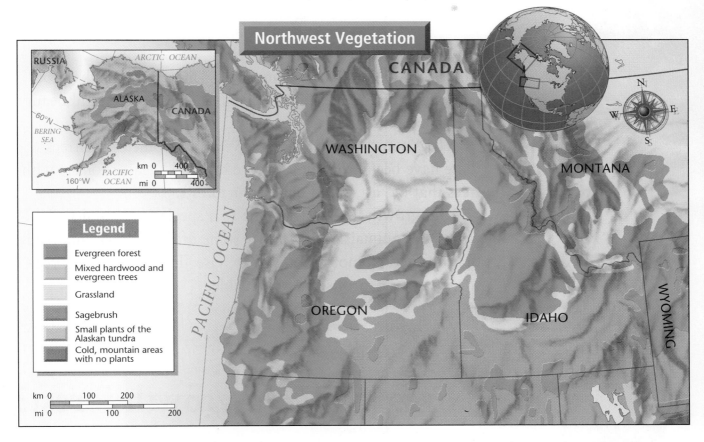

Northwest Vegetation

Legend

- Evergreen forest
- Mixed hardwood and evergreen trees
- Grassland
- Sagebrush
- Small plants of the Alaskan tundra
- Cold, mountain areas with no plants

Making a Living from Forests

The Northwest's forests bring jobs and money to the states where they grow. There, thousands of people work in the timber industry. **Timber** is a word for trees that are used for wood.

Some people who depend on forests to make their living cut down trees. Others work in sawmills, cutting trees into lumber. **Lumber** is wood cut into boards. Still other people are truck drivers. They haul lumber to warehouses to be stored. Later, factory workers turn it into products we need.

Oregon produces more wood than any other state. Every year, Oregon produces enough wood to make about 500,000 houses! Much of the wood from Oregon and other states in the Northwest stays here in the United States. Logging companies sell the rest of it to countries like Japan, which don't grow enough wood for their own uses.

This map shows the different kinds of trees and other plants that grow in the West. **Map Skill:** *What kinds of plants shown on this map are resources? Can you explain why some kinds are not?*

A logger cuts down a tree in a national forest in Oregon.

The Ancient Trees

These forests, however, are more than material to make products we need. They are also a precious source of natural beauty and a home to plants and animals.

Forests in the Northwest are very old. Some of the trees there have been growing for more than 200 years. Forests with trees that old are called **old-growth forests**.

Old-growth forests are home to a special community of plants and animals. *(See below.)* Some of the animals and birds that live here do not live anywhere else. They are another reason why these forests are so valuable.

· Tell Me More ·

Who lives in an old-growth forest?

Pileated (PIH lee ay tihd) woodpeckers eat insects from dead or dying trees.

In forests that have not been logged, some trees grow to great heights. Others fall and rot on the forest floor. Still others die but remain standing. In this tangle of living, dead, and dying trees, a community of plants and animals has flourished for thousands of years.

Fallen logs create pathways for mice and other small animals, homes for insects, and beds for moss and mushrooms to grow.

A fallen tree can become a nurse log — a home to plants and insects.

Moss hangs from trees in a rain forest in Washington.

Working on Solutions

Focus *How can people preserve both the logging industry and the old-growth forests?*

Some people think that no one should log old-growth forests. That way, animals in these forests will be protected. The huge trees there, however, make the best lumber. People in the Northwest depend on logging for their jobs.

For years, people have argued about which is more important — preserving wildlife or preserving jobs. Today, they are finding solutions to this problem.

A Renewable Resource

Trees are a renewable resource. If you cut down one tree, you can plant another in its place. Many logging companies do just that. However, it takes at least 200 years for a forest to reach the old-growth stage. The timber industry can't wait that long. To make money, they must cut the trees they plant after only 40 to 70 years.

Forests that are planted and cut in this way are called managed forests. Though they help loggers, managed forests cannot replace old-growth forests. The plants and animals living in these old-growth forests cannot always survive in managed forests.

These tall plants are called kenaf (KUH naf). They can be used to make paper and other products usually made from wood. Kenaf grows much faster than trees do. It reaches full size in just six months! **Economics:** *How can kenaf help save both jobs and forests in the West?*

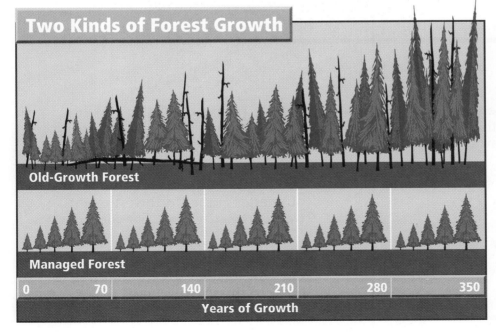

Two Kinds of Forest Growth

Old-Growth Forest

Managed Forest

| 0 | 70 | 140 | 210 | 280 | 350 |

Years of Growth

Managed forests are planted and then harvested every 70 years. This chart shows how a managed forest can be cut and planted five times during the life of one old-growth forest. **Chart Skill:** *How do these forests grow differently?*

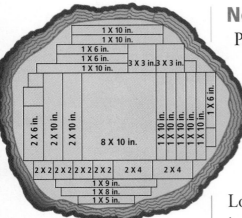

		1 X 10 in.		
		1 X 10 in.		
	1 X 6 in.			
	1 X 6 in.			
	1 X 10 in.	3 X 3 in.	3 X 3 in.	

2 X 6 in. 2 X 10 in. 2 X 10 in. 8 X 10 in. 1 X 10 in. 1 X 10 in. 1 X 10 in. 1 X 10 in. 1 X 6 in.

2 X 2 2 X 2 2 X 2 2 X 2 2 X 4 2 X 4

1 X 9 in.
1 X 8 in.
1 X 5 in.

A sawmill slices logs into boards of many sizes. This log could be cut as the diagram *(above)* shows. **Technology:** *Why do you think people use computers to help cut logs?*

New Methods for a Modern Industry

People in the Northwest are learning ways both to use and preserve the forests. Today, loggers use more wood from the trees they cut than ever before. Sawmills now use computers to find out the best way to slice each log into boards. People have even invented ways to build houses that use less wood.

Some loggers are also changing the way they cut trees. Loggers often cut down all the trees in one area of forest. This is called **clear-cutting.** Old ways of clear-cutting can cause problems. If loggers clear-cut a whole hillside, for example, the soil on the hill may wash away. Today, many loggers clear-cut only narrow bands of forest. They follow the outlines of the land's shape. These outlines are called **contours.** Clear-cuts along contours don't cause as much soil to wash away. They also allow the forest to grow back more quickly.

Recently, the federal government decided to set aside areas of old-growth forests. Those areas won't be cut. The government may also set aside areas that have already been cut. They will become old-growth forests again someday.

There is still a lot of work to be done. The future of the forests and the timber industry is not yet certain. If everyone works together, however, both the Northwest's old-growth forests and jobs in the timber industry can be protected.

Lesson Review

1 **Key Vocabulary:** Use these words in a paragraph about the Northwest: **timber, lumber, old-growth forest, clear-cutting, contour.**

2 **Focus:** What makes the Northwest's forests valuable?

3 **Focus:** How can people preserve both the logging industry and the old-growth forests?

4 **Critical Thinking: Decision Making** Which is more important, preserving forests or using them to make products people need? Explain why.

5 **Geography:** How do you think businesses in the Northwest might transport lumber to other countries?

6 **Citizenship/Science Activity:** Choose a tree growing near your school. Find out how long it took for that tree to grow to the size it is now.

Distinguishing Fact from Opinion

Is That a Fact?

As you walk through the Northwest's old growth forests, you might hear the hoot of the rare northern spotted owl. These forests are one of the only places where this species of owl lives. Some people think logging should be stopped to save the owls. Others believe that the forest can be both used and protected.

An **opinion** tells what someone believes or feels. A **fact** is a statement that can be proven. Whether you read a newspaper, watch the news, or listen to a speech, it is important to tell facts from opinions.

1 Here's How

- Listen or read for facts. Facts can and should be checked. A statement can sound like a fact but be only partly true. If you need to, use another source to check the facts.

- Listen or read for clues to the speaker's or author's opinion. Words that signal an opinion include *I think, I believe,* and *should.*

- Find descriptive words that tell the speaker's or author's feelings. Look for words such as *perfect, best,* or *difficult,* which show a judgment or opinion of something.

2 Think It Through

How does an author's opinion about a topic affect his or her choice of facts?

The northern spotted owl has become the symbol of the fight over the Northwest's old growth forests. There are only 4,000 to 6,000 of these birds left, which makes the spotted owl a threatened species. In 1990, the government said that seven million acres of forest was off limits to the timber industry. This would save the owls, but could cost 33,000 jobs. But I don't think the debate is just about jobs and owls. It's about saving an important natural resource. If we aren't careful with our resources, we could upset the balance of our beautiful blue planet.

3 Use It

Find the facts in the passage above. Then find the opinions. List them on a separate piece of paper. Explain how you decided which was which.

Farming the West

Main Idea Farms in the West use the resources of the region to supply people with the food they eat every day.

One evening, your family goes out for dinner. You order a hamburger and a plate of French fries. Then you wait. You're starving! Finally, your meal arrives, steaming hot. It sits before you. You feel like eating that whole burger in one bite.

Wait! Before you bite into it, did you ever wonder where the foods in that meal came from? Chances are, they came from the West. The cattle for the beef might have been raised in Colorado. The wheat for the buns could have been grown in Montana. The lettuce and tomatoes probably came from California. The potatoes for the French fries most likely grew in Idaho. When the meal is over and the bill has been paid, you can thank our Western farms, as well as your parents.

California grows tons of tomatoes.

Western farmers grow wheat in Montana, Washington, Idaho, Colorado, and Oregon.

Idaho harvests more potatoes than any other state.

A Wealth of Farms

Focus *What do farms in the West produce?*

The landscape of the West is filled with farms. Some are small. They are usually owned and run by families. Other farms are huge. They are often owned by large companies which hire workers to grow crops. Some people call these giant farms "factories in the field." They seem to produce food as constantly as factories produce things like cars.

Agriculture and Geography

In Chapter 12, you read about the many climates and landforms of the West. They allow farmers to grow an amazing variety of crops.

Colorado and Montana have level plains. Washington and Oregon have wide plateaus. Those areas are good for growing wheat. Southern California and parts of Arizona have warm weather all year. Fruits such as oranges and grapefruits grow well in those states. Two-thirds of California's crops come from a place called the Central Valley. This valley runs down the middle of the state. It boasts rich soil and a sunny climate. The Central Valley is one of the reasons why California makes more money from farming than any other state in the country.

Montana, Colorado, and California raise cattle for beef.

Much of our lettuce is grown and harvested in California and Arizona. **Geography:** *Why does so much of our food come from the West?*

These are some of the staples and specialty crops grown by farmers in the West.

Making a Living on the Land

Farming is a big part of the West's economy. Farmers and their employees depend on crops to make money. The crops that farmers grow specifically to sell are called **cash crops.** Some of them are **staples** — foods that are the basic parts of people's diets. Staples grown in the West include wheat and corn.

Farmers in this region also sell crops that are not staples. These are called **specialty crops.** Washington grows more sweet cherries and apples than any other state. Oregon is a leading producer of strawberries and onions. Hawaii grows the most bananas. New Mexico is a leader in growing pecans. California is number one in almonds, apricots, broccoli, carrots, grapes, lemons, nectarines, peaches, pears, plums, tomatoes, walnuts, and more! The resources of the West allow farmers to grow this wide variety of crops.

The Search for Water

Focus *How do farmers in the West get water for their crops?* It takes more than sun and soil to grow crops, however. Much of the West has very little of one crucial ingredient for farming: water. (See *Think Like a Geographer,* pages 342–343.)

Most farmers in the West have to irrigate their fields to grow crops. Arizona and Southern California are naturally deserts. Farmers there get some of their water from hundreds of miles away.

One source of water for farms in many parts of the West is the Colorado River. You can see that river on the map at the right. Dams along the river create lakes of stored water. These are called **reservoirs.** Water from the reservoirs flows to farms through pipes and canals. Dams and reservoirs make the farms of this region possible. However, they also raise questions about water in the West.

The Hoover Dam on the Colorado River is the highest concrete dam in the United States. Behind it is Lake Mead.

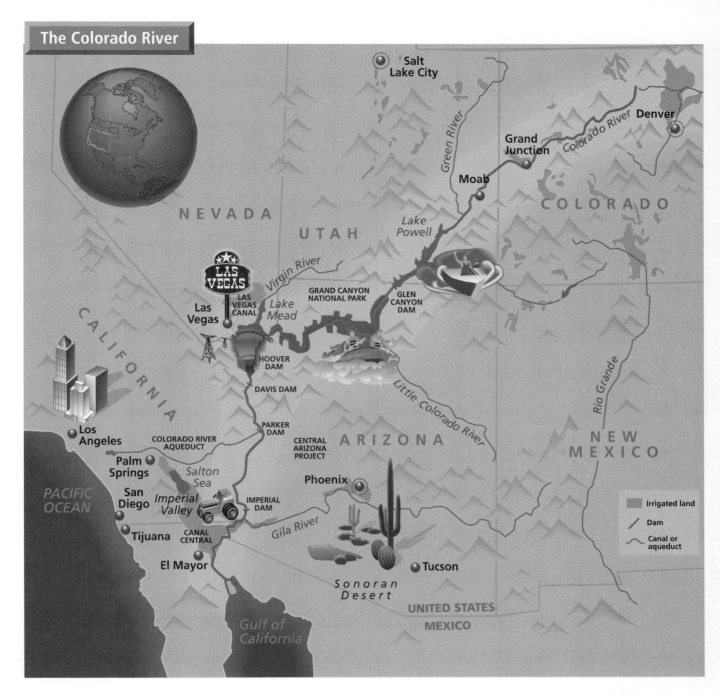

The Colorado River

Salt Lake City

Green River

Denver

Colorado River

Grand Junction

Moab

NEVADA

UTAH

Lake Powell

COLORADO

Virgin River

LAS VEGAS

GRAND CANYON NATIONAL PARK

GLEN CANYON DAM

Las Vegas

LAS VEGAS CANAL

Lake Mead

CALIFORNIA

HOOVER DAM

DAVIS DAM

Little Colorado River

Rio Grande

NEW MEXICO

Los Angeles

PARKER DAM

COLORADO RIVER AQUEDUCT

CENTRAL ARIZONA PROJECT

ARIZONA

Palm Springs

Salton Sea

Phoenix

San Diego

Imperial Valley

IMPERIAL DAM

PACIFIC OCEAN

Tijuana

CANAL CENTRAL

Gila River

El Mayor

Tucson

Sonoran Desert

Gulf of California

UNITED STATES

MEXICO

Legend:
- Irrigated land
- Dam
- Canal or aqueduct

About 21 million people in seven states get water from the Colorado River. Two million acres of farmland depend on it. All these people use up much of the water in the river. By the time it reaches the ocean, there is very little water left.

Lake Powell Over three million people a year go boating, fishing, or swimming in this lake.

Grand Canyon This mile-deep canyon was carved out by the Colorado River over millions of years.

Las Vegas Water for the homes and businesses in this city is taken from the river.

Hoover Dam Water from the reservoir behind the dam is used by cities in Arizona and California. Water rushing over the dam is used to produce electricity.

Southern California Cities use water from the river. Canals carry water to farms that once were desert.

Sonoran Desert Residents here have learned to conserve their water use.

Map Skill: *Why do people depend so heavily on the Colorado River? Are there any other rivers in the area?*

How Much Water Does It Take?

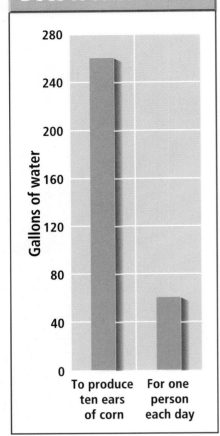

This chart compares the amount of water needed to grow corn with the water an average person uses each day. **Chart Skill:** *How many days worth of water does it take to grow 10 ears of corn?*

The Price of Water

Western water comes at a price. Consider dams. They cost a lot to build and to run. The federal government provided money for building many dams in the West. That means that people all over the United States have helped pay for them. Western farms depend on these dams. Still, the cost is high.

The environment pays a price for dams, too. Damming a river can change its temperature. Dams alter the amount of water that flows in the river. These changes can harm wildlife that live in or near the river.

There are also other difficulties. While water sits in reservoirs, it evaporates. This makes the water saltier. Irrigation adds to this problem. Water flowing in and out of a field evaporates even more quickly than it does in reservoirs. After a while, the water becomes too salty to drink or to grow crops.

Finding Answers to Western Water Problems

Today, people are working to solve these problems. Farmers are trying new ways of irrigating fields. To reduce waste, they give the crops just enough water. They also irrigate at night. That keeps the sun from evaporating the irrigation water. In Arizona, a kind of factory takes extra salt out of river water.

People are also learning to conserve water in their homes. Some states and cities even have laws about saving water. All of these methods help make sure that the West will have enough water for its farms and for its future.

Lesson Review

1 **Key Vocabulary:** Write a paragraph about irrigation in the West, using these words: **cash crop, staple, specialty crop,** and **reservoir.**

2 **Focus:** What do farms in the West produce?

3 **Focus:** How do farmers in the West get water for their crops?

4 **Critical Thinking: Predict** What do you think will happen if people stop trying to solve water problems in the West?

5 **Theme: From Desert to Tropics** Are any of your favorite foods grown in the West? In what climates do they grow?

6 **Citizenship/Math Activity:** Try to keep track of how many gallons of water you use in one week. Make a chart like the one on this page. Can you use less water? Make a chart for the next week, showing how much you saved.

A Region of High Technology

Main Idea High technology is a fast-growing industry in the West.

In the darkness of a stormy night, the captain flies a plane toward an airport. The plane passes through a thick cloud. He feels it bump and shake. Rain streaks past the windows. Then the clouds clear. The runway lights lie ahead.

Suddenly, alarms sound. An engine has failed! The pilot struggles to keep control. Finally, he lands the plane safely on the wet runway. He breathes a sigh of relief. Then he steps out of the cockpit into the bright lights of the training center.

The pilot has been working in a flight simulator. It looks just like the cockpit of an airplane. It has a special difference, though. The plane's "windows" are really computer screens. They can also show many situations that pilots might face. Flight simulators teach pilots to handle dangerous situations.

Key Vocabulary
silicon
computer chip
computer graphics
special effect

Key Places
Silicon Valley

A pilot in Denver, Colorado, shows a student how a flight simulator works.

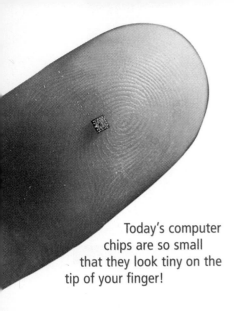

Today's computer chips are so small that they look tiny on the tip of your finger!

How a Chip Works

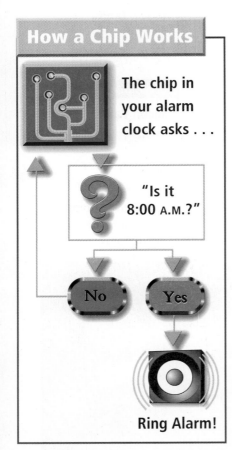

The chip in your alarm clock asks . . .

"Is it 8:00 A.M.?"

No   Yes

Ring Alarm!

Whatever a computer chip is used in, the basic way it operates is still the same. It answers questions "yes" or "no." This chart shows how a chip rings an alarm at eight o'clock. **Chart Skill:** *What answer did the chip give at seven o'clock?*

Silicon Valley

Focus *Why is Silicon Valley a center of high technology?*
Computer technology makes flight simulators possible. Much of this technology was created in the West, in a place called Silicon Valley.

Silicon Valley stretches south from San Francisco to San Jose (sahn hoh ZAY), California. The valley gets its name from an element called **silicon**. People use silicon to make Silicon Valley's most famous product: the computer chip.

A **computer chip** is a package of pathways for electricity. Each pathway can be either open or closed. Because of this, a computer chip is like a person who says only two words, "yes" or "no." You can see how this works in the chart at the left.

A computer chip is very small — about 1/4 of an inch on each side. Yet it can hold more than a million pathways of electricity. It can answer millions of yes-or-no questions every second! Chips are what make computers work so quickly.

The First Chip

The modern computer chip was created in 1959. Businesses began looking for a place to manufacture these chips, and Silicon Valley had a lot to offer. Sunny weather and cheap land helped bring companies there. Local colleges like Stanford University attracted scientists to the area and provided skilled workers.

At first, only a few high-technology companies did business in the valley. Then people around the world began to use more computers. These companies made a lot of money. During the 1960s, 1970s, and 1980s, thousands of businesses came to the valley. They wanted to share in the new industry's success.

Today, Silicon Valley is home to thousands of high-technology companies. In addition to computer chips, these companies make computers and other machines that use computer chips.

Creating and Using High Technology

Technology from Silicon Valley is part of how you work and play every day. Have you ever used a computer or a calculator? If so, then you've used technology that started here.

In fact, you probably use technology from Silicon Valley all the time — without even knowing it! When you ride in a car, you use a computer. How? Most cars today have computers in their engines. They help the cars work better. Computers also keep your phone lines running. Even some toys have computer chips in them.

People in Silicon Valley are always thinking about new ways to use high technology. T.J. Rodgers is president of a high-technology company. As he says:

> "**F**or turning some interesting idea . . . into a real product, there's no place in the world where you can do it faster."

Rodgers and many other people in the West know that Silicon Valley is a place where ideas come to life.

Computer chips are made in rooms without dust or dirt, known as "clean rooms." Workers in these rooms have to wear special suits. *(above)*

High-technology companies are close together in San Jose, California — a city in Silicon Valley. *(left)*

High-Tech Images

Focus | *What are some ways people use computer graphics?*
Some people in the West make ideas come alive on computer screens. They do this with **computer graphics** — pictures made on computers. Some of these graphics are in the movies. They are special effects. **Special effects** are pictures or sounds that people add to a movie after it has been filmed. *(See below.)*

• Tell Me More •

Bringing Dinosaurs to Life

Computer graphics help movie-makers create special effects that seem real. Look at the photo on the bottom of the page. It shows a special effect from a movie. When the movie was filmed, it included only the man and the car. A special effects team in San Rafael, California, drew the dinosaur on a computer. Then they added the picture of the dinosaur to the film.

Artists draw sketches and make models of a dinosaur. *(above)* Then they use powerful computers to make these images look real.

The computer graphic is added to the scene that has already been filmed. *(right)* This scene shows a tyrannosaurus rex (tih RAN oh saw ruhs reks).

Images for Science and Architecture

Special effects are just one way people use computer graphics. You read about another at the beginning of this lesson: flight simulators. These use computer graphics to teach pilots how to deal with emergencies. Today, people also use computer graphics in science, medicine, and many other fields.

Astronomers study outer space. They get information about stars and planets from different kinds of telescopes, as well as from satellites and spaceships. Computer graphics help astronomers turn this information into pictures.

Doctors also have machines that use computer graphics. They show the inside of the human body. Doctors can see how parts of the body work. Architects design buildings. They draw computer graphics of things they want to build.

Much of the technology behind computer graphics comes from the West. Computers can be used for much more than creating images, however. People all over the country find new ways to use computers every day. Computers have already changed the world. How have they changed your life?

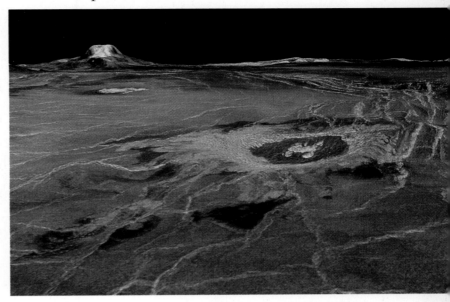

Scientists used information gathered by a spaceship to create this computer image. It shows the surface of the planet Venus. **Technology:** *Do you think this image is as accurate as a photograph? Why or why not?*

Lesson Review

1 **Key Vocabulary:** Use these words to write about a movie: **silicon, computer chip, computer graphics, special effect.**

2 **Focus:** Why is Silicon Valley a center of high technology?

3 **Focus:** What are some ways people use computer graphics?

4 **Critical Thinking: Predict** Do you think high technology will continue to change movies in the future? How?

5 **Geography:** What if the computer-chip industry had started in another region? Would it have grown as much as it did in Silicon Valley? Explain why or why not.

6 **Citizenship/Research Activity:** Find out how computers have changed your local government. How have they affected the way people communicate with their government leaders?

Chapter Review

Summarizing the Main Idea

1 Copy and complete the chart below, indicating how each resource affects the West today.

Resource	Effect on the West
Forests	
Farmland	
Water	

Vocabulary

2 Using at least 10 of the following terms, write a brief dialogue between two people who live in the West.

refugee (p. 349)

employee (p. 350)

self-employed (p. 350)

chamber of commerce (p. 351)

timber (p. 359)

lumber (p. 359)

old-growth forest (p. 360)

clear-cutting (p. 362)

contour (p. 362)

cash crop (p. 366)

staple (p. 366)

specialty crop (p. 366)

reservoir (p. 366)

silicon (p. 370)

computer chip (p. 370)

computer graphics (p. 372)

special effect (p. 372)

Reviewing the Facts

3 Why have people moved to the West from other countries?

4 Why would someone join a chamber of commerce?

5 How do westerners use their forests?

6 Why is it important to preserve old-growth forests in the West?

7 What is the purpose of a managed forest?

8 How are people preserving both the West's forests and the lumber industry?

9 Which western state earns the most money from farming? Why is this so?

10 How is water a problem in parts of the West? How are people solving it?

11 Why did high-technology businesses come to Silicon Valley?

Skill Review: Distinguishing Fact from Opinion

12 Explain the difference between fact and opinion. Use the controversy over the spotted owl to give some examples of each.

13 Find a newspaper article. Distinguish between fact and opinion. Use quotations from the article to explain how you know the difference between them.

Geography Skills

14 Look at the map on page 348. What if your family was moving to the West from Central America? What state would you go to? How would your family earn a living?

15 How is farming in the West different from farming in the Midwest? How is it similar?

Critical Thinking

16 **Compare** What is the difference between being an employee and being self-employed? Why would some people prefer one over the other?

17 **Conclude** How do you think people in the West can conserve water? Prepare a speech suggesting ways to use less water.

Writing: Citizenship and History

18 **Citizenship** Prepare an information booklet for new immigrants to Denver, Colorado. What information might be useful? Include illustrations.

19 **History** What would you put in a time capsule about the West today? Write a list of items that you think best represent the West.

Activities

Economics/Math Activity
Interview someone who owns his or her own business. What problems have they faced in running the business? How did they overcome them? Use what you learn to create a report with graphs or charts about this business.

Cultures/Research Activity
How do people live in Vietnam, Thailand, or Laos? Learn more about one Asian culture. What do people emigrating from Asia face when they move to the United States? Write a report about how their lives might change.

Internet Option

Check the **Internet Social Studies Center** for ideas on how to extend your theme project beyond your classroom.

THEME PROJECT CHECK-IN

Include information about life in the West today in your guidebook. Answer these questions:
- What are some reasons why people are still moving to the West?
- What foods do we eat that were grown in the West?
- How do high-technology industries affect our lives?

The United States and the World

"What we call foreign affairs is no longer foreign affairs. It's a local affair. Whatever happens in Indonesia is important to Indiana."

· THEME ·

Making Connections

❝ *It's important to cooperate with other countries. If we all work together, we might be able to keep Earth clean.* ❞

Stephanie Means, Fourth Grade
North Little Rock, AR

People who live on your street or in your town are your neighbors. In the same way, regions of the United States are neighbors to each other. The United States is also a neighbor to other countries. In this unit, you'll learn how regions and countries depend on each other. You'll see how different people in different places can all cooperate to help one another.

Theme Project

Design a Bulletin Board

On a bulletin board, show connections between places in the United States and places around the world.

• Put a world map on the bulletin board. Mark some of the places in the unit on the map.

• Find pictures of ways that different regions or countries work together. Draw lines to connect the pictures to those places.

• Write descriptions of some ways people cooperate.

RESEARCH: Choose two places mentioned in the unit and find out more about the activities that connect them.

◀ The control tower at San Francisco International Airport

WHEN & WHERE
ATLAS

The world is full of connections! Different regions and different countries buy and sell goods to and from each other. They share their cultures and their ideas. This map shows you many countries and some important cities of the world.

In this unit, you'll learn how communities within the United States work together and how the United States works with other countries. You'll also learn about special groups that some countries have formed to help each other. You'll see that people in different countries often turn out to have many things in common.

Unit 7 Chapters

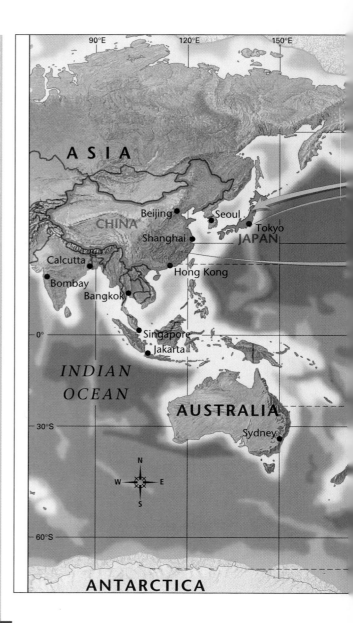

Unit Timeline

1500	1600	1700

Small Businesses

Find out how worms helped John Andrews start a business. *Chapter 14, Lesson 1*

Telecommunications

How many ways can you use a phone? *Chapter 14, Lesson 2*

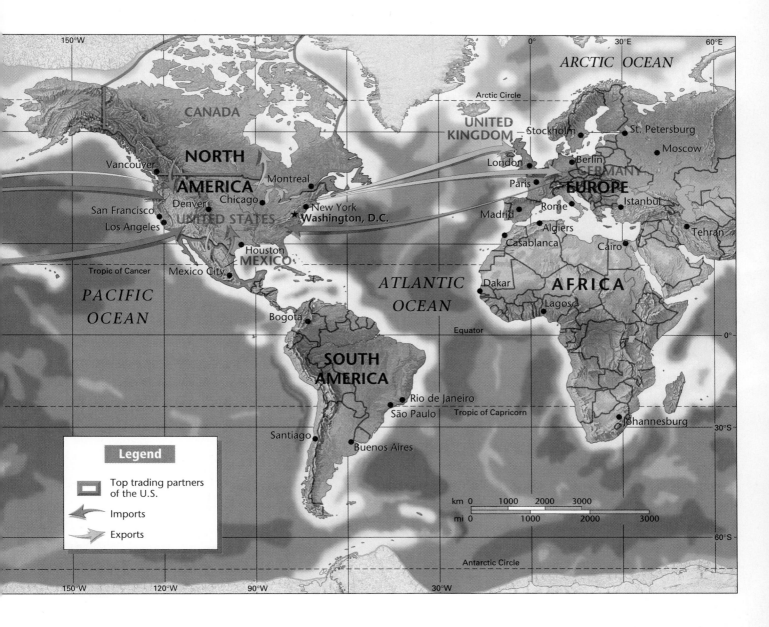

ARCTIC OCEAN

CANADA

NORTH AMERICA

UNITED STATES

UNITED KINGDOM

EUROPE

GERMANY

AFRICA

PACIFIC OCEAN

ATLANTIC OCEAN

MEXICO

SOUTH AMERICA

Vancouver
San Francisco
Los Angeles
Denver
Chicago
Montreal
New York
Washington, D.C.
Houston
Mexico City
Bogotá
Santiago
Buenos Aires
São Paulo
Rio de Janeiro
Dakar
Lagos
Johannesburg
Casablanca
Algiers
Madrid
Rome
Paris
London
Berlin
Stockholm
St. Petersburg
Moscow
Istanbul
Cairo
Tehran

Tropic of Cancer
Equator
Tropic of Capricorn
Arctic Circle
Antarctic Circle

150°W 120°W 90°W 30°W 0° 30°E 60°E
0° 30°S 60°S

km 0   1000   2000   3000
mi 0   1000   2000   3000

Legend

- ☐ Top trading partners of the U.S.
- ← Imports
- → Exports

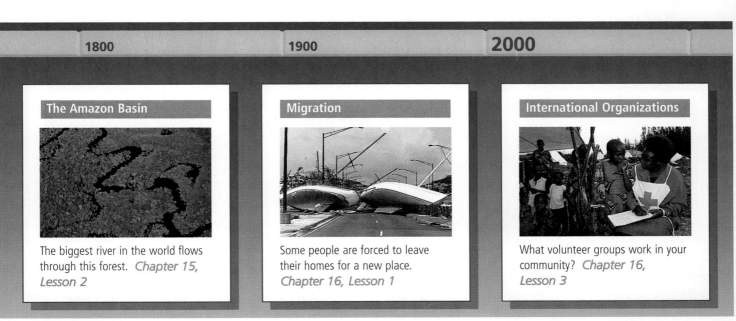

1800   1900   **2000**

The Amazon Basin

The biggest river in the world flows through this forest. *Chapter 15, Lesson 2*

Migration

Some people are forced to leave their homes for a new place. *Chapter 16, Lesson 1*

International Organizations

What volunteer groups work in your community? *Chapter 16, Lesson 3*

14 Regions Relying on Each Other

Chapter Preview: *People, Places, and Events*

1800	1850	1900

Truck Carrying Goods

Some goods travel all the way across the country. Find out why.
Lesson 1, Page 384

Portable Tape Player

Is $200 too high a price for this product? How can you tell?
Lesson 1, Page 387

Building Train Tracks

How did trains change the U.S. economy? *Lesson 2, Page 391*

Trading Goods and Services

Main Idea People across the regions of the United States rely on each other for goods and services.

Key Vocabulary
trade
profit
specialization
market
free enterprise
consumer

J & J Bait and Tackle in Clinton, Connecticut, was a busy place when a boy named John Andrews stood behind the counter. Customers found a store full of fishermen and twelve-year-old John selling supplies. Many adults asked him for advice about fishing and listened to what he told them. When they asked for the owner, however, John's answer surprised them. The fishing store was his own business.

John had seen that there was no store on the Clinton seashore that sold only fishing equipment. He borrowed $300 from his father to buy supplies and opened his store in June. By July he had paid his father back and earned enough money to buy his own motorboat. Pretty good for a summer job!

◀ A four-level overpass on a modern highway

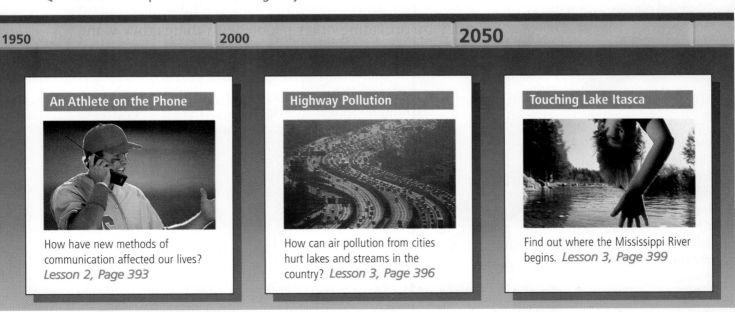

1950   2000   **2050**

An Athlete on the Phone

How have new methods of communication affected our lives? *Lesson 2, Page 393*

Highway Pollution

How can air pollution from cities hurt lakes and streams in the country? *Lesson 3, Page 396*

Touching Lake Itasca

Find out where the Mississippi River begins. *Lesson 3, Page 399*

A Regional Business

Focus *How does one business contribute to the economy?*

A small store such as John's is one of the thousands of businesses that make up the U.S. economy. An economy is all the different ways in which people earn money and get the things they want or need. One way people do this is through trade. **Trade** once meant exchanging goods for other goods. Now it means selling and buying things. John did this in his store. His customers gave him money, and he gave them fishing supplies.

The trades that happened in John's store were really the end of a long chain of other trades. John did not make the items he sold himself. He had to buy them from someone else. A business in a nearby town sold him lures and hooks. He also bought supplies from other states in his region. A business in Maine sold him bait and delivered it twice a week.

John had to buy everything he sold from someone else. So how did he make any money? He sold his supplies for a higher price than he paid for them. *(See chart.)* Part of the money he earned went to pay for his other expenses, such as shelves for supplies and freezers for bait. The money he had left over was his profit. A **profit** is what someone earns from running a business, after paying the expenses.

This is how an economy works. People like John make money by providing other people with things they want.

Twelve-year-old John Andrews poses in front of his store.

This chart shows how stores make money on each thing they sell. Part of the money from each sale must go to other expenses, which can include rent and electric bills. **Chart Skill:** *Which item makes the most money for the owner? Which makes the least?*

Making a Profit

Fishing Supplies	Price	Cost	Profit
swimmer lure	$4.00	$2.25	$1.75
popper lure	$6.50	$4.50	$2.00
hooks	$0.95/doz.	$0.57/doz.	$0.38
worms for bait	$3.75/doz.	$1.50/doz.	$2.25
mackerel for bait	$1.20/lb.	$0.50/lb.	$0.70

U.S. Regions and Industries

West	Midwest	South	Northeast
Airplanes	Trains	Furniture	Cameras
Computers	Cars and trucks	Textiles	Books
Sawed lumber	Heavy equipment	Chemicals	Footwear
Movies	Telephones	Heating and cooling equipment	Scientific instruments

Networks of Trade

Focus *How does trade connect regions of the United States?*
Throughout the United States, businesses buy goods in one place, just as John did, and sell them to people who live in another place. Why do people buy things? Because they cannot provide themselves with everything they need. The same is true of regions. Regions trade with each other because no single region can provide everything for all the people who live there.

One way regions help each other is through specialization. **Specialization** happens when a business concentrates on making or selling one kind of product. The map above shows some of the specialized businesses in each region. Workers in these industries make things that people in other regions buy.

Some U.S. regions are known for certain industries. This map shows some of the industries in each region that specialize in making one kind of product. **Map Skill:** *What industries does the map show for your region? Do you know someone who works in these businesses?*

Exchanging Goods

The exchange of goods connects people across the country. At home in Chicago, a girl needs to practice long division. She sits down at a computer made in California. She inserts a diskette made in Massachusetts and plays a math game invented in Texas. Networks of trade have helped her do better in school.

Networks of trade also help businesses. They bring factories materials they need to make their products. *(See photos.)*

The food we eat has often traveled farther in the past few weeks than we have! Depending on the time of year, your salad might have vegetables in it from Florida, California, and Texas, as well as some grown in your home state.

Because regions depend on each other for food, a problem with crops in one state can affect people living somewhere else. In 1994, tropical storm Gordon flooded farms in Florida. The heavy rains and fierce winds destroyed pepper, cucumber, tomato, and strawberry crops. David Holmes, a Florida official, said, "If you live in New York City you're going to be paying more for your fruits and vegetables. . . ."

Making Furniture

1 **Natural Resources** Loggers cut down a tree growing in the forests of a state such as Michigan or Oregon.

2 **Transportation** Trucks and trains carry the lumber to another region, perhaps to a furniture factory in South Carolina.

Exchanging Services

Businesses do more than provide people with goods like furniture or automobiles. They also sell services, which are jobs that people pay someone else to do. At J & J Bait and Tackle, John sold goods, but if someone hired you to shovel the snow off their sidewalk, you would be selling a service.

Doctors, lawyers, and teachers sell their services. People can provide a service just by talking or writing. Someone in West Virginia can use the telephone to sell a service in Colorado. People also sell services through computers and by mail. Some workers make a living without leaving home.

A Free Market

Focus *What are the benefits of a free-enterprise system?*

John opened his store because he knew that fishermen in his town wanted a place on the seashore to buy supplies. John saw there was a market for bait and tackle. A **market** is a group of people who need or want certain goods or services.

❸ **Manufacturing** Factory workers make the wood into chairs, tables, and other furniture. **Geography:** *Can you find out where your family's furniture was made?*

❹ **Retail** Retail stores sell products directly to consumers. Furniture made in the factories of one region is often sold in the cities of another region.

What is money?

Have you ever wondered how complicated life would be if there was no money? What if you wanted to buy a bike? Without money, you would have to trade with the store owner for something he wants.

Maybe the owner wants a microwave oven. You would have to go trade with someone for an oven, then carry the oven all the way back to the store, and trade it at last for the bike. Money is a simple way of exchanging things — it makes trading easier.

Anything can serve as money as long everyone agrees on how much it is worth. Most countries today use a combination of paper money and metal money (coins).

Two girls choose toys in a department store.

Some Native Americans used shells for money.

These coins and paper money come from countries around the world.

Laws did not keep John from providing that group of people — his market — with the goods it wanted. The same is often true for other businesses. Like many countries around the world, the economy of the United States is based on a free-enterprise system. **Free enterprise** means that businesses are free to choose the products they want to sell. The people who buy these goods and services are called **consumers**.

Businesses may be free to sell anything they want, but consumers are also free not to buy it. What if a store charged $20 for a pack of gum? What would you do? Most of us would go somewhere else, no matter how badly we wanted a piece of gum. John did not have the only bait-and-tackle store in Connecticut. If he charged too much, his customers might have driven to another town to buy their supplies. Part of making a profit in a free-enterprise system is setting the right price.

The Best Product for the Lowest Price

In a free-enterprise system, many businesses try to sell the same goods or services. They compete with each other for customers. What do most of their customers want? They want the best product for the lowest price. The business that offers this will usually get the most customers. This is one of the most important benefits of a free-enterprise system. Competition brings consumers quality goods and services at fair prices.

The government watches over our free-enterprise system. It sets rules about how different products should be made and sold. All cars made and sold in the United States, for example, must have seat belts. All meat and poultry must be inspected by government officials, who check that the food is healthy to eat. Laws also help businesses conserve our resources, such as water. Through government, we work to make sure that the networks of trade benefit everyone in the country.

Ask Yourself

How do you know a price is too high? Suppose you were grocery shopping and saw tomatoes you thought were too expensive. How would you decide if you were right? What if you thought a CD was too expensive? What would you do?

????????????????

Lesson Review

1. **Key Vocabulary:** Use the following words in a paragraph: trade, profit, market, free enterprise, consumer.

2. **Focus:** How does one business contribute to the economy?

3. **Focus:** How does trade connect regions of the United States?

4. **Focus:** What are the benefits of a free-enterprise system?

5. **Critical Thinking: Predict** What might happen if people could not trade?

6. **Theme: Making Connections** What products does your family use that come from another region?

7. **Citizenship/Math Activity:** What could you sell to raise money for school? How much would it cost for you to buy it? How much could you charge? Draw a chart showing your profit.

By Land, Water, and Air

Main Idea Networks of transportation and communication connect regions and help the U.S. economy.

The United States is a big country, and we have tried many different ways of traveling around it. By the early 1800s, people knew how to build railroad tracks, but they still did not know the best way to power the trains to run on them. The Baltimore & Ohio Railroad tried putting a horse on a treadmill inside a railroad car, like a mouse inside a cage. They also tried a "sail car" — a sailboat with wheels. Neither of these experiments worked. Yet they show how badly people wanted new ways of traveling. They would try almost anything once.

Transportation Changes America

Focus *How did transportation help the United States grow?*

People need transportation in order to trade with one another. Native Americans created a network of paths and trails for trading. They used these routes to exchange shells, tobacco,

The Life of the National Road

1750	1800	1850

1806 Congress decides to build the National Road on an old Native American path called Nemacolin's Trail.

1830s Settlers are now traveling the National Road to Ohio. Later, they will travel the road across Indiana and into Illinois.

flint, and hides. After the 1500s, Europeans used these same routes to trade furs.

On the Road

These paths changed when settlers began moving west in the late 1700s. Wagons and horses widened them into roads. Traveling was still difficult. Often wagons had to drive over tree stumps a foot high.

Settlers who wanted to reach the West asked the U.S. government to build better roads. In 1811, the government began the National Road. *(See map.)* At first the road ran from Cumberland, Maryland, to the Ohio River. Eventually, it reached Illinois.

Pioneers were not the only ones who traveled the National Road. It was also used by people trading livestock and other goods. One traveler recorded the scene at a stopping place along the way:

> **"** *. . . there would be thirty six-horse teams in the wagon yard . . . one thousand hogs in other enclosures, and as many fat cattle from Illinois in adjoining [nearby] fields.* **"**

The National Road still exists. It has been paved over and renamed U.S. Route 40. *(See timeline below.)*

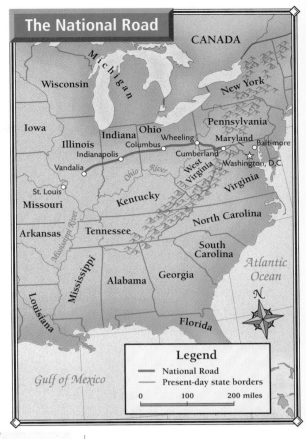

The National Road

The National Road was one of the first roads built by the U.S. government. **Map Skill:** *Why do you think the U.S. government helped pay for this road?*

1900   1950   **2000**

1920s More and more people are driving cars, and they begin asking for paved roads. The government turns part of the old National Road into U.S. Route 40.

1990s Today, U.S. Route 40 is one of the many interstate roads that connect regions of the United States.

Traveling by Waterway

A waterway is any body of water that a ship or a boat can use. The ocean is the world's most important waterway. Hundreds of years ago, both Native Americans and Europeans used the ocean to ship their goods up and down the coast.

Inland, traders and settlers used natural waterways, such as the Mississippi and Ohio rivers. As the United States grew, however, these waterways were no longer enough. Rivers did not run everywhere people needed to go, and many could only carry small boats. So states began building canals.

Canals changed the way people in different regions did business with one another. New York completed the Erie Canal in 1825. Before the canal, it took 20 days to move a ton of freight by wagon from Albany to Buffalo. The trip cost businesses around $100. Once the canal was finished, the same amount of freight made the trip in eight days. It only cost $20.

Canals made it cheaper to move goods, which increased the amount of trade across the country. By 1852, canals were carrying nine million tons of freight between regions. Canals were king — but not for long.

Canals in the 1800s

Most U.S. canals were built in the area between the Midwest and the East. They usually began and ended at a lake or a river.

Locks The land canals travel across is often not all the same height. Boats have to go up and down. This is why canals have locks. Locks are like steps of water. Gates let water in and out to raise or lower ships.

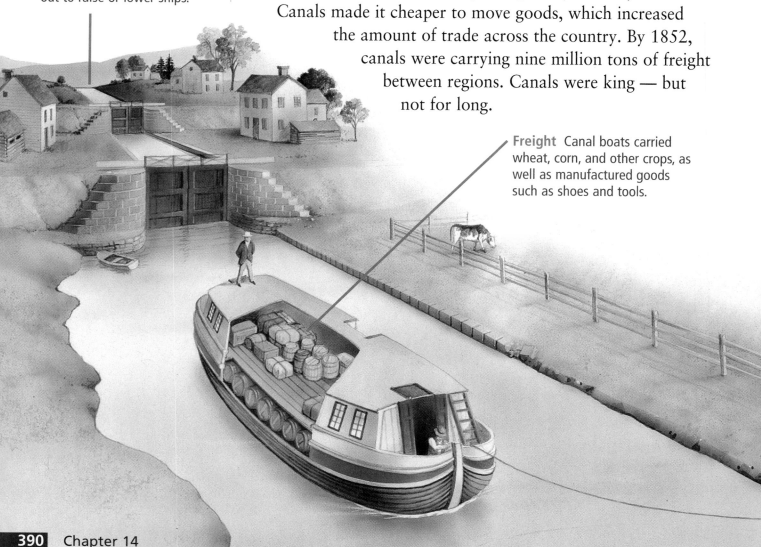

Freight Canal boats carried wheat, corn, and other crops, as well as manufactured goods such as shoes and tools.

The Railroad

In 1825, the same year the Erie Canal opened, John Stevens operated the first steam-powered locomotive in the United States. A **locomotive** is an engine built for pulling railroad cars. Stevens' engine did not leave the half-mile circle of track he ran it on. Even so, he saw a great future for it. He believed that railroads, not canals, would link America's growing towns and cities.

Stevens was right. In 1835, just 10 years after his first run, locomotives carried about 100,000 passengers on the Baltimore & Ohio Railroad. Between 1840 and 1860, over 27,000 miles of track were laid down across the United States.

Railroads changed the country. Trains moved faster than anything else at that time. They could also carry heavy loads, such as iron ore or coal. Factories got the materials they needed more easily and moved their products into stores more quickly. This helped the economy grow.

Today, trains still carry freight from region to region. Many businesses send their goods by train rather than by truck, because a modern locomotive can pull more weight. Trains still carry passengers, too. Many people take commuter trains to work. Trains are an important part of American life.

A construction crew (above) poses in front of a locomotive in 1885. The pick and shovel (below) were used to build the Union Pacific Railroad. **History:** *Do you think as many trains run today as 100 years ago?*

Power Early canal boats were often pulled by horses, mules, or oxen on shore. Later, steamboats were used in some canals. Diesel engines push boats through modern canals.

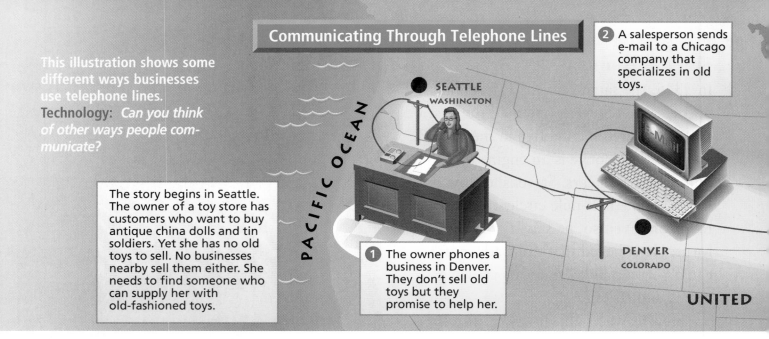

Communicating Through Telephone Lines

This illustration shows some different ways businesses use telephone lines.
Technology: *Can you think of other ways people communicate?*

The story begins in Seattle. The owner of a toy store has customers who want to buy antique china dolls and tin soldiers. Yet she has no old toys to sell. No businesses nearby sell them either. She needs to find someone who can supply her with old-fashioned toys.

PACIFIC OCEAN

SEATTLE
WASHINGTON

1 The owner phones a business in Denver. They don't sell old toys but they promise to help her.

2 A salesperson sends e-mail to a Chicago company that specializes in old toys.

DENVER
COLORADO

UNITED

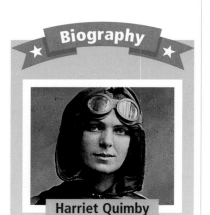
Keeping in Touch

Focus *How do airmail and telecommunications connect people across different regions?*

Businesses in different regions need to exchange more than goods. They also have to exchange information. In the 1900s, this has become faster than ever before.

Airmail

Everything went wrong on the first airmail flight from New York to Washington, D.C., in May 1918. First, someone discovered the fuel tank was empty. Then the pilot flew off in the wrong direction. The mail finally had to be delivered by train.

By August 1918, the post office began regular airmail service. In the years that followed, the U.S. government encouraged the airplane industry to improve their planes. This helped the post office deliver mail more quickly. Airplanes became faster. In 1930, it took 36 hours to fly from New York to Los Angeles. By 1953, the same flight took only eight hours.

Telecommunications

As airlines improved speed, mail delivery times became faster. Delivery companies began offering overnight service. Today, a person can send a package from Pennsylvania to Oregon in less than 24 hours. Even so, many businesses need to send information instantly — in the time it takes to make a phone call.

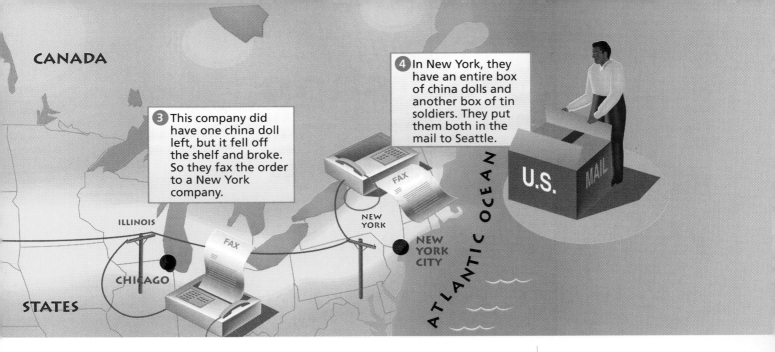

CANADA

3 This company did have one china doll left, but it fell off the shelf and broke. So they fax the order to a New York company.

4 In New York, they have an entire box of china dolls and another box of tin soldiers. They put them both in the mail to Seattle.

ILLINOIS

STATES

CHICAGO

NEW YORK

NEW YORK CITY

ATLANTIC OCEAN

U.S. MAIL

FAX

FAX

Improvements in telecommunications have allowed businesses to do just that. Telecommunications are electronic ways of communicating that include telephones, radios, televisions, and computers. Businesses today can send a message using a **fax machine**, which is like sending a letter over telephone wires.

Many people now use another kind of telecommunication. They travel the "information superhighway" known as the Internet. The **Internet** is a network of computers around the country, connected by telephone wires. People use the Internet to send and receive electronic mail, follow the news, and exchange information. With telecommunications, people in every region can be almost as close as next door.

Lesson Review

1 **Key Vocabulary:** Use these terms in a paragraph about communication: fax machine, Internet.

2 **Focus:** How did transportation help the United States grow?

3 **Focus:** How do airmail and telecommunications connect people across different regions?

4 **Critical Thinking: Generalize** How is transportation useful to businesses?

5 **Citizenship:** Do you think the Internet makes it easier to know what is happening in our government? Explain.

6 **Geography/Math Activity:** How might you have traveled from New York to Chicago in 1800? In 1900? How might you travel in 2000? Which method is fastest? Find out the distance between the cities. Create a chart to compare your journeys at these three dates.

Skills Workshop

Using Time Zones

Set Your Watches

If you live in Chicago, and you telephone your cousin in Seattle at 8:00 in the morning, you'll probably wake the entire family. When it's 8:00 A.M. in Chicago, it's only 6:00 A.M. in Seattle. Why? Seattle and Chicago are each in a different **time zone**. What is the reason for time zones?

In the 1800s, each town set its clocks by the sun. There were many different "local times." When train travel became popular, this system no longer worked. People needed to know exactly when their trains would arrive and depart.

In 1884, a system of standard time zones was developed. Time zones made travel, trade, and communication easier for everyone.

Why We Have Day and Night

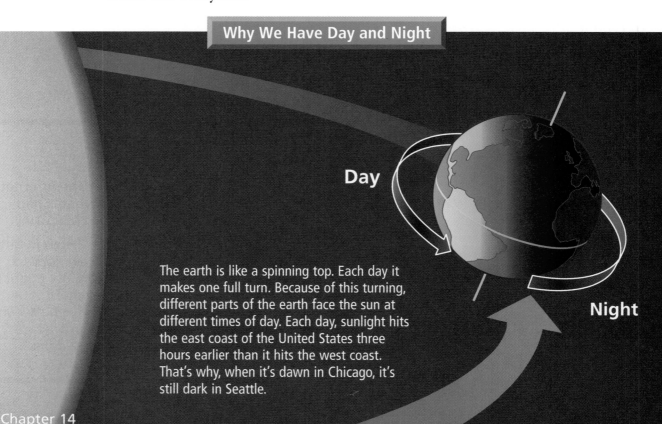

Day

Night

The earth is like a spinning top. Each day it makes one full turn. Because of this turning, different parts of the earth face the sun at different times of day. Each day, sunlight hits the east coast of the United States three hours earlier than it hits the west coast. That's why, when it's dawn in Chicago, it's still dark in Seattle.

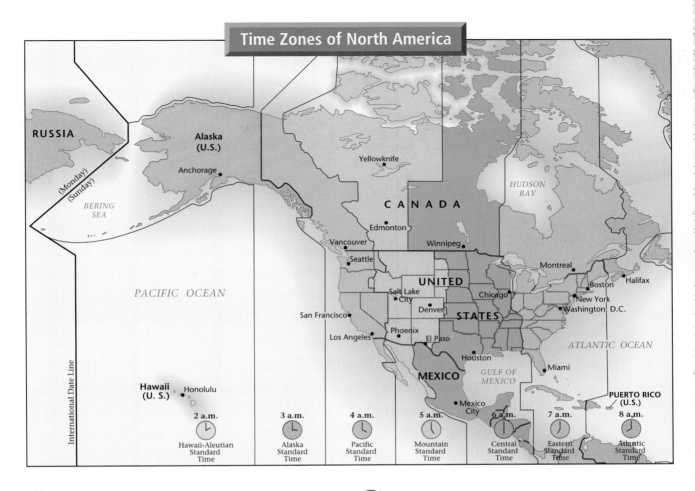

Time Zones of North America

RUSSIA

Alaska (U.S.)
Anchorage

(Monday)
(Sunday)

BERING SEA

Yellowknife

CANADA

HUDSON BAY

Edmonton

Vancouver
Seattle

Winnipeg

Montreal

Boston
Halifax

UNITED
Salt Lake City

Chicago

New York
Washington, D.C.

PACIFIC OCEAN

San Francisco

Denver

STATES

Los Angeles
Phoenix
El Paso

Houston

ATLANTIC OCEAN

Miami

MEXICO
GULF OF MEXICO

Hawaii (U. S.)   Honolulu

Mexico City

International Date Line

PUERTO RICO (U.S.)

2 a.m.	3 a.m.	4 a.m.	5 a.m.	6 a.m.	7 a.m.	8 a.m.
Hawaii-Aleutian Standard Time	Alaska Standard Time	Pacific Standard Time	Mountain Standard Time	Central Standard Time	Eastern Standard Time	Atlantic Standard Time

1 Here's How

The map above shows North American time zones.

- Find the seven time zones in North America from east to west. All places in the same time zone have the same time. What time zone do you live in?

- As you move west, subtract one hour for each time zone. Notice that it is an hour earlier in the Mountain time zone than in the Central time zone.

- As you move east, add one hour for each zone. You can figure out that it is three hours later in the Eastern time zone than it is in the Pacific time zone.

2 Think It Through

How would you explain time zones to a friend?

3 Use It

1. Suppose it is 11:00 A.M. in Chicago. What time is it in: a) New York b) Alaska c) Hawaii d) Florida?

2. When it is 6:00 P.M. in Denver, in what cities is it 5:00 P.M.?

3. Name five states in the Central time zone.

The sundial was the first tool used to measure time. The sun's rays cast a shadow that falls on different marks on the sundial during different times of the day.

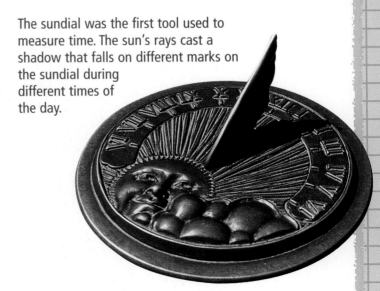

Working Together

Main Idea Regions can cooperate to use resources well.

In a lake high in the mountains, far from any city, fish start to die. Why? Pollution is killing them. Pollution happens when air or water is made dirty by wastes such as sewage, car exhaust, or factory smoke. Yet how can this lake be polluted, so far from houses, roads, and industries? Because pollution can travel. Smoke and exhaust rise above large cities and are carried away by the wind — sometimes to another region. The pollution mixes with rain clouds, and then rain brings it back to the earth. This polluted rain is called **acid rain**. It is an example of how a problem in one region can affect other regions.

Air pollution rises into the sky. Then it is carried long distances by wind currents.

As it travels, it mixes with the water in clouds and returns to the earth in rain.

Acid Rain Pollution travels! Air pollution from large cities is carried by the wind. It can cause problems in other regions.

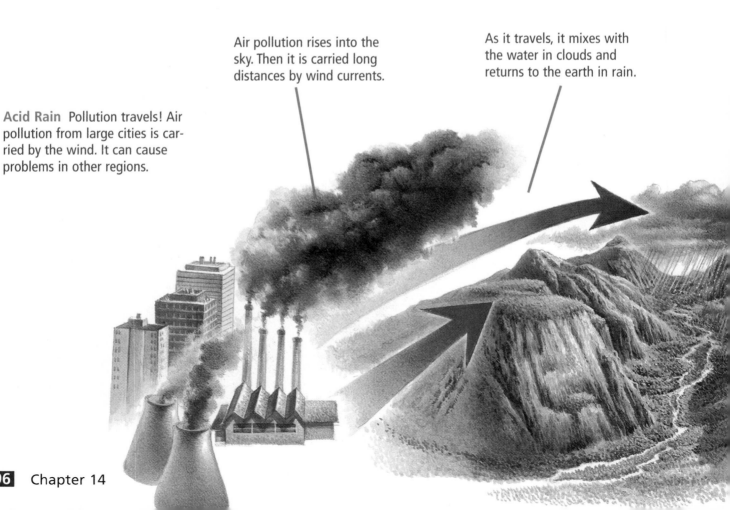

Using Our Resources Well

Focus *How are regions trying to conserve resources?*

The need to solve problems like acid rain brings regions together. People across the country consider conservation an important job. Many states, along with the national government, have passed laws to help protect resources. The Clean Water Act of 1977 is a law that keeps people from allowing too much sewage and waste products from industries into rivers, lakes, and other bodies of water.

Ordinary citizens have formed groups such as the Sierra Club and the Nature Conservancy to preserve forests, lakes, and rivers. There are also conservation groups for children. Students can join groups that plant trees. They can recycle and raise money to clean up the environment.

Business People and Scientists Fight Pollution

Many industries have worked to reduce the amount of pollution they produce. Factories in the Northeast have greatly reduced the chemicals that their smokestacks let into the air. Mining operations in the West create wastes that can damage water supplies as well as plants and wildlife. Some companies have found ways to contain these wastes while they mine.

Scientists are finding ways to clean up pollution that has already occurred. Recently, they discovered that tiny organisms called microbes will eat harmful waste. Now people use microbes to clean up some kinds of pollution. At a dump in Pennsylvania, microbes changed highly polluted soil to mostly clean soil in just two months.

Fourth graders *(top)* from Marietta, Georgia, study a stream as part of the Adopt-a-Stream program. Students can also join groups such as Global Releaf to plant trees *(bottom)*.

Acid rain changes the balance of chemicals in lakes and streams, hurting the plants and fish there. **Science:** *How might acid rain hurt birds?*

This island in the Mississippi River has been protected and improved by the Army Corps of Engineers. Located near Bellevue, Iowa, the area has been carefully managed to help birds and the other wildlife that live along the river.

In California, the Arcata Marsh and Wildlife Sanctuary uses microbes to clean the water. There, microbes eat the wastes that collect around the roots of marsh plants.

Down the Mississippi

Focus *How is the Mississippi River cleanup an example of cooperation between regions?*

Mississippi is a good name for the most important river in the United States. The word is Algonquian for "great water."

Passing through different regions, the Mississippi has long been used for trade and transportation. Every year, ships and barges still carry millions of tons of freight up and down it. About half of the freshwater fish in the United States live in the Mississippi. Many kinds of wildlife live along its shores. The river, and what happens to it, matters to people in all regions.

Governments Take Notice

The Mississippi is heavily used, and this has caused problems for years. Cities, businesses, and individuals polluted the river. Sewage and other wastes were dumped directly into it.

In the late 1960s, people realized that something was wrong. They found out that one important kind of insect called a mayfly had disappeared. Then scientists discovered that it wasn't healthy to eat fish caught in some parts of the river.

The Mississippi River

CANADA

Lake Itasca, Source of the Mississippi

Lake Superior

WISCONSIN

Minneapolis • ⊛ Saint Paul

MINNESOTA

Lake Michigan

Lake Huron

MICHIGAN

Des Moines River

IOWA

Davenport

Chicago •

Des Moines ⊛

Illinois River

ILLINOIS

INDIANA

Missouri River

• Kansas City

⊛ St. Louis

MISSOURI

Cairo •

Ohio River

KENTUCKY

TENNESSEE

ARKANSAS

Mississippi River

Little Rock ⊛

• Memphis

Arkansas River

Tennessee River

MISSISSIPPI

ALABAMA

Shreveport •

Vicksburg •

Red River

⊛ Baton Rouge

LOUISIANA

New Orleans •

N
W E
S

km 0   100   200
mi 0   100   200

Gulf of Mexico

A child touches Lake Itasca in Minnesota, where the Mississippi begins. As the river travels south, it flows past Wisconsin, Iowa, Illinois, Missouri, Arkansas, Kentucky, Tennessee, Mississippi, and Louisiana.

The Mighty Mississippi

Water from as far west as the Rocky Mountains and as far east as the Appalachian Mountains drains into the Mississippi. Great rivers, such as the Missouri, the Arkansas, and the Ohio, flow into the river, making it larger and larger as it travels south. At the end, the river carries millions of gallons of water per second. **Map Skill:** *Why do you think large cities grew along the river?*

The Mississippi ends in Louisiana, 2,350 miles after it begins. Here the "Big Muddy" joins the Gulf of Mexico. Can you see the difference between the ocean and the river?

How can mud hurt a river?

Mud is almost as important to the health of a river as the water that flows in it.

Chemicals that were once dumped into the Mississippi are still hidden in the mud at the bottom of the river. DDT, a chemical that has been illegal for over 20 years, can still be found here.

Even mud that does not contain harmful chemicals can hurt the river. Water that is too muddy does not allow sunlight to shine through it. Without light from the sun, plants beneath the surface cannot grow. The fish who need these plants die, and this hurts the birds and the other animals that live along the shore.

A scientist (above) measures mud in the river using a strobe light. As the Mississippi spreads out into the ocean (left), it slows down and drops the mud it carries. This creates a bank of sand and mud called a delta. Plants and animals live in the marshes that form in the delta.

Conservation groups have helped egrets and other birds.

National and state governments wanted to clean up the river. They also knew that one state could not do it alone.

Just as different regions contributed to the problem, different regions worked together to solve it. In 1981, the governors of Illinois, Iowa, Minnesota, Missouri, and Wisconsin created the Upper Mississippi River Basin Association. This group recommended ways to improve water quality in the northern part of the river. **Water quality** is the level of pollution in a lake, river, or other body of water.

Their effort is paying off. John F. Sullivan, a water-quality expert from Wisconsin, says, "The river has improved and continues to do so." Now, people from Arkansas, Tennessee, Mississippi, and Louisiana have formed the Lower Mississippi River Committee. They are looking at doing a similar project on the southern half of the river, where it crosses their states.

Individuals and Businesses Cooperate

Individuals and businesses from different states have also affected the river. Lloyd Spriggle, a resident of Wisconsin, started writing letters to officeholders in 1963, encouraging them to help protect the waters he loved so much. He said:

> **"The** river was always good to me, and so I wanted to be good to it.**"**

Wilfred Greene lives in Wallace, Louisiana, and he formed a group called River Area Planning. A chemical company had decided to build a plant near the shore, and Greene's group convinced the company to change its plans.

When citizens speak up, they encourage businesses to take action. Companies have taken up their challenge. The Louisiana Chemical Association tries to cooperate with citizens to keep the river clean. Dan Borné, its president, says, "That's what the public wants. They're telling us to clean up our act, and . . . our guys are getting the message."

Cleaning up the Mississippi is one example of Americans cooperating on an important job. Whether the job is protecting resources, increasing trade, or improving transportation, we all benefit when regions work together. As you will read in the next chapter, we also benefit from cooperating with other nations.

Water quality can be measured by the level of oxygen in the water. This chart shows how the river's water quality improved below St. Paul, Minnesota. **Chart Skill:** *Did water quality improve every year?*

Water Quality in the Mississippi

Lesson Review

1 **Key Vocabulary:** Use the words **acid rain** and **water quality** in a sentence about pollution.

2 **Focus:** How are regions trying to conserve resources?

3 **Focus:** How is the Mississippi River cleanup an example of cooperation between regions?

4 **Critical Thinking: Cause and Effect** How can protecting our resources help both businesses and consumers?

5 **Theme: Making Connections** How can telecommunications help people improve the environment?

6 **Citizenship/Writing Activity:** Think of a pollution problem your town shares with one of its neighbors. Write a plan for cleaning it up.

Chapter Review

Summarizing the Main Idea

1 Copy and complete the chart below, explaining how each main idea helps regions work together.

Main Idea	Working Together
Goods and Services	*Regions exchange things they need.*
Transportation	
Communication	
Resources	

Vocabulary

2 Using at least seven of the following terms, write an advertisement to increase trade between regions of the United States.

trade (p. 382)　　　　free enterprise (p. 386)　　Internet (p. 393)

profit (p. 382)　　　　consumer (p. 386)　　　　acid rain (p. 396)

specialization (p. 383)　locomotive (p. 391)　　　water quality (p. 400)

market (p. 385)　　　　fax machine (p. 393)

Reviewing the Facts

3 Why was John Andrew's business successful?

4 Why do regions trade with each other?

5 How does free enterprise help keep prices fair?

6 What kinds of services do people provide for each other?

7 Why was the National Road so important in the early 1800s?

8 How did canals change the way people in America traded goods?

9 What impact did trains have on the U.S. economy?

10 How have better telecommunications helped businesses?

11 How can problems such as pollution bring regions together?

12 What is an example of regions working together to use resources well?

13 Look at the map on page 395. Do time zones change as people move from north to south? Why or why not?

14 How do time zones make it easier for people to trade across different regions?

Geography Skills

15 Look at the map on page 389. Why do you think the National Road first went just to the Ohio River? How did people travel west from there?

16 You and your family are sailing down the Mississippi River from St. Paul, Minnesota. Write a journal describing what you see on your trip.

Critical Thinking

17 **Cause and Effect** What if another store sold fishing supplies in Clinton, Connecticut? How might this affect John Andrew's business? What could he do to keep his store a success?

18 **Predict** What do you think would happen if the government did not set rules about how different kinds of products can be made and sold?

Writing: Citizenship and Economics

19 **Citizenship** You are a government official proposing a new law to protect a certain resource. What resource do you want to protect? Write a speech explaining why your law is necessary.

20 **Economics** What kind of business would be profitable in your home town? Write a plan proposing your idea and explain why you think it could be successful.

Activities

Geography/Research Activity
Use a computer to contact someone on the Internet who lives in another region. Ask questions about his or her state or region.

Economics/Math Activity
Choose a city in another region. Do research to learn how much it costs to travel there by airplane, by train, and by car. Which is cheaper? Make a chart showing what you learned.

Internet Option

Check the **Internet Social Studies Center** for ideas on how to extend your theme project beyond your classroom.

THEME PROJECT CHECK-IN

On your bulletin board, include information about cooperation among regions of the United States.
- How does business or trade connect people within the United States?
- What are the different ways that people get from one place to another?
- What are people doing to protect the resources that regions share?

Neighbors to the North and South

1500	1600	1700

Connected Continents

Geography, history, and economics have made North and South America neighbors. *Lesson 1, Page 405*

Neighbors to the North

These Native American students are one of many cultures in Canada today. *Lesson 1, Page 408*

The Landforms of Mexico

When you are in Mexico, you are never far from mountains. *Lesson 1, Page 409*

North American Neighbors

LESSON
1

Main Idea The United States is linked geographically, economically, and culturally with Canada, Mexico, and Central America.

> **"G**eography has made us neighbors. History has made us friends. And economics has made us partners."

What do you think President Kennedy meant when he said this to the people of Canada in 1961? Looking at a map of North America will tell you. Canada, the United States, and Mexico are like three houses on the same street. This street is the continent of North America.

Being good neighbors hasn't always been easy. Still, history and economics have made the people in these North American countries partners — and friends.

Key Vocabulary
province
multicultural
mestizo
NAFTA
isthmus

Key Places
Western Hemisphere
Canada
Mexico
Central America

◀ Mountains, like these in Argentina, are found all over North and South America.

1800	1900	2000

Visit Central America

This forest is in Costa Rica. Read more about the countries of Central America. *Lesson 1, Page 411*

Bustling Cities

Learn about South American cities like this one — Caracas, Venezuela. *Lesson 2, Page 421*

Meet Your Neighbors

Come meet some of the people of South America! *Lesson 2, Page 422*

Shared Land, Shared Histories

Canada has many natural resources. The map below shows some of the important ones.
Map Skill: *What features do timber-producing areas share?*

Focus *What do countries in North America have in common?*

Canada, the United States, Mexico, and Central America are on the continent of North America. The continents of North America and South America are in the Western Hemisphere.

Countries in North America share many features. The Cordilleras (kawr dihl YAIR ahs) is a mountain system that runs from Alaska to the tip of South America. In the United States, this range is known as the Rocky Mountains. Plains are another feature

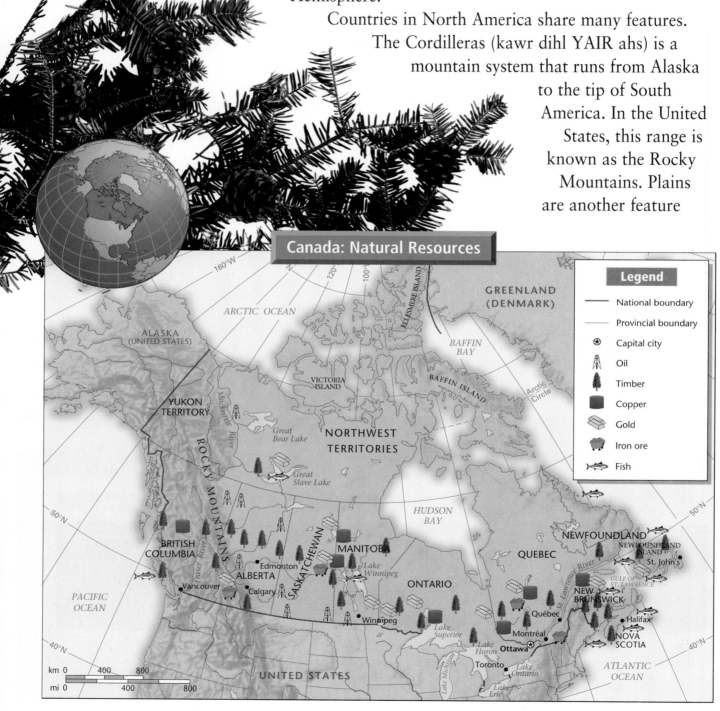

Canada: Natural Resources

Legend

⬟	National boundary
	Provincial boundary
⊛	Capital city
🛢	Oil
🌲	Timber
■	Copper
◈	Gold
⬛	Iron ore
🐟	Fish

GREENLAND (DENMARK)

ARCTIC OCEAN

ALASKA (UNITED STATES)

BAFFIN BAY

VICTORIA ISLAND

BAFFIN ISLAND

Arctic Circle

YUKON TERRITORY

Mackenzie River

Great Bear Lake

NORTHWEST TERRITORIES

ROCKY MOUNTAINS

Great Slave Lake

HUDSON BAY

50°N

50°N

NEWFOUNDLAND

NEWFOUNDLAND ISLAND

BRITISH COLUMBIA

SASKATCHEWAN

MANITOBA

QUEBEC

St. John's

Edmonton

Lake Winnipeg

St. Lawrence River

GULF OF ST. LAWRENCE

Fraser River

ALBERTA

ONTARIO

NEW BRUNSWICK

PACIFIC OCEAN

Vancouver

Calgary

Winnipeg

Québec

Halifax

40°N

40°N

Lake Superior

Montréal

NOVA SCOTIA

km 0   400   800

Lake Huron

Ottawa ⊛

ATLANTIC OCEAN

mi 0   400   800

UNITED STATES

Toronto

Lake Ontario

Lake Michigan

Lake Erie

that you'll find in the interior of much of North America. Beaches can be found along the eastern and western coasts. The Pacific Ocean is on the west coast. To the east lies the Atlantic Ocean.

Canada, the United States, Mexico, and Central America also share similar histories. As you learned in Chapter 4, Native Americans were already living in the Americas when European settlers arrived in the 1500s. The settlers created colonies throughout North America. In time, most of these colonies became independent countries. These countries sometimes disagree, but they have learned to be good neighbors.

Tall mountains like this one in Banff National Park are a common sight in Canada.

Canada

Focus *What are some characteristics of the land and people of Canada?*

Canada has the second largest land area of any country in the world. (Can you find out which country has the largest?) Canada has ten provinces and two territories. A **province** is a division of a country. It's a lot like a state.

Like the United States, Canada can be divided into several landform regions. If you traveled east from Canada's western coast, you'd soon reach the Canadian Rockies. Farther east, you would pass through the Interior Plains. They are north of the Great Plains in the United States. Some of the provinces in this region, such as Alberta, Saskatchewan, and Manitoba, have important agricultural and mining industries.

Continuing your journey, you'd pass the Great Lakes region. Sound familiar? The United States shares all of the Great Lakes with Canada except Lake Michigan, which is

This chart shows some of Canada's crops. **Chart Skill:** *Does Canada produce more wheat or more corn?*

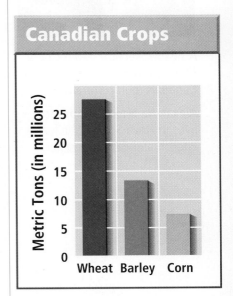

Canadian Crops

Metric Tons (in millions)

Wheat Barley Corn

entirely within the United States. Lush forests of spruce, balsam fir, and pine trees are resources for the timber and paper industries.

Finally, you'd reach the Appalachian region. The Appalachian mountain range stretches south to Alabama in the United States. The Atlantic Ocean is to the east of Newfoundland and New Brunswick, two of the provinces in this region.

Temperatures in Canada vary widely, as they do in the United States. Because Canada is farther north, the climate is usually cooler than in the United States or Mexico.

The People

In a letter to her North American neighbors, 11-year-old Canadian Alexandra Malone asks,

> "**H**ave you ever been to Canada? Canada is a multicultural country."

A historic section of the city of Montreal *(top)* reflects Canada's multiculturalism.

Alexandra Malone *(bottom)* lives in Nova Scotia. She learns English and French in school.

Multicultural means "having many cultures." Most Canadians have British or French heritage. Some, like the Inuit, are Native American. Others have Asian or African ancestors.

The French were the first Europeans to settle in Canada. They came in the 1600s. The British won control of the government in the 1700s, but French Canadians kept their culture. Today, both English and French are official languages in Canada. Government publications and street signs are written in both languages.

Canada's Native American heritage is very important. In 1999, the eastern part of the Northwest Territories will become a separate territory called Nunavut. The name means "our land" in the Inuit language.

Most Canadians live near the nation's southern border where the climate is warmer. Most industries are along the U.S.–Canada border. Canadians export many manufactured goods to the United States and Mexico.

Mexico and Central America

Focus *What are some characteristics of the land and people of Mexico and Central America?*

Mexico and Central America are south of the United States. Mexico is divided into 31 states. Central America includes the countries of Guatemala, Belize, El Salvador, Honduras, Nicaragua, Costa Rica, and Panama.

Mexico

Mexico is a land of many mountains. The Sierra Madre Occidental (ahk sih DEHN tuhl) range runs along Mexico's west coast. The Sierra Madre Oriental (awr ee ehn TAHL) lies along Mexico's east coast. Between them is the Central Plateau, which is high and fairly flat. Mexico City, the capital, is in the southern part of the Central Plateau.

Mexico City is one of many cities in Mexico's Central Plateau. Find Mexico City on the map. **Map Skill:** *What resources are found near Mexico City?*

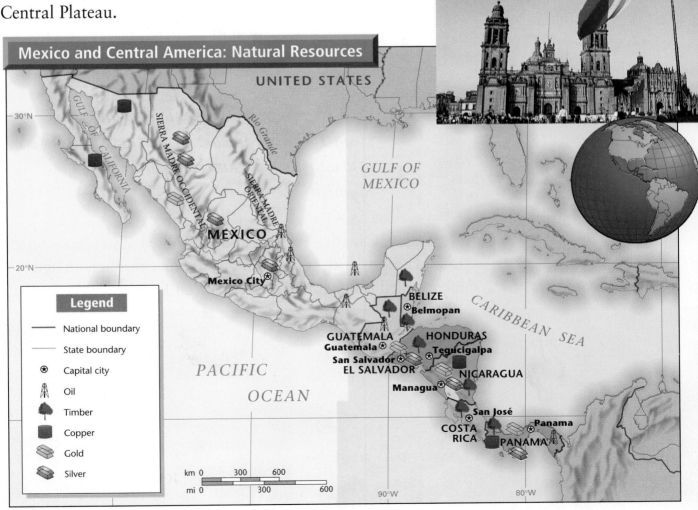

Mexico and Central America: Natural Resources

UNITED STATES

GULF OF CALIFORNIA

SIERRA MADRE OCCIDENTAL

Rio Grande

SIERRA MADRE ORIENTAL

MEXICO

GULF OF MEXICO

Mexico City

BELIZE
Belmopan

CARIBBEAN SEA

GUATEMALA
Guatemala

HONDURAS
Tegucigalpa

San Salvador
EL SALVADOR

NICARAGUA

Managua

PACIFIC OCEAN

San José

Panama

COSTA RICA

PANAMA

Legend

— National boundary
— State boundary
⊛ Capital city
⚲ Oil
🌲 Timber
▪ Copper
▭ Gold
▱ Silver

km 0   300   600
mi 0   300   600

90°W   80°W

30°N

20°N

Mexico's many mountains and plateaus are rich in mineral resources like silver and lead. Oil is also an important resource.

The climate of Mexico varies with the elevation of each region. The higher the land, the colder the climate.

The People of Mexico

Like the United States, Mexico is a country where different cultures come together. Most people in Mexico are **mestizo**. Mestizos have both Spanish and Native American ancestors. Other Mexicans are Native Americans. Some Mexicans have Spanish ancestors only. The Aztecs and Maya — Native American peoples — controlled most of Mexico and Central America before the Spanish came. They built great empires. When the Europeans came, they took the land from the empires and began colonies.

Most people in Mexico speak Spanish. Because Mexico is near the United States, many also speak English. Nine-year-old Luis Pablo Hernández Espino writes:

Luis Pablo Hernández Espino *(shown below)* and his family speak two languages.

"I *live in Juárez,[Mexico] right across from El Paso, Texas. My father, who is a journalist, writes in English and Spanish.*"

In some places in Mexico, you might see land that looks like this. **Science:** *What do the land and plants in the picture tell you about the climate?*

Today, Canada, Mexico, and the United States have agreed to make it easier to trade with one another through an agreement called **NAFTA**, the North American Free Trade Agreement.

Central America

Central America is an isthmus. An **isthmus** is a narrow strip of land with water on both sides. It connects two larger land areas. Like Mexico, Central America is a region of mountains. It also has a similar history. Most Central American countries were settled by the Spanish and gained independence in the 1800s. Belize, however, was claimed by the British.

Many people in Central America work in agricultural jobs. Coffee, cocoa, bananas, cotton, meat, and sugar are some major exports. There are also some manufacturing industries, usually related to agricultural products. For example, cotton is grown in Chinandega (chee nahn DAY gah), Nicaragua. You can find textile mills nearby. In the province of San José, Costa Rica, coffee processing plants prepare the coffee grown in the area.

Central America's location is a key transportation route. Since Panama is a narrow isthmus, it is a good place for a waterway. The United States built the Panama Canal in 1914. It allows ships to cross between the Atlantic and Pacific oceans. So, just as Central America bridges the continents of North and South America, it now also connects these two great oceans.

Guatemala and other Central American countries are famous for their colorful fabric *(top)*.

The Panama Canal *(bottom)* was an amazing feat of engineering. **History:** *How did the Canal make it easier for people to travel by ship?*

Lesson Review: Geography

1 **Key Vocabulary:** Write a paragraph about Canada, Mexico, and Central America using the terms, **province**, **mestizo**, **multicultural**, **NAFTA**, and **isthmus**.

2 **Focus:** What do countries in North America have in common?

3 **Focus:** What are some characteristics of the land and people of Canada?

4 **Focus:** What are some characteristics of the land and people of Mexico and Central America?

5 **Critical Thinking: Compare** How are the histories of Canada and Mexico similar? How are they different?

6 **Citizenship:** Why should neighboring countries work together?

7 **Theme: Making Connections/Research Activity:** Read about Mayan astronomy in an encyclopedia or other books. Present your research to the class.

POETRY

If you're not from the prairie . . .

By David Bouchard
Illustrated by Henry Ripplinger

The kids and the scenes from this book about Canada's prairie land should look familiar to American readers. There are many more similarities between the United States and Canada than there are differences. That's an important thing to remember, and it's one of the reasons our countries are such good neighbors.

If you're not from the prairie,
You don't know the wind,
You can't know the wind.

Our cold winds of winter cut right to the core,
Hot summer wind devils can blow down the door.
As children we know when we play any game,
The wind will be there, yet we play just the same.

If you're not from the prairie,
You don't know the wind.

If you're not from the prairie,
You don't know the sky,
You *can't* know the sky.

The bold prairie sky is clear, bright and blue,
Though sometimes cloud messages give us a clue.
Monstrous gray mushrooms can hint of a storm,
Or painted pink feathers say goodbye to the warm.

If you're not from the praire,
You *don't* know the sky.

If you're not from the prairie,
You don't know what's flat,
You've *never* seen flat.

When travellers pass through across our great plain,
They all view our home, they all say the same:
"It's simple and flat!" They've not learned to see,
The particular beauty that's now part of me.

If you're not from the prairie,
You *don't* know what's flat.

If you're not from the prairie,
You've not heard the grass,
You've never *heard* grass.

In strong summer winds, the grains and grass bend
And sway to a dance that seems never to end.
It whispers its secrets — they tell of this land
And the rhythm of life played by nature's own hand.

If you're not from the prairie,
You've never *heard* grass.

Meet the Author

David Bouchard was born on Canada's Great Plains. He has written four other children's books. Henry Ripplinger grew up in Canada and is a painter and an art gallery owner.

Additional Books to Read

Fiesta! Mexico's Great Celebrations by Elizabeth Silverthorne Learn about Mexican feasts and festivals.

Communication by Piero Ventura This book describes communication throughout history.

Response Activities

1. **Compare Literature and Geography:** How does David Bouchard's description of the prairie add to your understanding of life on the Canadian prairie?

2. **Expressive: Write a Poem** Use "If you're not from the prairie. . ." as a model for a poem about the land or the weather in your region.

3. **Geography: Make a Collage** Use pictures from magazines or newspapers to make a collage that compares life in the countryside with life in the city.

★ CITIZENSHIP ★

Resolving Conflicts

How Can We Cooperate?

Have you ever tried to solve a problem that involved several people? If so, you probably know how hard it can be to make everyone happy. But it can be done, as this case study shows.

Case Study

Keeping the Rio Grande Clean

The United States and Mexico share a border that is almost 2,000 miles long. About 1,000 miles of this border is a river called the Rio Grande. Over 100 years ago, both countries realized they needed to work together to care for the river. They needed to figure out how to solve boundary problems when the river changed course, and how to use the water.

In 1944, they formed the International Boundary and Water Commission (IBWC) to deal with water power, flood control, and rules that make sure no untreated sewage, or

human waste, goes into the river. The United States helped Mexico pay for a new sewage treatment plant. Both nations want to make sure that the water they share stays clean for everyone.

Take Action

Now is your chance to agree on something that crosses boundaries. Your school principal wants you to plan a lunch "Menu of the Week" that reflects the different cultures and tastes of the kids in your school. Your menu must also meet guidelines for good nutrition. What will you plan?

1 In small groups, make three lists: foods that are nutritious, foods kids love to eat, and foods from different cultures that kids in your school eat.

2 From your lists, pick different foods for different days. Pick two main dishes, two drinks, and two desserts for each day. Try to vary your selection.

3 Look over the menu. Is everybody happy with at least some part of the menu? Discuss and change the choices until everyone in your group is satisfied.

4 Make a poster of your group's "Menu of the Week." Share it with the class. How is your menu like other groups' menus? How is it different?

Tips for Resolving Conflicts

- Agree on what needs to be done.
- Consider everyone's interests.
- Make a list of several ideas and then see which is best.
- Sometimes changing one part of an agreement can satisfy someone who isn't happy with the whole plan.

Research Activity

What is the United Nations? How does it help nations work together to solve international problems? In a reference book, find an example of how the United Nations has helped solve a problem in a peaceful way. Share your findings.

South American Neighbors

Main Idea People throughout the Americas can benefit from the exchange of goods, services and ideas.

Machu Picchu (MA choo PEEK choo) and Huayna (HWAY nah) Picchu are two peaks in the Andes, a mountain system in South America. Their names mean "Old Peak" and "Young Peak" in the Quechua (KEHCH wah) language of the Inca. The Incan city of Machu Picchu lies between these peaks.

The Inca, Native Americans who ruled Peru before the Spanish arrived in the 1500s, built this magnificent city. Stone buildings, streets, and stairways seem to rise out of the mountainside. The Inca built the city in terraces. A **terrace** is a raised, flat bank of earth with sloping sides. Machu Picchu's remarkable layout is still a model for city planners today.

Machu Picchu is in the Andes in Peru. The Inca built this city high in the mountains. The picture on the right shows the surrounding area.

South America

The 13 countries in South America have many kinds of land. Volcanoes like the one in the top picture dot the Andes. This volcano *(top)* is in the country of Ecuador. The southern tip of the continent is close to Antarctica and has glaciers and ice fields. The ice field in the bottom picture is in Chile. **Map Skill:** *How many countries have borders with Brazil?*

South America

Focus *What are some important geographic features of South America?*

The Andes stretch the length of South America from north to south. They start in Venezuela and run through Colombia, Ecuador, Peru, Argentina, and Chile. This system of many mountain ranges runs for 5,500 miles. If you flew over the Andes, you would see high peaks and low plateaus, icy glaciers and even volcanoes.

While the Andes stretch from north to south, the Amazon River crosses the continent from west to east. It starts where glaciers and snow melt in the Andes. The river flows from Peru through Brazil into the Atlantic Ocean.

The Amazon Basin

The Amazon basin crosses nine countries in South America. Native Americans who live along the Amazon River have been there for at least 12,000 years.

They live in perhaps the richest biological area in the world. Over 2,000 species of fish are believed to live in the Amazon River. Many other animals live in the forests.

The people who live in the Amazon rain forest use many of the plants and trees for medicine, food, clothing, and shelter. Now many other people are using the products of the rain forest, too.

Ask Yourself

There have been many influences from Latin American culture in the United States. Spanish words are one of them. What are some words you know in Spanish?

? ? ? ? ? ? ? ? ? ? ? ? ? ? ?

Much of the river runs through the Amazon rain forest. A rain forest is a thick, evergreen forest where it rains for hours each day.

The landscape changes southeast of the Amazon River. Flat, grassy plains called **pampas** are an important cattle raising area in Argentina and Uruguay.

People in South America

Focus *What are some characteristics of the people of South America?*

The people of South America, like the people of North America, have diverse backgrounds. The earliest people in South America were Native Americans, like the Inca and

Aymara (eye muh RAH) in Peru and Bolivia. In the 1500s, Europeans began to set up colonies, bringing enslaved Africans with them. The Spanish settled most of the colonies, while the Portuguese settled the area that is now Brazil.

In the 1800s, many people in South America wanted freedom. They fought for their independence from Spain just as American colonies had struggled against British rule. From 1810 to 1824, a general named Simón Bolívar (see MOHN boh LEE vahr) led an army to drive the Spanish out.

Bolívar's victories won independence for Bolivia, Colombia, Ecuador, Peru, and Venezuela. Like many U.S. leaders, Bolívar believed that education was necessary for democracy. He hoped nations in South America would unite to form one country. Bolívar's dream, however, was never realized. Today, there are 13 separate nations in South America.

The People Today

Languages spoken in South America reflect many cultures. Native American languages such as Guarani (gwa rah NEE) are official languages in some countries. People speak Spanish, Portuguese, English, French, and Dutch, too. African words have also contributed to South American languages.

Many people in South America live in cities. Buenos Aires (BWAY nohs EYE rehs) in Argentina and Rio de Janeiro (REE oh day zha NAY roh) in Brazil are two important cities.

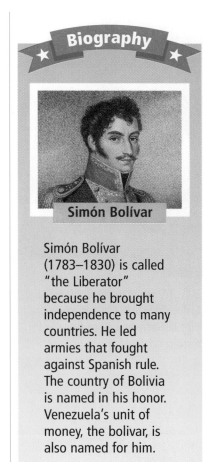

Biography

Simón Bolívar

Simón Bolívar (1783–1830) is called "the Liberator" because he brought independence to many countries. He led armies that fought against Spanish rule. The country of Bolivia is named in his honor. Venezuela's unit of money, the bolivar, is also named for him.

São Paulo, Brazil *(left)*, is South America's largest city. Buenos Aires, Argentina *(below)*, is another important city.

421

Sara María Campo lives in Colombia. She likes to play the piano. Sara wants to be a veterinarian when she grows up.

Sara María Campo, age nine, lives in Cali, Colombia. She writes, "The area near Cali is very sweet. We export a lot of sugar. The capital of Colombia is Bogotá." She adds,

> "**I** invite you to learn more about South America so you can make friends around the world."

Trading with South America

Focus *How does trade help relations between North and South America?*

Trade between the Americas helps people in both places. The United States buys about one third of South America's exports.

· **Tell Me More** ·

Trade Between Sister Cities

Atlanta, Georgia, and Rio de Janeiro, Brazil, are sister cities. Sister cities are cities in different places that trade and share their cultures with each other. One way in which Atlanta and Rio de Janeiro promote trade is through the Atlanta Caribbean Trading Co. This is a program at the North Atlanta High School. Students plan to import products from Brazil for their school store. They also hope to export products like school supplies and T-shirts to a school in Rio de Janeiro.

Students make announcements to tell others about their new products.

Students from Atlanta learn about Brazilian goods like this jewelry.

In turn, about one third of South America's imports of machinery, paper, chemicals, and other goods come from the United States.

Sugar, bananas, coffee, beef, and corn are some of the agricultural exports of the countries in South America. Minerals are also important. Petroleum can be found around Lake Maracaibo (mah rah KY boh) in Venezuela. There is more copper at Chuqicamata (choo kee kah MAH tah) in Chile than anywhere else in the world. The chart on the right tells more about South America's important exports.

People in North and South America are working to become better neighbors. In 1994, leaders met in Miami, Florida, for the Summit of the Americas. They talked about making trade easier in the Western Hemisphere. Some wanted to extend NAFTA to include countries in South America. They also talked about improving education and health.

It's important for the countries in the Western Hemisphere to work together to solve problems that affect them all. Connections with other countries don't stop in the Western Hemisphere, though. The nations of the Americas are also connected with other countries around the world.

South American Exports - 1990

U.S. Dollars (in billions)

	Meat	Copper	Coffee	Sugar

Coffee is one South American export. The chart above shows others. **Chart Skill:** *Does South America export more copper or more meat?*

Lesson Review

1 **Key Vocabulary:** Describe the geography of South America using **terrace** and **pampas**.

2 **Focus:** What are some important geographical features of South America?

3 **Focus:** What are some characteristics of the people of South America?

4 **Focus:** How does trade help relations between North and South America?

5 **Critical Thinking: Interpret** Why is South America an important neighbor to the United States?

6 **Theme: Making Connections** How are people in North and South America interdependent?

7 **Geography/ Writing Activity:** Find out about a city in South America. Write to a student in that city telling what makes your communities similar.

Skills Workshop

Identifying Primary and Secondary Sources

Were You There?

Deep in the rain forest, over 100 feet above ground, narrow bridges form a treetop walkway. This walkway helps people explore the canopy, or top level, of the rain forest. On the next page are two accounts of a visit to the canopy walkway. One is a **primary source**, written by someone who was there. The other one is a **secondary source**, which is written by someone who wasn't there. How can you tell which type of source you're reading?

1 Here's How

Read the two accounts of what it was like to be part of the Children's Rain Forest Workshop Program.

- Look for clues that the author was part of the event. Does the author use the words *I, me, we,* or *our*? This is a sign that you're reading a primary source.

- Does the author leave out personal comments or give information someone at the scene wouldn't have known? If so, it's probably a secondary source.

- Think about how the author might have collected this information. Did it come from being at the event or from talking to people or reading about it?

The canopy walkway is like a narrow trail through the treetops. It starts at the top of a tower and zigzags through the rain forest canopy. It ends 1,600 feet away at another tower.

The kids knew the walkway was safe. But that first step onto it was still a little scary. Sarah said it was, "fun, exciting, wonderful, frightening, and every word that describes my mixed feelings."

Scientists have known for a long time that tropical rain forests have more species than any other place on Earth . . . they're sure that *millions* of unknown species live overhead without ever coming near the ground.

Discovering an unknown species would have been neat. But the kids were happy just seeing what they did.

by Susan Goodman

② Think It Through

How does knowing that a source is primary or secondary affect what you think about the content?

③ Use It

1. Identify the accounts on this page as either a primary or secondary source.

2. On a piece of paper, make two columns. In one, list the differences between the two passages. In the other, list the similarities.

Soon after our arrival, we walked a short distance to the canopy walkway. I was so excited. This was the main thing I was looking forward to. The walkways were very wobbly. . . . I must admit I was a little nervous. . . . The view became more breathtaking with every step. As I walked onto the highest platform, my jaw dropped in amazement at the spectacular sight. Rain forest stretched out into the horizon in all directions. Mist could be seen rising from the rivers. Evening was approaching so I stood there for what must have been a half hour and watched the sunset. It was honestly the most beautiful thing I've ever seen in my life.

by Allison Heyns

CHAPTER 5

Chapter Review

Summarizing the Main Idea

1 Copy and complete the chart below, giving one or two facts about the people and geographic features of each country.

Neighbor	People	Geographic Features
Canada	*speak both English and French*	
Mexico		

Vocabulary

2 Using each of the following terms, write descriptive sentences about the geographic neighbors of the United States.

province (p. 407)	**NAFTA (p. 410)**	**pampas (p. 420)**
multicultural (p. 408)	**isthmus (p. 411)**	
mestizo (p. 410)	**terrace (p. 418)**	

Reviewing the Facts

3 What are some things that Canada, the United States, and Mexico share?

4 Describe the geography and climate of Canada.

5 What makes Canada a multicultural country?

6 Describe the geography and climate of Mexico.

7 What cultural backgrounds do the people of Mexico have?

8 What are the major industries in Central America?

9 What are some important geographic features of South America?

10 Describe some of the people who live in South America.

11 How do people in North America and South America work together?

For questions 12 and 13, look back at the quotations in the Skills Workshop (pages 424–425).

12 What are some clues that tell you that one quotation is a primary source and one is a secondary source?

13 Which source do you think gives the most complete description of the trip to the rain forest? Why?

Geography Skills

For questions 14 and 15, use the map of South America on page 419.

14 Through which countries does the Amazon River flow? How do you think the river affects people's lives?

15 Choose one country on the map and find out some more interesting facts about it. Put the facts together in a booklet about the place.

Critical Thinking

16 **Compare** Make a chart that compares two of the places you have read about. How are they different? How are they the same? Which place would you rather visit? Why?

17 **Interpret** What are the benefits of trade between the United States and its neighbors? What are some of the challenges?

Writing: Citizenship and Culture

18 **Citizenship** Research some of the things your community and a community nearby share. Write a paragraph describing how you can work together.

19 **Culture** Write a letter to a fourth grade student who lives in Mexico. Ask the student any questions you have about life in Mexico.

Activities

Economics/Math
Practice trade within your classroom. Organize the classroom into regions. If you need something that is in a region other than your own, trade for it with something a student in that region may need.

Culture
Work with several other students to make a mural that celebrates your combined heritages. Sketch a design on a long piece of paper. Then fill it in with details and color.

Internet Option

Check the **Internet Social Studies Center** for ideas on how to extend your theme project beyond your classroom.

THEME PROJECT CHECK-IN

Check your bulletin board. Have you included connections with the countries that are neighbors to the United States?
- How do the United States, Mexico, and Canada work together under NAFTA?
- What are some connections between North and South America?

Neighbors Around the World

Chapter Preview: *People, Places, and Events*

1925	1950	1975

World Environments

Find out about the different places people live around the world. *Lesson 1, Page 430*

People on the Move

Why do people like these refugees move? *Lesson 1, Page 432*

Exchanging Goods

Ships like these carry all kinds of products between different countries. *Lesson 2, Page 436*

A Home to All

Main Idea People live in places where they can meet their needs and wants.

How often does anyone get to see the earth from a distance of 250,000 miles? Not very often. Only astronauts have looked at the earth from this far away — from the surface of the moon.

If you could view the earth as astronauts have, how would you describe it? Alfred Worden, an American astronaut who looked at the earth from space, said,

Key Vocabulary

emigrate

involuntary
migration

voluntary migration

trend

> **"N**ow I know why I am here, not for a closer look at the moon, but to look back at our home, the earth.**"**

The earth looks small from far away. Yet billions of people share this planet, and call it home. Seeing the earth from space reminds people that they have neighbors around the world.

 From space, you can see many places on the earth.

2000	2025	2050

Sharing Information

Television can teach people far away. Learn other ways to share information. *Lesson 2, Page 438*

People Who Help

Read about international organizations that help children like these. *Lesson 3, Page 444*

Working Together

It's up to all the people on the earth to help one another. *Lesson 3, Page 447*

People and Places

Focus *What are some environments around the world, and how do people live in them?*

If you were orbiting the earth in a spacecraft, you would be able to see different parts of the globe. Some of the first features you might notice are continents. Then you might see mountains, lakes, valleys, canyons, rivers — even the Great Wall of China! You could watch smoke rising from volcanoes, hurricanes swirling over the oceans, and dust storms rolling over deserts. You could also see signs of people and their activities. City lights twinkle on the side of the earth where it is night. Where it is day, bridges, roads, and airport runways appear as straight and curved lines along the earth's surface.

If you looked at the earth in even more detail, you would see signs of human life almost everywhere on the planet. People live in cities and villages, on cold mountains, and in scorching deserts. People make their homes in forests and on

An ecoregion is an area with one kind of environment. The colors on the map show different climates. **Map Skill:** *What are some geographic features of each ecoregion?*

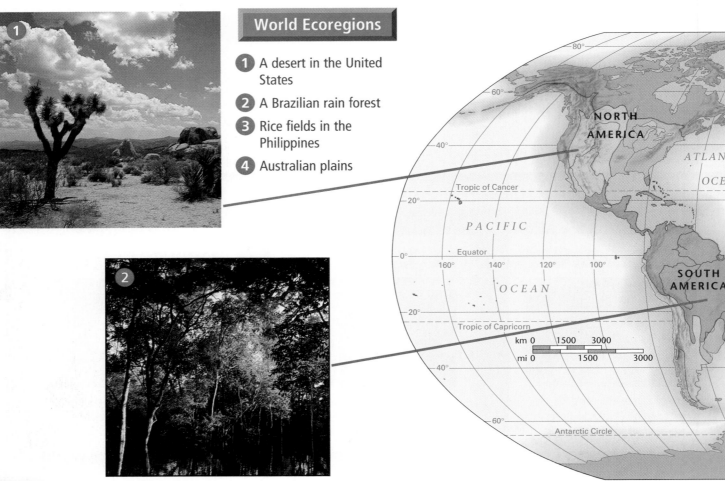

World Ecoregions

1 A desert in the United States

2 A Brazilian rain forest

3 Rice fields in the Philippines

4 Australian plains

islands, along coastlines, and in grasslands. People build homes in thick jungles and wide plains. Only the harshest environments, like most of icy Antarctica, keep people away entirely.

These different environments influence the way people dress, build their homes, and work. In the mountains, for example, people build sturdy homes as protection from cold weather. They also wear warm clothing. People who live along rivers often build their homes up on stilts in case of floods. They plant crops that need a lot of water, such as rice, or catch fish for food. In deserts, some people make homes with mud walls to keep rooms cool during the hot day. People who live in the desert dress in light clothing. Fresh water may be hard to find, so people use it carefully.

Although people around the world live and dress differently, they have the same basic needs. Everyone needs a place to live, food and water, and a way to provide for their other needs. People have to find ways to meet these needs in their specific environments. Otherwise, they have to move.

Curious Facts

Have you ever sailed in the high seas? The "high seas" refers to the area in the open ocean where no one nation's laws apply. In ancient times, the high seas began one league, or three miles, from the shore, which was the length of a cannon shot.

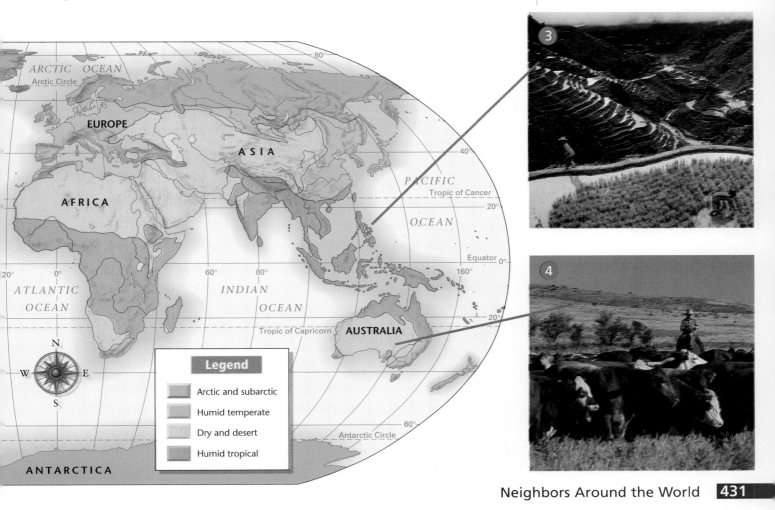

Wars in countries like Rwanda
(top, right) and Bosnia-
Herzegovina *(above)* have
forced many people to become
refugees. They leave their homes
to try to find a peaceful place to
live.

Natural disasters, like the hurricane that damaged this trailer
in Homestead, Florida, can also
cause people to move.

Changing Places

Focus *What are some of the reasons people move?*

People have moved, or migrated, from place to place since the beginning of human history. Some people **emigrate**. That means they leave their own country. Others move within a country from rural areas to cities, or from cities to suburbs.

Involuntary Migration

People migrate for many reasons. When people are forced to move, it is called **involuntary migration**. They might have to move because of harsh living conditions, political change, or war. People who leave their homes to find help and safety in other places are called refugees. Around the world today, refugees migrate to other countries or within their own countries.

A "push factor" is something that makes people want to leave a place. War is often a push factor for involuntary migration. For example, in the former country of Yugoslavia, war started when two regions in that country declared independence in the early 1990s. Different groups fought for territory and control of the government. Thousands of people left their homes to avoid being killed.

Harsh living conditions or natural disasters are also push factors for involuntary migration. Sometimes people's homes are destroyed because of hurricanes, earthquakes, or droughts. Without rain, people cannot grow enough food to feed themselves. Ethiopia and other countries in Africa have experienced droughts that have driven people from their homes.

Voluntary Migration

Some people are not forced to move, but choose to migrate to new places. This is called **voluntary migration**. Better jobs are one "pull factor" for voluntary migration. Pull factors make people want to move to a particular place. Better education and health care are also pull factors for many people.

As you learned in Chapter 4, many people have migrated to the United States. The United States is not the only place where voluntary migration has occurred. In the past 20 years, people have moved to countries with growing industries. Those industries provide jobs. In France and Great Britain, many people have found jobs in stores and factories. People move to Saudi Arabia to work in the oil industry. South Africa's mines have attracted people, too. The chart on the right shows which countries have high populations of people born in other countries.

The chart below shows the six countries with the highest population of immigrants in 1990. **Chart Skill:** *Which country has the most immigrants? Why do you think this is so?*

Immigrant Population

Immigrants (in millions)

20
15
10
5
0

United States · India · Pakistan · France · Germany · Canada

Countries

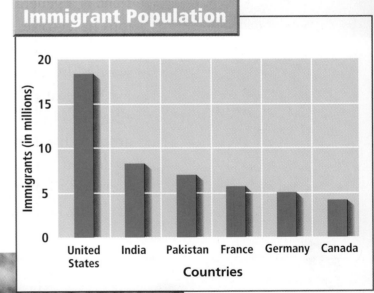

Jobs have attracted many people to South Africa. Many of the jobs, like the ones people are doing in the photo, are in the mining industry.

Many modern cities are very crowded. More than 12 million people live in Shanghai, China *(right)*. In some big cities, there are so many people that cars can't get through. People use motorcycles *(below)* or bicycles to travel.

Crowded Cities

Migration to cities has been a trend throughout history. A **trend** is a general pattern. The Industrial Revolution created jobs in factories. Many people wanted these jobs. Cities became very crowded. Overcrowding caused problems. There wasn't always enough housing or clean water.

Some of these problems still exist in cities today. However, cities also bring people together. People from different backgrounds live together. This means that cities offer many things to do and ways to live. People can find things in cities that they don't find in other places. As time goes on, people will probably keep moving to cities to find new opportunities.

Lesson Review

1. **Key Vocabulary:** Write sentences about different types of migration using the words **emigrate, involuntary migration, voluntary migration,** and **trend.**

2. **Focus:** What are some environments around the world, and how do people live in them?

3. **Focus:** What are some of the reasons people move?

4. **Critical Thinking: Cause and Effect** How do people's lives change when cities become overcrowded?

5. **Theme: Making Connections** What are some features that all people need in their environments?

6. **Citizenship/Writing Activity** Write a letter to a student who lives in one of the environments shown in this lesson. Ask any questions you have.

Links Around the World

Main Idea People around the world rely on one another for ideas, goods, and services.

Key Vocabulary

international trade
European Union
translate
World Wide Web
on-line

If you want to buy something, what do you do? You probably go to the store. But what if you lived in Sydney, Australia, and wanted something in New York? It'd be a long trip — more than 9,900 miles — to the store! Moving goods and information between distant places used to be difficult.

Today, you don't always have to travel to get what you need from other places. Networks of trade and communications link people all over the earth. A person in Sydney can use a phone or a computer to buy goods or get information from someone in New York. The person in New York can send goods or information quickly by plane, ship, Internet, or fax machine. Distant places don't seem so distant anymore.

Students in the United States *(left)* can communicate with students in South Africa *(right)* by computer.

Neighbors Around the World **435**

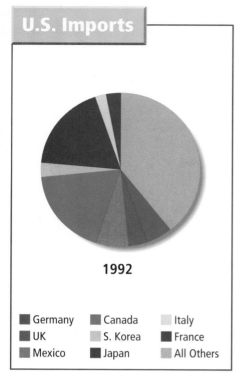

1992

- Germany
- UK
- Mexico
- Canada
- S. Korea
- Japan
- Italy
- France
- All Others

The chart above shows some countries from which the United States imports goods. The pictures below show some imported goods. **Chart Skill:** *Does the United States import more goods from Canada or Mexico?*

Exchanging Goods and Services

Focus *How do nations benefit from trading goods and services?*

As you know, people in the United States import and export goods and services. Today, international trade networks link nations around the world. **International trade** refers to buying and selling between two or more nations.

Every day, you probably see goods that have been imported from other countries. The photographs at the bottom of this page show some products the United States imports from other places. The United States exports goods to many countries, too. You can see some of those goods on the next page.

Even if nations have some of the resources they need, they may not have enough of a particular resource. For example, the United States makes newsprint (paper used to make newspapers) from its forests, but papermakers in the United States can't meet the country's needs. So the United States imports newsprint from Canada.

Crude oil is one of the world's most valuable raw materials. Cars, airplanes, trucks, and other machines run with fuel made from oil. Many nations, including the United States, need this valuable resource to keep their economies running. They buy oil from Middle Eastern countries like Saudi Arabia and Iran. Over half of the world's known oil reserves are found in the Middle East. Other countries, like Venezuela and Mexico, also export oil and oil products.

Trading Partners

To buy and sell products more easily across national borders, nations often form trading partnerships. In Chapter 15, you read about a trading partnership called NAFTA. Another partnership is the EU or **European Union**. Many countries in Europe, including France, Germany, and Great Britain, are members of the EU.

In Asia, countries such as Thailand, Singapore, Indonesia, and Malaysia have formed a group called the Association of South East Asian Nations (ASEAN). They are working to form a larger trading partnership with China, Japan, and Korea. It will be called AFTA (ASEAN Free Trade Area). They hope to have it set up by the year 2008.

Countries that belong to trade organizations charge each other lower taxes to sell their products. They also have fewer trading rules. These nations hope that lower taxes and fewer laws will help their businesses trade more goods. More trade helps the economies of all the member countries.

Nations depend on one another for services as well as goods. Countries that don't have good health care may ask doctors from other nations to help them. Trained people travel to show other people how to build houses, dig wells, grow better crops, and raise livestock. Scientists exchange ideas across borders. Countries also exchange movies, television shows, and other entertainment.

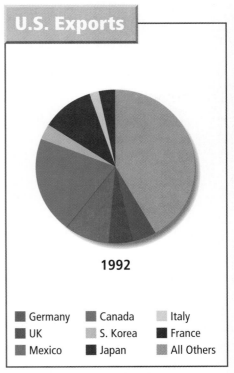

U.S. Exports

1992

- Germany
- UK
- Mexico
- Canada
- S. Korea
- Japan
- Italy
- France
- All Others

The chart above shows countries to which the United States exports goods. The pictures below show some exports.
Chart Skill: *Which country buys the most from the United States? Why do you think that is?*

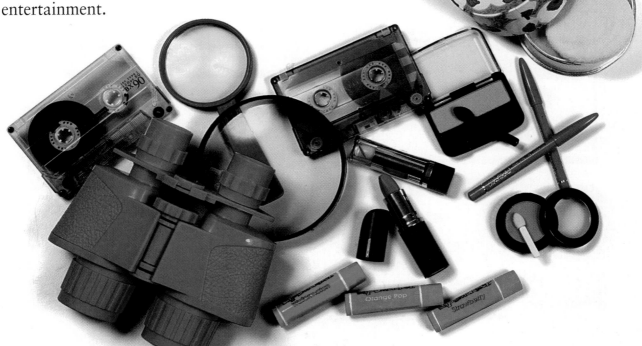

Exchanging Words and Ideas

Focus *How have improvements in communications helped people around the world exchange ideas?*

To trade with other people, you have to be able to communicate. Telecommunications makes that easier. Telephones, television, and computers are just some of the tools people use.

Quick communication helps people in many ways. Some businesses in the United States are now testing software that will translate messages. To **translate** means to restate something in another language. This way, you could send a message in English, but a person in France could read it in French.

New kinds of communication help individual people, too. They can learn more about products and companies. People can communicate with friends in places all around the world.

The World Wide Web

The **World Wide Web** is a tool that helps people to use the Internet. In addition to text, users can see pictures and hear sounds. Suppose you wanted to do research on the Antarctic. You could get information from places as different as

The World Wide Web finds information on the Internet. Each page links you to other pages. The address of this page is http://www.hmco.com/hmco/school/School.html.

California and Australia. One document links you automatically with more information. Most of the information you can find on the Web travels on-line. **On-line** means that the information moves through telephone lines.

A World of Neighbors

Communications networks have brought the world's citizens closer together. People who are far apart can communicate easily. Bill Gates, owner of one of the world's largest software businesses, says,

These California students are using the Internet to communicate with people in other places. They're part of a program called the Global Schoolhouse Project. Schools all over the world are using computer networks to share their ideas.

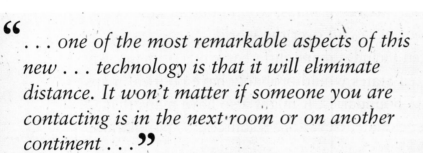

> *. . . one of the most remarkable aspects of this new . . . technology is that it will eliminate distance. It won't matter if someone you are contacting is in the next room or on another continent . . .*

People everywhere are becoming like neighbors. It's important for neighbors to understand each other. When people understand each other, it's easier for them to work together, too. Finding new ways to communicate can make this easier.

Lesson Review

1. **Key Vocabulary:** Write a paragraph about nations exchanging goods and services, using the words **international trade, European Union,** and **translate.**

2. **Focus:** How do nations benefit from trading goods and services?

3. **Focus:** How have improvements in communications helped people around the world exchange ideas?

4. **Critical Thinking: Interpret** Why are good relations among countries important in today's global economy?

5. **Geography:** Why do countries on the same continent form trading partnerships like the EU?

6. **Theme: Making Connections/Technology Activity:** Choose a form of communication and research its history. Share what you find with your class.

Skills Workshop

Using Atlases

All Around the World

If you orbit the earth in a spacecraft, you might see every continent and every ocean on the planet. There's a much easier way, though, to look for the places you hear or read about. Just open an **atlas,** a book of maps, to find out all kinds of information about places all over the world.

An atlas often includes many different kinds of maps. An atlas of the United States would probably have political maps, which show state boundaries. It might also have maps that show landforms, climate, elevation, resources, or population. The atlas and the atlas's index are your keys to finding what you're looking for.

INDEX | 109

Eleuthera

① **Here's How**

Decide if an atlas might tell you what you want to know, such as what the land is like between Santa Fe, New Mexico, and Durango, Mexico.

- Turn to the index at the back of the atlas.

- Look up the place you want to find out about. Write down the page number. Also jot down the letter and number coordinates, or grid numbers. The index will also tell you the exact latitude and longitude of a place.

- Turn to the page. Use the map's grid to help you locate the place. Remember, when you use a grid, point to the numbers or letters on the grid. The numbers and letters of the grid can be found along the map's edges. Follow the number and letter until you reach the area where the two meet. The place you're looking for is in that area.

Understanding an Atlas Index

Indexes provide many different types of information. They are arranged alphabetically and indicate the page of the map. Usually they list the grid number, latitude and longitude of the location, and sometimes the population.

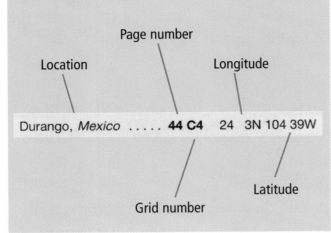

Page number

Location

Longitude

Durango, *Mexico* **44 C4**   24   3N 104 39W

Grid number

Latitude

❷ Think It Through

Suppose an atlas didn't have page numbers, coordinates, or an index. How would this make a place more difficult to find?

❸ Use It

Use an atlas in your classroom or library to find the answers to the questions below. For each one, write down the type of map you looked up, the place you looked up in the index, and the grid coordinates for the place.

1. What is the capital city of Arkansas?

2. What are the temperatures like in Sydney, Australia?

3. Where is the highest region in Asia?

4. Where is Addis Ababa located?

5. What is the most crowded area of South America?

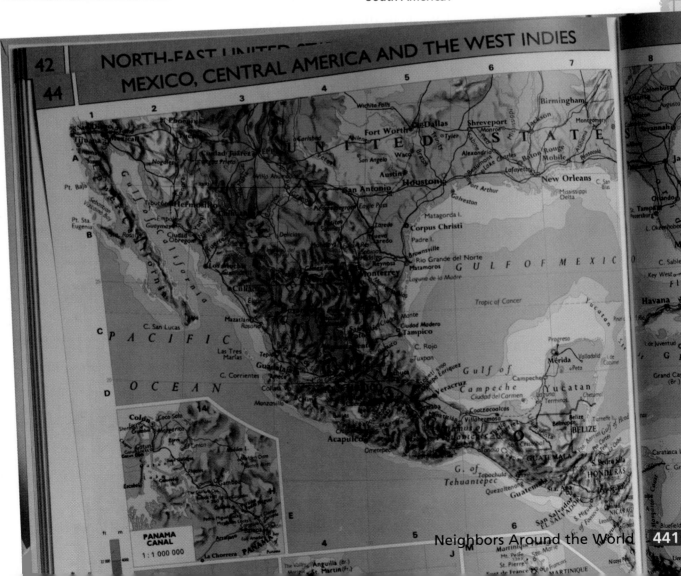

A Peaceful World

interdependent

Main Idea Nations and individuals can cooperate to make the earth a peaceful and prosperous home for everyone.

> "*We have learned . . . that our well being is dependent on the well being of other nations, far away. . . .*"

President Roosevelt said these words in 1945 at the end of World War II. The United States and many other nations fought in that war. When the war ended, people everywhere welcomed peace. The war had affected everybody deeply.

Today, governments realize that people around the world are **interdependent** — that is, they must work together and rely on each other. By learning more about other nations, you can begin to understand how people think, speak, and act. People need to understand each other to make a peaceful world.

Nations Working Together

Focus *In what ways do nations work together to create peace?*

In 1945, nations from around the world formed an organization called the United Nations. These countries wanted a place where they could meet to discuss world issues and make treaties to keep the peace. Treaties are formal written agreements made between countries.

The United Nations works for peace, security, and equal rights around the world. Member nations meet to discuss and vote on world issues. Any country can apply for membership. Today most countries in the world are members.

The United Nations is one organization that lets nations work together.

Nations also work together outside of formal organizations. One place where people from different nations have come together is in space. You can read more about international efforts in space in the Tell Me More on this page. Sharing the knowledge and technology gained from space exploration helps nations work toward peace.

• Tell Me More •

Cooperating in Space

In 1975, astronauts from the United States and the Soviet Union met high above the earth. Twenty years later, Russian and American astronauts met again (below).

In those 20 years, there have been many international efforts in space. The Hubble Space Telescope (above) has a camera built by the European Space Agency. Parts of the space shuttle were made in Canada. Japan, Saudi Arabia, Russia, and other countries have all worked with the United States on space missions.

Many countries launch satellites on the European Space Agency's Ariane rocket.

Alfred Nobel

Alfred Nobel (1833–1896) was a Swedish scientist and businessman. When he died, he left money for a worldwide prize called the Nobel Prize. It's given to people who contribute to the good of humanity.

UNICEF is a branch of the United Nations. It provides food, clothing, and education to children like these all over the world. UNICEF's work is supported by donations from people around the world. **Citizenship:** *Why is education important for all people?*

People Working Together

Focus *How can the actions of organizations and individuals today affect the future of the world?*

While governments work together toward peace, the people who live in countries around the world have worked together to help each other, too. Sometimes people join large international organizations. Other times, individuals work on their own and make a difference through their actions.

International Organizations

Some branches of the United Nations give people an opportunity to work together. The United Nations Children's Fund (UNICEF) helps children around the world who need health care, food, and education. It also trains nurses and teachers who work with children.

Other international organizations also do their part to improve life for people all over the world. The International Red Cross, for example, helps people caught in natural and human-made disasters. War victims receive medical care and help in moving to safe areas. In addition to helping people during wartime, the Red Cross has aided people caught in natural disasters like earthquakes, storms, and floods.

Sometimes organizations help people who can't meet their basic needs. Oxfam, which stands for Oxford Committee for Famine Relief, provides worldwide aid to poor communities.

This group of people in Bangladesh *(left)* are learning new farming techniques. Oxfam sends teachers to help poor people in many countries learn how to produce more food. **Economics:** *How can better farming techniques help people?*

Volunteers from the International Red Cross work in many places. These volunteers are helping refugees from the war in Bosnia-Herzegovina. Other volunteers help people who have lost their homes in natural disasters.

Based in the United Kingdom, Oxfam began programs during the 1960s to help people grow crops and produce more food. In the dry lands of Burkina Faso, a country in Africa, the group successfully showed farmers how to catch rain to support young trees. The farmers then used this idea to water food crops. People from all over the world now visit Burkina Faso to see the results of this project.

Organizations like UNICEF, the Red Cross, and Oxfam depend on volunteers. Some volunteers give money or buy products that support the organizations' programs. Others teach classes or donate the things that people in trouble need. Without the work of individuals, these organizations couldn't carry out their programs.

Actions of Individuals

The actions of individuals can be as important as those of nations and international organizations. People all over the world care about issues that affect them.

One individual who made a difference was Zlata Filipovic (fee LEE poh vik). She lived in Sarajevo (SAR uh YAY voh), in Bosnia-Herzegovina (formerly Yugoslavia). When Zlata began

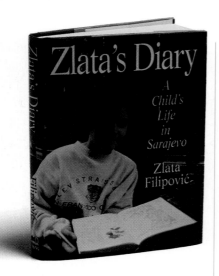

Zlata's diary about life in Sarajevo during the war was published as a book. Her book inspired other people to send supplies like food and medicine.

her journal in September 1991, life seemed normal. She was starting fifth grade. Then war broke out. *(See page 432.)*

Life became very difficult for Zlata and her family during the war. Often there was no running water, heat, or electricity. Zlata wrote about what she saw and experienced. In June of 1992, she wrote, "Despair!!! Hunger!!! Misery!!! Fear!!! That's my life! The life of an innocent 11-year-old schoolgirl!!"

UNICEF helped publish Zlata's diary to show the world what life was like in Sarajevo. When Zlata spoke to a group of journalists, she told them how important peace was.

> "The only thing I want to say to everyone is PEACE!"

After her journal was published, Zlata traveled to many countries to tell people about her experiences. In the United States she talked to a Senate committee. The committee used her comments as they talked about what the United States could do to help end the war in Bosnia and Herzegovina.

What Can You Do?

Your actions today influence your future. They also influence the future of other people and nations. Whether exploring space or working for peace around the world, nations and people can achieve more through cooperation. Everyone in the United States and around the world can contribute to make the earth a safe home for all.

Is there a world issue that you care about? Talk to your classmates, teachers, and family to find more information. Read the newspaper or watch the news on television to learn about all viewpoints. Write a letter to the editor of your school or town newspaper, or to your representatives in Congress. Tell other people what you think. If you disagree with each other, try to find out why.

Volunteering is another good way to contribute to the world. There are many ways you can help in your community and around the world. In this book, you've read about many people who got involved and made a difference. Giving your time to a cause you care about is one of the best ways to make a difference. You can also support international organizations that help people around the world.

People everywhere want and need to live in a safe and peaceful world. To make the world a peaceful place, all those people need to work together. By learning about important issues, speaking your mind, and getting involved, you can help build that world.

Working together makes the world a better place for everyone. It's important to help others locally and around the world.

Lesson Review

1 Key Vocabulary: Use the word **interdependent** in a sentence about the world today.

2 Focus: In what ways do nations work together to create peace?

3 Focus: How can the actions of organizations and individuals today affect the future of the world?

4 Critical Thinking: Generalize Why do countries need to learn about each other to make treaties?

5 Theme: Making Connections How can sharing ideas among nations make the planet a better place to live?

6 Citizenship/Arts Activity: Make a collage of words and pictures showing people and nations working together.

GEOGRAPHER

The Uses of Geography

What Can Antarctica Tell Us About the Earth?

Until 1820, no human being had ever seen Antarctica, the frozen landmass that surrounds and covers the South Pole. Serious exploration of this continent — the world's fifth-largest — did not begin until the early 1900s.

Because it is cut off from the rest of the world, Antarctica is still fairly unpolluted. Many scientists see the continent as a giant laboratory for studying important questions about the planet's past and future. By studying Antarctica's layers of ice, for example, reseachers have already learned when changes in the earth's climate occurred. They have also pinpointed when volcanoes erupted. Research may eventually allow scientists to detect early warning signs of global pollution or predict changes in the planet's weather patterns. The better human beings understand Antarctica, the better they may be able to plan for the earth's future.

1 South Pole

Amundsen-Scott Station
The United States set up the Amundsen-Scott South Pole Station in the late 1950s. Managed by the National Science Foundation, this scientific station is located about one-fifth of a mile from the South Pole.

The ozone layer is a region of the upper atmosphere that protects living things from the sun's ultraviolet rays. Satellite photographs *(above)* helped scientists discover a hole in the ozone layer above Antarctica. Many scientists believe pollution is a major cause of this hole.

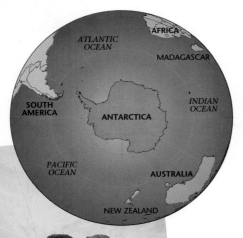

By drilling cylinders of ice, called ice cores, scientists can learn much about the history of the earth's climate. Ice cores also indicate periods of high volcanic activity.

Science Connection

Twelve countries signed the original Antarctic Treaty, which took effect in 1961. This 30-year agreement required that Antarctica be used only for peaceful, scientific purposes. Many more nations have since signed the treaty, which was renewed in 1991. Why do you think so many countries operate scientific stations on Antarctica?

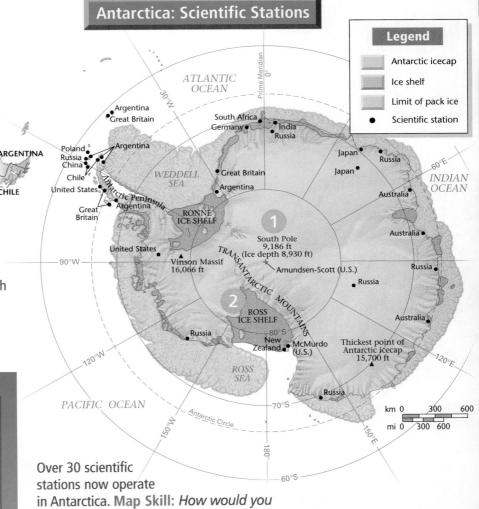

Antarctica: Scientific Stations

Legend
- Antarctic icecap
- Ice shelf
- Limit of pack ice
- • Scientific station

Over 30 scientific stations now operate in Antarctica. **Map Skill:** *How would you explain the location of these stations?*

Research Activity

Do further reading on the race to the South Pole between Robert Scott and Roald Amundsen.
❶ Why was Amundsen able to win this race?
❷ Write a diary entry of either Scott or Amundsen. Describe seeing the South Pole for the first time.

FROM THE PAGES OF
People

PEOPLE

By Peter Spier

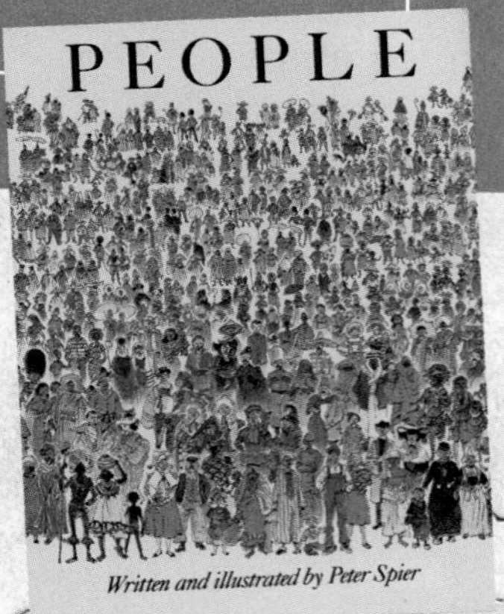
PEOPLE
Written and illustrated by Peter Spier

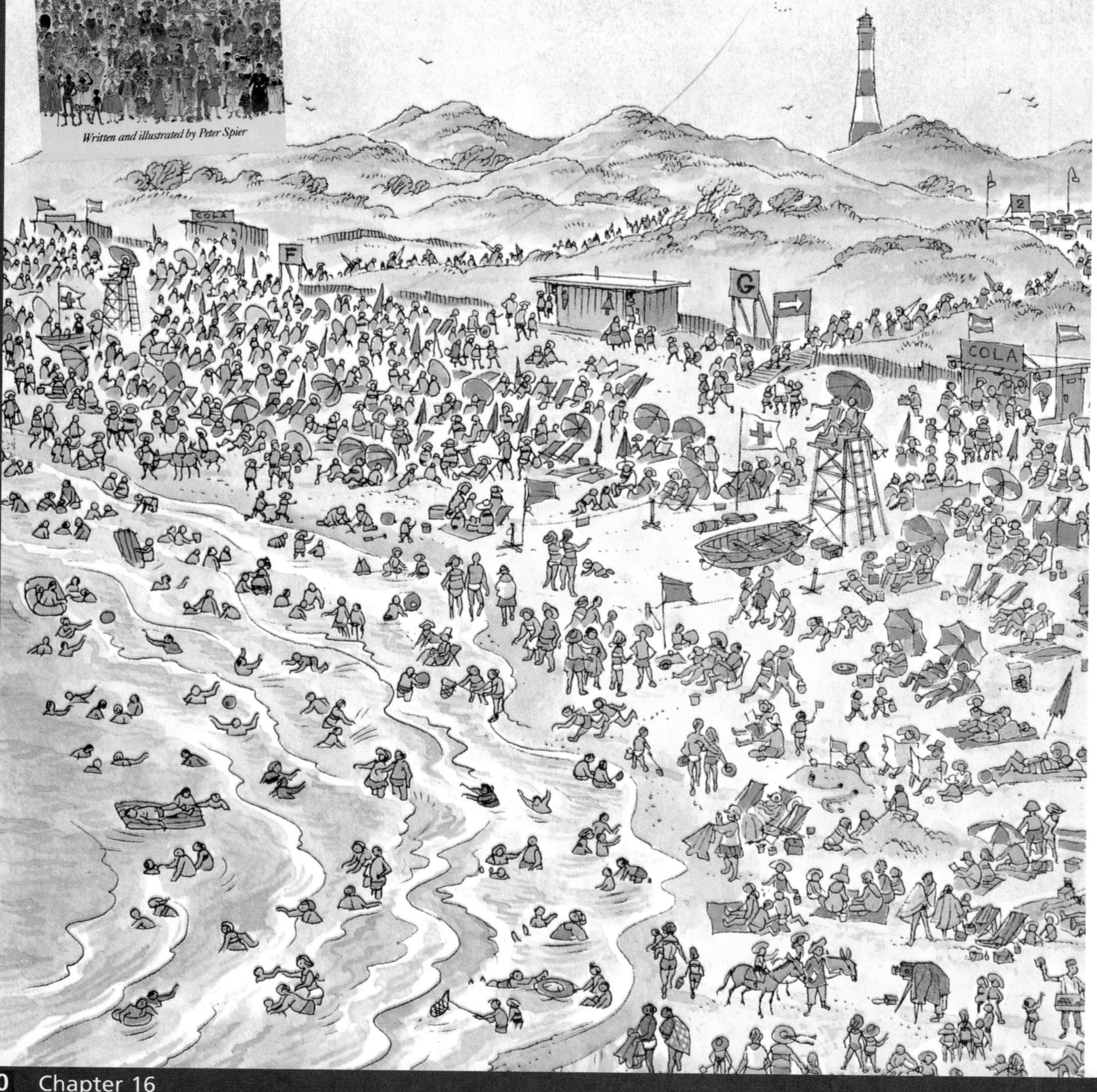
COLA
F
G
COLA
2

Who's to say what's unusual? Who's to say who's different or what looks strange?

Americans have had to learn tolerance because people in the United States have come from many different cultures. The diversity of our people has helped to make this a great country — ". . . with liberty and justice for all."

We all know that there are lots and lots of people in the world — and many more millions each year.

There are now over 5,000,000,000 human beings on earth, and if it takes you an hour to finish looking at this book, there will be over 4,000 more!

By the year 2000 there will be 6,000,000,000 people on earth. If we all joined hands, the line would be 3,805,871 miles long and would stretch 153 times around the equator.

Or sixteen times the distance to the moon. More than 5,000,000,000 people . . . and no two of them alike! Each and every one of us different from all the others. Each one a unique individual in his or her own right.

It is very strange: Some people even hate others because they are unlike themselves. Because they are different. They forget that they too would seem different if they could only see themselves through other people's eyes.

But imagine how dreadfully dull this world of ours would be if everybody would look, think, eat, dress, and act the same!

Now, isn't it wonderful that each and every one of us is unlike any other?

Response Activities

1. **Generalize:** How can organizations like those described on pages 444 and 445 help all people to better understand what they have in common?

2. **Descriptive: Write a Biography** Interview a student in your class that you don't know very well. Then write a paragraph describing what is unique about that person.

3. **National Heritage: Make a Poster** Choose a place in the world that is very different from your town. Learn about the people there and make a poster showing how they are both similar to and different from you.

Chapter Review

Summarizing the Main Idea

1 Copy and fill in the chart below. Give some examples of how each group contributes to world peace.

	How They Contribute to World Peace
Nations	cooperate in the United Nations
International organizations	
Individuals	

Vocabulary

2 Using at least nine of the following terms, write a speech about the importance of cooperation among nations.

emigrate (p. 432)

involuntary migration (p. 432)

voluntary migration (p. 433)

trend (p. 434)

international trade (p. 436)

European Union (p. 437)

translate (p. 438)

World Wide Web (p. 438)

on-line (p. 439)

interdependent (p. 442)

Reviewing the Facts

3 How do wet and dry environments influence the houses people build?

4 What are some of the reasons why people migrate to other countries?

5 What is the difference between involuntary migration and voluntary migration?

6 Why do many people move to cities?

7 What is the purpose of trade organizations?

8 How do telecommunications help people trade goods and services around the world?

9 How does the United Nations work to encourage world peace?

10 What are some examples of organizations that work to improve life for people all over the world?

11 How can individuals contribute to a peaceful world?

12 Use an atlas to find the Ross Ice Shelf. What continent is it part of?

13 Would an atlas be the best source for information about your state's government? Why or why not?

Geography Skills

14 Look at the map on pages 430 and 431. What ecoregions are in Australia? Which ecoregion do you think is shown in the photo of Australia?

15 Find out which countries are in the European Union. Trace a map of Europe and use colors to show these countries.

Critical Thinking

16 **Decision Making** Look back at the international organizations described in Lesson 3. Which one would you choose to support? Why? How would you participate in the organization?

17 **Conclude** What would you do if you were forced to leave your country because of harsh living conditions? How would you decide where to go? What would you bring with you?

Writing: Citizenship and Economics

18 **Citizenship** Look in the newspaper for articles about refugees. Write a summary of each article.

19 **Economics** Write a newspaper article about international trade. How can cooperation among nations increase world trade?

Activities

Geography/Science Activity
Choose one of the environments pictured on pages 430 and 431. Find out about the kinds of plants and animals that live there. Make a poster to present what you learn to your class.

Citizenship/Music Activity
Write a song about the importance of cooperation. Draw a picture to go with your song. Hang your song and picture in the classroom to share with others.

Internet Option

Check the
Internet Social Studies Center
for ideas on how to extend your theme project beyond your classroom.

THEME PROJECT CHECK-IN

As you finish your bulletin board, look to see if you've included information about countries all over the world.
• How can you show the movement of people around the world?
• Does your map show connections between the United States and other countries?
• Have you included descriptions of how different countries cooperate?

Reference Databank

Handbook for Learners

If you flip through this book, you'll see many maps, graphs, and photographs. One map can show you the different climates of an entire continent. One graph can give you information about a town's population. Pictures of all kinds add to our understanding of other places, times, and people.

This handbook will help you with the skills you need for your social studies journey. You may already know some of these skills. Others may be new to you. Use this handbook to practice skills you know or to learn new ones. Then you'll be ready to start your adventure in social studies.

Contents

Reviewing Map and Globe Skills

Reading Maps

Every map is different. One map may show the United States. Another map may show South America. One map may show the climate of Texas. Another may show the resources of Mexico.

Political maps, like the one at right, are maps that show the borders and boundaries of states and nations. However, there are some ways in which all maps are alike.

The **map key** or **legend** tells you what the symbols on the map mean. How does the map at right show state and national boundaries?

Map Key

Key

—— National boundaries

—— State boundaries

◉ National capital

★ State capital

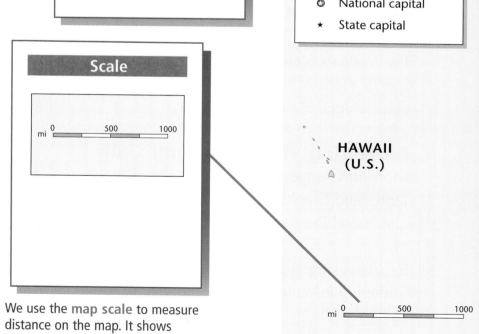

Key

—— National boundaries

—— State boundaries

◉ National capital

★ State capital

P
C

HAWAII
(U.S.)

Scale

mi 0   500   1000

We use the **map scale** to measure distance on the map. It shows distance in miles.

mi 0   500   1000

Use It

Take a piece of string and measure the distance between two cities on the map to the right. Then measure your string against the scale shown in the lower left corner of the map. How many times does the scale fit into the length of string you measured? Multiply this number by the miles which the scale stands for. How far apart are the two cities?

A **locator map** is the small map found within or near the main map. It tells you where the area of the main map can be found on the earth. A locator map helps you see how large or small the area on the main map is. It also shows you what places are near the area shown on the main map.

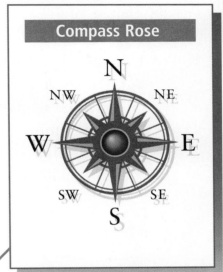

Map Titles

Map titles tell you what the map is about. They can also tell you what kind of map it is.

Compass Rose

The compass rose shows direction. Most compass roses label the four main directions 0 — north, south, east, and west. These are usually marked N, S, E, and W. The intermediate directions — northwest, southwest, southeast, and northeast — are between the four main directions.

Map Title

ARCTIC OCEAN

ALASKA (U.S.)

PACIFIC OCEAN

CANADA

Ottawa ○

UNITED STATES

Washington, D.C. ○

ATLANTIC OCEAN

TEXAS
Austin ★

MEXICO

Mexico City ○

CARIBBEAN SEA

Going Further

As you can see on this map, Austin, Texas is southwest of Washington, D.C. Where is your community in relation to Washington, D.C.? On a map of your state, find where your community is in relation to your state capital.

The World in Globes and Maps

Look at the photograph, the globe, and the maps on these two pages. They all show us the earth, but they do it in different ways. The photograph shows the earth as it looks from outer space. The globe is a model of the earth. It shows the shape of the planet, but it cannot show the whole earth in one view.

The flat map gives us a view of the whole planet in one image. Flat maps are useful for locating and comparing places.

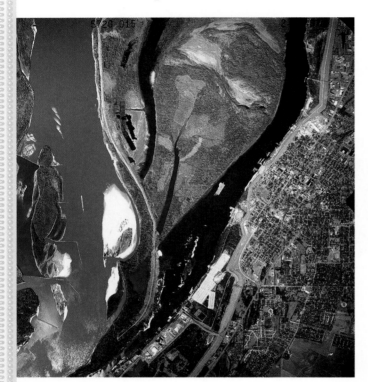

Satellite Photography

This photograph of Greenville, Mississippi, on the Mississippi River, was created by a satellite. Satellites also help make maps. They receive signals from places on the earth. These signals are used to pinpoint the exact location and shape of a place or country.

Globes

Globes show us that the earth is shaped like a sphere, or ball. At the top of the globe is the **North Pole**. It is the northernmost place on the earth. The North arrow on the compass rose points toward the North Pole.

At the bottom of the globe is the **South Pole**. It is the southernmost place on the earth.

Use It

Write down the names of the four hemispheres. Then write down which continents are located in each. Why do some of the names appear more than once?

Going Further

There are many different ways to show the earth. Sometimes it's hard to know which one to use. Pick one of the ways on these pages — globe, satellite photograph, hemispheres, flat map — and list reasons to use it.

The Equator and the Hemispheres

The **equator** is an imaginary line around the middle of the earth. It is equally distant from the North Pole and the South Pole. Geographers use the equator to divide the earth into halves, or hemispheres. These are the **Northern** and **Southern Hemispheres**.

Another imaginary line runs from the North Pole to the South Pole. Geographers use this line to divide the earth into the **Eastern** and **Western Hemispheres**.

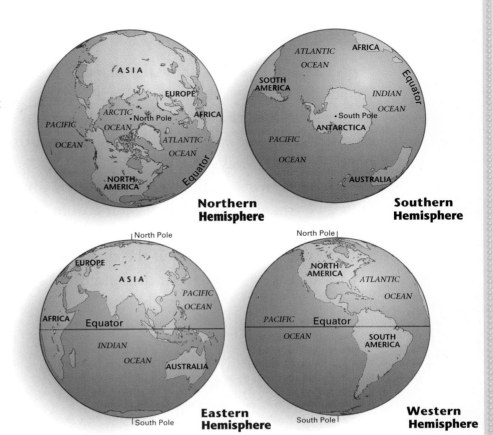

Northern Hemisphere

Southern Hemisphere

Eastern Hemisphere

Western Hemisphere

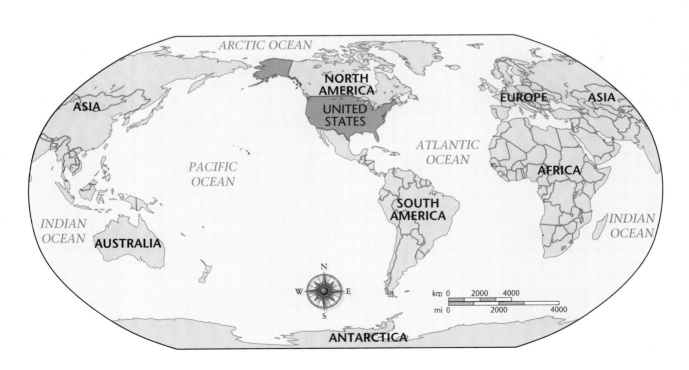

This kind of flat map is called a **Robinson Map**. It was made by an American mapmaker named Arthur Robinson in 1963. This map is different from other flat maps because the sizes, shapes, and distances of land and water areas on this map are closest to the ones found on a globe.

Special Kinds of Maps

Maps can do more than show the shape of the land and the boundaries of states and nations. Each kind of map has a special purpose. It might be to give you information about the resources of the land, to show natural features, or to show where major highways are located.

The three maps on these pages are called physical maps. They give you information about physical features of the land. One map tells you about the energy resources of the United States. Another tells you about the climate of South America. The third map tells you about the landforms of Alaska. Each map uses a different set of symbols to show its information.

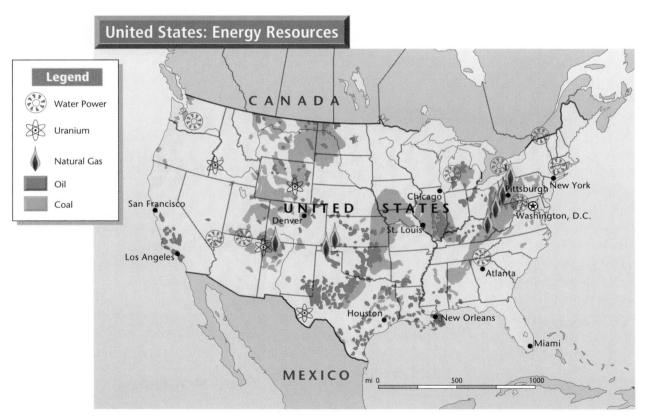

United States: Energy Resources

Legend

- Water Power
- Uranium
- Natural Gas
- Oil
- Coal

Resource Maps

A resource map has information about one or more resources, such as minerals or crops, in a region. A resource map can help you understand how people in that region earn a living. This map shows the energy resources of the United States. What symbol is used for uranium? Where is uranium found in the United States?

Climate Map

A climate map tells you about the average weather at a place over a period of years. Some climate maps show specific information like temperature or rainfall. Others use special names to describe types of climate.

South America: Climate

Caracas
Santa Fe de Bogotá
Amazon River
Lima
PACIFIC OCEAN
Tropic of Capricorn
São Paulo
Rio de Janeiro
Santiago de Chile
Buenos Aires
ATLANTIC OCEAN
mi 0   500   1000

Legend

- Tropical rainforest
- Tropical savanna
- Semiarid
- Desert (arid)
- Mediterranean
- Humid subtropical
- Marine
- Highland

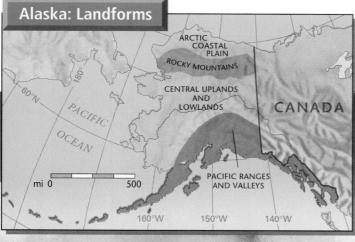

Alaska: Landforms

ARCTIC COASTAL PLAIN
ROCKY MOUNTAINS
CENTRAL UPLANDS AND LOWLANDS
CANADA
PACIFIC OCEAN
PACIFIC RANGES AND VALLEYS
mi 0   500

Landform Maps

A landform map shows the different types of natural features in an area. This map does not have a legend. Instead, the different landforms are labeled in their general location.

Use It

The climate map shows the types of climate found in South America. How many different types of climate are there in this region? What color is used to show a marine climate?

Going Further

Find climate, resource, or landform maps of your state. What landforms and energy resources are found in your state?

Calculating Distance

If you've ever done any traveling or sightseeing by car, you have probably seen a road map. Road maps show routes that connect cities and towns. They use symbols to identify different kinds of roads and points of interest. With a road map, you can figure out how to get from one place to another.

City Maps

City maps, like this one of Toronto, Canada, show streets instead of highways. They also show places of interest. These maps help tourists plan their visits and find their way around the city with ease.

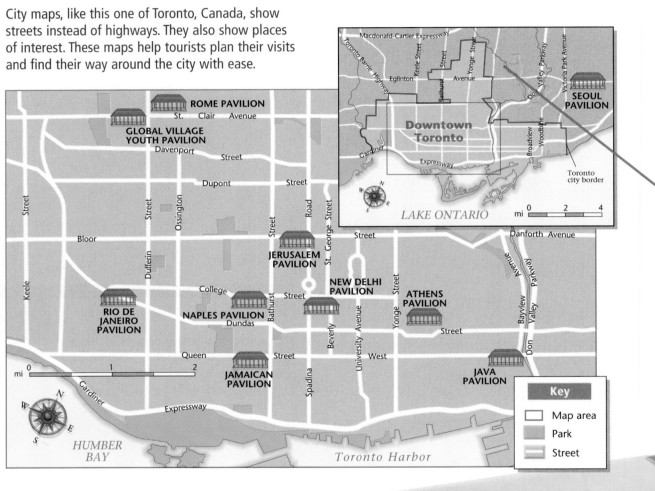

Use a piece of string to measure distance on the map. Lay the string along a route or between places. Then measure your string against the scale shown in the lower left corner. How many times does the scale fit into the length of string you measured? Multiply this number by the miles which the scale stands for.

Using map scales, you can also figure out how far it is from one place to another. The downtown Toronto map and the inset map both have scales. Map scales are different when maps show different areas. Look at the scale on the inset map. How is it different from the scale on the main map?

Inset Map

Many maps have inset maps. Some inset maps enlarge an area on a main map to give you more detail. Some inset maps, like this one, act like locator maps. This inset map shows you where downtown Toronto is located. You can also see Toronto in the photograph above.

Use It

Select two sights on the main map that you would like to see if you were in Toronto. Measure the distance between them, using the map scale. How much more is it if you measure only along the roads that go from one to the other?

Going Further

On a map of your area, pick two places, like the town hall and the park, or the library and your house. Write down the directions to get from one to the other. How far is the distance between them?

Reviewing Visual Learning Skills

Showing Change

How can we show change? A road map of the United States from 100 years ago and one from today would be different. Roads, towns, and cities have changed. Pictures can also show change. Photographs and other pictures can show details more clearly than a written account can. They also give us first-hand views of places and things. Pictures let us compare how things looked in an earlier time with how they look today.

Pictures

These two pictures of Boston Harbor show how much the harbor and the city have changed. There are more ships in the older picture. What could that mean about the use of the harbor? What's the biggest difference you see between the painting and the photograph?

Use It

Look at the two pictures of Boston Harbor again. Make a list of the things that have changed, and the things that are the same. Write a paragraph about how the harbor has changed over time.

Tables and Graphs

As you have seen, we can learn about change in many ways. Maps and pictures can show change. We can also arrange information in ways that make it easier to see change. Timelines, tables, and graphs are tools for showing change.

Timelines

Another way to show change is to list the important dates and events in the history of a person, place, or thing. This list of dates and events is called a timeline. A timeline puts events in order from earliest to most recent along a line. The timeline here lists events in the history of Dubuque, Iowa. How many years passed between the Land Office opening and three public schools opening?

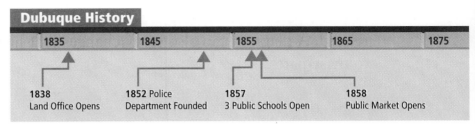

Dubuque History

1835	1845	1855	1865	1875

1838 Land Office Opens

1852 Police Department Founded

1857 3 Public Schools Open

1858 Public Market Opens

Tables

Tables take number data, or statistics, and organize this information into rows (across) and columns (up and down). The title and headings tell you what the table is about. What is this table about? What does the information in it show?

Population Table

	1989	1990	1991	1992	1993
Colorado	3,276,000	3,294,000	3,370,000	3,456,000	3,586,000
Arkansas	2,346,000	2,351,000	2,371,000	2,394,000	2,424,000

Graphs

Graphs can also show statistics. One type of graph is a bar graph. Bar graphs use bars of different heights or lengths to show data. Using them, you can compare information or see change.

Each side of a graph, called an axis, presents one kind of information. The vertical axis on this graph shows population measured in thousands. The horizontal axis shows the cities for which the statistics are being supplied.

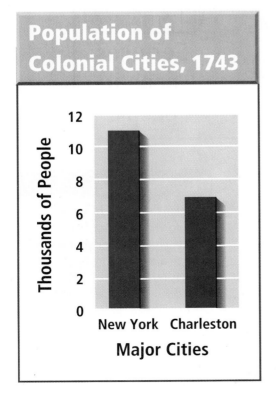

Population of Colonial Cities, 1743

Thousands of People
12 10 8 6 4 2 0

New York   Charleston

Major Cities

Going Further

Find out some information about your community, such as how many boys and girls are in each grade at school. Make a table or graph showing the information.

Charts and Diagrams

There are other ways pictures can show information. Sometimes we need to show a process, not just its result. A good way to do this is to make a flow chart. The arrows in a flow chart show which way the action is moving. Follow them and you'll see the process. Diagrams are drawings that show how the parts of something are arranged, or how the parts are related. A diagram can also show changes that have been made to these parts.

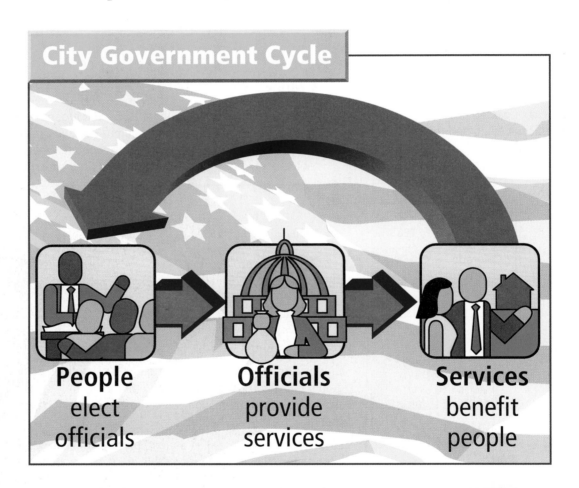

City Government Cycle

People
elect
officials

Officials
provide
services

Services
benefit
people

Flow Charts

In this flow chart, you can see how the cycle of city government works. Flow charts are diagrams with arrows that show the flow of action from one step to the next.

Use It

Follow the steps of the flow chart above. Is it clear how each leads to the next? Write a short caption explaining each step. What would happen if one of the steps were left out?

Going Further

Make a diagram of something you use a lot, like a bike, your desk, or your room. Remember to label all the parts.

A diagram uses labels, and sometimes a key, to explain what it shows. Below is a diagram of a lead mine.

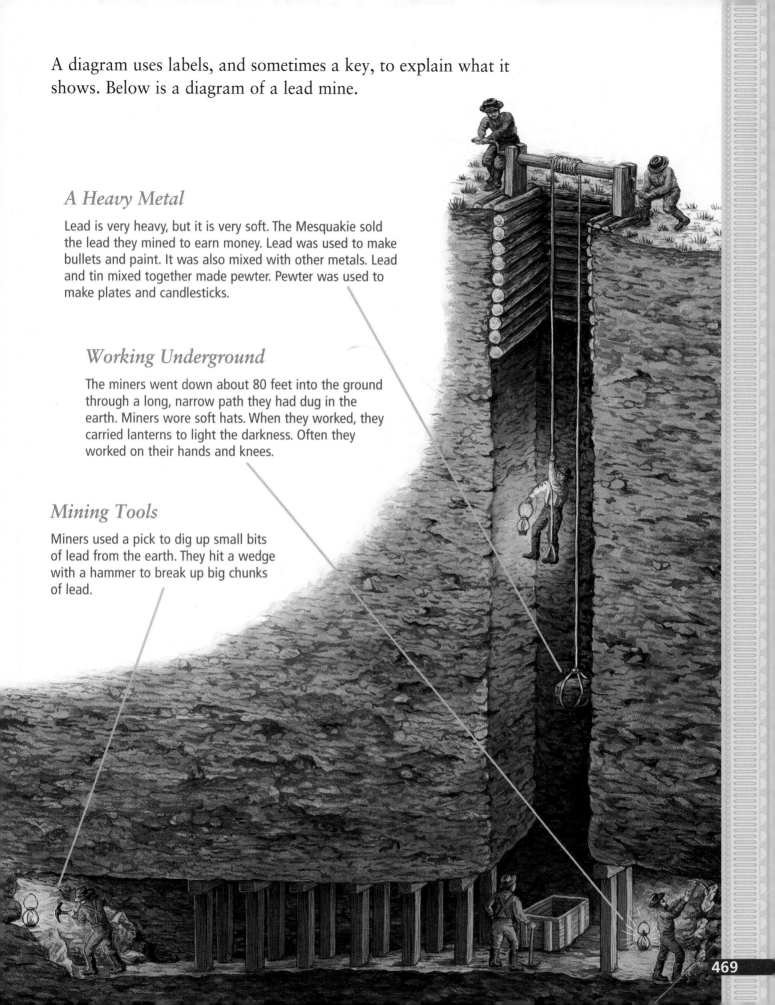

A Heavy Metal

Lead is very heavy, but it is very soft. The Mesquakie sold the lead they mined to earn money. Lead was used to make bullets and paint. It was also mixed with other metals. Lead and tin mixed together made pewter. Pewter was used to make plates and candlesticks.

Working Underground

The miners went down about 80 feet into the ground through a long, narrow path they had dug in the earth. Miners wore soft hats. When they worked, they carried lanterns to light the darkness. Often they worked on their hands and knees.

Mining Tools

Miners used a pick to dig up small bits of lead from the earth. They hit a wedge with a hammer to break up big chunks of lead.

Reviewing Social Studies Research Skills

Gathering Information

Every year for more than 200 years Americans have celebrated our nation's independence on the Fourth of July. How do Americans celebrate this holiday? There are several ways of gathering information from people to find out. You could take a survey, interview someone, or write a letter.

Survey

In a **survey** you ask a series of questions of a number of people. Most surveys offer people a choice of answers: Do you celebrate the Fourth of July — yes or no? How do you celebrate this holiday — go on a picnic, watch a parade, visit a war memorial, watch fireworks? When you complete the survey and add up the answers, you can see what the majority of people surveyed think or do.

Letter

A **letter** can ask someone for information. Perhaps you want to find out how your senators celebrate the Fourth of July. In your letter, explain why you are writing and include a list of the questions you would like the senator to answer. As with an interview, be sure to end your letter with a thank you.

Interview

An **interview** gives you in-depth information from one person. Plan in advance. Decide what you want to find out and write down your questions. It helps to organize your questions into categories or groups. During the interview, write down the answers you are given. When the interview is over, don't forget to say thank you!

Jefferson School
Third Grade

Dude Ranchers Association
Box 471
La Porte, CO 80535

Dear Association Members:

We are studying great trips. We found your address in a book. It looks interesting to us. Could you please send us some information?

First of all we would like to know what a dude ... What happens there? How would we

Using the Library

One of the best places to find information on any subject is in a library. There you'll find all kinds of resources, from books to encyclopedias to magazines. These sources can be useful for writing reports or working on projects. You'll also find people who will help you — the librarians.

Books are another place to look for information. Every library has a catalogue of its books. The catalogue is arranged alphabetically. If you look up your topic in the catalogue, you will find the titles of books that may help you.

Encyclopedias

Check encyclopedias first for information and answers. Encyclopedias arrange information alphabetically. They contain so much information that they are divided into many volumes. To locate information about Independence Day, you should look for the volume that has the letter "I" on its spine. Then skim through the volume until you find the article under the heading "Independence Day." Read the article and write down any information that helps answer your questions.

Use It

If you were writing a report on Independence Day, you'd need to prepare first. Make a list of the questions you would want answers to, such as, "Why do we celebrate Independence Day when we do?"

Going Further

Go to the library and find an encyclopedia article about the Statue of Liberty. Read the article to find out why it was built. Write down the answer.

Atlas

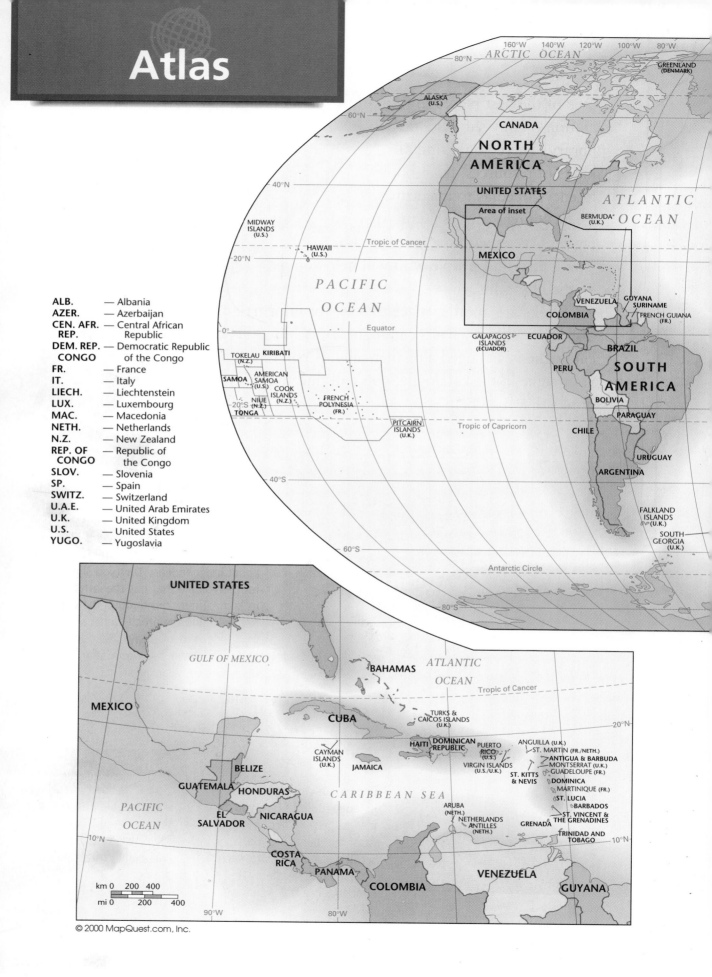

ALB. — Albania
AZER. — Azerbaijan
CEN. AFR. REP. — Central African Republic
DEM. REP. CONGO — Democratic Republic of the Congo
FR. — France
IT. — Italy
LIECH. — Liechtenstein
LUX. — Luxembourg
MAC. — Macedonia
NETH. — Netherlands
N.Z. — New Zealand
REP. OF CONGO — Republic of the Congo
SLOV. — Slovenia
SP. — Spain
SWITZ. — Switzerland
U.A.E. — United Arab Emirates
U.K. — United Kingdom
U.S. — United States
YUGO. — Yugoslavia

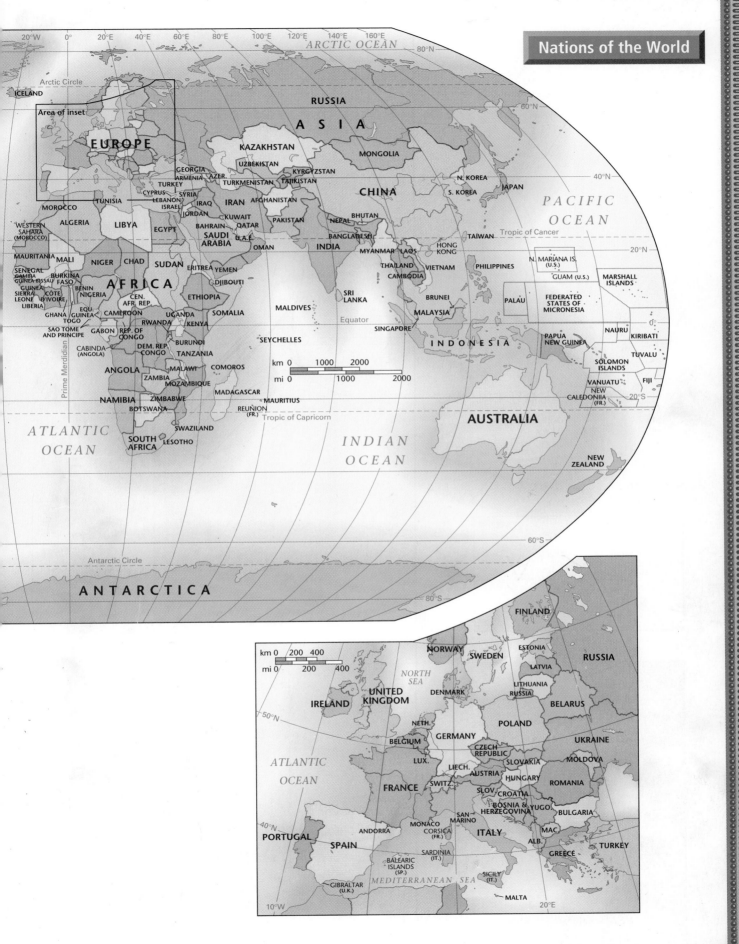

ARCTIC OCEAN

RUSSIA

A S I A

EUROPE

ICELAND

Arctic Circle

Area of inset

KAZAKHSTAN

MONGOLIA

UZBEKISTAN

GEORGIA
ARMENIA
TURKEY
AZER.
TURKMENISTAN
TAJIKISTAN
KYRGYZSTAN

N. KOREA
JAPAN
S. KOREA

CHINA

PACIFIC OCEAN

CYPRUS
LEBANON
ISRAEL
SYRIA
IRAQ
IRAN
AFGHANISTAN

TUNISIA

MOROCCO

JORDAN
KUWAIT
BAHRAIN
QATAR

PAKISTAN

NEPAL
BHUTAN

TAIWAN

Tropic of Cancer

ALGERIA
LIBYA
EGYPT
SAUDI ARABIA
U.A.E.

BANGLADESH

HONG KONG

N. MARIANA IS.
(U.S.)

20°N

WESTERN SAHARA
(MOROCCO)

OMAN

INDIA

MYANMAR
LAOS

GUAM (U.S.)

MARSHALL ISLANDS

MAURITANIA
MALI
NIGER
CHAD
SUDAN
ERITREA
YEMEN

THAILAND
VIETNAM

PHILIPPINES

SENEGAL
GAMBIA
GUINEA-BISSAU
BURKINA FASO
BENIN
NIGERIA

DJIBOUTI

CAMBODIA

BRUNEI

PALAU

FEDERATED STATES OF MICRONESIA

AFRICA

CEN. AFR. REP.

ETHIOPIA

SRI LANKA

SIERRA LEONE
LIBERIA
CÔTE D'IVOIRE
GHANA
TOGO
EQU. GUINEA

MALDIVES

MALAYSIA

NAURU

KIRIBATI

SAO TOME AND PRINCIPE

CAMEROON

UGANDA

SOMALIA

Equator

SINGAPORE

TUVALU

GABON
REP. OF CONGO

RWANDA
KENYA

SEYCHELLES

INDONESIA

PAPUA NEW GUINEA

SOLOMON ISLANDS

CABINDA (ANGOLA)

DEM. REP. CONGO

BURUNDI
TANZANIA

VANUATU

NEW CALEDONIA (FR.)

FIJI

ANGOLA
MALAWI
COMOROS

ZAMBIA
MOZAMBIQUE

km 0   1000   2000

mi 0   1000   2000

20°S

NAMIBIA
ZIMBABWE
MADAGASCAR

BOTSWANA

MAURITIUS
RÉUNION (FR.)

Tropic of Capricorn

AUSTRALIA

ATLANTIC OCEAN

SOUTH AFRICA
SWAZILAND
LESOTHO

INDIAN OCEAN

NEW ZEALAND

60°S

Antarctic Circle

A N T A R C T I C A

80°S

FINLAND

NORWAY
SWEDEN

ESTONIA

RUSSIA

km 0   200   400

mi 0   200   400

NORTH SEA

IRELAND
UNITED KINGDOM

DENMARK

LATVIA

LITHUANIA
RUSSIA

BELARUS

50°N

NETH.

BELGIUM
GERMANY

POLAND

UKRAINE

ATLANTIC OCEAN

LUX.

LIECH.

CZECH REPUBLIC

SLOVAKIA

MOLDOVA

AUSTRIA
HUNGARY

FRANCE

SWITZ.

SLOV.
CROATIA

ROMANIA

40°N

MONACO

SAN MARINO

BOSNIA & HERZEGOVINA

YUGO.

BULGARIA

ANDORRA

CORSICA (FR.)

ITALY

MAC.

PORTUGAL

SPAIN

ALB.

TURKEY

BALEARIC ISLANDS (SP.)

SARDINIA (IT.)

GREECE

GIBRALTAR (U.K.)

MEDITERRANEAN SEA

SICILY (IT.)

MALTA

10°W

20°E

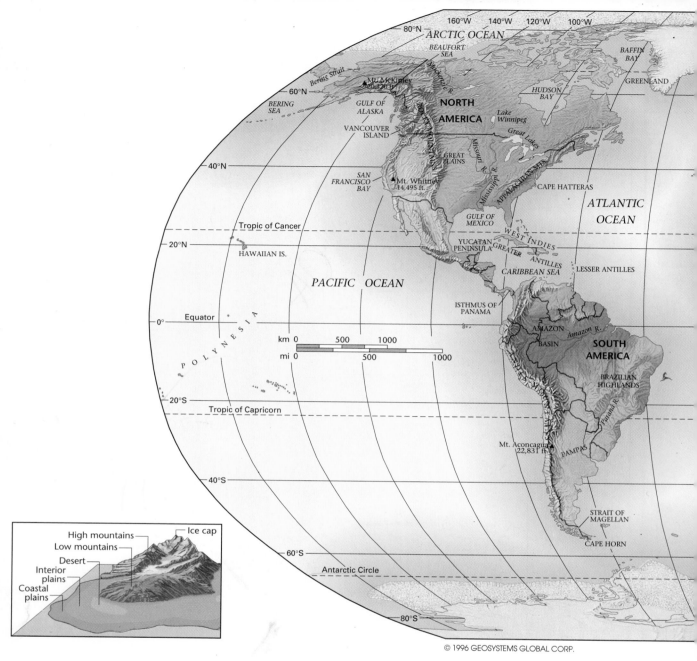

160°W 140°W 120°W 100°W

80°N

ARCTIC OCEAN

BEAUFORT
SEA

BAFFIN
BAY

Bering Strait

Mt. McKinley
20,320 ft.

Mackenzie R.

GREENLAND

60°N

HUDSON
BAY

BERING
SEA

GULF OF
ALASKA

NORTH
AMERICA

Lake
Winnipeg

VANCOUVER
ISLAND

Great Lakes

40°N

GREAT
PLAINS

Missouri R.

SAN
FRANCISCO
BAY

Mt. Whitney
14,495 ft.

APPALACHIAN MTS.

CAPE HATTERAS

ATLANTIC
OCEAN

Mississippi R.

Tropic of Cancer

GULF OF
MEXICO

WEST INDIES

20°N

HAWAIIAN IS.

YUCATAN
PENINSULA

GREATER
ANTILLES

CARIBBEAN SEA

LESSER ANTILLES

PACIFIC OCEAN

P O L Y N E S I A

ISTHMUS OF
PANAMA

AMAZON
BASIN

Amazon R.

SOUTH
AMERICA

Equator 0°

km 0   500   1000

mi 0   500   1000

BRAZILIAN
HIGHLANDS

20°S

Tropic of Capricorn

Paraná R.

Mt. Aconcagua
22,831 ft.

PAMPAS

40°S

STRAIT OF
MAGELLAN

CAPE HORN

60°S

Antarctic Circle

80°S

© 1996 GEOSYSTEMS GLOBAL CORP.

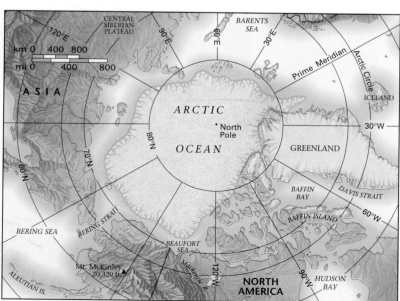

Ice cap
High mountains
Low mountains
Desert
Interior
plains
Coastal
plains

km 0   400   800
mi 0   400   800

CENTRAL
SIBERIAN
PLATEAU

120°E

90°E

60°E

BARENTS
SEA

30°E

Prime Meridian

Arctic Circle

ASIA

ARCTIC

OCEAN

+ North
Pole

80°N

GREENLAND

ICELAND

30°W

70°N

BAFFIN
BAY

DAVIS STRAIT

60°N

BERING SEA

BERING STRAIT

BEAUFORT
SEA

BAFFIN ISLAND

60°W

Mackenzie R.

ALEUTIAN IS.

Mt. McKinley
20,320 ft.

120°W

90°W

NORTH
AMERICA

HUDSON
BAY

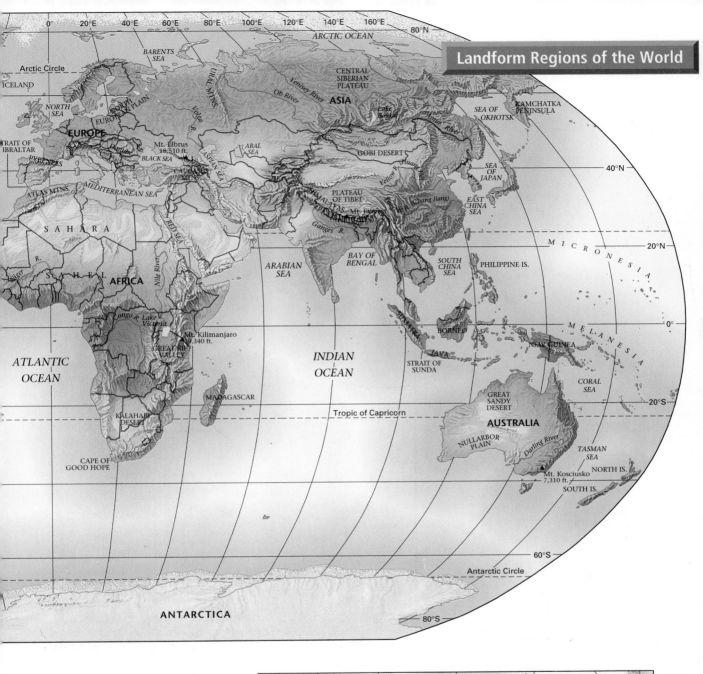

0°   20°E   40°E   60°E   80°E   100°E   120°E   140°E   160°E

ARCTIC OCEAN   80°N

ICELAND   CENTRAL
                                           SIBERIAN
Arctic Circle   BARENTS   PLATEAU
                       SEA
                                  URAL MTNS.   Yenisey River
NORTH   NORTH   Ob River
SEA   EUROPEAN PLAIN   ASIA
                                                        KAMCHATKA
EUROPE   PENINSULA
STRAIT OF   Mt. Elbrus   Amur River   SEA OF
GIBRALTAR   18,510 ft.   ARAL   OKHOTSK
PYRENEES   Danube BLACK SEA   SEA   GOBI DESERT   SEA
         CAUCASUS   SEA OF   40°N
ATLAS MTNS.   CASPIAN SEA   Yellow R. (Huang He) JAPAN
      MEDITERRANEAN SEA   EAST
                             HIMALAYAS   PLATEAU   CHINA
SAHARA   RED SEA   Mt. Everest OF TIBET Chang Jiang) SEA
                                         Fang River
                             Ganges R.
Niger R.   SAHEL   Nile River   MICRONESIA   20°N
              AFRICA   ARABIAN   BAY OF
                             SEA   BENGAL   SOUTH
                                                 CHINA   PHILIPPINE IS.
                                                 SEA
        Congo R. Lake   SUMATRA   MELANESIA   0°
ATLANTIC Victoria   BORNEO
OCEAN   Mt. Kilimanjaro   NEW GUINEA
          19,340 ft.   INDIAN   JAVA
          GREAT RIFT   OCEAN   STRAIT OF
          VALLEY   SUNDA
                    MADAGASCAR   CORAL
                                                         SEA   20°S
                                         GREAT
                             Tropic of Capricorn SANDY
                                         DESERT
          KALAHARI   AUSTRALIA
          DESERT   NULLARBOR   Darling River TASMAN
                                   PLAIN   SEA
CAPE OF   Mt. Kosciusko NORTH IS.
GOOD HOPE   7,310 ft.
                                                         SOUTH IS.

                                                                 60°S

                             Antarctic Circle

ANTARCTICA   80°S

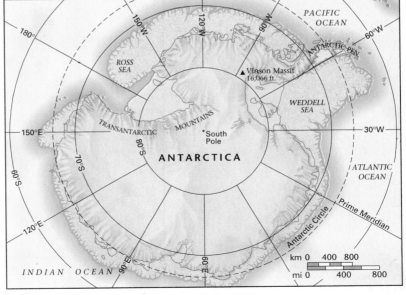

                                   PACIFIC
                                   OCEAN
        180   150°W   120°W   90°W   60°W
                                            ANTARCTIC PEN.
        ROSS
        SEA   Vinson Massif
                        16,066 ft.   WEDDELL
150°E   SEA
        TRANSANTARCTIC MOUNTAINS
                        +South   30°W
                         Pole
        ANTARCTICA   ATLANTIC
120°E   OCEAN
                                    Antarctic Circle Prime Meridian
                        90°E   60°E
        INDIAN OCEAN   km 0   400   800
                              mi 0   400   800

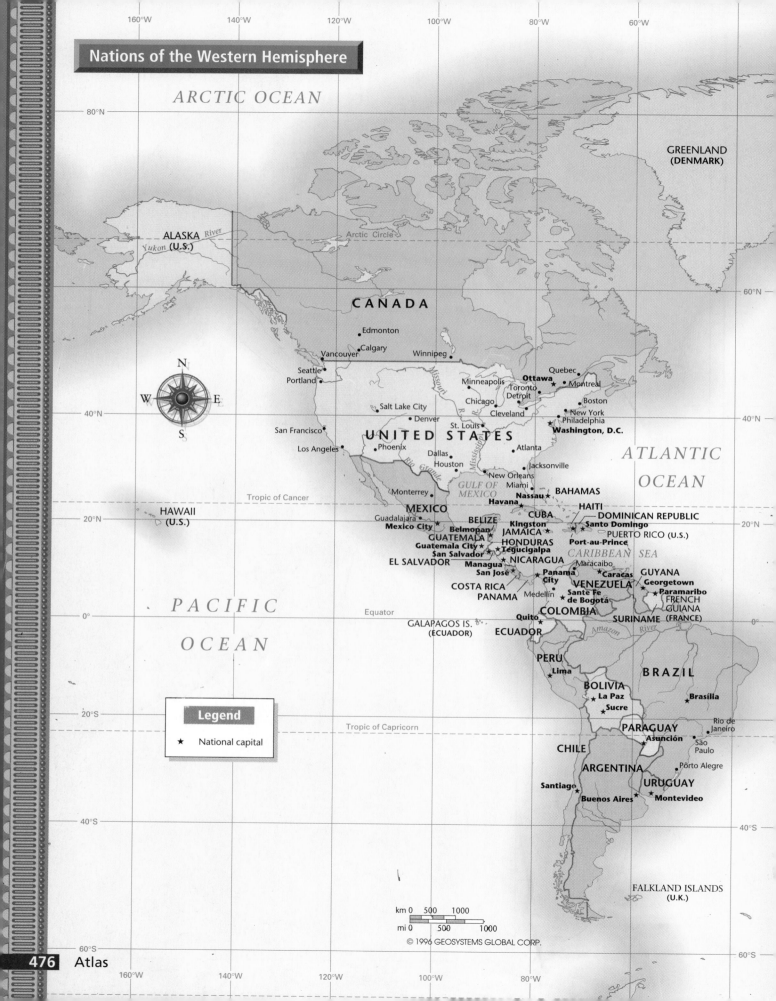

Nations of the Western Hemisphere

ARCTIC OCEAN

GREENLAND
(DENMARK)

80°N

60°N

ALASKA *Yukon River*
(U.S.)

Arctic Circle

CANADA

• Edmonton
• Calgary
Vancouver •
Seattle •
Portland •

• Winnipeg

Quebec •
Ottawa ★ • Montreal
• Minneapolis
Chicago • Toronto
Detroit
• Boston
• New York
• Philadelphia
★ Washington, D.C.

40°N

Salt Lake City •
• Denver
San Francisco •
• St. Louis
Cleveland

UNITED STATES

Los Angeles •
• Phoenix
• Dallas
• Atlanta
• Houston
• Jacksonville
Rio Grande
• New Orleans
Mississippi R.
Missouri R.

ATLANTIC
OCEAN

Tropic of Cancer

GULF OF
MEXICO
Miami
BAHAMAS
Nassau ★

HAWAII
(U.S.)

20°N

• Monterrey

Havana ★
MEXICO
Guadalajara •
Mexico City ★
BELIZE
Belmopan ★
GUATEMALA
Guatemala City ★
El Salvador
San Salvador ★
Kingston ★
JAMAICA
HONDURAS
Tegucigalpa ★
NICARAGUA
Managua ★
San José ★

CUBA
HAITI
DOMINICAN REPUBLIC
Santo Domingo ★
PUERTO RICO (U.S.)
Port-au-Prince ★

CARIBBEAN SEA

PACIFIC

COSTA RICA
PANAMA
Panama City ★
Medellín •
Maracaibo •
VENEZUELA
Sante Fe
de Bogotá ★
Caracas ★
GUYANA
Georgetown ★
Paramaribo ★
SURINAME
FRENCH
GUIANA
(FRANCE)

OCEAN

Equator

GALAPAGOS IS.
(ECUADOR)
ECUADOR
Quito •
COLOMBIA
Amazon River

20°S

PERU
Lima •

BRAZIL

BOLIVIA
La Paz ★
Sucre ★
Brasília ★

Tropic of Capricorn

Rio de
Janeiro

PARAGUAY
Asunción ★
São
Paulo

CHILE

ARGENTINA
Pôrto Alegre

URUGUAY
Santiago ★
Buenos Aires ★
Montevideo ★

40°S

Legend
★ National capital

FALKLAND ISLANDS
(U.K.)

60°S

km 0   500   1000
mi 0   500   1000

© 1996 GEOSYSTEMS GLOBAL CORP.

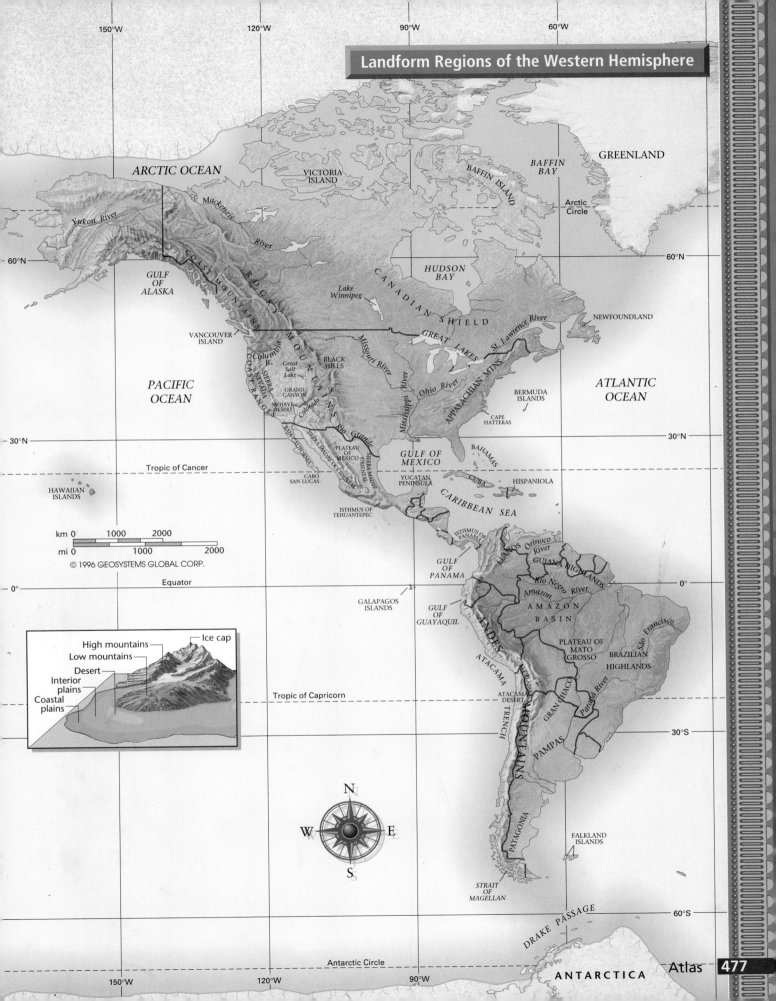

150°W   120°W   90°W   60°W

GREENLAND

ARCTIC OCEAN

VICTORIA ISLAND

BAFFIN ISLAND

BAFFIN BAY

Arctic Circle

Mackenzie River

Yukon River

60°N

GULF OF ALASKA

HUDSON BAY

CANADIAN SHIELD

Lake Winnipeg

NEWFOUNDLAND

60°N

COAST MOUNTAINS

ROCKY MOUNTAINS

VANCOUVER ISLAND

COAST RANGES

Columbia R.

Great Salt Lake

SIERRA NEVADA

GRAND CANYON

MOJAVE DESERT

BLACK HILLS

Missouri River

R.

Colorado

GREAT LAKES

St. Lawrence River

Mississippi River

Ohio River

APPALACHIAN MTNS.

BERMUDA ISLANDS

PACIFIC OCEAN

ATLANTIC OCEAN

CAPE HATTERAS

30°N

BAJA CALIFORNIA

SIERRA MADRE OCCIDENTAL

Rio Grande

PLATEAU OF MEXICO

SIERRA MADRE ORIENTAL

GULF OF MEXICO

BAHAMAS

CABO SAN LUCAS

CUBA

HISPANIOLA

30°N

Tropic of Cancer

HAWAIIAN ISLANDS

YUCATAN PENINSULA

CARIBBEAN SEA

ISTHMUS OF TEHUANTEPEC

km 0   1000   2000
mi 0   1000   2000

© 1996 GEOSYSTEMS GLOBAL CORP.

ISTHMUS OF PANAMA

LLANOS

Orinoco River

GUIANA HIGHLANDS

Equator

GULF OF PANAMA

Rio Negro

Amazon River

0°

GALAPAGOS ISLANDS

GULF OF GUAYAQUIL

AMAZON BASIN

São Francisco

0°

ANDES

PLATEAU OF MATO GROSSO

BRAZILIAN HIGHLANDS

High mountains — Ice cap
Low mountains
Desert
Interior plains
Coastal plains

ATACAMA

ATACAMA DESERT

GRAN CHACO

Paraná River

Tropic of Capricorn

ATACAMA TRENCH

PAMPAS

MOUNTAINS

30°S

N

W   E

PATAGONIA

FALKLAND ISLANDS

S

STRAIT OF MAGELLAN

60°S

DRAKE PASSAGE

Antarctic Circle

150°W   120°W   90°W   ANTARCTICA

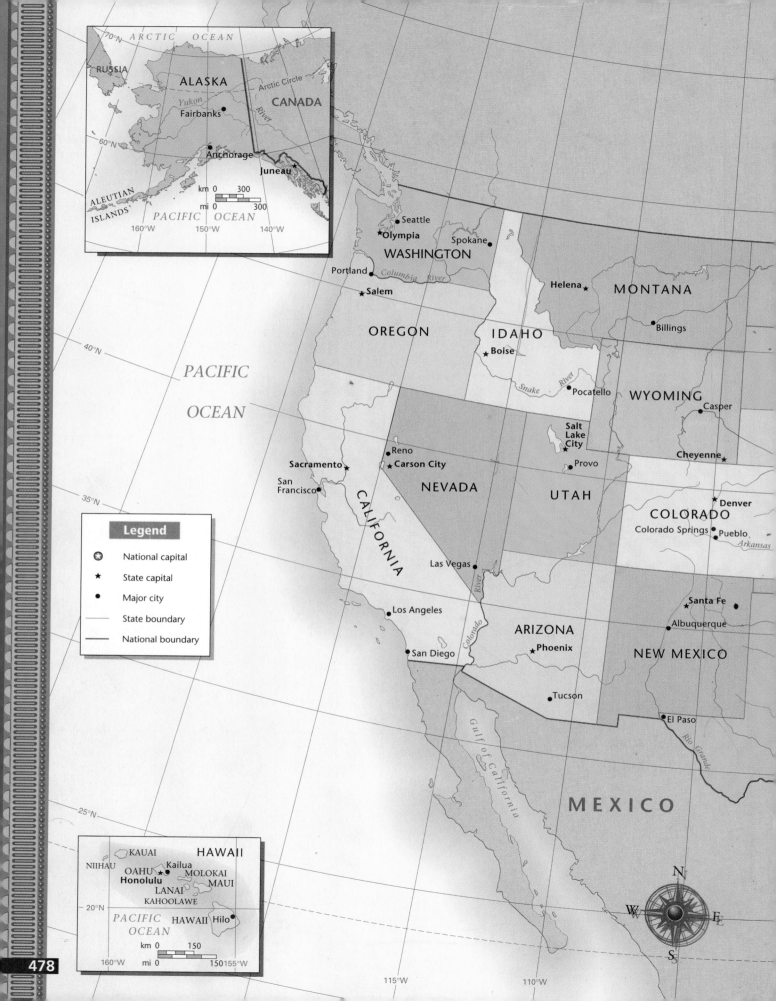

Legend

- ⊕ National capital
- ★ State capital
- ● Major city
- —— State boundary
- —— National boundary

ARCTIC OCEAN

70°N

RUSSIA

ALASKA

CANADA

Arctic Circle

Yukon River

Fairbanks

60°N

Anchorage

Juneau

ALEUTIAN ISLANDS

PACIFIC OCEAN

km 0   300
mi 0   300

160°W   150°W   140°W

Seattle

Olympia   Spokane

WASHINGTON

Portland   Columbia River

Salem

OREGON   IDAHO

Helena   MONTANA

Billings

Boise

PACIFIC

OCEAN

40°N

Snake River

Pocatello   WYOMING

Casper

Salt Lake City

Reno   Provo   Cheyenne

Sacramento   Carson City

35°N   San Francisco   NEVADA   UTAH   Denver

CALIFORNIA   COLORADO

Colorado Springs   Pueblo

Arkansas

Las Vegas

Colorado River

Los Angeles

Santa Fe

Albuquerque

San Diego   ARIZONA   Phoenix

NEW MEXICO

Tucson

El Paso

Rio Grande

Gulf of California

MEXICO

25°N

N

HAWAII

KAUAI

NIIHAU   OAHU   Kailua

Honolulu   MOLOKAI   MAUI

LANAI

KAHOOLAWE

HAWAII   Hilo

PACIFIC OCEAN

20°N

km 0   150
mi 0   150

160°W   155°W

115°W   110°W

W   E

S

478

CANADA

Lake Superior

NORTH DAKOTA
Bismarck ●
Fargo ●

SOUTH DAKOTA
Pierre ★
Sioux Falls ●

MINNESOTA
St. Paul ★
Minneapolis ★

Missouri River

WISCONSIN
Madison ★
Milwaukee ●

MICHIGAN
Grand Rapids ●
Lansing ★

Lake Michigan
Lake Huron

MAINE
Augusta ●

Burlington ●
Montpelier ★
VERMONT
NEW HAMPSHIRE
Portland ●
Concord ★
Manchester ●
Boston ●

St Lawrence River

Lake Ontario
Rochester ●
NEW YORK
Buffalo ●
Albany ★
MASSACHUSETTS
Hartford ★
New Haven ●
Bridgeport ●
Newark ●
New York ●
Providence ★
RHODE ISLAND
CONNECTICUT

NEBRASKA
Omaha ●
Lincoln ★
Platte River

IOWA
Cedar Rapids ●
Des Moines ★

Chicago ●
Detroit ●
Lake Erie
Cleveland ●

OHIO
Fort Wayne ●
Columbus ★

PENNSYLVANIA
Harrisburg ★
Pittsburgh ●
Philadelphia ●
Trenton ★
NEW JERSEY
Wilmington ●
Dover ★
DELAWARE

ILLINOIS
Springfield ★
Indianapolis ★
INDIANA
Cincinnati ●

WEST VIRGINIA
Charleston ★

Baltimore ●
Annapolis ★
Washington, D.C. ◉
MARYLAND

KANSAS
Topeka ★
Kansas City ●
Wichita ●

Kansas City ●
St. Louis ●
Jefferson City ★
MISSOURI

Ohio River
Louisville ●
Frankfort ★
Evansville ●
KENTUCKY

Richmond ★
VIRGINIA
Norfolk ●

OKLAHOMA
Oklahoma City ★
Tulsa ●

ARKANSAS
Fort Smith ●
Little Rock ★

Memphis ●

Nashville ★
TENNESSEE

Greensboro ●
Raleigh ★
NORTH CAROLINA
Charlotte ●

ATLANTIC OCEAN

TEXAS
Dallas ●
Austin ★
San Antonio ●

Mississippi River

LOUISIANA
Baton Rouge ★
New Orleans ●

Birmingham ●
ALABAMA
Montgomery ★
Mobile ●

JACKSON ★
MISSISSIPPI

Atlanta ★
GEORGIA
Columbus ●

SOUTH CAROLINA
Columbia ★
Charleston ●
Savannah ●

Jacksonville ●
Tallahassee ★
FLORIDA
Tampa ●

GULF OF MEXICO
Houston ●

Miami ●

Tropic of Cancer

BAHAMAS

CUBA

85°W 80°W
40°N
35°N
30°N
25°N
95°W 90°W 85°W 80°W

km 0   200   400
mi 0   200   400

© 1996 GEOSYSTEMS GLOBAL CORP.

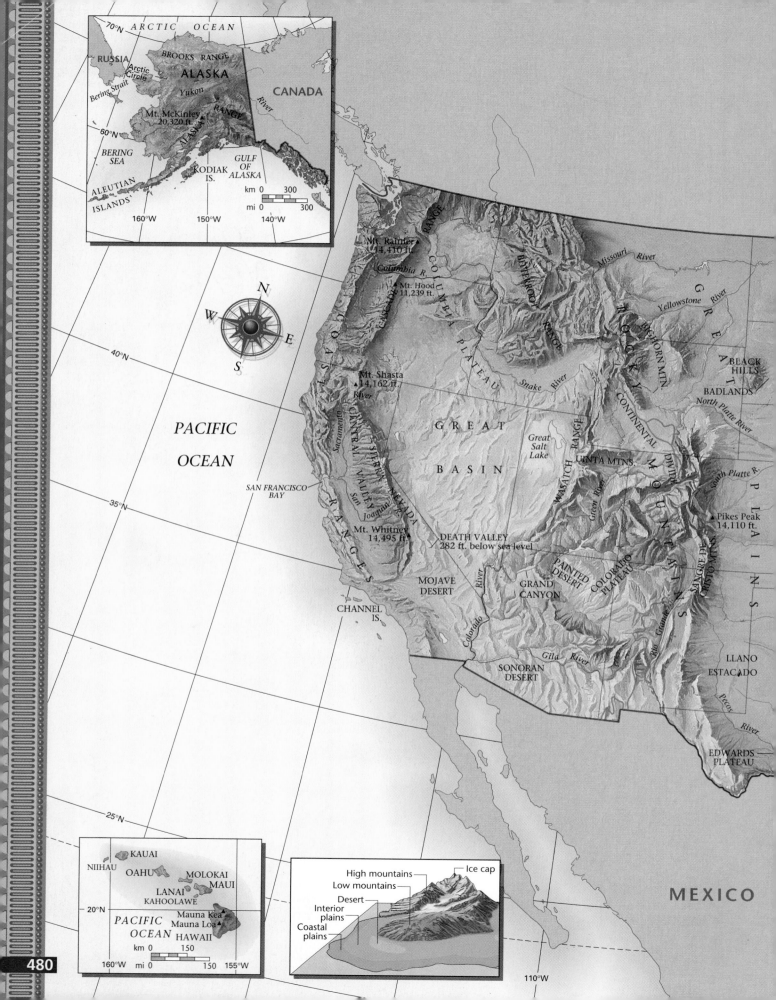

Inset Map — Alaska

ARCTIC OCEAN
70°N
RUSSIA
BROOKS RANGE
ALASKA
Arctic Circle
Bering Strait
Yukon
River
CANADA
ALASKA RANGE
Mt. McKinley
20,320 ft.
60°N
BERING SEA
KODIAK IS.
GULF OF ALASKA
ALEUTIAN ISLANDS
km 0 300
mi 0 300
160°W 150°W 140°W

Main Map

PACIFIC OCEAN

N
W E
S

40°N

35°N

SAN FRANCISCO BAY

CHANNEL IS.

COAST RANGE
Mt. Rainier 14,410 ft.
Columbia R.
Mt. Hood 11,239 ft.
CASCADE RANGE
COLUMBIA PLATEAU
BITTERROOT RANGE
Missouri River
Yellowstone River
Mt. Shasta 14,162 ft.
Sacramento River
CENTRAL VALLEY
SIERRA NEVADA
San Joaquin R.
Mt. Whitney 14,495 ft.
GREAT BASIN
Snake River
Great Salt Lake
WASATCH RANGE
UINTA MTNS.
Green River
ROCKY MOUNTAINS
BIGHORN MTN.
CONTINENTAL DIVIDE
GREAT PLAINS
BLACK HILLS
BADLANDS
North Platte River
South Platte R.
Pikes Peak 14,110 ft.
COAST RANGES
DEATH VALLEY 282 ft. below sea level
MOJAVE DESERT
River
Colorado
PAINTED DESERT
GRAND CANYON
COLORADO PLATEAU
SANGRE DE CRISTO MTNS.
SONORAN DESERT
Gila River
Rio Grande
LLANO ESTACADO
Pecos River
EDWARDS PLATEAU

MEXICO

Inset Map — Hawaii

KAUAI
NIIHAU
OAHU
MOLOKAI
MAUI
LANAI
KAHOOLAWE
Mauna Kea
Mauna Loa
HAWAII
PACIFIC OCEAN
25°N
20°N
km 0 150
mi 0 150
160°W 155°W

Inset Diagram — Landforms

Ice cap
High mountains
Low mountains
Desert
Interior plains
Coastal plains

110°W

Landform Regions of the United States

CANADA

MESABI RANGE

Lake Superior

Lake Michigan

Lake Huron

Lake Erie

Lake Ontario

St. Lawrence River

Mt. Washington 6,288 ft.

WHITE MTNS.

ADIRONDACK MTNS.

GREEN MTNS.

CATSKILL MTNS.

Hudson River

Connecticut River

Mississippi River

Missouri

Des Moines River

SAND HILLS

Platte River

CENTRAL PLAINS

Wabash R.

Ohio River

River

Susquehanna River

Delaware River

ALLEGHENY PLATEAU

NANTUCKET
MARTHA'S VINEYARD
LONG ISLAND

40°N

DELAWARE BAY

Arkansas River

OZARK PLATEAU

Mississippi River

CUMBERLAND PLATEAU

Tennessee River

APPALACHIAN MOUNTAINS

BLUE RIDGE MOUNTAINS

Mt. Mitchell 6,684 ft.

CHESAPEAKE BAY

35°N

OUACHITA MOUNTAINS

Tombigbee R.

Chattahoochee R.

Savannah River

FALL LINE

ATLANTIC COASTAL PLAIN

ATLANTIC OCEAN

Brazos River

Sabine River

Alabama R.

Pearl River

Altamaha River

30°N

Colorado River

GULF COASTAL PLAIN

GALVESTON BAY

MOBILE BAY

PENSACOLA BAY

TAMPA BAY

EVERGLADES

Rio Grande

GULF OF MEXICO

BAHAMAS

25°N

FLORIDA KEYS

km 0   200   400
mi 0   200   400

Tropic of Cancer

CUBA

© 1996 GEOSYSTEMS GLOBAL CORP.

85°W   80°W   95°W   90°W   85°W   80°W

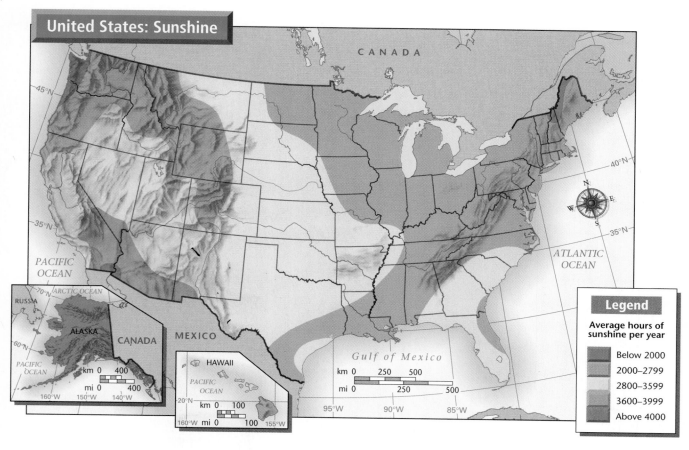

United States: Sunshine

CANADA

PACIFIC OCEAN

RUSSIA
ARCTIC OCEAN
ALASKA
CANADA

MEXICO

HAWAII
PACIFIC OCEAN

Gulf of Mexico

ATLANTIC OCEAN

Legend

Average hours of sunshine per year

Below 2000
2000–2799
2800–3599
3600–3999
Above 4000

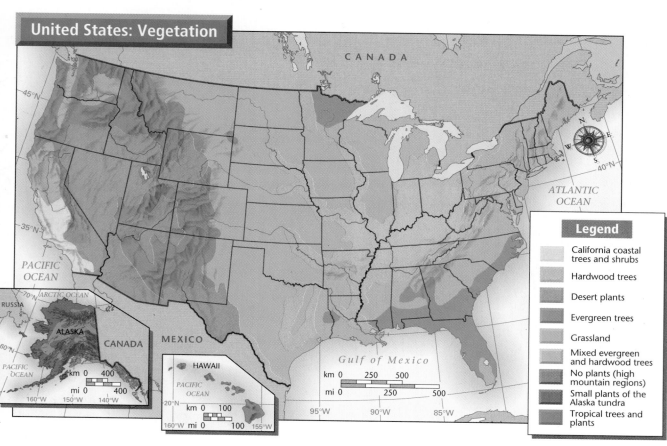

United States: Vegetation

CANADA

PACIFIC OCEAN

RUSSIA
ARCTIC OCEAN
ALASKA
CANADA

MEXICO

HAWAII
PACIFIC OCEAN

Gulf of Mexico

ATLANTIC OCEAN

Legend

California coastal trees and shrubs

Hardwood trees

Desert plants

Evergreen trees

Grassland

Mixed evergreen and hardwood trees

No plants (high mountain regions)

Small plants of the Alaska tundra

Tropical trees and plants

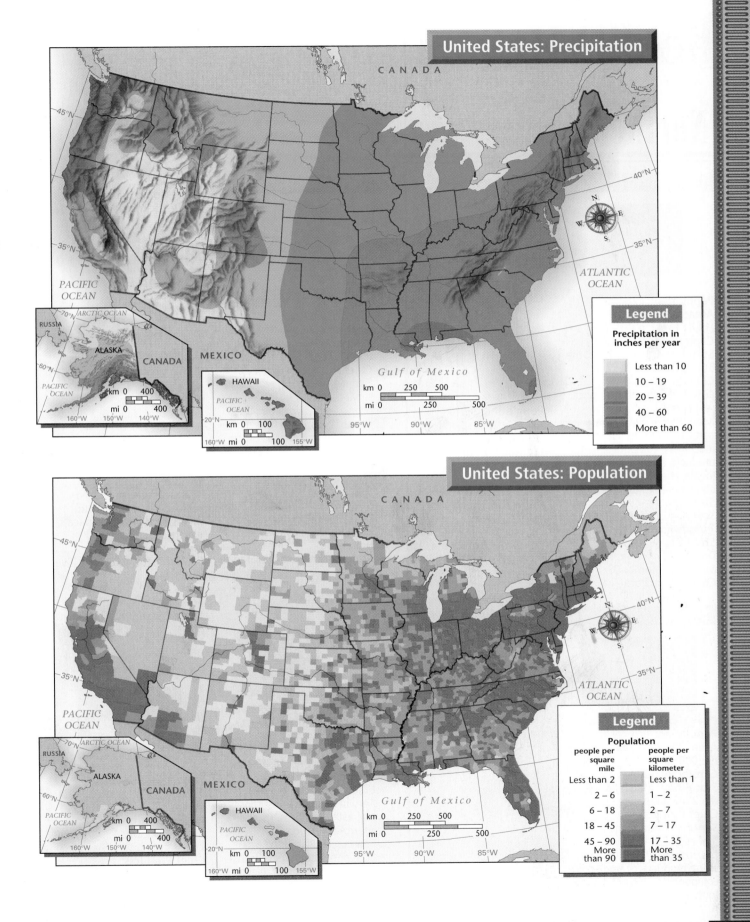

REGIONAL DATABANK

Northeast

Connecticut

Population: 3,287,116
Area: 5,544 sq. mi. (14,414 sq. km.)
Capital: Hartford
Statehood: Jan. 9, 1788, the 5th state
Chief Products:
Services: Finance, insurance, real estate services.
Manufacturing: Aircraft parts, helicopters, submarines, machinery, computers, metal products, scientific instruments, chemicals, electrical equipment, printed material.
State Motto: *Qui Transtulit Sustinet* (He Who Transplanted Still Sustains.)
State Song: "Yankee Doodle" Composer unknown.
State Nickname: The Constitution State

Maine

Population: 1,227,928
Area: 35,387 sq. mi. (92,006 sq. km.)
Capital: Augusta
Statehood: March 15, 1820, the 23rd state
Chief Products:
Services: Finance, insurance, real estate services.
Manufacturing: Paper and wood products, computer components, ships and boats, footwear.

Agriculture: Fish, milk, potatoes, eggs.
State Motto: *Dirigo* (I guide)
State Song: "State of Maine Song" by Roger Vinton Snow.
State Nickname: The Pine Tree State

Massachusetts

Population: 6,016,425
Area: 10,555 sq. mi. (27,443 sq. km.)
Capital: Boston
Statehood: Feb. 6, 1788, the 6th state
Chief Products: *Services:* Finance, insurance, real estate services, medical services, educational services.
Manufacturing: Computers, scientific instruments, electrical equipment, printed materials.
Agriculture: Fish, cranberries.
State Motto: *Ense petit placidam sub libertate quietem* (By the sword we seek peace, but peace only under liberty)
State Song: "All Hail to Massachusetts" by Arthur J. Marsh.
State Nickname: The Bay State

New Hampshire

Population: 1,109,252
Area: 9,351 sq. mi. (24,312 sq. km.)
Capital: Concord
Statehood: June 21, 1788, the 9th state
Chief Products: *Services:* Finance, insurance, real estate services.
Manufacturing: Computers, scientific instruments, electrical equipment, plastic products, printed material and paper products.
State Motto: *Live Free or Die*
State Song: "Old New Hampshire" Words by John F. Holmes, music by Maurice Hoffmann.
State Nickname: The Granite State

New Jersey

Population: 7,730,188
Area: 8,722 sq. mi. (22,677 sq. km.)
Capital: Trenton
Statehood: Dec. 18, 1787, the 3rd state
Chief Products:
Services: Finance, insurance, real estate services.
Manufacturing: Pharmaceuticals, food products, printed materials, transportation equipment, electrical equipment.
State Motto: *Liberty and*

Prosperity
State Song: none
State Nickname: The Garden State

New York

Population: 17,990,455
Area: 54,475 sq. mi. (141,635 sq. km.)
Capital: Albany
Statehood: July 26, 1788, the 11th state
Chief Products: *Services:* Finance, insurance, real estate services, medical, legal, advertising services.
Manufacturing: Printed materials, scientific instruments, machinery, chemicals, electrical equipment.
Agriculture: Milk, fish.
State Motto: *Excelsior* (Ever Upward!)
State Song: "I Love New York" by Steve Karmen.
State Nickname: The Empire State

Pennsylvania

Population: 11,881,643
Area: 46,058 sq. mi.(119,750 sq. km.)
Capital: Harrisburg
Statehood: Dec.12, 1787, the 2nd state
Chief Products:
Services: Tourism, health care facilities.
Manufacturing: Machinery,

clothing, foods, printed materials, textiles, transportation equipment, metals, natural gas.
Agriculture: Milk, eggs, chickens.
State Motto: *Virtue, Liberty, and Independence*
State Song: "Pennsylvania" by Eddie Khoury and Ronnie Bonner.
State Nickname: The Keystone State

Rhode Island

Population: 1,003,464
Area: 1,545 sq. mi. (4,017 sq. km.)
Capital: Providence
Statehood: May 29, 1790, the 13th state
Chief Products:
Services: Medical and legal services, computer programming services, financial, real estate, and insurance services.
Manufacturing: Jewelry and silverware, metal products, scientific instruments.
Agriculture: Fish and shellfish.
State Motto: *Hope*
State Song: "Rhode Island" by T. Clarke Brown.
State Nickname: The Ocean State

Vermont

Population: 562,758
Area: 9,615 sq. mi. (24,999 sq. km.)
Capital: Montpelier
Statehood: March 4, 1791, the 14th state
Chief Products:
Services: Real estate services, tourism services.
Manufacturing: Electrical equipment, fabricated metal products, printed materials.
Agriculture: Milk, maple syrup.
State Motto: *Freedom and Unity*
State Song: "Hail, Vermont!" by Josephine Hovey Perry.
State Nickname: The Green Mountain State

South

Alabama

Population: 4,040,587
Area: 52,423 sq. mi. (136,299 sq. km.)
Capital: Montgomery
Statehood: Dec. 14, 1819, the 22nd state
Chief Products:
Services: Wholesale and retail trade services.
Manufacturing: Paper products, chemicals, steel, textiles and clothing.
Agriculture: Chickens.
State Motto: *Audemus Jura Nostra Defendere* (We Dare Defend Our Rights)
State Song: "Alabama" Words by Julia S. Tutwiler, music by Edna Gockel Gussen.
State Nickname: The Heart of Dixie

Arkansas

Population: 2,350,725
Area: 53,182 sq. mi. (138,273 sq. km.)
Statehood: June 15, 1836, the 25th state
Capital: Little Rock
Chief Products:
Services: Wholesale and retail trade.
Manufacturing: Food products, especially poultry, electrical equipment, paper products, metal products, machinery, natural gas, petroleum, coal.

Agriculture: Chickens, beef cattle, eggs, peanuts, cotton.
State Motto: *Regnat Populus* (The People Rule)
State Song: "Arkansas" by Eva Ware Barnett.
State Nickname: The Natural State

Delaware

Population: 666,168
Area: 2,489 sq. mi. (6,471 sq. km.)
Capital: Dover
Statehood: Dec. 7, 1787, the 1st state
Chief Products:
Services: Finance, insurance, and real estate services.
Manufacturing: Chemicals, food products, especially poultry, automobiles.
Agriculture: Chickens.
State Motto: *Liberty and Independence.*
State Song: "Our Delaware" Words by George B. Hynson, music by William M.S. Brown.
State Nickname: The First State

Florida

Population: 12,937,426
Area: 65,758 sq. mi. (170,971 sq. km.)
Statehood: March 3, 1845, the 27th state
Capital: Tallahassee

Chief Products:
Services: Medical services, tourism services.
Manufacturing: Food products, especially citrus products, communication equipment, printed materials, search and navigational equipment, computers, fertilizer.
Agriculture: Citrus fruits, greenhouse and nursery products, shellfish.
State Motto: *In God We Trust* (unofficial)
State Song: "Old Folks at Home" ("Swanee River") by Stephen Foster.
State Nickname: The Sunshine State

Georgia

Population: 6,478,216
Area: 59,441 sq. mi. (154,546 sq. km.)
Capital: Atlanta
Statehood: Jan. 2, 1788, the 4th state
Chief Products:
Services: Wholesale and retail trade services.
Manufacturing: Automobiles, airplanes, carpeting, food processing, paper products, chemicals, clothing, printed materials, electrical equipment.
Agriculture: Chickens, peanuts, tobacco, peaches, shellfish.
State Motto: *Wisdom, Justice, and Moderation.*
State Song: "Georgia on My Mind" Words by Stuart Gorrell, music by Hoagy Carmichael.
State Nicknames: The Empire State of the South, The Peach State

Kentucky

Population: 3,685,296
Area: 40,411 sq. mi. (105,068 sq. km.)
Capital: Frankfort
Statehood: June 1, 1792, the 15th state
Chief Products:
Services: Wholesale and retail services, finance and real estate services.
Manufacturing: Automobiles, trucks, machinery, appliances, tobacco products, food products, chemicals, printed materials, coal.
Agriculture: Tobacco, beef cattle, horses, milk, corn, hay.
State Motto: *United We Stand, Divided We Fall*
State Song: "My Old Kentucky Home" by Stephen Foster.
State Nickname: The Bluegrass State

Louisiana

Population: 4,219,973
Area: 51,843 sq. mi. (134,792 sq. km.)
Capital: Baton Rouge
Statehood: April 30, 1812, the 18th state
Chief Products:
Services: Medical and legal services, hotel services.
Manufacturing: Petroleum, and natural gas, pharmaceuticals, fertilizers, paints, plastics, soap, ships, paper products, coffee, soft drinks, sugar.
Agriculture: Soybeans, beef cattle, cotton, milk, rice, corn, sugar cane, shrimp.

State Motto: *Union, Justice, and Confidence.*
State Songs: "Give Me Louisiana" by Doralice Fontane, "You Are My Sunshine" by Jimmy H. Davis and Charles Mitchell.
State Nickname: The Pelican State

Maryland

Population: 4,781,468
Area: 12,407 sq. mi. (32,250 sq. km.)
Capital: Annapolis
Statehood: April 28, 1788, the 7th state
Chief Products:
Services: Private health care, computer programming, consulting, data processing.
Manufacturing: Communication equipment, food products, soaps and detergents, newspapers and documents.
Agriculture: Fish and shellfish.
State Motto: *Fatti Maschii Parole Femine* (Manly Deeds, Womanly Words)
State Song: "Maryland! My Maryland!" sung to the tune of "O, Tannenbaum" Words by James Ryder Randall.
State Nickname: The Old Line State

Mississippi

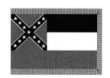

Population: 2,573,216
Area: 48,434 sq. mi. (125,928 sq. km.)
Capital: Jackson
Statehood: Dec. 10, 1817, the 20th state

Chief Products:
Services: Wholesale and retail trade services.
Manufacturing: Meatpacking, poultry processing, beverages, ships, motor vehicle parts, electrical equipment.
Agriculture: Chickens, beef, milk, cotton, soybeans.
State Motto: *Virtute et Armis* (By Valor and Arms)
State Song: "Go Mississippi" by Houston Davis.
State Nickname: The Magnolia State

North Carolina

Population: 6,628,637
Area: 53,821 sq. mi. (139,934 sq. km.)
Capital: Raleigh
Statehood: Nov. 21, 1789, the 12th state
Chief Products:
Services: Wholesale and retail trade services.
Manufacturing: Tobacco products, textiles, pharmaceuticals, synthetic fibers, electrical equipment.
Agriculture: Poultry, tobacco, corn, soybeans, peanuts, sweet potatoes.
State Motto: *Esse Quam Videri* (To Be, Rather Than to Seem)
State Song: "The Old North State" Words by William Gaston, music by Mrs. E. E. Randolph.
State Nickname: The Tarheel State

Oklahoma

Population: 3,145,585
Area: 69,903 sq. mi. (181,747 sq. km.)
Capital: Oklahoma City
Statehood: Nov. 16, 1907, the 46th state
Chief Products:
Services: Wholesale and retail trade services.
Manufacturing: Military aircraft, aircraft parts, rocket parts, automobiles, machinery, electrical equipment, petroleum, natural gas.
Agriculture: Beef cattle, other livestock, wheat, corn, cotton.
State Motto: *Labor Omnia Vincit* (Labor Conquers All Things)
State Song: "Oklahoma!" Words by Oscar Hammerstein II, music by Richard Rogers.
State Nicknames: The Sooner State, The Boomer State

South Carolina

Population: 3,486,703
Area: 32,007 sq. mi. (83,218 sq. km.)
Capital: Columbia
Statehood: May 23, 1788, the 8th state
Chief Products:
Services: Wholesale and retail trade services.
Manufacturing: Textiles, pharmaceuticals, soaps, paper products.
Agriculture: Tobacco, beef cattle, shrimp.
State Mottoes: *Animis*

Opibusque Parati (Prepared in Mind and Resources), *Dum Spiro Spero* (While I Wait I Hope)
State Song: "Carolina" Words by Henry Timrod, music by Anne Custis Burgess.
State Nickname: The Palmetto State

Tennessee

Population: 4,877,185
Area: 42,146 sq. mi. (109,576 sq. km.)
Capital: Nashville
Statehood: June 1, 1796, the 16th state
Chief Products:
Services: Insurance, printing, music recording.
Manufacturing: Industrial chemicals, synthetic fibers, food products, machinery, electrical equipment, clothing, fabricated metals, paper products, coal, stone, zinc.
Agriculture: Tobacco, soybeans, greenhouse and nursery products, cotton, beef, dairy products, pork, hardwood lumber.
State Motto: *Agriculture and Commerce*
State Songs: "Tennessee Waltz" by Redd Stewart and Pee Wee King, "When It's Iris Time in Tennessee" by Willa Mae Waid, "My Tennessee" by Francis Hannah Tranum.
State Nicknames: The Volunteer State, The Big Bend State

Texas

Population: 18,986,510
Area: 261,914 sq. mi. (696,576 sq. km.)
Capital: Austin
Statehood: Dec. 29, 1845, the 28th state
Chief Products:
Services: Wholesale and retail trade services, banking and insurance.
Manufacturing: Industrial chemicals, rubber and plastic, computers, calculators, food processing, machinery, automobiles, natural gas, petroleum, coal.
Agriculture: Beef cattle, milk, chickens, cotton, greenhouse and nursery products, sorghum, grain, corn, wheat, vegetables, fish, shellfish.
State Motto: *Friendship*
State Song: "Texas, Our Texas" Words by Gladys Yoakum Wright, music by William J. Marsh.
State Nickname: The Lone Star State

Virginia

Population: 6,187,358
Area: 42,769 sq. mi. (111,199 sq. km.)
Capital: Richmond
Statehood: June 25, 1788, the 10th state
Chief Products:
Services: Government services.
Manufacturing: Synthetic fibers, pharmaceuticals, ships, motor vehicle parts, trucks, tobacco products, food pro-

cessing, electrical equipment, coal.
Agriculture: Tobacco, beef cattle, milk, chickens, crabs, oysters.
State Motto: *Sic Semper Tyrannis* (Thus Always to Tyrants)
State Song: "Carry Me Back to Old Virginia" by James B. Bland.
State Nicknames: Old Dominion, Mother of States

West Virginia

Population: 1,793,477
Area: 24,231 sq. mi. (62,759 sq. km.)
Capital: Charleston
Statehood: June 20, 1863, the 35th state
Chief Products:
Services: Finance, insurance, and real estate services, wholesale and retail trade services.
Manufacturing: Dyes, detergents, paints, plastics, rubber, salt cake, steel, glassware, pottery, coal, natural gas.
State Motto: *Montani Semper Liberi (*Mountaineers Are Always Free)
State Song: "The West Virginia Hills" Words by David King, music by H.E. Engle.
State Nickname: The Mountain State

Midwest

Illinois

Population: 11,430,602
Area: 57,918 sq. mi. (150,586 sq. km.)
Capital: Springfield
Statehood: Dec. 3, 1818, the 21st state
Chief Products:
Services: Medical, legal, business services.
Manufacturing: Construction equipment, farm machinery, food products, fabricated metal products, electrical equipment, chemicals, printed materials, coal, petroleum, crushed stone.
Agriculture: Corn, soybeans, hogs, beef cattle, milk.
State Motto: *State Sovereignty, National Union*
State Song: "Illinois" music by Archibald Johnston, words by Charles H. Chamberlin.
State Nicknames: The Land of Lincoln, The Prairie State

Indiana

Population: 5,544,159
Area: 36,420 sq. mi. (94,692 sq. km.)
Capital: Indianapolis
Statehood: Dec. 11, 1816, the 19th state
Chief Products:
Services: Wholesale and retail trade services.
Manufacturing: Steel, aluminum, motor vehicles, aircraft parts, chemicals, coal.
Agriculture: Corn, soybeans, hogs.
State Motto: *The*

Crossroads of America
State Song: "On the Banks of the Wabash, Far Away" by Paul Dresser.
State Nickname: The Hoosier State

Iowa

Population: 2,776,755
Area: 56,276 sq. mi. (146,317 sq. km.)
Capital: Des Moines
Statehood: Dec. 28, 1846, the 29th state
Chief Products:
Services: Finance and insurance services, wholesale and retail trade services.
Manufacturing: Meatpacking, corn products, cereal, farm machinery, electrical equipment.
Agriculture: Hogs, corn, soybeans, beef cattle.
State Motto: *Our Liberties We Prize and Our Rights We Will Maintain*
State Song: "The Song of Iowa" sung to the tune of "O Tannenbaum" words by S.H.M. Byers.
State Nickname: The Hawkeye State

Kansas

Population: 2,477,574
Area: 82,282 sq. mi. (213,933 sq. km.)
Capital: Topeka
Statehood: Jan. 29, 1861, the 34th state
Chief Products:
Services: Wholesale and retail trade services, finance and insurance services.

Manufacturing: Airplanes, missiles, railroad cars and locomotives, automobiles, animal feed, meatpacking, printed materials, petroleum, natural gas.
Agriculture: Beef cattle, wheat, grain sorghum, hay, hogs, corn, soybeans.
State Motto: *Ad Astra per Aspera* (To the Stars Through Difficulties)
State Song: "Home on the Range" Words by Brewster Higley, music by Daniel Kelley.
State Nicknames: The Sunflower State, The Jayhawker State

Michigan

Population: 9,295,297
Area: 96,810 sq. mi. (251,706 sq. km.)
Capital: Lansing
Statehood: Jan. 26, 1837, the 26th state
Chief Products:
Services: Financial and insurance industries, private health care facilities, research and engineering services.
Manufacturing: Motor vehicles, machine parts, computers, engines, cutlery, tools, pharmaceuticals, paints, soaps, cereal, iron, steel, aluminum, natural gas, iron ore, petroleum.
Agriculture: Fruit, vegetables, milk.
State Motto: *Si quaeris peninsulam amoenam, circumspice* (If you seek a pleasant peninsula, look about you)
State Song: "My Michigan" words by Giles Kavanagh, music by H.J. O'Reilly Clint
State Nicknames: The Wolverine State, The Great Lakes State

Minnesota

Population: 4,375,099
Area: 86,943 sq. mi. (226,051 sq. km.)
Capital: St. Paul
Statehood: May 11, 1858, the 32nd state
Chief Products:
Services: Wholesale and retail trade services, real estate and financial services.
Manufacturing: Computers, farm and construction machinery, meatpacking, poultry processing, printed materials, iron ore.
Agriculture: Milk, corn, soybeans, beef cattle, hogs.
State Motto: *L'Etoile du Nord* (The Star of the North)
State Song: "Hail! Minnesota" Words by Truman E. Rickard and Arthur E. Upson, music by Truman E. Rickard.
State Nicknames: The Gopher State, The North Star State, Land of Sky-Blue Waters, Land of Ten Thousand Lakes, Bread and Butter State

Missouri

Population: 5,117,073
Area: 69,709 sq. mi. (181,243 sq. km.)
Capital: Jefferson City
Statehood: Aug. 10, 1821, the 24th state
Chief Products:
Services: Private health care facilities, data processing services, wholesale and retail trade.
Manufacturing: Airplanes, barges, railroad cars, truck

and bus bodies, automobiles, trucks, fertilizer, insecticide, paint, pharmaceuticals, soap, butter, cheese, flour, lead, limestone, coal.
Agriculture: Soybeans, beef cattle, hogs, corn, hay.
State Motto: *Salus populi suprema lex esto* (The Welfare of the People Shall Be the Supreme Law)
State Song: "Missouri Waltz" Words by J.R. Shannon, music from a melody obtained from John V. Eppel.
State Nicknames: The Show Me State, Mother of the West

Nebraska

Population: 1,578,385
Area: 77,358 sq. mi. (201,130 sq. km.)
Capital: Lincoln
Statehood: March 1, 1867, the 37th state
Chief Products:
Services: Insurance and real estate services, wholesale and retail trade services.
Manufacturing: Meatpacking, cereal, livestock feed, electrical equipment, farm equipment, petroleum.
Agriculture: Beef cattle, corn, hogs, soybeans.
State Motto: *Equality Before the Law*
State Song: "Beautiful Nebraska" by Jim Fras.
State Nickname: The Cornhusker State

North Dakota

Population: 638,800
Area: 70,704 sq. mi. (183,830 sq. km.)
Capital: Bismarck
Statehood: Nov. 2, 1889, the 39th state
Chief Products:
Services: Real estate services, wholesale and retail trade services.
Manufacturing: Food processing, machinery, petroleum, coal, natural gas.
Agriculture: Wheat, beef cattle, barley, hay, sunflower seeds, milk, sugar beets.
State Motto: *Liberty and Union, Now and Forever, One and Inseparable*
State Song: "North Dakota Hymn" Words by James W. Foley, music by C.S. Putnam.
State Nicknames: The Flickertail State, The Peace Garden State

Ohio

Population: 10,847,115
Area: 44,828 sq. mi. (116,552 sq. km.)
Capital: Columbus
Statehood: March 1, 1803, the 17th state
Chief Products:
Services: Private health care facilities and other social and personal services, wholesale and retail trade, financial and real estate services.
Manufacturing: Motor vehicles, aircraft parts, machinery, soaps and cleansers, paints, steel, food processing, coal, natural gas, petroleum.

Agriculture: Corn, soybeans, milk, hogs, beef cattle, hay.
State Motto: *With God, All Things Are Possible*
State Song: "Beautiful Ohio" Words by Ballard MacDonald, music by Mary Earl.
State Nickname: The Buckeye State

South Dakota

Population: 696,004
Area: 77,121 sq. mi. (200,514 sq. km.)
Capital: Pierre
Statehood: Nov. 2, 1889, the 40th state
Chief Products:
Services: Financial and real estate services, wholesale and retail trade services.
Manufacturing: Food products, farm and construction equipment, medical instruments, gold.
Agriculture: Beef cattle, hogs, corn, hay, wheat, milk, sunflowers.
State Motto: *Under God the People Rule*
State Song: "Hail! South Dakota" by Deecort Hammitt.
State Nicknames: The Sunshine State, The Coyote State

Wisconsin

Population: 4,891,769
Area: 65,503 sq. mi. (170,307 sq. km.)
Capital: Madison
Statehood: May 29, 1848, the 30th state
Chief Products:
Services: Real estate, insurance, and financial services, wholesale and retail trade services, social and personal services.
Manufacturing: Machinery, dairy products, other food processing, paper products, electrical equipment, metal products.
Agriculture: Milk, beef cattle, hogs, vegetables, fruits.
State Motto: *Forward*
State Song: "On, Wisconsin!" Words by J.S. Hubbard and Charles D. Rosa, music by William T. Purdy.
State Nickname: The Badger State

West

Alaska

Population: 550,043
Area: 656,424 sq. mi.
(1,706,702 sq. km.)
Capital: Juneau
Statehood: Jan. 3, 1959, the
49th state
Chief Products:
Services: Government, trans-
portation services.
Manufacturing: Fish process-
ing, petroleum products, wood
and paper products, fur,
petroleum.
Agriculture: Salmon.
State Motto: *North to the
Future*
State Song: "Alaska's Flag"
Words by Marie Drake, music
by Elinor Dusenbury.
State Nickname: The Last
Frontier

Arizona

Population: 3,665,228
Area: 114,006 sq. mi.
(296,415 sq. km.)
Capital: Phoenix
Statehood: Feb. 14, 1912, the
48th state
Chief Products:
Services: Private health care
facilities, legal services,
tourism, wholesale and retail
trade.
Manufacturing: Aircraft,
space vehicles, electronic components, machinery, copper,
gold.
Agriculture: Beef cattle, cotton, milk.
State Motto: *Ditat Deus*
(God Enriches)

State Songs: "Arizona" Words
by Margaret Rowe Clifford,
music by Maurice Blumenthal.
"I Love You Arizona" by Rex
Allen, Jr.
State Nickname: The Grand
Canyon State

California

Population: 29,760,021
Area: 163,707 sq. mi.
(425,638 sq. km.)
Capital: Sacramento
Statehood: Sept. 9, 1850, the
31st state
Chief Products:
Services: Health care
providers, legal and engineer-
ing services, tourism and
entertainment, real estate ser-
vices.
Manufacturing: Aircraft,
motor vehicles, spacecraft,
computers, baked and canned
foods.
Agriculture: Milk, beef cattle,
greenhouse products, cotton,
grapes, hay, tomatoes, fish.
State Motto: *Eureka* (I Have
Found It)
State Song: "I Love You,
California." Words by F.B.
Silverwood, music by A.F.
Frankenstein.
State Nickname: The Golden
State

Colorado

Population: 3,294,394
Area: 104,100 sq. mi.
(270,660 sq. km)
Capital: Denver

Statehood: Aug. 1, 1876, the
38th state
Chief Products:
Services: Health care facili-
ties, tourism, data processing,
engineering, legal services,
wholesale and retail trade ser-
vices, banking and insurance
services.
Manufacturing: Scientific
instruments, food processing,
machinery, petroleum, coal,
natural gas.
Agriculture: Beef cattle, hay,
wheat, milk, corn.
State Motto: *Nil sine
Numine* (Nothing Without
Providence)
State Song: "Where the
Columbines Grow" by A.J.
Flynn.
State Nickname: The
Centennial State

Hawaii

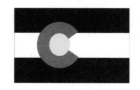

Population: 1,108,229
Area: 10,932 sq. mi. (28,423
sq. km.)
Capital: Honolulu
Statehood: Aug. 21, 1959,
the 50th state
Chief Products:
Services: Military bases,
schools, and hospitals,
tourism, health care facilities.
Manufacturing: Food prod-
ucts, printed materials,
petroleum products.
Agriculture: Sugar cane,
pineapples, flowers.
State Motto: *Ua mau ke ea
o ka aina i ka pono* (The Life
of the Land Is Perpetuated in
Righteousness)
State Song: "Hawaii Ponoi"
("Hawaii's Own") Words by
King Kalakaua, music by
Henry Berger.
State Nickname: The Aloha
State

Idaho

Population: 1,006,749
Area: 83,574 sq. mi. (217,292
sq. km.)
Capital: Boise
Statehood: July 3, 1890, the
43rd state
Chief Products:
Services: Wholesale and retail
trade services, private health
care facilities, tourism, engi-
neering services, legal ser-
vices.
Manufacturing: Potato pro-
cessing, paper and wood
products, machinery, chemi-
cals, electrical equipment,
gold, silver, phosphate rock.
Agriculture: Potatoes, hay,
wheat, sugar beets, beef cat-
tle, milk, barley.
State Motto: *Esto Perpetua*
(Let It Be Perpetual)
State Song: "Here We Have
Idaho" Words by McKinley
Helm and Albert J. Tompkins,
music by Sallie Hume Douglas.
State Nickname: The Gem
State

Montana

Population: 799,065
Area: 147,046 sq. mi.
(380,848 sq. km.)
Capital: Helena
Statehood: Nov. 8, 1889, the
41st state
Chief Products:
Services: Real estate services.
Manufacturing: Lumber and
wood products, food products,
coal, petroleum, printed mate-
rials.

Agriculture: Beef cattle, wheat, hay, barley.
State Motto: *Oro y Plata* (Gold and Silver)
State Song: "Montana" Words by Charles C. Cohan, music by Joseph E. Howard.
State Nicknames: The Treasure State, Big Sky Country

Nevada

Population: 1,201,833
Area: 110,567 sq. mi. (287,474 sq. km.)
Capital: Carson City
Statehood: Oct. 31, 1864, the 36th state
Chief Products: *Services:* Recreation and tourism services, private education and health care services, advertising services, data processing services.
Manufacturing: Gold, silver, diatomite, petroleum, computers, electronic components, concrete, printed materials, food products.
State Motto: *All for Our Country*
State Song: "Home Means Nevada" by Bertha Raffetto.
State Nicknames: The Silver State, The Sagebrush State

New Mexico

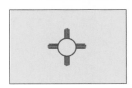

Population: 1,515,069
Area: 121,598 sq. mi. (316,154 sq. km.)
Capital: Santa Fe
Statehood: Jan. 6, 1912, the 47th state
Chief Products:
Services: Research facilities, military bases, health care facilities, tourism, engineering services.
Manufacturing: Natural gas, petroleum, coal, copper, electrical equipment, food products, printed materials.
State Motto: *Crescit Eundo* (It Grows as It Goes)
State Song: "O, Fair New Mexico" by Elizabeth Garrett.
State Nickname: The Land of Enchantment

Oregon

Population: 2,842,321
Area: 98,386 sq. mi. (255,803 sq. km.)
Capital: Salem
Statehood: Feb. 14, 1859, the 33rd state
Chief Products:
Services: Real estate and banking services.
Manufacturing: Wood products, food products, electrical equipment, scientific instruments, machinery, paper products, metals.
Agriculture: Timber, beef cattle, milk, greenhouse products, wheat, hay, shrimp, salmon.
State Motto: *Alis Volat Propriis* (She Flies with Her Own Wings)
State Song: "Oregon, My Oregon" Words by J.A. Buchanan, music by Henry B. Murtagh.
State Nickname: The Beaver State

Utah

Population: 1,722,850
Area: 84,904 sq. mi. (220,750 sq. km.)
Capital: Salt Lake City
Statehood: Jan. 4, 1896, the 45th state
Chief Products:
Services: Health care facilities, tourism, legal services, engineering services.
Manufacturing: Petroleum, coal, natural gas, rocket propulsion systems, dairy products, baked goods, scientific instruments, printed materials, machinery.
Agriculture: Beef cattle, milk.
State Motto: *Industry*
State Song: "Utah, We Love Thee" by Evan Stephens.
State Nickname: The Beehive State

Washington

Population: 4,866,692
Area: 71,303 sq. mi. (185,387 sq. km.)
Capital: Olympia
Statehood: Nov. 11, 1889, the 42nd state
Chief Products:
Services: Wholesale and retail trade, health care facilities, computer programming, engineering and legal services.
Manufacturing: Airplanes, space vehicles, ships, food products, paper and wood products, chemicals.
Agriculture: Timber, milk, beef cattle, wheat, apples, salmon.
State Motto: *Alki* (By and By)
State Song: "Washington, My Home" by Helen Davis.
State Nickname: The Evergreen State

Wyoming

Population: 435,588
Area: 97,818 sq. mi. (254,327 sq. km.)
Capital: Cheyenne
Statehood: July 10, 1890, the 44th state
Chief Products:
Services: Pipeline, railroad, telephone, and utility companies, real estate and banking services.
Manufacturing: Petroleum, coal, natural gas, chemicals.
Agriculture: Beef cattle.
State Motto: *Equal Rights*
State Song: "Wyoming" Words by Charles E. Winter, music by G.E. Knapp.
State Nickname: The Equality State

Territories and Commonwealths in the Caribbean

Puerto Rico

Population: 3,533,037
Capital: San Juan
Area: 3,515 sq. mi. (9,104 sq. km.)
Became Territory: 1898
Became Commonwealth: July 25, 1952
Chief Products:
Services: Tourism.
Manufacturing: Clothing industry, food processing, furniture, paper products, rubber and plastic products, scientific instruments, and machinery.
Agriculture: Sugar cane, coffee, tobacco, poultry, and vegetables.
Commonwealth Anthem: *La Borínqueña*

Virgin Islands

Population: 101,809
Capital: Charlotte Amalie
Area: 136 sq. mi. (352 sq. km.)
Became Territory: 1917
Chief Products:
Services: Tourism.
Manufacturing: Oil refining, aluminum.
Agriculture: Vegetables, cattle, commercial fishing.

Territories and Commonwealths in the Pacific

American Samoa

Population: 46,773
Capital: Pago Pago
Area: 77 sq. mi. (199 sq. km.)
Became Territory: 1899
Chief Products:
Services: Tourism.
Manufacturing: Tuna canning, coconut products.
Agriculture: Commercial fishing, coconuts.

Guam

Population: 133,152
Capital: Agana
Area: 209 sq. mi. (541 sq. km.)
Became Territory: 1898
Chief Products:
Services: US military, tourism.
Manufacturing: Food processing, watch assembly, furniture making.
Agriculture: Commercial fishing, vegetables, fruits, poultry, eggs, hogs, cattle, carabao (water buffalo).

Johnston Atoll

Population: Uninhabited
Area: less than 0.5 sq. mi. (1.3 sq. km.)
Became Territory: 1898

Midway Islands

Population: 453 (US military personnel)
Area: 2 sq. mi. (5 sq. km.)
Became Territory: 1867

Northern Mariana Islands

Population: 43,345
Capital: Saipan
Area: 246 sq. mi. (637 sq. km.)
Became Territory: 1947
Became Commonwealth: 1978
Chief Products:
Services: Tourism.
Manufacturing: Clothing.
Agriculture: Coconuts, breadfruit, tomatoes, melons.

Palau

Population: 12,116
Area: 192 sq. mi. (497 sq. km.)
Became Territory: 1947
Chief Products:
Services: Tourism.
Manufacturing: Fish processing.
Agriculture: Commercial fishing, coconuts.

Wake Island

Population: 195
Area: 3 sq. mi. (8 sq. km.)
Became Territory: 1900

Our National Heritage

Students say the Pledge of Allegiance.

Americans pledge allegiance to the American flag because it is a symbol of the United States. Pledging allegiance means promising loyalty.

The Pledge of Allegiance

I pledge allegiance to the Flag
of the United States of America
and to the Republic for which it stands,
one Nation under God, indivisible,
with liberty and justice for all.

Francis Scott Key wrote the words to our national anthem. The song tells how the American flag still flew after a night of battle. To show love and respect for our nation, Americans sing the anthem at many public events.

The Star-Spangled Banner

O say, can you see, by the dawn's early light,
What so proudly we hailed at the twilight's last gleaming,
Whose broad stripes and bright stars, through the perilous fight,
Oe'r the ramparts we watched were so gallantly streaming?
And the rockets' red glare, the bombs bursting in air,
Gave proof through the night that our flag was still there.
O say, does that Star-Spangled Banner yet wave
O'er the land of the free and the home of the brave?

On the shore, dimly seen through the mists of the deep,
Where the foe's haughty host in dread silence reposes,
What is that which the breeze, o'er the towering steep,
As it fitfully blows, half conceals, half discloses?
Now it catches the gleam of the morning's first beam,
In full glory reflected now shines on the stream;
'Tis the Star-Spangled Banner, O long may it wave
O'er the land of the free and the home of the brave!

O thus be it ever when free men shall stand
Between their loved homes and the war's desolation!
Blest with vict'ry and peace, may the heav'n-rescued land
Praise the Power that hath made and preserved us a nation.
Then conquer we must, for our cause it is just,
And this be our motto: "In God is our trust."
And the Star-Spangled Banner in triumph shall wave
O'er the land of the free and the home of the brave.

The Great Seal

The Great Seal of the United States is used on legal documents to show that they are official. The seal was first adopted in 1782, but the design that we use today was created in 1904. Each part of the Great Seal, even its colors, means something important.

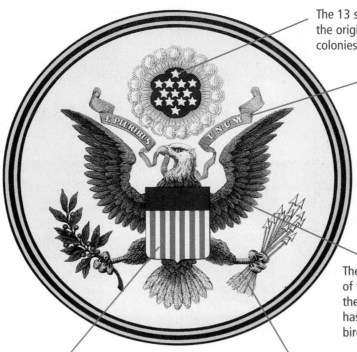

The 13 stars stand for the original 13 colonies.

On the ribbon in the eagle's beak is the Latin phrase, *E Pluribus Unum,* which means "From Many, One." The United States is made up of many states and people, but together they form one nation.

The eagle is a symbol of the independence of the United States. It has been the national bird since 1782.

The shield stands for the United States flag. The red in the shield means bravery and strength. The blue represents alertness, justice, and determination. The white is for purity and innocence.

The arrows in this claw and the olive branch in the other claw represent the power of the United States to make both war and peace.

Uncle Sam

Uncle Sam was a real man named Samuel Wilson who sold salted beef to the American soldiers during the War of 1812. He stamped each crate *U.S.*, meaning the "United States." The soldiers joked that *U.S.* meant "Uncle Sam." They called themselves Uncle Sam's soldiers. Their joke turned Uncle Sam into a national figure.

Liberty Bell

The Liberty Bell was made in London and was first rung in 1752 in Philadelphia, Pennsylvania. It cracked during that first ring. The bell was repaired, but later it cracked again. The last time it was rung was on George Washington's birthday in 1846. Now it is on display in Independence Hall so that everyone can read the words on it: "Proclaim Liberty throughout all the land unto all the inhabitants thereof."

The Flag

The United States flag didn't always look the way it does now. It was not until 1777 that the Second Continental Congress approved a national flag. This design changed several times before 1818, when Congress chose the design we see today. The 13 red and white stripes represent the original 13 American colonies. The stars represent the states. Today there are 50 states, so the flag has 50 stars.

U.S. Presidents

George Washington (1st)

(1732–1799)
President from 1789–1797
party: Federalist
home state: Virginia
first lady: Martha Dandridge Custis
   Washington

John Adams (2nd)

(1735–1826)
President from 1797–1801
party: Federalist
home state: Massachusetts
first lady: Abigail Smith Adams

Thomas Jefferson (3rd)

(1743–1826)
President from 1801–1809
party: Democratic–Republican
home state: Virginia
first lady: Martha Jefferson
   Randolph (daughter)

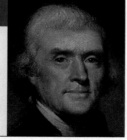

James Madison (4th)

(1751–1836)
President from 1809–1817
party: Democratic–Republican
home state: Virginia
first lady: Dolley Payne Todd
   Madison

James Monroe (5th)

(1758–1831)
President from 1817–1825
party: Democratic–Republican
home state: Virginia
first lady: Elizabeth Kortright
   Monroe

John Quincy Adams (6th)

(1767–1848)
President from 1825–1829
party: Democratic–Republican
home state: Massachusetts
first lady: Louisa Catherine Johnson
   Adams

Andrew Jackson (7th)

(1767–1845)
President from 1829–1837
party: Democratic
home state: Tennessee
first lady: Emily Donelson (late
   wife's niece)

Martin Van Buren (8th)

(1782–1862)
President from 1837–1841
party: Democratic
home state: New York
first lady: Angelica Singleton Van
   Buren (daughter–in–law)

William H. Harrison (9th)

(1773–1841)
President 1841
party: Whig
home state: Ohio
first lady: Jane Harrison
   (daughter–in–law)

John Tyler (10th)

(1790–1862)
President from 1841–1845
party: Whig
home state: Virginia
first lady: Letitia Christian Tyler

James K. Polk (11th)

(1795–1849)

President from 1845–1849
party: Democratic
home state: Tennessee
first lady: Sarah Childress Polk

Zachary Taylor (12th)

(1784–1850)

President from 1849–1850
party: Whig
home state: Louisiana
first lady: Margaret Mackall Smith
    Taylor

Millard Fillmore (13th)

(1800–1874)

President from 1850–1853
party: Whig
home state: New York
first lady: Abigail Powers Fillmore

Franklin Pierce (14th)

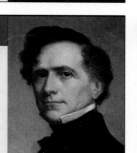

(1804–1869)

President from 1853–1857
party: Democratic
home state: New Hampshire
first lady: Jane Means Appleton
    Pierce

James Buchanan (15th)

(1791–1868)

President from 1857–1861
party: Democratic
home state: Pennsylvania
first lady: Harriet Lane (niece)

Abraham Lincoln (16th)

(1809–1865)

President from 1861–1865
party: Republican
home state: Illinois
first lady: Mary Todd Lincoln

Andrew Johnson (17th)

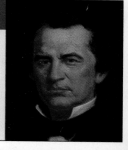

(1808–1875)

President from 1865–1869
party: Democratic
home state: Tennessee
first lady: Eliza McCardle Johnson

Ulysses S. Grant (18th)

(1822–1885)

President from 1869–1877
party: Republican
home state: Illinois
first lady: Julia Dent Grant

Rutherford B. Hayes (19th)

(1822–1893)

President from 1877–1881
party: Republican
home state: Ohio
first lady: Lucy Ware Webb Hayes

James A. Garfield (20th)

(1831–1881)

President 1881
party: Republican
home state: Ohio
first lady: Lucretia Rudolph
    Garfield

Chester A. Arthur (21st)

(1830–1886)

President from 1881–1885
party: Republican
home state: New York
first lady: Mary Arthur McElroy
    (sister)

Grover Cleveland (22nd, 24th)

(1837–1908)

President from 1885–1889 and
    1893–1897
party: Democratic
home state: New York
first lady: Frances Folsom Cleveland

Benjamin Harrison (23rd)

(1833–1901)
President from 1889–1893
party: Republican
home state: Indiana
first lady: Caroline Lavina Scott
Harrison

William McKinley (25th)

(1843–1901)
President from 1897–1901
party: Republican
home state: Ohio
first lady: Ida Saxton McKinley

Theodore Roosevelt (26th)

(1858–1919)
President from 1901–1909
party: Republican
home state: New York
first lady: Edith Kermit Carow
Roosevelt

William Howard Taft (27th)

(1857–1930)
President from 1909–1913
party: Republican
home state: Ohio
first lady: Helen Herron Taft

Woodrow Wilson (28th)

(1856–1924)
President from 1913–1921
party: Democratic
home state: New Jersey
first lady: Edith Bolling Galt Wilson

Warren G. Harding (29th)

(1865–1923)
President from 1921–1923
party: Republican
home state: Ohio
first lady: Florence Kling Harding

Calvin Coolidge (30th)

(1872–1933)
President from 1923–1929
party: Republican
home state: Massachusetts
first lady: Grace Anna Goodhue
Coolidge

Herbert Hoover (31st)

(1874–1964)
President from 1929–1933
party: Republican
home state: California
first lady: Lou Henry Hoover

Franklin D. Roosevelt (32nd)

(1882–1945)
President from 1933–1945
party: Democratic
home state: New York
first lady: Anna Eleanor Roosevelt
Roosevelt

Harry S. Truman (33rd)

(1884–1972)
President from 1945–1953
party: Democratic
home state: Missouri
first lady: Elizabeth Virginia Wallace
Truman

Dwight D. Eisenhower (34th)

(1890–1969)
President from 1953–1961
party: Republican
home state: New York
first lady: Mamie Geneva Doud
Eisenhower

John F. Kennedy (35th)

(1917–1963)
President from 1961–1963
party: Democratic
home state: Massachusetts
first lady: Jacqueline Lee Bouvier
Kennedy

Lyndon B. Johnson (36th)

(1908–1973)
President from 1963–1969
party: Democratic
home state: Texas
first lady: Claudia Alta (Lady Bird) Taylor Johnson

Ronald Reagan (40th)

(1911–)
President from 1981–1989
party: Republican
home state: California
first lady: Nancy Davis Reagan

Richard M. Nixon (37th)

(1913–1994)
President from 1969–1974
party: Republican
home state: New York
first lady: Thelma Catherine (Pat) Ryan Nixon

George Bush (41st)

(1924–)
President from 1989–1993
party: Republican
home state: Texas
first lady: Barbara Pierce Bush

Gerald R. Ford (38th)

(1913–)
President from 1974–1977
party: Republican
home state: Michigan
first lady: Elizabeth Bloomer Ford

William Clinton (42nd)

(1946–)
President from 1993–2001
party: Democratic
home state: Arkansas
first lady: Hillary Rodham Clinton

Jimmy Carter (39th)

(1924–)
President from 1977–1981
party: Democratic
home state: Georgia
first lady: Rosalynn Smith Carter

George W. Bush (43rd)

(1946–)
President from 2001–
party: Republican
home state: Texas
first lady: Laura Welch Bush

Gazetteer

PLACE	LAT.	LONG.	PAGE
Central Plateau area in Mexico between the Sierra Madre Occidental and the Sierra Madre Oriental	25°N	103°W	409
Central Valley valley running through the center of California from which two-thirds of California's crops come	41°N	122°W	365
Chapel Hill city in North Carolina	36°N	79°W	230
Charleston city in South Carolina	33°N	80°W	220
Chesapeake Bay inlet of the Atlantic Ocean; important Southern waterway	38°N	76°W	202
Cheyenne city in Wyoming	41°N	104°W	339
Chicago large city in Illinois	42°N	88°W	308
Chile country on western coast of South America	35°S	72°W	419
China country in East Asia; capital: Beijing	37°S	93°E	68
Coast Ranges a part of the Pacific Ranges	41°N	123°W	38
Coastal Plains flat area east of the Appalachians extending to the Atlantic Ocean	35°N	80°W	39
Colorado River river in the southwest United States; carved the Grand Canyon	46°N	124°W	14
Columbia capital of South Carolina	34°N	81°W	118
Columbia River river in the Northwest	46°N	120°W	27
Continental Divide line along the top of the Rockies that divides rivers and streams that flow west from those that flow east	50°N	114°W	39
Cordillera Mountains part of the Andes	13°S	75°W	406
Cumberland city in Maryland that is a shipping area for a coal mining area	39°N	78°W	389

D **Death Valley** desert basin in California; lowest point in North America · 36°N · 117°W · 41

PLACE	LAT.	LONG.	PAGE
Denver capital of Colorado	40°N	105°W	350
Detroit large city in Michigan	42°N	83°W	291
Duluth port city on Lake Superior in northern Minnesota	46°N	92°W	286
Durham city in North Carolina	36°N	78°W	230

E **Eastern Hemisphere** the half of the earth made up of Europe, Africa, Asia, and Australia · 0° · 75°E · 16

PLACE	LAT.	LONG.	PAGE
Egypt country in northeast Africa; capital: Cairo	27°N	30°E	72
Ellis Island island in New York	41°N	74°W	85
England country in Western Europe; part of the United Kingdom; capital: London	52°N	2°W	150
Erie Canal waterway between Albany and Buffalo	43°N	78°W	152
Ethiopia country in Africa; capital: Addis Ababa	9°N	39°E	433
Europe 6th largest continent	50°N	15°E	85
Everett city in Washington	48°N	122°W	337
Everglades wetlands in southern Florida	26°N	81°W	238

F **France** country in Western Europe; capital: Paris · 47°N · 1°E · 84

G **Gary** city in Indiana, built by U. S. Steel. · 42°N · 87°W · 45

PLACE	LAT.	LONG.	PAGE
Germany country in western Europe; capital: Berlin	51°N	10°E	84
Grand Canyon deep gorge in Arizona formed by the Colorado River	36°N	112°W	13
Great Basin desert area covering a large part of the Western United States	40°N	117°W	38
Great Britain England, Scotland, and Wales	55°N	5°W	84

PLACE	LAT.	LONG.	PAGE
Great Lakes five freshwater lakes in the United States and Canada	45°N	83°W	**144**
Great Plains in central North America; high grassland region	45°N	104°W	**39**
Gulf of Mexico body of water along the southern United States and Mexico	25°N	94°W	**39**
Harrisburg capital of Pennsylvania	40°N	77°W	**63**
Hartford capital of Connecticut	41°N	72°W	**229**
Hollywood part of Los Angeles	34°N	118°W	**337**
Honolulu capital of Hawaii	21°N	158°W	**50**
Hoover Dam dam on the Colorado river	36°N	114°W	**366**
Houston city in Texas	30°N	95°W	**220**
Hudson River river in New York	43°N	74°W	**152**
Huntsville city in Alabama	34°N	86°W	**220**
Hutchinson city in Kansas	38°N	98°W	**45**
India country in south Asia	23°N	78°E	**151**
International Date Line imaginary line through the Pacific Ocean where everything east is one day earlier than anything to the west	0°	180°	**16**
Ireland country in the North Atlantic; capital: Dublin	53°N	8°W	**235**
Italy country in southern Europe; capital: Rome	44°N	11°E	**436**
Jackson Hole valley through which the Snake River runs	44°N	110°W	**36**

PLACE	LAT.	LONG.	PAGE
James River river flowing through central Virginia to the Chesapeake Bay	37°N	77°W	**211**
Jamestown city in Virginia; first permanent English settlement in North America	44°N	76°W	**211**
Japan island country off northeast coast of Asia; capital: Tokyo	37°N	134°E	**16**
Kitty Hawk city in North Carolina; site of first successful motorized flight	36°N	76°W	**246**
Lake Erie one of the Great Lakes	42°N	81°W	**287**
Lake Huron one of the Great Lakes	44°N	82°W	**286**
Lake Mead reservoir formed by the Hoover Dam in Nevada and Arizona	36°N	114°W	**366**
Lake Michigan 3rd largest Great Lake	44°N	87°W	**286**
Lake Nasser formed by the construction of the Aswan High Dam on the Nile River	44°N	87°W	**286**
Lake Okeechobee lake in south central Florida	27°N	80°W	**238**
Lake Ontario one of the Great Lakes	43°N	78°W	**287**
Lake Powell lake on the Colorado River in Colorado used for recreation	37°N	110°W	**367**
Lake Superior largest Great Lake	48°N	88°W	**286**
Lansing city in Michigan	42°N	84°W	**63**
Las Vegas city in Nevada	36°N	115°W	**367**
Latin America the countries of the Western Hemisphere south of the United States	0°	60°W	**86**
Los Angeles city in California	34°N	118°W	**134**
Louisville city in Kentucky where the Kentucky Derby is run	38°N	85°W	**220**
Marietta city in Georgia with an aircraft industry	39°N	81°W	**397**

PLACE	LAT.	LONG.	PAGE
Marquette Range area in Michigan mined for iron ore	46°N	87°W	**277**
Mexico country bordering the United States to the south; capital: Mexico City	24°N	104°W	**409**
Mexico City capital of Mexico	19°N	99°W	**409**
Miami city in Florida	26°N	80°W	**423**
Middle East area including the countries of southwest Asia and northeast Africa	30°N	38°E	**86**
Minneapolis largest city in Minnesota	45°N	93°W	**274**
Mississippi River principal river of the United States and North America	32°N	92°W	**39**
Missouri River one of the longest rivers in the United States	40°N	96°W	**98**
Mojave Desert desert in southern California southeast of the Sierra Nevada	35°N	117°W	**51**
Mount McKinley mountain in Alaska; highest mountain in North America	63°N	152°W	**321**
Mount Rainier mountain in Washington State; highest mountain in the Cascade Range	47°N	122°W	**28**
Mount St. Helens volcano in Washington that erupted in 1980	46°N	122°W	**26**
Mount Waialeale mountain in Hawaii that can have 350 rainy days a year	22°N	159°W	**51**
Mount Washington mountain in New Hampshire	44°N	71°W	**143**
N **Nashville** capital of Tennessee	36°N	86°W	**235**
Netherlands country in northwestern Europe; also called Holland; capital: Amsterdam	52°N	6°E	**84**
New Orleans city in Louisiana	30°N	90°W	**97**
New York City large city in New York state	41°N	74°W	**50**
Nigeria country in Africa; capital: Lagos	10°N	8°E	**212**

PLACE	LAT.	LONG.	PAGE
Nile River world's longest river	30°N	31°E	**72**
North America northern continent of Western Hemisphere	45°N	100°W	**16**
North Pole most northern point of the earth's axis	90°N	0°	**16**
Northern Hemisphere the half of the earth north of the equator	30°N	0°	**16**
O **Ohio River** flows from Pennsylvania to the Mississippi River	37°N	88°W	**268**
Ohio River Valley farming region west of the Appalachian Mountains	37°N	88°W	**270**
Okefenokee Swamp wetlands in southeast Georgia and northeast Florida	31°N	82°W	**238**
Olympic Peninsula area in Washington that can get 150 inches of rain a year	48°N	124°W	**325**
P **Pacific Ocean** largest ocean; west of the United States	0°	170°W	**39**
Pacific Ranges contains the Coast Ranges, the Cascades, and the Sierra Nevada; some of the youngest mountains in the country	45°N	120°W	**38**
Panama Canal canal extending across the Isthmus of Panama connecting the Atlantic and the Pacific Oceans	10°N	80°W	**411**
Peru country on the Pacific coast of South America; capital: Lima	10°S	75°W	**418**
Philadelphia large port city in Pennsylvania	40°N	75°W	**175**
Phoenix city in Arizona	33°N	112°W	**343**
Piedmont area of rolling hills between the Appalachians and Coastal Plains	35°N	80°W	**200**
Platte River river of central Nebraska that flows into the Missouri River	39°N	100°W	**59**
Plymouth Colony in Massachusetts; site of first Pilgrim settlement	42°N	70°W	**150**

PLACE	LAT.	LONG.	PAGE
Presidential Range in New Hampshire; part of Appalachian Mountains	44°N	71°W	**144**
prime meridian the zero meridian used as a reference line for longitude east and west; passes through Greenwich, England	51°N	0°	**16**
Princeton city in New Jersey	40°N	74°W	**161**
Promontory Point the place in Utah where the two halves of the Transcontinental Railroad met in 1869	38°N	112°W	**334**
R **Raleigh** capital of North Carolina	35°N	78°W	**230**
Rio de Janeiro city in Brazil	22°S	43°W	**421**
Rio Grande river forming part of the Texas-Mexico border	26°N	97°W	**58**
Rocky Mountains mountain range in the western United States	50°N	114°E	**39**
Russia formerly part of the Soviet Union; capital: Moscow	61°N	60°E	**68**
Rwanda country in Africa; capital: Kigali	2°S	30°E	**432**
S **St. Augustine** city in Florida; oldest permanent European settlement in the United States	29°N	81°W	**211**
St. Lawrence Seaway system of canals connecting St. Lawrence River above Montreal to Lake Ontario	45°N	75°W	**286**
St. Louis city in Missouri on Mississippi River	39°N	90°W	**98**
St. Paul capital of Minnesota	45°N	93°W	**279**
Salem an early English settlement in Massachusetts	43°N	71°W	**151**
San Andreas Fault place in California where two of the earth's plates meet	37°N	122°W	**323**

PLACE	LAT.	LONG.	PAGE
San Antonio city in Texas	29°N	98°W	**211**
San Francisco a major port city in California	38°N	122°W	**329**
San Jose city in California	37°N	121°W	**370**
San Rafael city in California	38°N	122°W	**372**
São Paulo city in Brazil	23°S	46°W	**421**
Sarajevo city in Bosnia-Herzegovina	44°N	18°E	**445**
Sault Sainte Marie a city in Michigan	46°N	84°W	**286**
Scotland part of Great Britain; capital: Edinburgh	57°N	4°W	**235**
Seattle large city in Washington State	48°N	122°W	**28**
Sierra Madre Occidental mountain range that runs along Mexico's western coast	25°N	107°W	**409**
Sierra Madre Oriental mountain range that runs along Mexico's eastern coast	25°N	100°W	**409**
Sierra Nevada mountain range mainly in eastern California	39°N	120°W	**38**
Silicon Valley nickname for region in California known for computer technology	37°N	121°W	**370**
Snake River river near the Teton Range	46°N	119°W	**36**
Sonoran Desert desert area in Arizona	33°N	113°W	**327**
South Africa country in Africa; capital: Cape Town	30°S	26°E	**433**
South America southern continent of the Western Hemisphere	15°S	60°W	**418**
South Pole most southern part of the earth's axis	90°S	0°	**16**
Southern Hemisphere the half of the earth south of the equator	30°S	0°	**16**
Spain country in Western Europe; capital: Madrid	40°N	5°W	**84**

PLACE	LAT.	LONG.	PAGE
Springfield capital of Illinois	39°N	89°W	**278**
Suwannee River river flowing from southeast Georgia across northern Florida to the Gulf of Mexico	30°N	83°W	**238**
T **Tacoma** city in Washington near Mt. Rainier	47°N	122°W	**28**
Taos a town in New Mexico	36°N	106°W	**332**
Tennessee River river beginning in Tennessee and flowing through Alabama and Kentucky to the Ohio River	36°N	88°W	**219**
Tennessee Valley area around the Tennessee River	36°N	88°W	**219**
Teton Range mountains in Wyoming	44°N	111°W	**36**
U **United States** country in central and northwest North America	38°N	110°W	**16**

PLACE	LAT.	LONG.	PAGE
V **Vineland** city in New Jersey	39°N	75°W	**168**
W **Washington, D.C.** capital of the United States	39°N	77°W	**97**
Waynesboro city in Virginia with textile factories	38°N	79°W	**229**
Western Hemisphere the half of the earth made up of North America, Central America, and South America	0°	75°W	**16**
Wichita city in Kansas	37°N	97°W	**276**
Williston city in North Dakota	48°N	103°W	**51**
Y **Yakima** city in Washington State	46°N	120°W	**325**
Yugoslavia an Eastern European country	44°N	19°E	**445**

Geographic Glossary

basin
a bowl shaped area of land surrounded by higher land

▲ **bay**
part of a lake or ocean extending into the land

cliff
the high, steep, edge of a hill, mountain, or plain

1 coast
the land next to an ocean

desert
a dry area where few plants grow

▼ **glacier**
a large ice mass that moves slowly down a mountain or over land

2 harbor
a sheltered body of water where ships can safely dock

3 hill
a raised mass of land, smaller than a mountain

▼ **island**
a body of land completely surrounded by water

isthmus
a narrow strip of land connecting two larger bodies of land

lake
a body of water completely surrounded by land

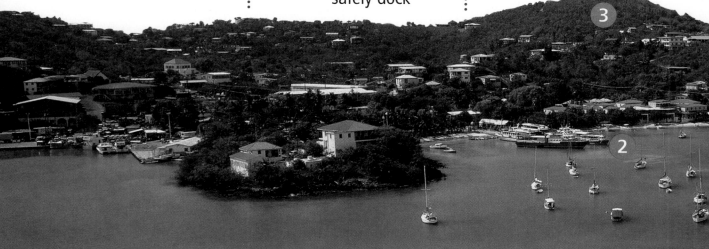

▲ mesa
a wide flat topped mountain with steep sides, found mostly in dry areas

mountain
a steeply raised mass of land, much higher than the surrounding country

mountain pass
a gap between mountains

▼ mountain range
a row of mountains

④ ocean or sea
a salty body of water covering a large area of the earth

⑤ peninsula
land mostly surrounded by water but connected to the mainland

plain
a large area of flat or nearly flat land

prairie
a large, level area of grassland with few or no trees

river
a large stream that runs into a lake, ocean or another river

sea level
the level of the surface of the ocean

strait
a narrow channel of water connecting two larger bodies of water

tree line
on a mountain, the area above which no trees grow

valley
low land between hills or mountains

volcano
an opening in the earth, often raised, through which lava and gasses from the earth's interior escape

Biographical Dictionary

The page number refers to the place where the person is first mentioned. For more complete references to people, see the Index.

A **Aldrin, Edwin "Buzz"** 1930– , second man to walk on the moon (p. 250).

Andropov (ahn DROH puhv)**, Yuri** 1914–1984, former leader of the Soviet Union (1982–1984) (p. 125).

Anthony, Susan B. 1820–1906, reformer who fought for women's rights (p. 123).

Armstrong, Louis 1901–1971, leading jazz trumpeter; helped spread New Orleans jazz nationwide (p. 232).

Armstrong, Neil 1930– , first man to walk on the moon (p. 250).

B **Bell, Alexander Graham** 1847–1922, invented the telephone (p. 170).

Bessemer (BEHS uh muhr)**, Henry** 1813–1898, English scientist; invented process to convert iron to steel (p. 310).

Bolívar (boh LEE vahr)**, Simón** 1783–1830, helped several South American countries gain independence from Spain (p. 421).

Brown, Linda 1947– , African American who was not allowed to go to a school in Topeka, Kansas, reserved for white students; Supreme Court decided in her favor in *Brown v. Board of Education* in 1954 (p. 117).

C **Carson, Rachel** 1907–1964, writer, biologist, and conservationist who helped start the environmental movement (p. 146).

Carter, Jimmy 1924– , 39th President of the United States (1977–1980); now works with Habitat for Humanity (p. 88).

Carter, Rosalynn 1928– , former First Lady; now works with Habitat for Humanity (p. 89).

Chapman, John 1774–1845, better known as Johnny Appleseed; traveled throughout the Midwest planting and tending apple trees (p. 60).

Clark, William 1770–1838, explored Louisiana Purchase with Meriwether Lewis (p. 259).

Clinton, DeWitt 1769–1828, governor of New York (1817–1822; 1824–1828); favored building the Erie Canal (p. 181).

Coltrane, John 1926–1967, jazz musician who made improvisation popular (p. 233).

D **Douglas, Marjory Stoneman** 1890– , author who worked to protect the Everglades through her writings; founder of Friends of the Everglades (p. 240).

du Sable (dyu SAH bl)**, Jean Bapiste Pointe** (zhahn bah TEEST pwah) 1745?–1818, known as the founder of Chicago (p. 270).

E **Edelman, Marian Wright** 1939– , founded Children's Defense Fund in 1973 (p. 88).

Edison, Thomas A. 1847–1931, inventor of the light bulb, the moving-picture camera, and the phonograph (p. 107).

F **Faulkner** (FAWK nuhr)**, William** 1897–1962, American novelist who wrote about the South (p. 208).

Fitzgerald, Ella 1918– , American singer most famous for her "scat" style (p. 233).

Ford, Henry 1863–1947, automobile manufacturer; first to mass produce cars on assembly line (p. 107).

G **Gordy, Berry, Jr** 1929– , started the Detroit-based record company, Motown Industries, Inc., in 1959 (p. 292).

Greeley, Horace 1811–1872, journalist who urged Americans to move west (p. 348).

J **Jefferson, Thomas** 1743–1826, wrote Declaration of Independence; third President of the United States (1801–1809) (p. 121).

Joplin, Scott 1868–1917, known as the "King of Ragtime" (p. 232).

K **Kennedy, John F.** 1917–1963, 35th President of the United States (1961–1963) (p. 405).

King, Martin Luther, Jr. 1929–1968, prominent civil rights leader (p. 89).

L **Lewis, Meriwether** 1774–1809, explored Louisiana Purchase with William Clark (p. 259).

Liliuokalani (lee lee uh woh kuh LAH nee), **Lydia Kamekeha** (kah MAY kay ah) 1838–1917, last queen of Hawaii (1891–1893) (p. 331).

Lincoln, Abraham 1809–1865, 16th President of the United States (1861–1865); issued Emancipation Proclamation in 1863 (p. 214).

M **Madison, James** 1751–1836, known as "Father of the Constitution"; fourth President of the United States (p. 115).

McCormick, Cyrus 1809–1884, invented the mechanical reaper (p. 106).

McCoy, Elijah 1843–1929, invented a "lubricating cup" in 1920 (p. 293).

Monroe, Bill 1911– , father of bluegrass (p. 235).

N **Nobel, Alfred** 1833–1896, Swedish scientist and businessman; endowed Nobel Prize (p. 444).

Noyce (nois), **Robert** 1927–1990, inventor of the computer chip (p. 371).

P **Powell, John Wesley** 1834–1902, American geologist who conducted an exploration of the western United States (p. 13).

Q **Quimby** (KWIHM bee), **Harriet** 1875–1912, first female pilot to fly across the English Channel (p. 392).

R **Roker, Al** 1954– , weather forecaster who wrote a program to help predict the weather (p. 50).

Roosevelt, Franklin D. 1882–1945, 32nd President of the United States (1933–1945) (p. 442).

S **Smith, Samantha** 1972–1985, wrote a letter to Soviet leader, Yuri Andropov, in 1983 and was invited to visit the Soviet Union (p. 125).

Stevens, John 1749–1838, operated first steam locomotive in the United States (p. 391).

Sullivan, Louis 1856–1924, architect considered the father of the skyscraper (p. 308).

Sutter, John 1803–1880, California farmer; gold found on his property in 1848 (p. 333).

T **de Tocqueville** (dee TOHK vihl)**, Alexis** 1805–1859, Frenchman who traveled in America and wrote a book about Americans and their government (p. 35).

W **Walker, Madam C. J.** 1867–1919, African American businesswoman who became America's first female independent millionaire (p. 107).

Washington, George 1732–1799, commanded Continental Army during Revolution; first President of the United States (1789–1797) (p. 213).

Watson, Thomas A. 1854–1934, assistant to Alexander Graham Bell (p. 170).

Whitney, Eli 1765–1825, inventor of the cotton gin (p. 106).

Wilkins, John 1614–1672, wrote about flying to the moon in 1638 (p. 248).

Worden, Alfred 1932–   , American astronaut; first American to walk in space (p. 429).

Wright, Frank Lloyd 1869–1959, midwestern architect famous for his original building designs (p. 307).

Wright, Orville 1871–1948, with help from brother, Wilbur, made first successful flight in motorized plane on December 17, 1903 (p. 246).

Wright, Wilbur 1867–1912, with help from brother, Orville, pioneered motorized flight (p. 246).

Glossary

acid rain (AS ihd rayn) rain that carries certain kinds of pollution (p. 396).

adapt (uh DAPT) to change in order to survive in a new environment (p. 19).

aeronautics (air uh NAW tihks) the science of building and operating aircraft (p. 247).

aerospace (AIR oh spays) a word used to describe businesses that make airplanes (p. 337).

agribusiness (AG ruh bihz nihs) a large company that raises and sells agricultural products (p. 298).

amendment (uh MEHND muhnt) a change made to the Constitution. (p. 122).

aquifer (AK wuh fur) a huge underground collection of water (p. 261).

archaeology (ahr kee AHL uh jee) the study of artifacts to learn how early people lived (p. 268).

architecture (AHR kih tek chur) the art of designing buildings (p. 306).

artifact (AHR tuh fakt) something that people from the past made, used, and left behind (p. 268).

assembly line (uh SEHM blee lyn) a method of manufacturing goods in which the thing being made moves from worker to worker and everyone does one job. (p. 107).

astronaut (AHS truh nawt) a person who is specially trained to travel in space (p. 247).

avalanche (AV uh lanch) a large amount of snow or earth that falls down a mountain (p. 26).

bay (bay) a piece of the ocean that is partially surrounded by land, where ships can be sheltered from storms (p. 202).

bayou (BY oo) a slowly moving stream that flows through a swamp (p. 203).

belt (behlt) a region that shares a special feature, such as good soil for growing corn (p. 62).

blizzard (BLIHZ urd) a storm with heavy snowfall and high winds (p. 145).

bluegrass (BLOO gras) music with roots in English, Irish, and Scottish fiddle music (p. 235).

blues (blooz) slow, often sad songs (p. 232).

border (BAWR dur) the line that divides one country, state, or region from another (p. 58).

boundary (BOUN duh ree) a line that marks the border of a country, state, or region (p. 56).

canal (kuh NAL) a waterway made by people (p. 152).

capital (KAP ih tl) a city where a state or country's government is located (p. 153).

cash crop (kash krahp) a crop that a farmer grows only to sell (p. 366).

chamber of commerce (CHAYM bur uhv KOM urs) a group of business people who work together to make their companies more successful (p. 351).

citizen (SIHT ih zun) a person who has the same rights as everyone else in their country (p. 123).

civil war (SIHV uhl wawr) a war fought between two groups or regions of a nation (p. 214).

clear-cutting (klyr KUT ing) cutting down all the trees in one area of a forest (p. 362).

climate (KLY miht) the usual pattern of weather in an area of the world (p. 50).

colony (KAHL uh nee) a settlement ruled by a another country (p. 114).

combine (KUHM byn) a machine for harvesting crops such as corn or wheat (p. 297).

committee (kuh MIHT ee) a group who works together to get something done (p. 132).

communications system (kuh myoo nih KAY shuhnz SIS tuhm) a way of sending and receiving messages, such as telephones (p. 170).

commuter (kuh MYOO tur) a person who travels on most days to work or school (p. 174).

computer chip (kuhm PYOO tur chihp) a package of pathways for electricity (p. 370).

computer graphics (kuhm PYOO tur GRAF iks) pictures made by computers (p. 372).

conflict (KAHN flihkt) fighting (p. 71).

conservation (kahn sur VAY shuhn) the careful use and protection of natural resources, such forests or mineral deposits (p. 46).

consumer (kuhn SOO mur) a person who buys goods and services (p. 386).

Continental Divide (kahn tuh NEHN tl dih VYD) a stretch of high land along the Rocky Mountains that separates water that flows east from water that flows west (p. 39).

contour (KAHN tur) a line that follows the shape of the land (p. 362).

cooperate (koh AHP uh rayt) to work together to achieve a goal (p. 132).

cost of living (kawst uv LIHV ing) the money that people pay for food, clothing, transportation, and housing (p. 228).

country and western (KUHN tree uhnd WEHS turn) American music that grew out of blues, folk, and religious music (p. 235).

craftsperson (KRAFTS pur suhn) a person who is skilled in a trade (p. 104).

crop (krahp) plants that people grow and gather (p. 72).

D **delta** (DEHL tuh) land that forms at the end of rivers, where rivers slow down and drop the mud they carry (p. 202).

democracy (dih MAHK ruh see) a government in which the people make political decisions by voting and the majority rules (p. 114).

descendant (dih SEHN duhnt) a person's child, grandchild, or great-grandchild (p. 212).

E **economy** (ih KAHN uh mee) the exchange of goods and services in a country, region, or state (p. 60).

ecosystem (EHK oh sihs tuhm) all the living and nonliving things that make up an environment and affect one another (p. 146).

election (ih LEHK shuhn) when a group makes a choice by voting (p. 113).

elevation (ehl uh VAY shuhn) the height of a landform above or below sea level (p. 36).

emigrate (EHM ih grayt) when people leave their own country to live in another (p. 432).

employee (ehm PLOI ee) a person who is paid to work for other people (p. 350).

endangered species (ehn DAYN jurd SPEE sheez) a kind of plant or animal that is in danger of dying out completely (p. 239).

enslaved (ehn SLAYVD) when someone works for no pay and can be sold as property (p. 84).

environment (ehn VY ruhn muhnt) everything that surrounds someone, including air, water, and land (p. 16).

erosion (ih ROH zhuhn) the process by which water, ice, and wind wear away soil and rock (p. 36).

erupt (ih RUPT) when melted rock inside a volcano bursts out from underground (p. 26).

ethnic group (EHTH nihk groop) a group of people who come from the same country or share the same way of life (p. 166).

European Union (yur uh PEE uhn YOON yuhn) a trading partnership in Europe that helps countries buy and sell products more easily across international borders (p. 437).

F **facade** (fuh SAHD) the front wall of a building (p. 310).

factory (FAK tu ree) a building or group of buildings in which goods are made (p. 159).

fault (fawlt) a crack in the large rock formations that lie under the surface of the earth (p. 322).

fax machine (fax muh SHEEN) a machine used to send messages over telephone lines (p. 393).

federalism (FEHD ur uhl ihzm) a system in which a central government shares power with the governments of separate regions (p. 116).

fertile (FUR tl) filled with the chemicals that plants need to grow (p. 72).

finance (fuh NANS) the management of money, especially by businesses and banks (p. 159).

forty-niner (FAHR tee NY nur) a person who went to look for gold in California during the gold rush of 1849 (p. 333).

fossil fuel (FAHS uhl FYOO uhl) a resource that comes from living things that died millions of years ago; includes petroleum and coal (p. 44).

free enterprise (free EHN tur pryz) when people and businesses are free to choose the products they want to make, buy, and sell (p. 386).

frontier (FRUHN tyr) land that settlers have just started moving into; any subject or other area that people are just starting to explore (p. 332).

G **geography** (jee AHG ruh fee) the study of the earth and its features (p. 14).

glacier (GLAY shur) a mass of ice that moves slowly over land (p. 145).

goods (gudz) things that people buy and sell, including both manufactured and agricultural products (p. 60).

government (GUHV urn munt) a system that has the power to make laws and keep order for a group of people (p. 114).

ground water (ground WAH tur) water that has collected beneath the surface of the earth (p. 238).

H **habitat** (HAB ih tat) a place where a certain kind of plant or animal lives (p. 326).

hemisphere (HEHM ih sfyr) any half of the earth, divided either between north and south or east and west (p. 16).

hurricane (HUR ih kayn) a very powerful storm with strong winds and heavy rain (p. 200).

hydroelectric power (hy droh ih LEHK trihk POU ur) electricity made by moving water (p. 219).

I **immigrant** (IHM ih gruhnt) a person who moves to another country (p. 84).

Industrial Revolution (ihn DUHS tree uhl rehv uh LOO shuhn) great changes in how people lived and worked during the 1800s that were caused by the invention of new machinery (p. 106).

industry (IHN duh stree) a business that makes and sells a product or offers a service (p. 106).

interchangeable part (ihn tur CHAYN juh buhl pahrt) a part that fits right into each thing being made in a factory, without having to be changed or adjusted (p. 290).

interdependent (ihn tur dih PEHN duhnt) relying on one another (p. 442).

international trade (ihn tur NASH uh nuhl trayd) buying or selling between two or more nations (p. 436).

Internet (IHN tur neht) a network of computers connected by telephone lines (p. 393).

involuntary migration (ihn VAHL uhn tehr ee my GRAY shuhn) when people are forced to move from one area to another (p. 432).

irrigation (ihr ih GAY shuhn) a method of moving water to grow crops in dry land (p. 276).

isthmus (IHS muhs) a narrow strip of land with water on both sides (p. 411).

J **jazz** (jaz) lively American music that is a mixture of spirituals, ragtime, blues, and marching music (p. 232).

jury (JOOR ee) a group of people who listen to evidence in a court case and then decide whether someone is innocent or guilty (p. 123).

L **labor force** (LAY bur fawrs) a supply of workers (p. 293).

landfill (LAND fihl) a place where garbage is buried (p. 186).

landform (LAND fohrm) a physical feature of the earth's surface, such as a mountain (p. 36).

livestock (LYV stahk) animals that people raise on farms; especially animals raised to sell (p. 278).

locomotive (loh kuh MOH tihv) an engine built for pulling railroad cars (p. 391).

lumber (LUHM bur) wood cut into boards (p. 359).

M **manufacture** (man yuh FAK chur) to make something, usually with machines (p. 229).

market (MAHR kiht) a group of people who need or want a kind of good or service (p. 385).

mass production (mas pruh DUHK shuhn) the making of goods in large quantities, using interchangeable parts and an assembly line (p. 290).

media (MEE dee uh) a way of communicating, such as newspapers or television (p. 171).

megalopolis (mehg uh LAWP uh lihs) many cities and suburbs connected together (p. 97).

mestizo (mehs TEE zoh) a descendant of a Spanish colonist and a Native American (p. 410).

metropolitan area (meht ruh PAHL ih tuhn AIR ee uh) an area that includes a large city and the suburbs around it (p. 97).

migration (MY gray shuhn) the movement of people from one area to another (p. 99).

militia (muh LIHSH uh) an army of ordinary citizens, not professional soldiers (p. 123).

mineral (MIHN ur uhl) a substance that can be dug up from the earth and sold or traded; examples include stone, coal, and gold (p. 44).

mining (MYN ing) taking minerals from the earth (p. 220).

mission (MIHSH uhn) a settlement of people who have come to a foreign country to teach about religion (p. 211).

motion picture (MOH shuhn PIHK chur) a movie (p. 337).

multicultural (muhl tee KUHL chur uhl) having many cultures (p. 408).

N **NAFTA** (NAF tuh) the North American Free Trade Agreement, which eliminates barriers to trade between the United States, Mexico, and Canada (p. 410).

network (NEHT wurk) a group of things that are connected in some way (p. 172).

nutrient (NOO tree uhnt) a chemical in soil that plants need for food (p. 297).

O **old-growth forest** (ohld grohth FAWR ihst) a forest with trees that are old and that have never been cut down (p. 360).

on-line (awn lyn) when information from a computer moves through telephone lines (p. 439).

opportunity (awp ur TOO nih tee) a good or fair chance (p. 87).

P **pampas** (PAM puhz) flat, grassy plains in parts of South America (p. 420).

pesticide (PEHS tih syd) a chemical used to kill insects (p. 297).

Pilgrim (PIHL gruhm) a Puritan who left England to settle in Plymouth Colony (p. 150).

pioneer (py uh NEER) a person who takes on new challenges, such as settling a frontier (p. 271).

plantation (plan TAY shuhn) a large farm where the planting and harvesting were done by enslaved African Americans (p. 213).

pollution (puh LOO shuhn) making something dirty or impure (p. 186).

port (pawrt) a place along the shore of a lake or ocean where ships can dock (p. 166).

prairie (PRAIR ee) a large, flat grassland (p. 262).

precipitation (prih sihp ih TAY shuhn) moisture that falls from clouds, including both rain and snow (p. 49).

profit (PRAHF it) what someone earns from running a business after paying expenses (p. 382).

province (PRAHV ihns) an area with its own government, much like a U.S. state (p. 407).

public transportation (PUHB lihk trahns pur TAY shuhn) transportation that all people can use, such as buses, trains, and subways (p. 174).

pueblo (PWEH bloh) an adobe town built by Native Americans in the Southwest (p. 331).

R **ragtime** (RAG tym) a type of American music that became part of jazz (p. 233).

rain forest (rayn FAWR ihst) a thick, evergreen forest where it is wet most of the year (p. 326).

rain shadow (rayn SHAD oh) an area where little rain falls because air passing over nearby mountains loses the moisture it carries (p. 325).

ranch (ranch) a farm where people raise animals, such as cattle, sheep, or horses (p. 338).

rangeland (RAYNJ land) grassy land where cattle are kept (p. 338).

raw materials (raw muh TYR ee uhlz) natural resources before they are made into products (p. 276).

recreation (rehk ree AY shuhn) an activity done for fun or relaxation (p. 287).

recycling (ree SY kling) reusing things instead of throwing them out (p. 47).

refugee (rehf yoo GEE) a person who flees home to find safety and help elsewhere (p. 349).

region (REE jehn) an area made up of places that have one or more features in common (p. 55).

representative (rehp rih ZEHN tuh tihv) someone chosen to speak or act for a group (p. 114).

republic (rih PUHB lihk) a government in which the people vote for representatives (p. 114).

research (rih SURCH) careful study of something (p. 230).

reservoir (REHZ ur vwahr) a lake of stored water created by dams along rivers (p. 366).

resource (REE sawrs) something that goes into making what people need (p. 42).

responsibility (rih spahn suh BIHL ih tee) something you should do; a duty (p. 123).

retail (REE tayl) the sale of goods or services directly to customers (p. 159).

right (ryt) a basic freedom (p. 121).

rodeo (ROH dee oh) an event in which cowhands compete for prizes (p. 338).

rural (ROOR uhl) coming from or belonging in the countryside (p. 96).

S **satellite** (SAHT l yt) a machine that flies in space, circling the earth (p. 29).

sea level (see LEHV uhl) the height of the surface of the world's oceans (p. 36).

secede (sih SEED) for a state to break away from the rest of the country (p. 214).

self-employed (sehlf ehm PLOYD) when people work for themselves, not others (p. 350).

service (SUR vihs) work someone is paid to do for someone else (p. 60).

silicon (SIHL ih kuhn) an element used to make computer chips (p. 370).

silt (sihlt) fine soil carried by a river (p. 202).

skyscraper (SKY skray pur) a very tall building (p. 308).

slavery (SLAY vuh ree) a system in which people can be sold and forced to work without pay (p. 84).

sod (sahd) slabs of earth held together by the roots of grass (p. 272).

software (SAWFT wair) instructions or programs for computers (p. 109).

sonar (SOH nair) a machine that finds objects underwater by bouncing sound off them (p. 285).

space shuttle (spays SHUHT l) a special kind of spaceship that can be used often (p. 247).

space station (spays STAY shuhn) a huge spaceship where people live and work (p. 250).

special effect (SPEHSH uhl ih FEKT) a picture or a sound that people add to a movie after it has been filmed (p. 372).

specialization (spehsh uh lih ZAY shuhn) when a business concentrates on making or selling one kind of product (p. 383).

specialty crop (SPEHSH uhl tee krahp) a farm product that people want but do not always need (p. 366).

staple (STAY puhl) a farm product that is a basic part of people's diets (p. 366).

stock (stahk) a share in the ownership of a business (p. 160).

suburb (SUHB urb) an area between the city and the country, designed mainly for homes (p. 97).

subway (SUHB way) an underground train (p. 174).

T **tax** (tahks) money that people and businesses give their government to help pay for services it provides them (p. 176).

technology (tehk NAHL uh jee) the use of scientific knowledge in industry (p. 108).

telecommunications (TEHL ih kuh myoo nih KAY shuhnz) sending messages across distances, often using phone lines or satellites (p. 172).

temperate (TEHM pur iht) a climate that is neither very hot nor very cold (p. 144).

temperature (TEHM pur uh chur) a measurement of hotness and coldness (p. 48).

terrace (TEHR ihs) a raised, flat bank of earth (p. 418).

textile (TEKS tyl) cloth (p. 219).

timber (TIHM bur) trees that can be used for lumber (p. 359).

tornado (tawr NAY doo) a huge, swirling windstorm (p. 261).

trade (trayd) selling and buying things (p. 382).

tradition (truh DIHSH uhn) a practice handed down from parents to children (p. 167).

transcontinental (trans kahn tuh NEHN tl) across a continent (p. 334).

translate (trans LAYT) to restate something in another language (p. 438).

transportation system (trahns pawr TAY shuhn SIHS tuhm) the different ways of traveling that people in an area can choose to use (p. 176).

trend (trehnd) a general pattern (p. 434).

U **urban** (UR buhn) coming from or belonging to cities (p. 96).

V **value** (VAHL yoo) an idea or belief that a person thinks is important (p. 166).

volcano (vahl KAY noh) a place where melted rock squeezes out from underground (p. 26).

voluntary migration (VAHL uhn tehr ee MY gray shuhn) when people choose to leave their homes and move to a new place (p. 433).

volunteer (vahl uhn TYR) a person who offers to do something without pay (p. 133).

W **water quality** (WAH tur KWAWL ih tee) the level of pollution in a lake, river, or other body of water (p. 400).

waterway (WAW tur way) a river or a lake on which boats can travel (p. 152).

weather (WEHTH ur) what is happening in the air that surrounds the earth — temperature, precipitation, and so on (p. 48).

wetland (WEHT land) a low-lying area, such as a marsh or bog, that is covered by water for all or most of the year (p. 238).

wholesale (HOHL sayl) the sale of large amounts of goods, usually to stores (p. 159).

World Wide Web (wurld wyd wehb) a tool that helps people use the Internet (p. 438).

writing system (RY ting SIHS tuhm) a way of writing down sounds or words (p. 68).

Z **zydeco** (ZY de koh) African American music from the Louisiana bayou (p. 234).

Index

Page numbers with *m* before them refer to maps. Page numbers with *p* refer to pictures. Pages numbers with *c* refer to charts.

Credits

Acknowledgments: American Voices

p. 2 Father Jeronimo de Zarate Salmeron; *Aztlan: An Anthology of Mexican American Literature,* Luis Valdez and Stan Steiner, eds., Alfred A. Knopf, 1972. p. 3 from "America the Beautiful," by Katharine Lee Bates. **p. 4** Thomas Jefferson; *Familiar Quotations,* fifteenth edition, by John Bartlett, Little, Brown and Company, 1980. **p. 5** from "Lift Every Voice and Sing," by James Weldon Johnson, 1900. Reprinted in The Poetry of the Negro, Langston Hughes and Arna Bontemps, eds., Doubleday, 1949. **p. 6** Woodrow Wilson; *The Harper Book of American Quotations,* by Gorton Carruth and Eugene Ehrlich, Harper & Row, 1988.

Unit Opener Quotes

Unit 1 from "Death Song of the Texas Kiowa"; *Lone Star: A History of Texas and the Texans,* by T.R. Fehrenbach, Collier Books, Macmillan, 1968. **Unit 2** from *The Invisible Man,* by Ralph Ellison, 1952. **Unit 3** from "Neither Out Far Nor In Deep," from *The Poetry of Robert Frost,* edited by Edward Connery Lathem. Copyright © 1916, 1923, 1928, 1930, 1934, 1939, 1947, ©1967, 1969 by Holt, Rinehart and Winston; copyright © 1964, 1967, 1970, 1975 by Lesley Frost Ballantine. Reprinted by permission of Henry Holt and Company and Jonathan Cape, Ltd. **Unit 4** from "The Negro Speaks of Rivers," from *The Weary Blues,* by Langston Hughes. Copyright © 1926 by Alfred A. Knopf, Inc. Reprinted by permission. **Unit 5** Isabella L. Bird; *A Lady's Life in the Rocky Mountains,* 1879. **Unit 6** Jessamyn West; *Woman's Home Companion,* May 1956. **Unit 7** President Dwight D. Eisenhower; Speech to graduating class of Foreign Service Institute, 1959.

Permissioned Material

Selection from *The Amazing Impossible Erie Canal,* by Cheryl Harness. Copyright © 1995 by Cheryl Harness. Reprinted by permission of Macmillan Books for Young Readers, Simon & Schuster Children's Publishing Division.

Selection from an article by Susan Goodman, from *Ranger Rick* magazine, October 1994. Copyright © 1994 by Susan Goodman. Reprinted by permission of the author. Susan Goodman is also the author of *Bats, Bugs, and Biodiversity,* Atheneum 1995.

Selection from *Blast Off to Earth!: A Look at Geography,* written and illustrated by Loreen Leedy. Copyright © 1992 by Loreen Leedy. Reprinted by permission of Holiday House.

Selection from *Bridges to Change: How Kids Live on a South Carolina Sea Island,* by Kathleen Krull, photographs by David Hautzig. Text copyright © 1995 by Kathleen Krull. Photographs copyright © 1995 by David Hautzig. Reprinted by permission of Lodestar Books, an affiliate of Dutton Children's Books, a division of Penguin Books USA, Inc.

Selection from *Corn Belt Harvest,* by Raymond Bial. Copyright © 1991 by Raymond Bial. Reprinted by permission of Houghton Mifflin Company. All rights reserved.

"The Cowgirl Way!" by Susan Brody, from *Kid City* magazine, October 1995. Copyright © 1995 by Children's Television Workshop. Reprinted by permission.

"Eye of the Tiger: How Hurricanes Work," by Lauren Graper, from *3-2-1 Contact* magazine, September 1993. Copyright © 1993 by Children's Television Workshop. Reprinted by permission.

Selection from *If you're not from the prairie...,* by David Bouchard, illustrated by Henry Ripplinger. Text copyright © 1995 by David Bouchard. Illustrations copyright © 1995 by Henry Ripplinger. Reprinted by permission of Raincoast Books Distribution Ltd.

Selection from *...If Your Name Was Changed at Ellis Island,* by Ellen Levine, illustrated by Wayne Parmenter. Text copyright © 1993 by Ellen Levine. Illustrations copyright © 1993 by Scholastic, Inc. Reprinted by permission of Scholastic, Inc.

"Made in the ... USA," from *3-2-1 Contact* magazine, July/August 1995. Copyright © 1995 by Children's Television Workshop. Reprinted by permission.

"New Orleans Jazz and Heritage Festival," brochure cover. Copyright © 1995 by the New Orleans Jazz and Heritage Foundation, Inc. Reprinted by permission.

"Jobs vs. Environment," cartoon by Joel Pett, as reprinted in *American Forests,* January/February 1995. Copyright © 1992 by Lexington *Herald-Leader.* Reprinted by permission.

Selection from *The Other Side: How Kids Live in a California Latino Neighborhood,* by Kathleen Krull, photographs by David Hautzig. Text copyright © 1994 by Kathleen Krull. Photographs copyright © 1994 by David Hautzig. Reprinted by permission of Lodestar Books, an affiliate of Dutton Children's Books, a division of Penguin Books USA, Inc.

Selection from *People,* written and illustrated by Peter Spier. Copyright © 1980 by Peter Spier. Reprinted by permission of Bantam Doubleday Dell Books for Young Readers, Bantam Doubleday Dell Publishing Group, Inc.

Selection from *Presidents: A Library of Congress Book,* by Martin W. Sandler. Copyright © 1995 by Eagle Productions, Inc. Reprinted by permission of HarperCollins Children's Books, a division of HarperCollins Publishers.

"Tallgrass Prairie," from "Wildflowers Across America," illustrated by Jack Unruh, text by Michael E. Long, from *National Geographic* magazine, April 1988. Copyright © 1988 by the National Geographic Society. *National Geographic* is the official journal for members of the National Geographic Society. Reprinted by permission.

Selection from student journal of Allison Heyns, from *The Children's Rain Forest Workshops Program.* Reprinted by permission of Children's Environmental Trust Foundation, International.

World Book Encyclopedia, copyright © 1995 by World Book, Inc. Reprinted by permission.

Selection from *Zlata's Diary: A Child's Life in Sarajevo,* by Zlata Filipovic. Copyright © 1993 by Fixot et editions Robert Laffont. Reprinted by permission of Fixot et editions Robert Laffont and Penguin Books USA, Inc.

Fair Use Quotes

p. 13 from *Canyons of the Colorado,* by John Wesley Powell. Flood & Vincent, 1895. **p. 35** from *Bartlett's Familiar Quotations,* Fifteenth and 125th Anniversary edition. Little, Brown & Company, 1980. **p. 47** from *National Geographic* magazine, July 1994. **p. 59** from *The Oregon Trail Diary of Amelia Stewart Knight,* Harold R. Carpenter ed. Clark County Historian, vol. 6, 1965. **p. 70** from *National Geographic* magazine, April 1990. **p. 86** from "The Changing Face of America," in *Time* magazine, July 8, 1985. **p. 107** from *Notable Black American Women,* by Jessie Carney Smith. Gale Research, Inc., Detroit, 1992. p. 135 from "Planting Seeds, Harvesting Scholarships," by Lester Sloan, *Newsweek* magazine, May 29, 1995. **p. 199** from *She Walks These Hills,* by Sharyn McCrumb. Charles Scribner's Sons, 1994. **p. 208** from *Go Down, Moses,* by William Faulkner. The Curtis Publishing Company, 1942. **p. 227** from "An Alien in Suburbia," by Fuad Faridi, from *Newsweek* magazine, October 9, 1995. **p. 231** from *The Book of American Negro Spirituals,* ed. by James Weldon Johnson and J. Rosamond Johnson. The Viking Press, Inc., 1925. **p. 241** from *National Geographic* magazine, April 1992. **p. 246** from *Respectfully Quoted: A Dictionary of Quotations Requested from the Congressional Research Service,* Suzy Platt ed. Library of Congress, 1989. **p. 259** from *The Journals of Lewis and Clark,* Bernard de Voto ed. Houghton Mifflin Company, 1981. **p. 288** from "Crow's Nest: The Big Cesspool Lessons," by Bruce R. Rosendahl. **p. 292** from *Current Biography Yearbook.* H.H. Wilson Company, 1976. **p. 293** from "The Resurgent Great Lakes Region: Ready to Compete in a Global Economy," by John Randy, from *Site Selection* magazine, February 1994. **p. 308** from *Who's Who in Architecture from 1400 to the Present,* J.M. Richards, ed. Holt, Rinehart and Winston, 1977. **p. 323** from *Anchorage Earthquake,* by Bryce S. Walker. Time Life Books, 1982. **p. 330** from *House Made of Dawn,* by N. Scott Momaday, HarperCollins, 1966, 1967, 1968. **p. 347** from *Hoang Anh: A Vietnamese-American Boy,* by Diane Hoyt-Goldsmith. Holiday House, 1992. **p. 371** from *Design News* magazine, p. 69, May 17, 1993. **p. 389** from *Traveling the National Road,* by Merritt Ierlay. The Overlook Press, Woodstock, NY. **p. 401** from "The Mississippi River Under Siege," by William S. Ellis, from *National Geographic* magazine, November 1993. **p. 408** Letter from Alexandra Malone, September 27, 1995. **p. 410** Letter from Luis Pablo Hernández Espino, September 7, 1995. **p. 422** Translated from a letter from Sara María Campo, October 29, 1995. **p. 439** from "Bill's New Vision," by Steven Levy, from *Newsweek* magazine, November 27, 1995.

Cover/Title Page

Front Cover: Photography by Donovan Reese/Tony Stone Images (background); Comstock (m). **Back Cover:** Photography by The Granger Collection (m); Earth Imaging/Tony Stone Images (r). **i:** Comstock. **ii-iii:** Donovan Reese/Tony Stone Images (background); Kunio Owaki/ The Stock Market (inset). **iii:** Earth Imaging/Tony Stone Images (br).

Photo Credits

vi: Tony Stone Images (t); Grant Heilman/Grant Heilman Photography (b). **ix:** Illinois State Fair. **x:** © Cheyenne Frontier Days, Cheyenne, WY (t). **xi:** Mary Kate Denny/Tony Stone Images. **xiii:** Tim Davis/Tony Stone Images. **2:** Gary Holscher/Tony Stone Images (l). **2-3:** © Marc Muench. **4-5:** © Robert Llewellyn. **5:** Martin R. Jones/Unicorn Stock Photos (br); J. Whitmer/Superstock (tl). **6:** Phoebe Ferguson/Gamma-Liaison (l). **6-7:** Terry Vine/Tony Stone Images (m); Donovan Reese/Tony Stone Images (background). **8-9:** David Muench. **10:** © Zandria Muench Beraldo 1995 (t); J. Lotter/Tom Stack & Associates (bl); Steve Smith/Westlight (br). **11:** Arthur Tilley/FPG International (l); D.E. Cox/Tony Stone Images (r). **12:** © Zandria Muench Beraldo 1995 (t); Larry Ulrich/Tony Stone Images (l); Bob Daemmrich (r). **13:** Kenneth W. Fink/Bruce Coleman, Inc. (m); © Bill Curtsinger (r). **14-15:** © Liz Hymans/Panoramic Images, Chicago 1995. **16:** Courtesy of Dr. Ricki Sanders. **18:** Joseph H. Bailey/National Geographic Image Collection. **19:** Animals Animals/E.R. Degginger. **21:** David Parker/Science Photo Library/Photo Researchers. **27:** © 1996 Gary Braasch. **28:** Janet Jakoda Rogers/Photo Researchers (t); Calvin Larsen/Photo Researchers (tr); Jim Corwin/Tony Stone Images (b). **29:** © Bill Curtsinger. **30:** NASA/Mark Marten/Science Source/Photo Researchers (l); Tony Stone Images (r). **31:** Library of Congress (tl)(b); Smithsonian Institution (tr). **34:** David Muench (t); Rich Buzzelli/Tom Stack and Associates (l); John Shaw/Bruce Coleman, Inc. (m); Larry Lee/Westlight (r). **35:** Jeff Greenberg/The Picture Cube (l); Gay Bumgarner/Tony Stone Images (m); William L. Wantland/Tom Stack and Associates (r). **36-37:** © David Lawrence/Panoramic Images, Chicago 1995. **37:** Steve Smith/Westlight (t). **39:** Annie Griffiths/Woodfin Camp and Associates (t); Russell Munson/The Stock Market (b). 40: H. Wendler/The Image Bank (t); A. & L. Sinibaldi/Tony Stone Images (b). **41:** Larry Ulrich/Tony Stone Images. **42:** Steve Satushek/The Image Bank (r). **43:** Mark Tomalty/Masterfile (t); Jack Dyklinga/Bruce Coleman, Inc. (inset). **45:** Peter Pearson/Tony Stone Images (t); Jonathan Kim/Gamma-Liaison (b). **46:** Brian Parker/Tom Stack and Associates (tl); Bruce Hands/Tony Stone Images (tr); O. Franken/Sygma (bl). **47:** Hank Morgan (t). **48:** Hans Reinhard/Bruce Coleman, Inc. (tl). **49:** Arthur Tilley/FPG International. **50:** Courtesy of NBC. 51: Bob Abraham/The Stock Market (t); Larry Ulrich/Tony Stone Images (b). **54:** Chris Huskinson/F-Stock Photo Agency (t); Superstock (l); David Ball/Tony Stone Images (m); *The Oregon Trail* by Albert Bierstadt, The Butler Institute of American Art, Youngstown, Ohio (r). **55:** Dennis Stock/Magnum Photos (l); Epix/Sygma (m) Martin Barraud/Tony Stone Images (r). **56:** Bachmann/Photo Researchers. **58:** © Willard Clay 1995/Dembinsky Photo Associates (t); Michael Yamashita (b). **60:** F. Davis/Granger Collection (t). **63:** Grant Heilman/Grant Heilman Photography (l); Bill Ross/Westlight (r). 64: Alex S. MacLean/Landslides (b); Jeff Hunter/The Image Bank (l). **65:** Jeff Hunter/The Image Bank (r). **66:** John Elk/Tony Stone Images. 68: D.E. Cox/Tony Stone Images (m). **69:** Kenneth Gabrielsen Photography/Gamma-Liaison. **71:** Anthony Suau/Gamma-Liaison (ml); Chip Hires/Gamma-Liaison (br). **72:** Don Smetzer/Tony Stone Images. **73:** Rohan/Tony Stone Images (l); The Bettmann Archive (r). **74:** © Walt. Disney Co. (tl, background); Peter Brauné (tl, inset). **74-75:** U.S. Geological Survey. **78-79:** Fred J. Maroon. **80:** Greg Pease/Tony Stone Images (tl); Wai Murata Konishi & Bessie Konishi, courtesy Ellis Island Immigration Museum/NPS (bl); Jeff Zaruba/The Stock Market (br). **81:** ©1995 Louis Psihoyos/Matrix International (l); University of Illinois at Chicago/The University Library/Jane Addams Memorial

U.S. Army Corps of Engineers, Rock Island District (b). **404:** Alan Kearney/Viesti Associates, Inc.(t); Science Photo Library/Photo Researchers (bl); Joe Viesti/Viesti Associates Inc.(bm); Bob Thomason/Tony Stone Images (br). **405:** Chip & Jill Eisenhart/Tom Stack and Associates (bl); D. Donne Bryant (bm); Joe Viesti/Viesti Associates, Inc.(br). **407:** Tony Stone Images. **408:** George Hunter/Tony Stone Images (t). **409:** Brian Atkinson/Tony Stone Images. **410:** Robert Frerck/Tony Stone Images (b). **411:** Frank Rosotto/The Stock Market. **416:** Bob Daemmrich (b); Jeff Hunter/The Image Bank (l). **417:** Jeff Hunter/The Image Bank (r). **418:** Don Mason/The Stock Market (b); Robert Frerck/Odyssey (inset). **419:** Guido Rossi/The Image Bank (tr); Luis Padilla/The Image Bank (br). **420:** Tim Davis/Tony Stone Images (l); Art Wolfe/Tony Stone Images (m); Jaques Jangoux/Tony Stone Images (r). **421:** The Granger Collection (tr); Fred McKinney/FPG International (bl); Jose Fuste Raga/The Stock Market (br). **422:** North Atlanta High School, Center for International Studies/Atlanta Carribbean Trading Company (bl)(bm). **424-425:** Jim Cronk/Children's Environmental Trust International. **428:** Earth Imaging/Tony Stone Images (t); Anne B. Keiser, ©National Geographic Society Image Collection (bl); P. Robert/Sygma (bm); Jack Rendulich/Frozen Images (br). **429:** Kevin Kelley/Tony Stone Images (t); Raghu Rai/Magnum Photos (bl); J. Horner/UNICEF (bm); NASA (br). **430:** Tony Craddock/Tony Stone Images (t); Will and Deni McIntyre/Tony Stone Images (b). **431:** Steve McCurry/Magnum Photos (t); Peter M. Fisher/The Stock Market (b). **432:** Malcom Linton/Black Star (t); P. Robert/Sygma (inset); Frank Siteman/Viesti Associates (b). **433:** P. Durand/Sygma. **434:** Owen Franken/Tony Stone Images (l); Jeffrey Aaronson/Network Aspen (r). **435:** Mary Kate Denny/Tony Stone Images (l); Brooks Kraft/Sygma (r). **439:** Alan Levenson/Tony Stone Images. **442:** Rotolo/Gamma-Liaison. **443:** NASA (tl,bl); Sygma (r). **444:** The Bettmann Archive (t); Sean Sprague/UNICEF (b). **445:** Oxfam (l); Jon Jones/Sygma (r). **446:** Paul Lowe/Magnum Photos (m). **447:** Photo Edit. **448:** George F. Mobley © National Geographic Society (t); NASA/Science Source/Photo Researchers (m); Hans Reinhard/Tony Stone Images (b). **449:** George F. Mobley © National Geographic Society (m); Roger Mear/Tony Stone Images (b). **456:** Bill Ross/Westlight. **460:** U.S. Department of Agriculture, Aerial Photography Field Office, Farm Service Administration. **463:** Olaf Soot/Tony Stone Images. **465:** David Frazier/Photo Researchers (l). **466:** The Granger Collection (t); Alex MacLean/Landslides (b). **494:** Robert E. Daemmrich/Tony Stone Images. **495:** The Granger Collection (t); John Elk III/Stock Boston (br); Ed Simpson/Tony Stone Images (bm); D.E. Cox/ Tony Stone Images (bl). **496-499:** White House Historical Association. **506-507:** © James Schwabel/Panoramic Images, Chicago 1995. **506:** Wolfgang Kaeler/Gamma-Liaison (l); Kurgan-Lisnet/Gamma-Liaison (m); Animals Animals/Breck Kent(r). **507:** Tim Bieber/The Image Bank; Alan Becker/The Image Bank (inset, b).

Assignment Photo Credits
178 (m): Robin M. Andersen. **346 (bl), 350, 351:** Eric L. Bakke/Mercury Pictures. **164 (bm), 168-169:** Brad Bower/Mercury Pictures. **67, 131 (bd), 217 (bd) 471:** Dave Desroches. **68 (bd), 158 (tr):** FayFoto. **417 (bd):** Glenn Kremer. **65 (bd), 189 (bd):** Allan Landau. **257 (bm), 285 (bl), 300 (tl, tr, br), 301 (tl, tr):** Bill Rowe/Mercury Pictures. **47 (m), 144 (b), 145 (t), 166 (bl), 210 (tl), 300-301 (bd):** Tony Scarpetta. **17 (br), 131 (insets), 357 (insets), 465 (r):** Dorey Sparre. **13 (bl), 26 (bl):** Bronia Sullivan. **65 (insets), 191 (insets), 470 (l):** Tracey Wheeler. **179 (r), 313:** David Witbeck/Mercury Pictures.

Text Maps
209, 264–265: Patrice Rossi Calkin. **61, 70, 85, 102–103, 260, 270–271, 343, 399:** DLF Group. **10, 27, 38, 41, 44, 50, 62, 68–69, 71, 72, 80–81, 97, 99, 118, 144, 145, 155, 178-179, 201, 204, 205, 219, 222, 230, 239, 256–257, 275, 280–281, 286-287, 324, 348, 359, 395, 406, 409, 419, 431, 449, 458–459, 461, 462, 463, 464–465, 482, 483:** Geosystems. **367:** Dale Glasgow & Associates. **57:** Ellen Kuzdro. **59, 175:** Ortelius Design.

Illustrations
15, 328–329: Pat Rossi Calkin. **261, 392–393:** Dale Glasgow & Associates. **98–99, 262–263, 269:** Wood Ronsaville Harlin. **396–397:** Robert Hynes. **146–147,222–223, 322, 323:** Carlyn Iverson. **291, 299:** Nenad Jakesevic. **210–211:** Steve Patricia **157, 309:** Matthew Pippin. **249:** Frederick Porter. **48–49:** Mark Seidler. **218–219, 291:** Steven Wagner